Jihad in My Saffron Garden

Jihad in My Saffron Garden

Roxy Arora

PRABHAT PAPERBACKS

Published by
PRABHAT PAPERBACKS
4/19 Asaf Ali Road,
New Delhi-110 002 (INDIA)
e-mail: prabhatbooks@gmail.com

ISBN 978-93-5186-871-2
JIHAD IN MY SAFFRON GARDEN
Novel by Roxy Arora

Edition
First, 2016

Price
₹ 250.00 (Rupees Two Hundred Fifty only)

Printed at
R-Tech Offset Printers, Delhi

This book is dedicated
to my loving parents
Mrs. Chanchal and Dr. Prabhat Mohan Gupta.
Papa, with All My Heart
I Miss You.

'Let not the fruits of action be your motive,
Nor let your attachment be to inaction.'
—Bhagawad Gita

Acknowledgements

With Deepest gratitude to my Eternal Mentor. You taught me to empower myself and recognize the writer inside me. I could not have done it without you.

My husband, Dr. Sachit Anand Arora. You have always insisted that my talent lies in, 'Narrating a story.'

My precious child, Pranav Arora. You were an inspiration to complete this manuscript as I watched you burn the midnight oil for your Eighth Grade Annual Examinations. Thanks for lending me your room.

My second set of parents, Mrs. Sudha and Mr. Krishan Arora. Thank you for all your affection and love.

My sister, Dr. Ramia and brother-in-law, Dr. Vijay Kangotra. Ramia, my distinguished publisher accepted my manuscript on your birthday.

My worthy alma maters. They have provided me an education which has nourished my soul and made me yearn for more. Hensingham Junior School, U.K.; St. Mary's Presentation Convent, Jammu; The Indian School, Kuwait and my dearest of all, College of Dental Surgery, Manipal.

I would like to thank, Dr. Sheetal Sahunja and Dr. Bhumija Gupta for holding my hand in the darkest moments of my life.

As for Dr. Komal Seth, thank you for always carrying my weighty problems on your slender shoulders.

I would like to acknowledge, Dr. Sarika Kalra who painstakingly went through my manuscript and gave me invaluable advice. Shalini Malhotra and Priya Lahiri for always being 'there.' You girls are my strength.

With heartfelt recognition for the efforts of Shalini Digvijay, my cousin and childhood friend.

The teachers who have influenced me the most in my life. With extreme appreciation for Mrs. Shanta Devdasan, English Teacher, Presentation Convent, Jammu. Thank you for gifting me 'Tess Of The D'Urbervilles' when I was twelve years old. Dr. K.S. Bhatt, Dean, CODS, Manipal. Thank you, Sir, for being a father figure when I needed one.

To the departed, Sister Loyala, Moral Science teacher, Presentation Convent, Jammu. May her soul rest in peace.

Prologue

Mr. Jimmy Carter, I was a little girl of eight when you fought United States Presidential elections for the second time.

I liked you with your grey hair and kind face. I wanted you to win. I was a bright-eyed and bushy-tailed little girl and couldn't take the thought of any one losing.

I cried, when Papa announced the next day that Mr. Ronald Reagan had won.

My father sat glued to the television set as the former Hollywood star spoke his famous lines, 'You ain't seen nothing yet.'

I informed my teacher in school about the new Mr. President. She was tight lipped and reluctant to admit that a non-white aka me, knew more than the Briton Whites. Those were the eighties. The days when 'The Now taboo N word, was not taboo then.' I was the 'Nigger' from India.

Between those lips ever so tight, my teacher in a manner most mild said that the classroom, a forum for international politics was not. If truth be told that was school policy.

We knew more, us lot, you know the one's tagged, 'The Now taboo N word, not taboo then.' Our parents had left their countries to see us shine and smile in lands where we could live the dream. They fed us all sorts of information which we had to assimilate. The Indian brain had descended from Aryabhatta. It would never let us down.

We were endowed with information our white comrades were denied.

How else do we prove our mettle?

How else do we hold our head high when we face the 'Now taboo N word, not taboo then?'

So over Weetabix (Cereal) and the *Daily Telegraph,* the following morning, Papa informed me of Jimmy Carter's defeat.

Tears streamed down my face, Mr. President, as I saw you on the morning BBC news. You were going to have to leave your enormous house which had a spotless coat of white. No one should have to leave their house. Not Presidents like you, not ordinary people like us. That was the first time I cried because of you. There was the look of the defeatist about you and it made me sad.

I also cried when I left my house in England. Though it was not as big as yours. But it was big and it was in the Lake District. My house was not just a house, it was my home.

And when I left England, my home since as long as I could remember, I cried as I hung on to my father's leg and pleaded with him to let me stay. Despite the ethnic slur, I had still managed to fit in.

And as we (my sister and I) shopped for chocolates and magazines, in W.H. Smith, at Heathrow Airport we pledged that one day we will be back. England was my home. I was in love with Adam Ant and adored Princess Di.

House leaving became a regular feature in my life so nomadic.

In the August of Nineteen Ninety, in the dark of the night, I fled from my house in Kuwait. Saddam Hussein had decided it was his new governorate. So, as Mum and me huddled under Burqas, and bullets were fired in the air, we left our 'Home' again First time in his life my father, 'A Man of Medicine' wandered so far without his stethoscope. It broke his heart, but we had false documents stating his profession as shopkeeper. Saddam and his merry men wouldn't need him that way. Another exodus! I thought.

All these house leavings, yours and mine have something in common...tears.

While researching for this book, I cried, Mr. Carter when I read the 'Carter Doctrines' and asked, 'why?'

I felt the world would be bereft of the slaughter of nine-eleven, seven-eleven and twenty-six eleven.

Come to think of it we wouldn't even have the ISIS.

If only there hadn't been the Carter Doctrines!

And as for the paradise we call 'Kashmir......'

And as for my story......

1

Pir Panjal Mountain Range, Jammu and Kashmir

These towering peaks of the princely state of Jammu and Kashmir, remain buried under snow and avalanches the whole year through. Intensely chilling winters and uninviting terrains render it impossible for modern man to consider civilization.

This is the abode of the people of the Bakerwal clan. It is what is called, 'Dera.'

Settlers in this area are the nomads who nimble wit their way around the soaring precipices, with a spryness characteristic of them.

Rahim, the shepherd boy is in deft pursuit of his sheep dog Qazim.

"Rahim, bring back the wood for the fire. Your sisters have gone to get the water. I have to prepare the evening meal." Rahim is Mama's first born and her only son. He is the bearer of the 'Dada Porta,' what we call lineage.

"Yes, Mama." He responds obediently and sets out. His mind is engaged with concern regarding the whereabouts of his beloved dog.

Rahim's gaze falls on the mountain yonder. Since the last few days, he has been witness to strange lights blinking from the tall masses.

Qazim has been dispensing his duties half heartedly, which is so uncharacteristic of his usual compliant self, and he has been temperamental.

Rahim hears a snarl and feels relieved that Qazim is somewhere around.

And now he is certain he can hear his dog bark from a distance. But it is sounding from the, 'Not to trespass area.' It is the abode of the 'undesirables.'

"Evil commands them. They want to snatch our *Jannat.*" Grandfather has always cautioned.

Rahim strains his ears as he can hear the muffled bark of his worthy friend.

What follows is an eerie silence in the same way as the blizzard reduces vision to naught.

Mama will get worried if I don't return on time. Will come back here with a search party. He grimaces.

He turns as he hears a sound. 'Qazim,' he thinks with a smile.

But alas, it is not his cherished animal. As the '*Watan Ke Dushman*' looms menacingly.

Rahim sprints blindly through the slippery ice. This Dushman is exactly who grandfather has warned him about.

There is a piercing noise and with a thud Rahim falls onto the flurry of snow. He unites with the convoluted flesh of his dog.

There will be no dinner tonight. Blood has been shed. Tears will gush forth.

The undesirable brandishes his Avtomat Kalashnikova and aims at the fresh target. The rifle has a firing precision of eight hundred metres. The 'Dera' of Rahim is just short of a kilometre away.

The undesirable has a purpose.
A purpose called Jihad.

Noor Aunty's father, Baba, was a saffron farmer and a very important person in Sopore, the saffron town of Kashmir.

When Mummy gave birth to Rohan, to make things easier for her, I was shipped off to this saffron town for a few days, with Heena and her family.

The town was Muslim dominated and at the tender age of seven, even me with my Hindu, thick skin felt a little of an outcast. Village children would gather outside the farm shouting out, '*Kafir*,' meaning one who does not believe in the Prophet. I wailed and wept. Heena was furious and complained to Baba. She went marching to the saffron pickers, snatched their tweezers and made a fine cut on her left hand. Blood spilled out and splashed into puddles. She then did the same to my hand, and yelled to the stunned mob of villagers, "Our blood is the same." The two hands reddened as the colour of blood was identical.

I was Heena's 'sister, by blood' and was never called *Kafir* again.

Except for the next day and another day and yet another day and so many days thereafter.

"This is your side of the garden," Heena affirmed kindly as she wiped my tears. "And this is my side of the garden." Her eyes kindled with a selfless love that is a rarity. My smile her way was hesitant. We sat in the porch of her grandfather's house, in Sopore, Kashmir. This was his saffron farm. The family had cultivated this crocus since generations. Today morning he had gifted this saffron bed to Heena. It was now officially hers. She had split it into two and given half to me. We sipped on the Kehva, garnished with bright fibers. It was October and the purple flowers were in full bloom. The saffron pickers were sorting them into large baskets. They would expertly remove the priceless threads with fingers ever so quick. The violet flowers would be tossed aside without a thought spared their way. Heena and I sprinkled the petals all over the floors. The aroma of saffron emanated the entire porch. We tossed the silken petals into tubs of water and dipped our feet into this 'pretty potion.' It couldn't have been possible for Royalty to be more privileged than us.

One day, a Hangul (deer) was found in our saffron garden. It had escaped from the nearby National Park. His majestic antlers had caught the greedy eye of a ruthless poacher who had gone ahead and shot it in its leg. It tottered all the way and lay down in our saffron enclosure. His pupils were dilated in fear, and his supple body lay writhing in pain. It made 'Baa' sounds, as if it were distressed and called out to its doe for solace. Baba scooped out the bullet, irrigated the wound and made some medicines with bunches of shrubs. He generously added the stamens and stigmas of mystical saffron. Gradually, it recovered its strength and we fed it milk, and fresh grass. But when the Hangul tried to skip up we could virtually see the tears in his eyes. Neither lissom nor agile were he. All our ministrations reduced to nothing. Rendered maimed and scarred forever, his lustrous eyes pleaded 'Moksh.' With a sorry stare, the Village Head and Baba decided to put him to sleep forever. "Give him a burial fit for a Mughal Emperor. The *Kafir* can also attend." The Village Head dictates. While the Hangul is lowered into the ground, Heena tries to hurl herself into the hole dug out for him. Baba grabs hold of her. She is burning hot, her body as if placed on the millions of coal, found only in hell. "Evil eye," the *Hakim* announces, with a grim shake of his head. Yet again, the saffron fibers enter the mortar, with a pestle they are minced and a tonic procured. She takes five nights to recover. Heena my Angel, with a heart of gold.

Once I had a Saffron Garden where we turned and tilled the soils. Heena and I, added compost to the fertile land, and we basked in the folk songs of Sopore. The rabbits frolicked. We chased them, delighting in their coats so furry. With sickle and spade, we shoveled at the mice tunnels and said shoo to the rodents as they nibbled at the flowers. We laughed with the sun as it emerged at dawn in a glittering exhibit. The breeze hollered and swept our hair around our face. The moon crooned us a lullaby. By the moon-lit porch, we would fling off our plimsoles, lie down on the settee and indulge in folk lore with Baba.

However, on a cold, dark night, where hung neither moon nor star, when the winds cut me to my bone. Neither flower nor fiber bloomed in my meadow. Banshees yelled at me and Demons chased me. Why?

'Heena, Roshina!' Who is calling us? I love this voice and its velvet quality. Its timbre never fails to fill me with warmth. 'Heena, Roshina,' I hear it again. Let's just call him, 'The Voice' for now. But for this magnificent place! This is Pehalgam, the most beautiful part of Kashmir. Look at that stunning red head. She is Heena Qazmi. What about that raven haired tomboy? That is me, Roshina Kapoor. I am here with my parents and Heena's family. Heena is my best friend and my sister, by blood. Our hotel is situated on the banks of the river Lidder. We lie awake at night, Heena and I, as we listen to the night calls of the migratory bird, European Hoopoe. The waters of the Lidder make a mellifluous sound which enthralls us. It is a totally unique feeling. We are the first ones to get up the next morning and make our way to the summoning elixir. The engorged liquid devours our feet greedily. It numbs us to the bone, and we let out squeals of delight. Across the pebbles, we scramble. Again the voice calls out to us uncompromisingly, "Heena, Roshina! Come back, right now." Our thrill is lost on him. "Heena, didn't Abbu tell you not to come here alone?" Mutinously, we leave the Azure froth. But our fun doesn't end here. We step on to mainland, and scream out our names, 'Heena, Roshina,' as loudly as we can. Sound waves, deflect back as what in Physics, are called echoes. We are in splits of laughter. What is so funny? It is an echo, a perfectly scientific phenomenon. We clap, giggle, jump up and down and hug each other. We make bracelets and anklets out of the wild daisies. And we meander through the thick carpet of grass, screaming out our names while we tease the amazed echo. The butterflies hover above us, and the birds flap their wings merrily. We have all been etched from a common Divinity. The mountains smile at us indulgently. How magnanimous they are to provide us such a resplendent playground. Their heads capped with snow, they seem to be nodding in acquiescence to our hearty abandon.

And now that is my baby brother, Rohan. I can hardly recognize him what with all that puppy fat. Heena and I hug him hard. Heena, chases my brother who she loves as much as I do, probably even more. The voice approaches us. His stance has softened. He just had our best interests in his heart anyway. As if sensing my stare he looks at me and takes in my dishevelled, dark hair, my rolled up jeans and my T-shirt, stained with grass and mud. He finally smiles and that, too, leniently. I smile back at him in open adoration. I am his most faithful devotee. He is my Aafaq Qazmi and this is my 'Kashmir.'

Why do I thrash out in pain as Heena screams at me? That is impossible. I look at her incredulously. I see the ravage in her eyes. She is covered in a shroud of black. "Heena, talk to me, tell me what troubles you?" "We were sisters in a previous life time, Rosha, you and I." She has always maintained. I hear those words again and again. "We were sisters, we were sisters." I cover my ears as I want to hear no more. I am in a dark tunnel, and there are masked men chasing me. There is no light at the end of the tunnel. It goes on endlessly. "Come away with me, Heena." I implore of her. "You are my sister, by blood. Your grief is mine." I reach out to her, to hug her, and provide her withering body warmth, but she eludes my grasp. She cruelly tells me she doesn't want to see me, ever again. The deceit of man has purged out the spark from my life.

I shout at the top of my voice, "No, you are not Aafaq. You are a sinister person, impersonating him." I want to destroy this pretender. "Look at my eyes, they are green." He declares forcefully. The bile rises inside me and fills me with revulsion. This repugnant, murderer. How dare he call himself Aafaq. I slap him hard and tear at the scarf covering his face. He laughs a cynical laugh. I look at his eyes. They are brown. "I told you so," I summon with all my contempt. Oh no! they are green as they astonishingly change their colour. This can't be happening. I slap him again. He hits me back. I fall down, to be cushioned by a soft mattress. It is spongy and wet. This is what it means to experience hell, here on earth. What else can you call a predicament so macabre? I am lying down on several corpses all stiffened with rigor mortis. A lifeless form stares at me with eyes wide open. The eyes are bright, brilliant and green. They are the eyes I have loved since as long as I can remember. I frantically search for the brown fleck in the right eye. I beat my chest and implore of God to exorcise the demons which have possessed me.

The dreams are back to haunt me, the highly evocative images which rip my body of its natural juices, leaving my skin cold and clammy. I get out of bed and walk to my window. From the eleventh floor of my high rise building, the city looks tiny. The roads bear a deserted look, except for a few, stray cars. I open the window as I welcome the cold, December air of New Delhi.

It takes me so little to come undone, I think, introspectively. On my wall hangs the mounted photograph of the most beautiful girl in the world, Heena Qazmi, aged seventeen. She smiles down at me as if reading my mind, something she can do, so easily. Her beauty so rare that it can be only termed ethereal.

The silken curls of her flaming, red hair tumble to her waist. The fine features of her exquisite face, sketched in perfection. Her alabaster complexion, the redness of her cheeks which could not be procured from the costliest jars of French rouge. I miss you, Heena, I say to myself, come back to me. With tremendous effort I tear away my gaze only to look at the tall, handsome boy by her side. Her brother Aafaq Qazmi, the man who made me a woman, his woman.

I had clicked this photo in our garden in Srinagar. It now seems to be another lifetime but the memory so distinct. It was Aafaq's new Nikon camera and he had been generous enough to let us use and hence abuse it. We had taken turns to click snaps of each other. I had even gone a step further and had sashayed in our garden, like a model performing a catwalk. It had not been a wasted effort as I had felt Aafaq look at me. His eyes hooded, the expression unreadable. I had taken full advantage of being behind the camera for I soaked up every inch of him. It had been a bright day, full of sunshine and warmth. But out of nowhere the clouds had appeared. Their shapes distorted and cruel. No cotton nor floss, but grey and eerie. Was Mother Nature sending me an ominous warning that she had the power to change my destiny, and my life would take a sinister turn? I know for sure now, what I could not have in my wildest dreams imagined, that the days of unrestraint were over. That this photo of Aafaq and Heena was taken for a reason. And that was to hang on my wall as a poignant reminder of a life in Kashmir.

I reflectively close my eyes while my arms reach out to snatch something. Something, which once, I had never valued. But my hands remain empty as 'Time' belongs to no one.

I decide to listen to Mozart. His 'Piano Sonata Number Sixteen In C Major' has never failed to lift my spirits. It provides me immense peace. What an incomparable genius! Like all that is dear to me, at the end of his sonatas, a melancholic halo announces its presence. Zohaib laughingly tells me that probably the long departed Mozart, was a miserable man. A smile lifts my face at the thought of my son, Zohaib, and the tension of the past fortnight is temporarily forgotten. Why only temporarily, as it is an extremely heavy cross I bear. And now this proposal of marriage, from an acquaintance so loved has taken me by surprise. I can't fathom where that has sprung from. Ironic, these men and their feelings, you feel brotherly about someone, and he throws a marriage proposal your way scaring the living daylights out of you. You feel insanely passionate about another, and he insists you are like his kid sister.

Zohaib has been upset with me. He is rather fond of this suitor of mine. And has implored me to at least give it a thought. Not that he needs a father figure or has ever had Daddy issues. Zohaib has become a Medical Intern after finishing rigorous training from a reputed institute in New Delhi. He is strong willed, compassionate and desperate to see me tie the knot. I know he feels deeply for me. His concern for my welfare is touching. But I remain taciturn. Sensitive as he is, my son has never loved anyone, the way I have. Hence, he cannot understand that you can't marry another person when your heart will always belong to your first love.

My hand inadvertently goes to the pendant hanging from a delicate chain, around my throat. It has never left my skin ever since it was planted there, decades ago. The warmth that suffuses me as my fingers play with it, is no different than the sensation which pervaded me the day it was placed.

I walk into my study. The Holy Quran, the Bhagavad Gita and the Holy Bible are the pride of this room. I have read them all and consider myself to be profoundly privileged. Not many people, in all honesty can profess to experience the joy of so many religions.

I glance at the screen of my mobile phone pensively. I read the message again. The message which delivered the most startling of revelations. Not that it was in any way offensive. But the very fact that the concerned gentleman had harboured such thoughts for me. It read as follows: I don't want you to feel any pressure. I know life has not been easy for either of us. I am aware that I can never be the love of your life and those are very large shoes to fill. I, too, have loved like you. All I request from you is to consider spending the rest of our lives together, not as good friends any more but in the institution of marriage. If your answer is no then I will still be there, to hold your hand, respecting the boundaries of our relationship. Just like always. Please do not misunderstand me and don't feel undue pressure. There is one more thing that I have to say, and if it helps you make your decision. I do love you.

The message has triggered the insomnia. For when I sleep, it is to dream. Dreams which always end in nightmares. I must have inspired the wrath of Lord Morpheus in some way.

My mobile phone rings, and I am beside myself with fear. I stare at the screen and read Zohaib's name. It is half past five in the morning. I pray silently for nothing to be wrong.

"Hi, Mum, I was sure you would be up, sipping your tea and reading a book." His voice brims with good cheer, dispelling any uneasy thoughts.

"Hello, Zohaib, I hope everything is okay in the hospital. I mean you don't usually call this early." "Well, I did when I was being ragged in my hostel," Zohaib counters amusedly. There is a contemplative silence as if he is weighing what he has to say next. "It's beautiful, Mum, I mean, there are no words to describe it." I hear him say. "What is? I don't understand what you are talking about." Curiosity to the necessity of this 'graveyard shift' telephone call leaving me very agitated indeed.

'Dal Lake,' comes his soft reply. "It's like how you described it, Mum."

My stomach tightens in knots and threatens the bile to rise upwards. "Oh God!" I cry, does this mean? No, it can't be possible.

"Mum, I am in Srinagar." His voice is clear so I definitely cannot be dreaming. "I can now fully comprehend why you find it so fascinating."

I clutch my mobile phone tightly, not just out of concern for its safety but to hold on to something for comfort. I see it so distinctly, Dal Lake on a summer morning. The air so clear and thin. The water lilies and lotuses brimming on its surface in a splendid myriad of colours. Dal lake, or Jamil as I once had called it. The Urdu word for beautiful.

"Mum, can you hear me?" His voice sounds alarmed. "What are you doing there, Zohaib?" I try to be stoic. "Relax, Mum, I know what you are thinking right now. Be rest assured, it is nothing like that at all." Despite the sincerity in his voice, I still find it hard to allay my deepest fears. I sit on my rocking chair as my legs threaten to give way. For years, I have kept myself and him away from the only place on earth, I ever wanted to belong to. All my efforts couldn't have been wasted. Is this really happening? I am being forged to confound the fear which has always made me look backwards. The fear which like an obsession in the few moments of joy and peace, has still kept me on the edge. As 'Time,' I know for sure will reach out and ruin me in my moment most unguarded.

"How did you get there?" I marvel at the composure in my voice. Images of him driving to that part of the country in his second-hand car, send my heart rate accelerating.

He speaks softly, rendering me speechless. "Can you repeat what you said?" I make no attempt to hide my disbelief.

"Mum, you heard me right the first time." His voice is still soft, but there is no denying its authoritative tone. "I want you to fly to Srinagar tomorrow morning. I have booked you on the eleven am flight. Remember that holiday you promised we will take together, once I pass my finals. Well, this is it. I have spoken to Sheetal, and she has cleared you till next Monday. In all seriousness, she was overjoyed and told me that she was going to suggest you, to take some time off. So don't give work as an excuse. Everyone takes a holiday, Mum, even best selling authors." Sheetal is my Senior Editor, my Girl Friday and a whole lot of things rolled into one. More or less an extension of the small family I have managed for myself, in the country's power capital.

"What do you want from Kashmir, Zohaib?" I ask him nervously.

"I don't want anything, Mum. You have given me everything a child could ask for. But I definitely want to give you something from here." I sigh, somewhat in helplessness. "And what is that, Aafaq?" I do admit to myself that things are a little bewildering.

'Mum,' his voice is a soft whisper. "I am Zohaib, not Aafaq."

My tears fall silently in twin rivulets down my cheeks. "Hush, Mum, nothing is going to happen to me."

For those who are single parents with an only child, you can relate to me when I say the apron strings remain a tight knot for a long time. I was sure that not so much as a whimper has left my mouth, but Zohaib sitting miles away, knows that I am sobbing.

"Come back to me, Zohaib." I plead with him. "I can't take another desertion." Oh my God, why had I not been more vigilant? Had Zohaib been attending 'Those Sort Of Meetings' which preach nothing but religious intolerance and communal violence? I have always encouraged secularism, fought for it, wrote about it. But I never knew I will pay such a high price. Was he being lured by ISIS or something equally nefarious? A piercing pain racks my skull. I clamp my hands over my ears to lessen the impact. There is a deafening noise. I can hear it again. It is the sound of gun shots. I see masked men with Kalashnikovs, militants on the roads. Blaring loud speakers warning Kashmiri Pandits and all Hindu minorities to leave Kashmir. Hand grenades and time bombs being detonated. And the dreaded slogan which has frequented my body and soul for what seems like forever. *'Jo Khuda se kare khauff, vo utha le Kalashnikov.'* (If you believe in Allah, pick up a Kalashnikov.)

I have been dreading this moment ever since I became a mother.

"I will be there at Srinagar airport tomorrow to pick you up. I love you." The line goes dead. What was it that Zohaib had wanted to give me? I wonder.

After what seems like forever. I open my closet and take out my thickest sweaters and jackets. After all Decembers in Kashmir are cold, yes, very cold indeed.

□

2

The flight from New Delhi to Srinagar will take over an hour. I am bone weary as I flop down on my seat in the aircraft. The past twenty-four hours have been busy. Sheetal because of her camaraderie with Zohaib has rescheduled all my important meetings and events. I am the owner and Editor of a small magazine called '*Relic.*' Being a proud Indian, I want to showcase our wonderful country through my words. It has been a rewarding journey for me, and the offices of Relic have come a long way. What started as a one-room office in a dingy basement, is now a full floor on one of the more recent business complexes in the so-called upscale part of the city. I have a capable and thorough team. I love my work and my magazine is at its zenith. I have also written a book. It is a work of fiction. Everyone has loved it, and it has made its way to the best seller list. My parents who reside abroad are my biggest fans. Zohaib remains dissatisfied. He says he would appreciate something, a little more, he used the word, 'Heartfelt.' "Make it a personal narrative, Mum." He keeps on urging me. "Next time," I promise, with a procrastinating smile.

Most of the passengers in the aircraft are Kashmiri. They are so distinct with their exceptionally fair colouring. The married Hindu women are discernible with their ears pierced from inside and enormous earrings. Some of the Muslim gentlemen are wearing a skull cap. These are the people I grew up with, I played marbles with them and went to school with them. But for some reason I now shy away from them. I don't possess enough courage to go to Kashmir and confront those memories of what now seems another life-time. What will happen when I hear Heena's melodious giggle? The dead 'Give away' that she is hiding behind the gnarled Walnut Tree in our garden on Raj Bagh Road. I don't want to hunt for her amongst the strawberry orchards, the cherries and the red, Kashmiri apples. A red so crimson, like the red blush in stark contrast to her white as snow cheeks. Whenever I stop to buy strawberries on the way back from work, something prevents me from doing so. It's the vision of Heena biting into an obese strawberry, with the juice trickling down her chin. I miss you, Heena. Why aren't we going to Srinagar together?

I can't believe I am going to Kashmir. Or should I say Kashmir and Kalashnikov? Sort of like Siamese twins now. Better not voice my thoughts aloud. Before Air Marshalls strap me to my seat. I never had the dare to question Aafaq about the Kalashnikov. Or so many other things I wanted to ask him like, why this smoldering rage? I was scared that he would offer in retaliation, "What would you have done if it had happened to you?" I still don't have an answer. I have acquired the art of rhetoric speaking and writing but I can't find an apt rejoinder.

I fasten my seat belt and shut my eyes. The gentle voice of the air hostess wakes me after some time. 'Kehva,' she offers. My eyes blink furiously in confusion. I was never aware of the fact that Kehva was served on the flight to Srinagar. "We do in the winter months." She answers gently as she reads the unspoken question in my eyes. My glance falls on a small Samovar in her hands. Kehva is one of the things I have left behind.

I step back in time, and I see myself sipping steaming, hot kehva (Kashmiri brew made with saffron and dry fruits) made by my Mum. It's a cold winter night. Even now separated by both time and distance I can smell the aroma from my Mum's kitchen. The door bell is going to ring any minute, and Heena will arrive from her house on the ground floor. Soon her parents will also pour in, armed with playing cards and a massive bowl of a sumptuous Kashmiri dessert. This is a daily ritual, our two families getting together after dinner. I will wait with bated breath for Aafaq to come or pray that he doesn't. As Mum is going to send me downstairs with a mug of kehva for him, now. A warmth engulfs me from deep inside. And no one can be the wiser, in knowing as to why.

He is alone, in his house, on the ground floor. He accepts the mug, totally oblivious to the storm raging inside me. The sight of him takes my breath away. Through lowered lashes, I look at him in open adoration. He is tall, above six feet, skinny, no lanky for want of a better word. He is very fair, fairer than me (so what, I shrug) and astoundingly good looking.

But when you look into his eyes, doom is inevitable. Nothing or no one can save you. His eyes are the colour of my beautiful Dal lake on a summer afternoon. They blaze a fierce green, like the finest emerald a Maharaja covets to give to his favourite concubine. And his right eye has a tiny brown fleck which is only visible when you stand real close to him.

I take out my Math book and ask him how to solve a sum. Unsuspectingly, he starts to explain it to me and I pretend not to understand. I stare at the back of his bent neck as he repeatedly does the calculation for my benefit. And now the best part, our hands touch and fingers brush. He immediately apologizes and looks sheepish. I play act as if I am unaware about anything occurring out of the norm. The accidental grazing of our fingers has actually been the finest cunning of my wicked mind. I, too, possess the knowledge of Eve.

Aafaq politely informs me that he has to study and to tell Mum that the kehva is delicious. Since I have run out of excuses by now, I will reluctantly start to leave. The confidence that, one day, I'm going to enter this room as Aafaq's bride and it will be my boudoir, makes me sail out breezily.

'Islam and Hinduism.' Both of these religions advocate non-violence. Those following the Holy Quran, believe in *Zakat*, those following the Bhagavad Gita, believe in *Daan*. Both literally meaning an obligatory alms giving. So we really can't claim to be as different as chalk from cheese.

I even know of a Kashmir, where a Muslim landlord suffered severe blood loss in an automobile accident. His Hindu friend was the first person to rush to the hospital. He concealed from the blood bank staff that he is a hypertensive patient and is endangering his own life, by donating blood. It was the life of a best friend at stake. There couldn't have been a wife prouder of her husband than my mother was at that moment. As that Hindu friend was my father, and the hospitalized victim was Aafaq's father, Abbas Qazmi.

The slim paperback I carry for the flight ceases to hold my interest. My heart is in too much of a turmoil, and the memories, they refuse to be thwarted.

When I was a little girl, like all little girls I loved listening to fairy tales. The exquisite princesses, the gallant princes and the castles with turrets, all never failed to bewitch me. And one thing stared at me, quite rudely in the face. In every fairy tale, there was a Prince Charming, coming to the rescue of the Princess. So I started scouting around for a prince. Aafaq did fit the bill but when it comes to these things, one can't be so sure. He was handsome, tall and all that for certain. But was he virtuous? My heart would ask. I would hide this intense streak with my tomboyish behaviour. I am sort of a women's libber. (Though I did try to squeeze into my mother's corset, and needed Heena to pull me out.)

It so happened one day, on the summer of my sixth birthday on Raj Bagh Road, Srinagar. There I was, dressed in my new T-shirt and jeans and with a six year old's flagrant disregard for parental authority. I wandered out of the gates of our house. I wanted to show off my new shoes, the ones with red lights. I was out to extract my pound of flesh, from our neighbour, Zubeida, who forever was teasing Heena and me about our scarcity of dolls.

But it was Zubeida who had the last laugh. As soon as I had stepped into the lane, her ferocious Alsatian dog, Jack bit my leg.

With an amazing twist of fate, Aafaq had been playing cricket in the garden when he heard my bloodcurdling scream. He rushed to my side and swooped me into his arms, giving Jack, a deft swing of his bat. Aafaq carried me all the way to my house on the first floor. All that time he was gently urging me not to cry. I still remember the tender words he quietly spoke, '*Rosha, meri jaan, ro mat.*' Roughly translated as 'Rosha, my life or love as I would like to think, don't cry.' Aafaq had passed the test, supplied by destiny with flying colours. That was the day I fell in love with Aafaq, my own gallant hero. Mum arrived on the scene and took over, splashing all sorts of antiseptics over me. I didn't feel the sting at all but out of the corner of my eye, I saw Aafaq wince. I realized then that he loved me, too, and though we were two bodies, we were one soul, like in all those fairy tales. In my love story, Jack surely played cupid. After that incident my attitude towards Aafaq was of total hero worship. I had finally found my prince. The prince who had all the requisite virtues.

My memories are interrupted by the shrill cry of a baby, crying in his mother's lap.

The mother tries to silence him with his pacifier. If only our worries could go away so easily, I think wishfully. I am dazed as I peer into the baby's face. He returns my stare with an intense look of his own. The green hue of his eyes spellbinds me.

I realize that I have forgotten to inform my parents and my uncle about this venture of mine. Subconsciously, I deliberately avoided saying anything lest it gets them into a panic mode. I am grateful that Mum and Papa both are healthy and still have each other.

My parents, Rishabh and Promilla Kapoor had done their Doctorates in Organic Chemistry from Jammu University. My parents had both studied and fallen in love in Jammu, while writing their thesis under the same Guide. Mum was an Army brat. She had practically lived all over the country and my Colonel grandad had once upon a time been posted in Srinagar. My mother had studied in Presentation Convent over there and had strong ties to the place. Then it so happened, my grandfather went to the United Kingdom as a Military Attaché. He took his family with him. Mum lived in the county of Cumbria, in England for three years and went to school there, in a little town called Whitehaven. She loved it for so many reasons but the real reason was, it was so much like Kashmir. It was pure heaven. What, with its transparent lakes and deep forests to adorn the panorama of valleys.

My mother's family had always been inclined to the times of the Crown Rule in India. And this trait never wore thin. My great-grandfather had in fact been an Officer in the British Army. And he had even witnessed 'Coming Out' ceremonies of Royalty, in Buckingham Palace. In England, Mum acquired all the makings of a lady, ever so refined. I can say from what we ate to what we wore and even to some extent, what, and how we thought and spoke, definitely bore the influence of the Raj. When she married Papa and demurely whispered the word Kashmir for their honeymoon, to my easy going father, Kashmir it was. For Mum, it was where she could live her childhood again. Cumbria and its poetry inspiring, Lake District had always been second best. Kashmir, would always be 'home.' Mum smiled a smile, all too knowing. She was fully aware of what was going to happen.

They honeymooned in Kashmir where they steered shikaras on the Dal and braved Gondola rides with broken cables. When newlyweds posed in Kashmiri garb for the shutterbugs, my folks skied and sledged. They even trekked all the way uphill to Sonmarg and with frostbitten feet trekked all the way down. By the end of their honeymoon, Papa was not only crazy about his gorgeous bride but madly in love with her even more intriguing dowry. A dowry called 'Kashmir.' They took up jobs as Lecturers in the Department of Chemistry, Kashmir University, Srinagar City.

Mum's family soon migrated to the United Kingdom. They could be accurately termed as multi-ethnic and multi-cultural. I could boast of a Tamillian aunt and a Bengali uncle. Mum's brother went a step further and married a Briton White. Hence, I even acquired a 'Blonde Aunt Sophie,' who was as pretty as a picture. Instead of being la-di-da, as we were meant to believe she was very down to earth. She loved coming to Srinagar and would pick up shawls and samovars, in all shapes and sizes. My Briton cousins are just smashing and we love it when they say, 'Oops a daisy,' and 'A cuppa tea.' Blonde Aunt Sophie taught English to High School children in Carlisle. When she would praise and encourage me after reading the short stories I had started to write, it would really mean a lot. I travelled to England a couple of times. Yes, the cleanliness and orderliness was very inspiring but I was an Indian all the way and always will be.

Papa's family was still in Jammu. We would visit them every year. I loved my grandparents. Unfortunately, they passed away within a year of each other when I was barely ten years old. But my father's younger brother, Rudratej Kapoor made up for not having any grandparents. He was a Colonel in the Army. And larger than life. Chachu (endearment used for father's younger brother) was a dyed in the wool bachelor. When I grew older, I was let on to the fact that he was a hit with the ladies. Chachu did love his women, alright, but more than them, he loved his independence. And I loved my Chachu as he was the world's best uncle. Heena and her family also went with us, to Jammu, a couple of times. Chachu would plan his vacation accordingly and join us there in our ancestral home. My uncle would be thrilled as Aafaq and Rohan would hang on to every word he said. Mum would try to hover around, and make sure his anecdotes were censored. Chachu, somehow would still manage to get his message across.

Sorry for juggling around the timeline. Back to Kashmir and all things Kashmiri. When my parents joined Kashmir University, they had a Principal, Faizal Qazmi. He took my parents under his wing and referred them as tenants to his nephew, Mr. Abbas Qazmi, who was an Engineer. Mr. Qazmi was from a privileged background, a little short of aristocracy and had inherited an enormous mansion on Raj Bagh Road. (A very posh locale) He lived there with his wife Noor, on the ground floor. The principal actually admired my young parents especially Mum who he found full of '*Janoon*.' An Urdu word, for spunk or brass. Just right tenants for his nephew. As Abbas Qazmi had studied in MIT, Boston and needed to have 'likeminded tenants.' The two families will blend well. Those were his thoughts. He was certainly right.

I don't think the two families ever had a single minute, as second is an exaggeration of a landlord-tenant relationship. Abbas Qazmi, his beautiful wife Noor and their politely shy two-year old son, Aafaq, welcomed the Kapoors with open arms.

I was born in Srinagar two years later in 1972. Abbas Uncle had spent the whole day in the hospital with my Dad pacing up and down the hospital floor. Noor Aunty, that plucky lady, nearly full-term pregnant, arrived an hour after I was born. She was the one who placed the customary drop of honey in my mouth, and sprinkled it over my head to thwart away the evil spirits. I did earlier mention something about similarity in our traditions. That 'Warding off Evil' bit with the honey was their custom. The Hindu custom is restricted to placing a drop on the newborn's tongue.

I came home to Raj Bagh wrapped in a pink blanket with white bunnies. Heena was born a month after me and she came home in the same pink blanket. When we were little girls, I would nastily tell Heena that she had been given a 'Hand me down blanket.' It would fetch a rather reproving look from Mum. I would squirm and immediately feel woebegone. Heena was someone who had always put my happiness, above her own. I loved her wholeheartedly. One look at her hurt face would make me want to roll up in shame and spend the whole day in bed. We had crawled together, walked together and gurgled on the same day. Point to ponder, Mum would say as I being a month older, should have had my milestones before her. "Does she ever tease you about that?" Mum would quiz. That would make me loathe myself, ever the more.

I have photos of us in frilly frocks with bows and bonnets, holding each other's hands for all we were worth. (With me looking more than a wee bit sore.) We got afflicted with Chicken pox, and German measles together. Perfectly understood, as both the maladies are infectious. But how we both got Appendicitis together and had to be operated on the same day, baffled the two surgeons who did our surgeries in adjacent operation theatres. We were in the same class in Presentation Convent. The major difference being, Heena was the Nun's pet and I was the hell-raiser. They couldn't wait to see my backside those 'Ladies of genteel bearing.' I was tolerated for Mum's sake and the accolades I won in debates and symposiums. Heena and I did our homework together, we practically spent every waking minute with one another. 'Joined at the hip' that's what we were. I was good with languages and Heena loved Science. 'Woe betide' anyone who threw in their lot with us.

Rohan was born when I was nearly seven years old. Though I had gotten used to being an only child and was rather set in my ways, I still welcomed him. 'Someone to boss over.' I thought with self-importance. The fact that I got to spend a lot of nights at Heena's place when he was born and Mum was in the hospital, made it easier to love him. Apart from the mid-night feasts, I had the privilege of visiting the 'Saffron Garden.'

Undoubtedly, My Saffron Garden was a playground for Farishtey and Djinns. The tiny flora in the lush meadow tiptoed upwards as lithe as ballet dancers while they hobnobbed with tinted winged butterflies. The gentle breeze would loan a quite momentum to all of God's creations.

Since I was the only Hindu child in that Muslim-dominated neighbourhood, I quickly acquired the name '*Kafir,' Dark Kafir*. As in comparison to Kashmiri Muslims as well as Hindus I did not possess the fair colouring. *Kafir*, someone who does not believe in the Prophet. I was made to feel, a misfit. The same as what my cousins in England used to suffer, in the seventies. When during school assembly, hymns like, "Your hand is black and mine is white, but we are friends, and we will hold them tight," would be hummed.

"My hand is as brown as yours, Rosha Jaan." Aafaq told me one afternoon when I went back to the Farm House, using my thirst as a ruse to go indoors. I had been called a *'Kafir'* again. I went and hid under the kitchen table, pushing away my tears.

"Am I that dark, Aafaq?" I asked him, my eyes guileless as they searched his, for an honest answer. He solemnly replied, "You are as beautiful as the *'farishtey'* who play in the garden of heaven. Never feel small if you are dark." But I wasn't one to give up and said in childhood honesty, "*Farishtey* have wings, Aafaq. I don't."

He took out his brushes and easel and painted two pairs of wings, one for me and one for Heena.

He then set forth to cut them out and decorate them with glitters. We flapped our wings, hopped, skipped and jumped around the farm, at sunset, all of us. We were children of this earth and lived for the day. The wings had taken the sting out of the *Kafir* episode, for a while. But anyone who has experienced racism will understand that it is a hurt that remains somewhere buried in your heart. *Kafir*, I cover my ears with my hands. It still has the power to disturb me. It's an awful feeling, to feel the odd one out. You start to rebel.

Rohan turned out to be a good child. He loved soccer, computers and Aafaq. And Aafaq also reciprocated this sentiment. I would feel envious when Rohan would get to piggy back on his bike. Heena, knowing her brother all too well, never asked to be taken. I would beg like a tramp. Bat my eyelashes at Aafaq and try out all my feminine wiles to ingratiate myself to him. To rid himself of me and my adulation, he would let me straddle behind him. We would go to Boulevard Road. I would hold on to him tightly and face the cold air spiralling over the Dal Lake, with exuberance.

Eid and Diwali would be celebrated with equal excitement and fervour on both our floors. I loved

Eid, especially Eid-ul-Fitr which came after the Ramzans. I would sleep over at Heena's house, both of us unable to grab our forty winks. We would be trying on our new clothes which Heena's parents had bought for us all. I loved eating the sumptuous *seviyyan*, the first thing in the morning while waiting for the *Iddi* money, (gifts of cash) uncle would generously shower us with.

Aunty would take us to the mosque to pray. There would be a separate entrance for women and children. Mum would also go. In fact, I would love to see my mother dressed up on Eid. She never did for Diwali but every Eid, aunty would gift Mum a lovely hand embroidered salwar shirt. Mum would never disappoint Noor aunty, certainly not at Eid. She would wear the suit with her natural elan and pray with devotion.

Why, then have we in the name of religion, chosen to defile our neighbour's property, to plunder and wipe out their lives?

How have we succumbed to the scheming of our leaders, their intent so Machiavellian?

It's about respecting your own religion because no Faith on this earth teaches us to hate and destroy. The tranquility I would experience sitting next to Heena, with a chador (a long scarf) draped around me, raising my head in prayer is incomparable to any sensation I have ever felt. I have trampled bare feet in temples, made earnest requests for penance in cathedrals, taken vows of silence but I have never encountered what I felt in the mosque beside Heena, my sister, by blood. Nothing can replicate that feeling of peace.

□

3

"What is a Guldasta, Papa?" I ask my father as I scramble onto his knee in the balcony of our house boat. "It means a big bouquet of flowers." My curiosity is not satisfied. "But why is Kashmir called a Guldasta, Papa?" "Because my dear child. We practise Kashmiriyat which means the true respect, of all people, of all religions. We are Hindus, but we respect Heena's religion, similarly they give regard to ours. Thus, like a big bouquet of flowers we all stay together and spread a lovely fragrance. Muslims, Hindus, Sikhs and Buddhists all reside in harmony in Kashmir. This is what we call Kashmiriyat." "One day we will have Kashmiriyat all over the world," I say to myself.

Though no one in my house was very religious, we were brought up to be God fearing. Mum and Papa instilled character shaping and moral values in us. Papa only took offense when we would lie. That would make him ballistic. 'I hate liars.' He would bellow our way. We were taught the difference between right and wrong. Since we had different religions and ethnic origins in our family itself, acceptance and reverence towards all beliefs was easy.

Heena had eyes only for Ruhail. He was her first cousin, and it was normal and natural for them to wed cousins. There was a sort of understanding between their respective families that one day they would be married.

It was as if they were already betrothed. Ruhail was a nice enough person and kind of cute, but my loyalties lay with Aafaq.

Often Heena would talk about Ruhail with longing. I would be tempted to bare my heart out to her, about 'My love knowing no bounds for Aafaq' but something would always hold me back. I still wasn't sure of what her reaction would be. At this moment, while she was talking about Ruhail's sister, Shireen's wedding, I could envision myself getting married to Aafaq. We were eating walnuts on the patio. "Well, you can get to see her today." I had been so lost in my thoughts that I hadn't been paying attention to Heena and stared at her blankly. "See who?" I asked full of regret that I had to snap out of my lovely daydream. "Rosha, why aren't you listening? Where do you wander to, when you get so absorbed." "I am a writer, Heena." I announced with as much aplomb as possible. "I have the privilege of being eccentric, whereas you are a woman of science and always have to have your wits around you."

"I was talking about Saira Hyder Ali. Her family has sent a marriage proposal to Ammi and Abu for Bhai Jaan. She is going to be there at Shireen's *Nikah* today, where they will meet each other, for the first time. Saira has seen Bhai Jaan somewhere before and has fallen head over heels in love with him. But then who wouldn't?" Heena announced with sisterly pride. With my heart bleeding and pride wounded, I managed. "Isn't it a little old fashioned? Getting married without actually being in love. I don't think Aafaq will agree. I am sure he would like to know the person." There was a defensive edge to Heena's tone as she spoke. "They will be given time to court and do all that mushy stuff. Her family is very educated and she has studied abroad." I felt jealousy raise its very ugly head. To think that not only was she from their community and must be as gorgeous as they come, she had even studied abroad. Heena looked at me closely as if trying to appraise what was going on in my mind. "You seem to know Bhai Jaan quite well." I flippantly ignored her and took long strides indoors.

This can't be happening! Aafaq is supposed to be mine. Where on earth has this Saira Hyder Ali come from? I raved and ranted to myself as I paced all over the floor of my room. What did Heena mean that they were going to meet each other? How pathetic is that? I pounded the pillows on my bed with annoyed fists.

Shireen looked exceptionally pretty in her red bridal clothes as we sat with her in one of the '*zenana*' rooms. I looked around trying to figure out who could be that dreadful girl, Saira Hyder Ali. I saw a young lady enter the room. I had a gut feeling that she is the one. She does look rather mature, I thought cattily. She was very conservatively dressed and had her head covered not just with a scarf but with her *chador* as well. I had to admit reluctantly, though in an austere manner, she was fetching. She was what they called a handsome woman as there was nothing delicate about her. She possessed a hardness. As if sensing my stare, she glared back at me with a look which would have made a more mellow person tremble with fear. 'Wouldn't like to get on her wrong side' I thought to myself. Soon I heard every one offering felicitations and realized the *Nikah* had been performed. It was later during dinner when we were all in the massive reception hall, I saw Saira staring at Aafaq quite openly. It were as if she would devour him, then and there. I had never seen such raw emotion spilling out of a pair of eyes. Heena nudged me excitedly. "That's her," she whispered, discretely pointing at Saira. I nodded with a semblance of a smile, dying inside.

Precisely two days after Shireen's wedding, a tear faced Heena entered my room. "He has said no, Rosha Jaan." I looked at Heena surprised to see her face all wound up. "Bhai Jaan has refused the proposal for Saira's hand in marriage. He has said that he doesn't want to marry anyone, and no way will he go to meet Saira if he doesn't want to get married. Ammi and Abu are relieved." She said in one breath. "Why? I thought they would have approved considering the family background and religion are all in order." Heena shook her head. "Ammi spoke to her on the evening of Shireen's *Nikah* and found her rigid in her outlook and far too opinionated. She actually had the discourtesy to tell Ammi that we were being non-Islamic by keeping Hindu tenants. Can you believe the cheek of the girl?" But I didn't hear a single word. I was delighted there were going to be no wedding bells. Who was bothered with what Saira had to say? When I thought of her eyes and the naked greed with which she had looked at Aafaq, I felt nauseous.

A couple of weeks had passed to this event when I witnessed Mum and Noor Aunty speaking in hushed tones to one another. And as I heard Aafaq's name being mentioned, I knew I was duty bound to eavesdrop. "I don't understand, how can someone spread such malicious lies about their own daughter?" That was Noor Aunty. I kept my ears glued to the door of my room. I furtively peeped through the open space. The door was ajar, and I saw Mum handover aunty a cup of tea. I didn't have the slightest idea what they were talking about but it all seemed very mysterious to me. It was evident that Noor Aunty was very upset about something and Mum was comforting her.

The next morning Heena revealed the sensational details while we were on our way to the bus stop. Apparently, Saira Hyder and her parents had been affronted with Aafaq turning down the marriage proposal. Between sobs, Heena told me that Ruhail's mother had told Noor Aunty that Saira's parents were going around accusing Aafaq of being involved with Saira in a 'No holds barred, torrid love affair.' "What, how sick, I mean how can they cast such false accusations?" I couldn't believe it. But it didn't stop at that. Heena revealed sorrowfully, "Bhai Jaan was roughed up by some boys outside his college, a couple of days ago. They were Saira's cousins and have threatened him with dire consequences. Abbu and Ruhail's father had gone to meet Saira's parents last night, but they have left the country. We have been informed that they are in Iran. Abu has gently told us all to put it behind us as an unpleasant episode. Bhai Jaan is very disturbed. I mean, what do you think his friends will say?" Heena declared fervently. I held her hand firmly. "We have had a narrow escape. Bhai Jaan says that in the party she came right up to him and admitted to be crazy for him. Bhai Jaan made himself scarce and had left soon." "It's over now." I placated Heena. "As for Aafaq's reputation, I think it is going to take more than the crazy accusations of a deranged mind to damage it. Everyone who knows Aafaq will never believe what Saira and her family have to say. Come on now, I want you to smile." I ordered Heena. Aafaq and me were meant to be. I thought. It is written in the stars. I pushed Saira out of my mind.

□

4

I soon became seventeen years old. I can't say that I was 'A looker.' But I had lost my puppy fat and had acquired a pair of shapely legs. My hair was shorn short in a page boy manner. I had a cute face with two identical dimples on either cheek. I still felt gauche and clumsy walking next to Heena, but so would Princess Di. Anyway, I was proud of Heena. I could swear to myself that I had caught Aafaq looking my way once or twice. And that's what mattered to me. Everything and everyone, paled in comparison. The expression on his face would be soft, bordering on the wistful. That didn't bother me as I felt I had aroused his interest. He was now studying to be a Computer Engineer from the Regional Engineering College, Srinagar. He had always been a Mathematics prodigy and was great with fixing blenders and television sets. I had started to feel that he was sort of distancing himself from us, me in particular. When I had mentioned it to Heena, she had brushed it aside saying that he was like that with her, too. I sensed she was just trying to make me feel better.

I guessed it was time for me, to have a tete-à-tete with Mum. We had our 'Birds and the Bees' chat a couple of years ago. Where Mum had been modest, Jackie Collins had filled in the blanks. Obviously, with the most graphical of scripts. I could affirm that I was well informed about the pleasures of the flesh. Mum had sweetly yet firmly reinforced they were pleasures only at the right time, with the right person and when the heart is involved.

I had two out of a scale of three. Right person, heart assuredly involved. Now where to get the right timing from?

Mum was making mutton curry. It was called Rogan Josh in Kashmir. I loved it and Mum would make it very often in the winters. The two men of the house had gone for a stroll. I sat across the small makeshift kitchen table thinking how I should steer the conversation towards Aafaq? Call it mother's intuition, the fact that I was playing with the mutton rather than greedily helping myself to my usual enormous helpings. Mum definitely sensed something was troubling me. She filled her plate and sat across the table giving me a rather pointed look.

"Come on, Rosha," Mum rolled her eyeballs in exasperation. "Spill it out. What have you done this time?" I realized Mum was referring to school. She had thought I had gotten into trouble with Sister Loyala again. The Nuns had always felt morally bound to inform their brilliant ex-student about her daughter's assumed wayward behaviour. Only last month the school had called Mum at work and complained that I was laughing during Morning Assembly. I had been, but then I didn't deserve to be branded a trespasser in the land of morality. "Mum," I said a bit hesitantly, clutching at straws, not knowing how to begin. She looked at me straight ahead without speaking. "Mum," I repeated this time a little louder, my confidence wavering under her unflinching stare.

"I heard you the first time, Rosha, no need to raise your voice." Her gaze narrowed and she came to the point. "Let me hazard a guess. Is this regarding Aafaq?" I wasn't surprised at all that Mum had realized what it was all about. She had a sixth sense about us, especially when it came to me. Probably due to my fetish for always landing into trouble.

"Darling, I've been wanting to speak to you for some time and I think it's very important that we talk, now that it's the two of us." I don't know how it came out of my mouth but I blurted, "I love Aafaq, and I am going to marry him." There, I had said it out loud, my expression belligerent. If I had meant to rattle her, it certainly hadn't worked. She looked at me without so much as a flicker of her lash.

"So, when are you going to tell him?" She gently parried. "Mum, why are you making fun of me?" She was acting rather nasty, I thought to myself.

"Why on earth should I do that?" Her voice carried the correct amount of surprise. "When you love someone, you should tell them." Mum's tone was equable but the intent was not lost on me. "Your father might be unaware, but I have guessed since some time that you have more than a childhood crush on Aafaq. I may not be a rocket scientist but do credit me with some adequate amount of intellect." I shifted nervously.

'Rosha', she said thoughtfully as if weighing her words. "Love is a very beautiful thing, and my darling daughter there is nothing like knowing the person you love, loves you back."

"You mean like you and Dad?" I questioned hesitantly. "Mum, you are petite and beautiful. Men always look at you protectively. Dad says he fell for you the moment he saw you." I heard the petulance in my voice and felt awful. I had always been proud of my charismatic mother, but now I had sounded so mean spirited.

She didn't reply but alighted from her chair and walked up to me. I saw her eyes looking at me pensively. "You are my first born, Rosha, and I never want to see you sad. The guy who falls in love with you is going to be the most fortunate person on this earth because you, my little minx, are one of a kind." She held me in a tight embrace as if trying to impart me some of her immense strength. I realized at that moment that I could discuss any topic under the sun, with my mother. I had never known that under her no-nonsense exterior, Mum was a softie.

'Sweetheart,' she continued. "Looks and clothes don't make a person, it's what lies beneath all the finery. It is the soul and the heart that are important." I loved my mother, but I don't think I've ever loved her, as much as I did then. I heard Mum's voice, as she asked me rather incredulously. "Please, do let me know who on earth has given you the impression that you are not pretty? Let me guess." She continued. "Sister Loyala. I think we will have to ignore her, won't we? She's ninety years old if not a day older. And I do agree, she is a defender of the laws a bit too draconian." Mum lovingly stroked the hair, back from my eyes. "I would advise you to do away with the fringe though. You are aware that their religion does allow them to keep more than one wife?" I could sense the graveness in Mum's tone. There was a pregnant silence. "Right now you probably think that such a situation will never arise but are you prepared to face the possibility?" I didn't realize it then, but my tone was definitely protective. "Mum, I have asked Heena, and it was sort of a feudal practice which has faded away with time. There is no one like that in their family. Besides, they can only do it only after the first wife gives some sort of consent."

"You do seem to have done your homework," she said casually looking my way, her brows a perfect arch.

"As for parental disapproval from his side, I don't think you will get any." I could sense she was being a tad too secretive or over confident so I asked her frankly. "Rosha dear," Mum said, her face softening. "Noor and I have been friends now since quite some time, and like all best friends, we grow on one another. And sometimes we can tell what our friends feel, deep in their heart. When my best friend makes a statement like, 'I would love to have a daughter-in-law like Rosha'. I do think I am entitled to read a bit into it."

My eyes lit up with hope. Except for my prospective groom of whom I was a bit unsure, things did not seem to be all that bleak. I got up and hugged my mother as hard as I could. She had a lot more than '*Janoon*', she had what you call the, 'whole package.'

"Tell him, Darling." Mum whispered into my ear. "Never keep the person you love in doubt regarding what you feel. I sometimes get the impression that he still thinks you are his kid sister." Mum's face was thoughtful as if she had mulled over that last rejoinder and found it necessary to express.

Later at night I lay on my bed, thinking, rather I plotted and planned. Sister, my foot! I already have a brat of a brother, and you, Aafaq, my hero, already have a sister. It is about time you set your gallantry aside. My mouth broke out into a naughty smile. I laughed out loud at what I had in mind.

I rummaged around in my closet and fished out my tightest pair of jeans. They were my pride and joy and fit like a glove, emphasizing my slim legs, while hanging snugly on my hips. Armed with a pair of shears, I unceremoniously cut both legs of the jeans, transforming them into shorts. Now they were shorts which would still fit like a glove, accentuating my curves and exposing my long legs to perfection. With the additional advantage of revealing bare flesh. 'If you've got it, flaunt it.'

After making sure everyone was fast asleep, I took out a bottle of depilatory cream which had been stolen from Mum's room, without guilt pricking at my conscience. The dipping mercury didn't stop me from peeling off my quilted nightwear and going into the bathroom. I breathed in and took out the applicator of the cream, evenly spreading it all over my arms and legs. I cringed as my virgin skin felt its first taste of chemicals. 'Operation

Deforestation,' was finally over. Result, under the most critical and microscopic scrutiny of mine, Roshina Kapoor looked sparky. Yes, a few blotches here and there. But it had been my first time.

After much deliberation in the night, I made up my mind that I had to make a clean breast of things with Heena. She had a major role to play in what I had planned, though no way was I going to use her as a pawn. Never! I drew the line very clearly when it was about being treacherous to Heena.

We were sitting in the garden the following afternoon, enjoying the sun. Noor Aunty had placed an enormous bowl of fresh strawberries in front of us and we were helping ourselves generously. I summoned my courage and told Heena about how hopelessly in love I was with Aafaq. After an enormous coughing fit which got her even more red faced, Heena burst into tears. I felt numb with pain. Does Heena not consider me a good enough soulmate for her brother?

She must have seen my chagrined expression. As she got up from her chair and sat next to me, her cough fortunately halting.

'Rosha,' she said, "You don't know how happy you've made me by telling me this. I've wanted you for a Bhabhi since ages. (Bhabhi meaning brother's wife in Hindi and Urdu both.) I never mentioned it to you as I wasn't really sure about how you felt. That's why I have repeatedly been talking about Ruhail in front of you. I've actually wanted you to open up. I have seen you look at Aafaq a couple of times," she added slyly. I blushed, and my dimples emerged with a bounce. Heena and I hugged and kissed as tears of joy trailed down our cheeks. Then like what we did as little girls, running after butterflies in Pehalgam. We jumped up and down, clapped our hands and giggled.

"My best friend Rosha, my sister, by blood, now legally will be my sister. Do you know that Ammi and Abu adore you? Ammi says that religion is to teach you how to love and tolerate. Abbu was mentioning what a fine, young woman you have turned out to be. And that he has some nice Hindu friends in the United States who are looking for girls from India for their sons. Furthermore, he is going to suggest it to your parents. This way you will get an opportunity to go and study over there. It was the same time Ammi casually mentioned how pretty you have become." Heena elaborated. I was all ears now at this interesting piece of information. I noticed how her face started to look uncertain and I realized she wasn't telling me some thing. "What is it, Heena? Did Aafaq say that he doesn't find me pretty?"

"Don't be stupid," Heena retorted sharply. "Whatever made you think that? It's when Ammi sort of directed the question Aafaq's way, he got up from the dining table. He curtly told Ammi that it is improper on her part to be talking about you like that in front of him as you are like a younger sister." Heena and I exchanged looks while we reached the same conclusion. There was only one serpent in my Paradise and his name was, Aafaq Qazmi.

Two brains were now working together to outsmart the unsuspecting Aafaq. Heena approved of the ripped jeans, though she couldn't stop giggling. Our plot thickened. I smile broadly to myself in the aircraft at the memory of that giggle.

We didn't have to wait long as the following Friday evening both set of parents went to the club. Somehow, we cajoled Rohan into staying back. We required his services for what we had in mind. Heena had decided to go to Zubeida's house. She was our friend now. Rohan had been lured along with her, after being tempted with Lebanese wraps which the vendor had started selling at the end of our road. Heena would spend an hour with

Zubeida and then go for the wraps. That would give me nearly a good two hours to execute my plan. Rohan would definitely demand to have an ice cream, keeping them out of the house for more time.

With Heena and Rohan gone, I immediately sprang into action. I took off my thick trousers and slipped into those self-designed, sexy shorts with a sleeveless tank top. It had seen better days and now with the weight I had lost, it emphasized my slim waist and young breasts. I then discarded my sensible moccasins for a pair of strappy sandals.

Heena had spent the afternoon painting my nails a pretty pink. I had found the colour totally repugnant. Heena had flashed me a silencing look and insisted I needed all the ammunition I could gather, to look feminine.

I went downstairs into Heena's room and snuggled into the thick quilt on her bed. I sneaked a look at my watch. Aafaq had called an hour ago informing Heena he would be back by seven in the evening. That should be any time now. Within a couple of minutes, I heard the front door open. I discarded the quilt and lay on top of the bed as elegantly as possible. With my eyes firmly closed, I gave a good performance of being asleep.

'Heena,' I heard Aafaq call out. His voice came from just outside my door, and I quickly switched off the table light. After a gentle knock he entered the room. 'Heena,' he said again, surprise in his voice that his sister would be asleep, with the lights off so early. "I hope you are feeling alright." I laughed to myself at his brotherly concern. His hand went to the light switch at the entrance of the room and he turned it on. He stopped short as he realized that it wasn't his sister but me, a semi-clad 'me.'

I started rubbing my eyes as if the harsh light had awoken me from a centuries old sleep. With my arms stretching wide, I curved my body backwards and gave an enormous yawn. 'Aafaq,' I said looking at him in wonder.

The absurdity of the situation shocked him, rendering him speechless. I was sure he was actually inculpating himself for opening his sister's bedroom door.

"Heena and I were preparing for this test, but Rohan insisted that he be taken for Lebanese wraps. He started howling like the baby he is. Heena had to take him. I must have fallen asleep while studying."

If Aafaq found it odd that on a cold night in the Switzerland of India, I was dressed for the beach. Or despite my repeated mention of studying, there wasn't a book next to me, he certainly didn't mention it. His face suddenly looked sullen. "You are going to catch pneumonia if you don't dress properly, Roshina." His voice was dry. He had never addressed me like that before, had always called me Rosha Jaan. I really liked the way my name sounded coming from his lips. With that he abruptly turned around and walked out of the room. "Was the guy only part human?" I thought, as a feeling of helplessness engulfed me. It wasn't supposed to be like this. He was supposed to be mesmerized with my bare arms and legs, not to mention my flat midriff. I had imagined him embracing me with passion, declaring how love for me is driving him crazy. Here he was sulking like a virgin who has been asked to kiss a bloke. I could have frozen to death. After my painful ablutions of the previous night is this what I get? I was inwardly seething with rage. But I was not about to give up like that. I hurriedly slipped on my sandals and followed him. We had planned every thing down to the minutest detail. It was time for 'Plan B.'

I knocked at his door, the feeling that it was just the two of us in this massive house giving me a thrill. The heady sensation being, I had caught his eyes, lingering for a second more than you could assuredly term 'brotherly' on my legs. Aafaq Qazmi, there is more to you than what meets the eye. His voice was brusque as he ordered me to enter.

I stepped inside his room, frissons of excitement shooting through me. "Aafaq, I need to borrow your essay 'Bapu and I.' We have got to write a paper on the Mahatma, and I need to be in Sister Loyala's good books desperately." "What have you done now?" Aafaq asked trying to hide his curiosity by keeping his voice sardonic. "Oh! nothing really, I was just reading a novel during the English period. A Mills and Boon." I told him with saccharine sweetness.

"I don't know where the essay is." He replied slowly not reacting to my statement which was a sort of double entendre from my end. I had deliberately mentioned those novels famous for their explicit love making scenes. Obviously, you don't know where your essay is, moron. I wanted to say, as it is safely locked in my closet upstairs. It has been since ages.

"Do you do it on purpose?" He finally decided to look at me as he spoke. I was inconveniencing him now, that was sure. "Do what?" I asked in a butter wouldn't melt in my mouth tone. "Get into trouble all the time. I mean you can read your ridiculous novel at home. No one is stopping you. But you have to do it in school. It's like now. Here we are in the middle of winter, and you are practically roaming around with no clothes on at all. Are these your cries for attention?" He was bristling with anger now. "What's wrong with you, Aafaq? I know you are older than us, but you don't have to be such a stick in the mud. Why are you so worked up about me dressing like this? You are practically my brother." I looked at him daringly. Our eyes met. Mine challenging, his burning with rage.

"Heena doesn't roam around like this." He snarled. "Have some sense. We are alone at home, the two of us.

And you are not a blood relative. The least you can do is put a sweater on. Here take this." He picked up his denim jacket from the bed and tried to drape it around me. I shrugged my slim shoulders in defiance and let it slide to the floor carelessly.

"What are you actually scared of, Aafaq, me catching a cold or the fact that I'm not your little sister? I already have a brother. I don't want another one. Let's face it you even have a problem looking at me. There can be only two reasons. One you find me ugly. And the other being," I added provocatively. I tossed my head backwards exposing my graceful neck to him. I paused for effect but said nothing. I waited patiently and completed the sentence. "You find me sexy and don't want to admit it and certainly not to yourself. As in your warped up brain you are trying to convince yourself that you are wrong to have less than brotherly thoughts about me."

Saying that, I walked out of the room. I certainly deserved an Oscar for my performance. Five more minutes of this sultry siren act would surely land me in hospital with hypothermia. I ran upstairs and put the heater on in my room and snuggled into my flannelled night clothes. I felt like the cat that got the cream.

Heena was in splits of laughter when I told her what had transpired between the two of us. 'My poor brother,' she said, holding her sides. I looked at her shrewdly. Aafaq was her one and only sibling and she loved him dearly. She couldn't be too thrilled with my harassment of him. As if she could read my mind she hurriedly extinguished my fears. "Of course, I'm feeling sorry for him. He is totally in love with you. He just has to come to terms with it. He is wallowing in self-denial, I am sure of that. Now let's chart out what to do next."

Thus, started a sequence of events to bring Aafaq around. To say that we put our nose to the grindstone, thinking of how to annoy him in every possible way, would be very accurate indeed.

I for one, wore clothes which were about three sizes small whenever Aafaq was around. I ransacked Rohan's wardrobe picking out clothes that were unisexual enough. And didn't I look lovely in those snug fitting T-shirts? For the love of God, Rohan couldn't figure out why I had developed a sudden fondness for his clothes and that, too, outgrown ones. I traded my old walkman with him and had to constantly finance his gourmand appetite. All for a 'Has Been' T-shirt, which looked groovy on me. My brother certainly didn't come cheap.

A fortnight had passed since the 'semi-nude episode.' Ever since then, Aafaq could hardly be seen in the house, as he was spending a lot of time at his campus on a project. I knew what the real reasons for his absences were. He was trying to stay away from me as much as possible. Yesterday something happened, and I couldn't tell which court the ball had rolled into.

Heena and I had gone for a walk the previous evening and so engrossed were we in our daily chatter that we lost track of time. We had also wandered a few lanes too far from our house. It had become quite dark, and we usually never stayed out till this late. We were relieved when we met Yaseer and his twin Junaid. The two brothers lived a few blocks away and were Aafaq's friends. We accepted their offer to drive us back home, without a murmur of protest.

Aafaq met us at the house gates and a very annoyed Aafaq indeed. He was glaring at us when we alighted from the car. One look at him and it was obvious that he was not going to tolerate any sort of explanation from us. We walked passed him quietly. Heena was petrified, but I held my head high and returned his severe glance with a very calm one of my own. Barely had we made it to Heena's room when he walked in muttering something under his breath. I realized he was indeed very furious. But with what? I nearly cried out in exasperation. It was just a measly lift back home.

He looked at both of us, his eyes stormy. "Are you two out of your mind?" We looked at each other and then back at him. I knew that though the question was directed at both of us, his accusation was meant for me.

"What do you mean?" Heena asked, her voice trembling.

"First of all, you go roaming around like ragamuffins with tiny clothes on, all over the house." Touché, was my instant thought. "Then, you step outside like hooligans and gallivant away to glory, way after sunset. To top it off, you have the audacity to get into a car with not one but two boys, and you take a little spin with them. Stop feigning ignorance. Both of you are not little girls any more. You are grown up. How stupid are the pair of you? What do you know about those boys?" His voice shook with rage, and he was not trying to conceal it at all. "If you had gotten lost, you should have gone into one of the houses and made a call home. Why do you have to walk so far away from home in the first place?" He was yelling at the top off his voice now, totally unconcerned that he could probably be heard miles away.

"But Aafaq," Heena managed defensively. "They are friends of yours. It was dark and...." Alas, he was in no mood to be reasoned with.

"So what if they are my friends, Heena? Do you know that both of them are doing drugs? Do you have any idea what happens to your thinking, your brain, when you are on a drug high?" I could tangibly feel the desperation in his voice which at that moment I hailed as an unfounded paranoia.

"We weren't supposed to know that were we?" I said softly. "I think you are over reacting. It's my fault. I told Heena that it is okay to come home with them. We didn't think of calling because we were not sure where you would be." I knew Heena wouldn't be able to bear his fury any more. It was clear that she was on the verge of tears. I wanted Aafaq away from us. He was behaving like an overbearing bully.

He looked at me for a long-time. "I'm not buying that story. No blaming games. You two have to grow up. There are consequences for your actions. How come you are not wearing one of Rohan's miniscule sweaters today?" He sneered.

At least my clothes had caught his attention. I thought wryly.

I blurted out in my most sarcastic tone, "Sorry, for being a bad influence on Heena."

He gave me a murderous look. "I don't know what's gotten into you, Roshina. I never said that at all." I wasn't going to let him off the hook so easily. "You did bring the matter of my attire up. Heena doesn't roam around semi-nude. You said that the other day, didn't you? All I am saying is that since you think I am to blame for every thing. It's okay by me." My tone was merciless. I had had enough of his high handedness. "Insult me all you want, Roshina Kapoor, but don't insult my sister's love for you." He snapped back. I wanted to hit him hard, the opinionated zealot. Heena's gaze flittered from Aafaq's face to mine. I recognized the amusement in her eyes as she realized Aafaq had a lot of issues to deal with right now. Us getting into the car with those assumed dopers was the least of them.

He left, realizing that when engaged in verbal assault with Roshina the great, don't ever expect to win.

Today I wasn't able to get a glimpse of him at all. Heena had told me he was in a foul mood before leaving for college. It was way after everyone was fast asleep that I heard Aafaq walk softly up the stair case that led to the terrace. I knew he smoked before going to bed and preferred the solace and isolation of the roof top. I waited for some time and followed him as quietly as possible. I stepped foot on the terrace and saw him silhouetted against the dark of the sky.

"What do you want now, Rosha?" Aafaq quipped without turning my way. His voice sounded weary and my heart overflowed with love for him. Since I had lately become a glutton for punishment, I walked up to him with purpose. He was taking the last few drags of his cigarette, and I snatched the butt out of his hand and inhaled on it deliberately. His eyes were fixed on me, and I made a tremendous effort to make sure my hands did not quaver under his keen stare. I looked into his eyes and knew for sure that both of us were remembering a similar incident of last year. It had been around the same time of night, and I had gone up after him, following him with the stealth of a spy. After constant pestering, he had reluctantly allowed me to take a drag of his cigarette. In fact, he had held it in between my inexperienced lips and watched curiously as I had inhaled. He had smiled indulgently at my cough which had followed. This time I did not cough, not because I had started smoking. Somehow lady luck which was definitely absent in my life had resurfaced, to spare me some humiliation. "What, no cough?" He derided. His brows rose as if expecting an answer. I pointedly ignored him, happy inside though, that he, too, remembered.

The wind tousled my hair, and I didn't know that I made a bewitching picture. I shivered as I was tired. These daily battles with Aafaq were both mentally and physically exhausting. I was drawing the conclusion that you can't force someone to love you back in return. I felt my behaviour was pushing him away from me. I did not have the strength to live without him. Better to have him in my life as a friend rather than not have him at all. I ventured softly. "Why are you doing this to me?"

I looked at his lips wondering what it would feel like, to be in his arms and to feel his lips pressed on mine. He was looking at me. I could not read his expression at all, but I did feel him inching towards me. His lips parted as if he was about to say something, but the moment, if there had been one, was lost as soon as it had come. As if regretting his momentarily display of emotion, he was back on his guard again. He turned away from me. "Go to bed, Rosha, or if you want to stay here, fetch a jacket. I'm going downstairs. Good night." My mind worked furiously, over time. There would never again be a moment like this. I held on to his arm forcing him to look at me. "Aafaq, what have I done to make you dislike me so much?" I had certainly underestimated his acting skills as he looked unshaken. "You are crazy, Rosha Jaan. You always have been. That's why it is so difficult to dislike you. Even when one wants to." He smiled at me, but it was a tender smile, I can tell you that. With that, he left, without looking my way at all. After staring at the sky for several minutes I hurried downstairs. Sleep eluded me for the better part of the night. I was reliving every minute of what happened between the two of us. Now had I received a mixed message from Aafaq? The thought unsettled me through dawn.

□

5

"He might have a girl friend or someone he likes. Have you ever considered that?" Chachu asked me while he puffed on his pipe. We were sitting in our balcony as I poured out my pain of 'love so unrequited.'

My dismal mood was made a little better since the arrival of Chachu. He was being assigned a new posting in Ambala and had come to spend a couple of days with us before he joined. I could make out from my parent's conversation that Chachu like always had made quite an impression in the club the previous evening. And not with the gentlemen, mind you.

When I came back from school I revealed all to Chachu. He heard me carefully. I even told him all about my 'shorts disaster' and how angry Aafaq had been after the infamous 'car dropping episode.' Chachu blew bubbles of smoke expertly and lent me a very practiced ear. (He was after all the confidant of many a lady.)

Chachu hugged me gently and wiped away the tears from my eyes with a red, silk handkerchief. "Kaju, I had never taken you for a coward," was all he said. Chachu had always called me Kaju, meaning cashew nut in Hindi, since the time I was a baby and would eat nothing but cashews, till I was sick and silly. 'Now we are Chachu and Kaju.' He had proudly informed a three-year old me as I sat, perched on his shoulders. Like Mum, he fondly ran his fingers through my hair trying to push the stubborn locks back from my eyes. "No, he doesn't have a girl friend." I told him in a wavering voice. "He would have confided to Ruhail, and Heena would have known." Chachu cupped my chin deftly and looked at me with paternal tenderness. "You do know that you are not a niece but a daughter to me so do you want me to take out my gun? Or run him under my new tank? Roshina, you have disappointed me."

If Chachu had wanted to cheer me up, he had definitely succeeded. I let out a guffaw of laughter.

"I am not a coward, it's just that I don't know what to do. You won't understand. It's easy for you to be judgmental as you have always been a lady killer. You have never faced rejection. Aafaq probably isn't interested in me. I don't look like Mum. I surely don't look like Heena. My legs are too long. No way am I delicate. I am never going to find a boy my height. Thanks to you." I grumpily stated. Chachu was well over six feet and had passed on the gene for tall, to Rohan and me. I saw him smile, as the tears threatened to run down my face again. I took gulps of air. "Kaju, I will not have you crying like this. Today this old man is going to beat the crap out of that scoundrel called Aafaq Qazmi." He spoke in all sincerity, and I smiled, despite my sorrow. I don't know whether it was Chachu calling himself old or Aafaq a scoundrel. Both the descriptions were far from the truth.

"Yes, I agree, you are not like your Mum, or like Heena. But beauty is skin deep. And Rosha, when a guy looks at you he immediately snaps you up as marriage material. My unit was head over heels in love with you last year. If only you knew how those Lieutenants and Captains have been sucking upto me ever since you visited Jabalpur." I looked at Chachu doubtfully. Did he think I am an idiot? "You are politely trying to tell me that I am ordinary looking." I was so low on self-esteem that moment. "If you cry so much, you are going to ruin your eyes and will need to wear glasses." He looked at me as he said ebulliently, "Men don't make passes at women who wear glasses. That's one thing I can say for a fact. Now let your Chachu take charge, you don't have to worry one bit as I am here." He kissed my forehead. "Rosha, what I would have done to have a daughter like you?" His voice was full of self-reproach.

As expected Chachu true to his word or a little untrue, as he didn't beat the crap out of Aafaq but took him out for some guy bonding. He did give me a conspiratorial wink before the two of them set out. They returned late in the evening and he came into my room before joining my parents. "Underneath the cover of the introvert boy lies someone very committed to his goals and family. The two of us got down to some real talking. I offered him a beer which he politely declined citing the respect for elders angle. I liked that. He told me about his course and how he wants to study further. I even asked him if he was keen on joining the Armed Forces. We are looking for sharp-minded, young professionals like him. He said he wasn't sure and will definitely let me know, in case. I threw the bait. I asked him if he liked anyone or was he seeing anyone. He said that he didn't have the time and hasn't really liked anyone to make all the effort. I sort of asked him about the qualities he looks for in a girl. Please listen," Chachu smiled at me smugly. "She should love his family, not just him. She needn't be a Madam Curie. But should possess some decent amount of intellect. I told him that we had been approached by some prospective suitors in Jammu for your hand in marriage. You should have seen the bugger's face then." I chuckled loudly. "And I didn't stop at that." Chachu continued, with a roar of laughter. "I casually stated, that last year you made quite an impact on some lieutenants who have declared celibacy if you don't accept their marriage proposals. He didn't like it one bit. I mean he tried to maintain a façade of bravado. I could see right through him. The cat surely caught his tongue then. He thought he could act smart, so he airily asked me what I felt about it.

I replied that we as a family want you to study and make an indelible mark on society.

I decided he needed to be taken down a peg or two and mentioned that you would love the Defence life as it suits your personality. I went on and added that we need a well-settled and broad-minded boy for Rosha. Someone who respects her individuality. There are so many Defence institutes from which she can study. And with me in the Army, no other chap can get the better of her. That really knocked the living daylights out of him, by Jove. I can swear to you that he was bristling with anger. Let me tell you, dear child, he is not that indifferent to you as he would like us all to believe. And with my experience, which is unquestionably vast in matters of the heart, Aafaq Qazmi is definitely interested in you."

I looked appreciatively at Chachu as my face lit up. He had done wonders for my flagging morale. Here I was, wallowing in self-pity and there he was conjuring up images to Aafaq, about me being some sort of super eligible catch, if not really a debutante. I planted a resounding kiss on Chachu's cheek. The door opened suddenly and Mum's gamine head appeared. "What are you two up to?" She gazed at me and then at Chachu as she entered my room. Chachu smiled at her and I nonchalantly shrugged my shoulders. Her glance was assessing as she looked back at me while she escorted my uncle towards the living room.

I barely saw Aafaq after that encounter on the terrace. I overheard aunty telling Mum that he was designing some new computer and was very busy. I decided to start preparing for my annual exams which were a couple of months away. I was sure I wanted to graduate in English Literature and needed a good grade to get through New

Delhi University. Seeing my sad face and the fact that it would soon be my time to leave the family nest, Papa gave us a surprise. "A weekend on the Dal Lake in a houseboat. Take your textbooks." He ordered a puzzled Heena and me with finality. "You girls need a break." I was packing my bag when Rohan entered my room. I was about to order him to get lost when I realized I was going to miss him when I went away to college. He looked at me and remained quiet so I ignored him, too. I prayed he wouldn't try to wangle some more money out of me. It came as a surprise when he stood next to me and whispered softly in my ears. "You are the best girl in the world. Aafaq Bhai Jaan is nuts not to be in love with you." It was a very touching gesture. My baby brother had grown up.

□

6

The world famous 'floating market' on the Dal Lake has started. The small boats called *shikaras* are laden with vegetables, fruits, exotic flowers and spices. My hands feel snug and warm as I tuck them under my fine poncho. It is adorned with flowers in exquisite designs, woven by finest needles belonging to the world's finest craftsmen. The rays of the sun glimmer through the morning mist. I pick up loaves of bread which have been baked at the crack of dawn and transferred from the Boulevard. I pay for a box of strawberries otherwise Heena will be disappointed. The sun's rays slant on the surface of the water. They disperse, splaying the entire spectrum of colours.

Nadeem steers the *shikara* back to the houseboat. I gaze at the Hazratbal shrine. It never ceases to fill me with respect for its sheer magnificence.

The waters of the Dal are so clear that I can see the forest like vegetation growing inside. Fishes of assorted sizes chase our boat, and I dip my hands occasionally into the water. I see a shikara bobbing on the waters as I approach our houseboat. 'Aafaq,' I realize at once. The high and mighty have decided to come. I, too, can play hard to get, and I look the other way.

Dinner is uneventful other than Heena and Rohan debating over the next vacation. It is our last night on the Dal. I am totally disinterested in this family banter now. I have to get out of here and make my life. Other than the cursory glance, polite smile or nod of my head, I remain silent.

This is my own, private 'starry night.' I think to myself as I step onto the balcony of the houseboat. Just like the 'Starry Night' painted by Vincent Van Gogh which is my favourite painting. The moon is crescent and slender. There is not a single patch of dark space available. Stars are splattered against the vast expanse of sky. Practically like diamonds. The thought of New Delhi with its reputed institutes fills me with awe, but for me, Kashmir will always be my home, and these people inside the houseboat my family, even Aafaq. With a sigh I realize it is time to go inside and start studying. All of a sudden I see green emeralds glowing in the dark. It is Aafaq. Our eyes meet. 'Here take this.' He says as he hands me Mum's shawl, breaking the calm. "Aunty told me you are out here." The look he flashes my way is searching as if he is trying to read what is going on in my mind.

"Rudra Chachu was mentioning that you have practically broken the heart of every young officer in this country." What game is he playing at? Aafaq has never spoken to me on these lines in his entire life. In fact, these days we barely speak at all. It had started to hurt, very much, this distance between us. But I wasn't going to give him the benefit of witnessing my despair.

"What does it have to do with you?" I speak in the most self-possessed tone I can feign.

"Nothing, but I don't believe you are interested in any of those fellows otherwise Heena would have known. And when I asked her the other day she said Chachu was pulling my leg." I square my shoulders, resentful that Aafaq has been able to see through the charade presented by Chachu. His mocking smile infuriates me further. I wish Heena had avoided parting that bit of vital information. I can wipe that smile of his dumb face, ever too easily, I muse. "I like the men from Defence." My voice has an unnatural shrill to it as I struggle to act haughty. "They have so much of exposure and are witty. They are confident enough to handle strong-minded women. There are massive libraries in their clubs. I will be able to study from one of their institutes. I will even be allowed to wear short skirts without being labelled a harlot." I looked at him challengingly. "I never called you a harlot." Now, was that a self-reproving tone I just heard?

"If I am lucky, I might get a chance to go abroad. My husband might be a military attaché like my Grandfather. We may go to New York, and then I will get to see the original 'Starry Night.' Papa told me it's there, in one of the museums." Let's hear what you have to say now, Aafaq Qazmi, I silently dare.

"Roshina Kapoor, I have known you since the day you opened your eyes to this world. I can proudly say that I know you better than you know yourself. You may travel all over the world and see all the places you have read about and be overjoyed. But you will always come back here as this is where you belong, this is your home." I am stunned that he could actually be echoing my own thoughts of nearly five minutes ago. He can't think that he can do what he damn well pleases with me. Be indifferent and distant one minute and pretend to be my bosom pal the next. I am not a pushover and he had better not think likewise. I turn around to go inside, but somehow he reaches the door and stands in front of me. "I had a word with your parents before coming out here." He calmly mentions.

I will not insult myself by fighting against his first-rate male strength, so I stand with my arms folded in front of me and meet his speculative look. "Stop messing around with me, Aafaq and move out of my way. Let me go inside. I want to study." If surprised by my onslaught he doesn't show it but says, "I better apologize to aunty and uncle. I wasn't fooling around with you, though, I just asked them how they feel. They said that I would have to ask you first."

I don't have the faintest idea what he is talking about. I push him as I am in such a hurry to go inside. If I hadn't known better I would have thought he is baiting me, though the appropriate word would be flirting. But that will be like character assassinating 'Mr. Goody Two Shoes.'

"Aafaq Qazmi, I never want to see you again in my life. I don't know what stupid game you're playing. But let me tell you, I am not interested. Not in you, not in your stupid games."

I am nearly screaming now. He softly holds me by both my elbows, and I feel myself being pulled towards him. He looks into my eyes, "Roshina Kapoor, I love you from the bottom of my heart. I don't know why you have been tormenting me, but I can't take it anymore. Since years, I have been trying to convince myself that I should be proud of the fact that I have not one but two lovely younger sisters. I was fighting a lost battle. I have gone through months of self-recrimination. However, you are the most mischievous and delightful person, I have ever come across, and without you my life is meaningless. I love your dimples, the way your hair refuses to be pulled back, and most of all I love you in those torn shorts of yours. I have asked your parents if I can marry you. I can't promise you New York, but I do promise you that I will do all that I can, to keep you deliriously happy for the rest of your life. I will never clip your wings. Study further as much as you want, but as long as you come back to me. Roshina Kapoor, will you marry me? If yes, then please tell me now. If your answer is no, then I will leave and go back to college. As I can't bear to be around you, if you don't love me the way I do. I can't waste more time."

I look at him, mystified by the turn of events. Surely, he cannot play a joke so cruel. I look into his eyes. The irises are as violet as the flowers of my saffron garden. Then I gaze with curiosity at the brown fleck in his right eye which is only visible when you are this near him. I can see what I have always wanted to see, love and adoration. He senses my confusion. "Yes, Rosha, Meri Jaan." The possessive endearment of those many years ago, when he had carried me in his arms. The day I had realized he was my Prince of valour. There is no stopping me now. Without hesitating I move closer to him and he softly pulls me into his arms in what will be our first embrace as lovers. I bury my head in the hollow of his neck, and the tension of the past couple of months finally leaves me. "Aafaq Qazmi, I have loved you since I was six years old. Don't you dare talk to me about wasted time." He looks at me with compassion. And for that moment Roshina Kapoor, for all her five feet ten inches feels tiny and cherished.

We step inside the houseboat. And for what everyone has to say, it's pure music to my ears. My prospective mother-in-law loudly proclaims 'taberkhallah' and wards away the evil eye. Heena jumps up and down.

And in the midst of the jubilations so effusive I hear Mum ask Aafaq. "I do hope you know what you have taken on?" And she gives me a winning smile. I look at Papa and run into his arms. And everyone of you female readers will second me when I remark, 'The real hero of a girl's heart will always be her father.'

We didn't have a whirlwind courtship or a whirlwind romance. Life on Raj Bagh Road remained more or less the same. I continued to go to school and devoted myself to my books. God had granted me my wish, it was now my turn to do my bit. I became determined to do amazingly well in my last few months of school.

New Delhi University was offering a two-year Graduation Course in English Literature. There was an In-Campus Girl's Hostel. New Delhi wasn't all that far from Srinagar, and maybe Aafaq could find a job as a Computer Engineer. Two years would pass in a jiffy, and I really would like to work for a good magazine or even do my Masters later. Neither of the families wanted a formal engagement as there was so much of understanding between us all. No need of a hullabaloo, Aafaq was firm about that and the matter was over. He displayed the same attitude when it came to the subject of religion and my conversion. He was very clear that he would never even request, leave alone insist that I convert. His parents left it at that. They wisely realized it would be tough to handle his one-upmanship. And to be honest, for them there were other priorities, like knowing me and my family so well. Their only son's happiness was too important. I was very relieved as I knew that I might not have had devout Hindus for parents, but I still was proud of the religion I had been born into. I wouldn't have been able to convert, even for Aafaq. But I do feel guilt-ridden at times.

□

7

We had a lot in common, Aafaq and I. On top of the list was our love for Kashmir. In our hearts both of us wanted to work in Srinagar. Abbas Uncle and Papa assured us that for educated, hard-working people like us there would be no shortage of employment. Aafaq and I would occasionally go for a movie together, just the two of us. It would be a heady experience, and now I think they were moments borrowed from Time. Aafaq would never so much as even touch my hand in the theatre, but the thrill of being with him alone would make me euphoric. We would go for long walks by the Dal Lake and usually bump into his friends or acquaintances. Sometimes Heena and Ruhail would also accompany us. I realized Ruhail was an easy-going and sweet natured fellow. The two of us got on quite well, and I was happy how supportive he was about Heena's academic aspirations. One glorious afternoon on the Dal Lake the four of us sat in a *shikara*. I saw Ruhail timidly hold Heena's hand. Just to let it go, when he saw Aafaq about to turn their way. It was an idyllic existence. But for the memory of one evening. We were coming back from Shankaracharya Mandir. It was Rohan's birthday and we were about to sit in the car.

Suddenly, out of nowhere, Saira Hyder Ali appeared. At first I didn't recognize her as she was wearing a Burqa, and her face was also covered. She pulled back her veil, and her eyes glowed dangerously. "You cheat," she screeched. "To think that you rejected me for this *Kafir*." She shouted at Aafaq oblivious to the passersby who had collected over there. Aafaq immediately pushed us all into the car. Rohan was totally stunned. "You ruin my life, defile me and enjoy yourself with this family of *Kafirs*. You will suffer." She banged on the car widow. And I was scared it might break under her hammering fists. Without further thought I stepped out of the car. "Listen, Saira, please don't get upset like this, but Aafaq hasn't done anything to you. He was never going around with you, he never encouraged you." Her face turned purple. "Shut up, before I skin you alive. You whore." She showered me with the choicest of abuses. "Aafaq will never be yours." She moved towards me threateningly. Aafaq literally dragged me back into the car and drove home as fast as possible. It was an appalling end to what had been a lovely day. We never spoke about it again, but it had left me very shaken. I sometimes wonder now that did she really love Aafaq, or was it the madness of a spurned suitor?

Heena and I had two months left of school. We decided to bury our nose behind our books and give it our best. Abbas Uncle had promised to take us to the Saffron Garden as soon as our exams got over. Everything was falling into place, I thought, while I studied determinedly. My hand would invariably go to the golden bangle that Noor Aunty had given me.

Heena and I passed our Annual exams with flying colours. Papa went to New Delhi, and secured my admissions for the upcoming academic year in English Literature from Saint Elizabeth's College. Heena cleared the Entrance Test for the Medical College in Srinagar enlarging the already ecstatic atmosphere. But then why were we begrudged the Saffron Garden?

The baby is quite annoyed now. He seems to be fed up of sitting in his mother's lap. He pulls at her arm which shackles him but cannot understand the futility of his act. Nobody likes restraints. We as humans have been born free. He manages to grab his pacifier and throw it to the floor in anger. The little children across the aisle can't stop laughing. Now the baby seems to be enjoying his audience. He gives a toothy grin and looks delicious. His irritation dims with the applause, and he preens with pride. Flattery appeals to all of us, irrespective of size.

Zohaib had never been a demanding child. His all-winning smile, his easy-going disposition had made it easy to nurture him, especially for his nanny. I had never had a personal hands-on experience with the terrible two syndrome or with the turbulent teens. Making this recent disappearing act of his all the more vexing. I had thought I was the most involved of mothers, then why hadn't I seen the telltale signs?

He had occasionally wanted to know about his roots and family tree. His questions were linked to his own identity. I had never imposed my religion on him. I had gently pushed him towards his own. I barely went to temples. I couldn't be held guilty of misleading him.

"Are you going to Kashmir for a white Christmas, Ms. Kapoor?" The stewardess genially interrupts my trail of thought. "I have read your book, and recognized you from your photograph." She smiles warmly at me. "Do you have family in Srinagar? I had a lot of Kashmiri friends in school." She refills my coffee cup.

I momentarily pause then say, "Yes, I have my family in Srinagar." "Oh! you are going home, Ms. Kapoor." She gushes.

'Home,' I repeat liking the sound of the word. It means a whole lot more to me than to others.

□

8

"Rudra, this is our home. What in God's name are you trying to say?" Mum's voice can be actually termed a scream, and Papa looks very disturbed.

Chachu had arrived this afternoon. And what he had to say shakes the ground under my feet. It terrified my parents, but I know for me there are going to be consequences of a very different kind. According to him, the madrassas on both sides of the border are not transparent in their education practices anymore. They are imparting religious teachings of a very extreme sort. *Jihad* or Holy War is being taught, and the works of the Holy Quran are being highly distorted and thus inflammatory. The ideologies that are being preached are very 'radical.' It was a word I had never heard. The Muslim, is being portrayed as a victim whose plight will be better in a separate Muslim state or by blending with Pakistan. The Hindus and other religious minorities like Buddhists and Sikhs in Kashmir have to be driven out of the state. Kashmir has to be converted into a completely Islamic state. In the mountains entire villages of Gujjar and Backerwal communities have been wiped out as they resisted these insurgents. The secular Muslims who till now coexisted in an exemplary manner with the Hindus are reducing in number. Some on their own, and some out of force. The first war between India and Pakistan which dated back to nineteen forty-eight and the subsequent one in nineteen sixty-five, both ended in defeat of Pakistan. Now they have blood thirsty and war hungry Afghans who have defeated the Soviets. Enormous funds of money were provided by Pakistan Secret Services, the rest of the Arab world and the United States to support the Afghans. The religious outfit 'Inquilaab Kashmir,' with its origins in the early eighties in Srinagar has ample of foreign backing. They have the most sophisticated ammunition like rocket launchers, grenades, explosives and kalashnikovs. Thanks to Pakistan. It cannot be suppressed nor ignored any more. They are already forcing conversions wherever they can. They are ready to kill and die. Rumour is strong, Chachu says succinctly that they are being trained in weapons by Pakistani Secret Service. The Afghan Mujahideen are practically 'War Mughals.' The Pakistanis have been shrewd enough to engage their services and are now motivating students towards *Jihad* in the *madrassas*. A generous compensation is being provided to those engaged in *Jihad*. A lot of the affluent Muslims of Kashmir are sending their sons abroad to study and the not so fortunate are enlisting in *Jihad*. Kashmir has always been a waterloo for Pakistan but this time they are determined to succeed and make our country bleed in the process.

I had realized things in the city were a little less than normal. I had assumed it was the usual, routine, non-serious affair I had been brought up around. After spending a life time in Kashmir, one was used to the celebrations when Pakistan won a cricket match against India. Sometimes such sort of dissidence would take a flair for the dramatics when Pakistan's National Flag would be hoisted on its Independence Day. Yes, it was a Muslim-dominated state, but it was a secular country nevertheless. We had thought it was a storm brewing in a tea cup. I don't remember listening to more only realizing that Chachu was telling us to leave the city and go to Jammu or Delhi for some time.

He looked my way in a protective fashion. "What you and Aafaq have is legendary. I am requesting you all to leave the city for a few days. Go home to Jammu, or all the better go to Delhi and get your admissions in order. As it is you were supposed to study in New Delhi, be away from Srinagar and Aafaq. All I am asking is to do it a little prematurely. Do you know that they, are in brazen words saying that the non-Islamic women are welcome to stay back, and be used as sex slaves? You won't believe what is happening to their own women. Girls as young as eleven are being married to self-styled commandos. And then being handed over to the rest of his men. I know this is tough for you to digest especially on the heels of what you and Aafaq have found. But you are my family and I won't mince words. There is too much of unrest. And we still haven't seen the worst of it. Aafaq is a signed-up member of our family now. Do you think he would want any thing happening to any one of you? You cannot be so blinded by love to think immaturely that you want to marry him now, without a College Degree. I am speaking on behalf of your parents that it will not be allowed. I know that it certainly does not fit in your scheme of things either."

I was totally and madly in love with Aafaq, but I had never thought of matrimony. I had always been prepared to leave the city to study. Actually the only difference would be my parents leaving Srinagar, too and the uncertainty. I did not want my parents and Rohan to be persecuted. Chachu was right, what difference does it make if I leave for New Delhi now or after a month. This will always be my home. And soon things will get better. What these insurgents did not know that this was Kashmir and we practiced Kashmiriyat.

I ran into my room, to block out everything. I was desperate to talk to Aafaq. I heard Chachu firmly telling my parents to leave Srinagar by the end of the week.

"A lot of the boys from college have mysteriously vanished into thin air. Some have left voluntarily and as for others, rumour is their families are being kidnapped or tortured." Aafaq told Heena and me on the terrace that night. "Computer and Electronic Engineers are being recruited by these militant organizations. They have very advanced technology systems with all sorts of microchips and satellites. This is a little different from your average terrorist. You have to contribute in whatever capacity you can." His tone was mournful as he relegated a whole lot of frightening incidents.

I was sure because of Chachu, we were jumping the gun.

It couldn't have been further from the truth.

After a couple of days, the word *Mukhbir* was painted in big, bold letters on our house walls. Literal meaning, 'informer of the Indian Government.' The name had been given to the Hindus of Kashmir, and it was being used for all non-Muslims now. To see your house walls being defiled so venomously was horrible. Peace-loving families were humiliated, spat on and brutally coerced to divulge details of Hindu tenants and friends alike. The miscreants were unscrupulous and would stop at nothing. All Hindu houses were marked, defaced and sabotaged. That would be a warning to leave or pay a price. Zubeida was devastated. Her elder brothers had gone overseas to work in some Middle Eastern country and were now incommunicado. We needed no wagging tongues to inform us about what had happened. Zubeida confessed to us that they had both emptied their bank accounts into off-shore banks and demanded their inheritances from her father, in a very heated argument before leaving. When he had refused, they had called him a sick, untrue Muslim. They had been very nasty to Zubeida before departing and had constantly chided her for being friends with me. They had scorned that the Qazmis were soon going to reach their downfall because of their proximity to us.

"What on earth was that?" Mum appeared scared as she placed her hands over her ears. "Batta chu marun, Battta Chu Marun"... A jeep full of young men went by in the lane outside our house. They were screaming at the top of their voices. It meant all Non-Muslims have to be killed. We were having our breakfast, and no one had a morsel to eat after that. I saw my parents exchange nervous looks. A couple of days ago their offices in the university had been cruelly vandalized. At work my parents were being ostracized. The respect that they had procured from their students and colleagues after years of selfless, hard work had come tumbling down. We stopped venturing out of the house. Papa would go with Abbas Uncle to buy the necessities. So many times, a group of radicals would stop them and order Papa to convert or leave. They would mock Abbas Uncle and call him a traitor to his community.

A couple of days ago I had seen a Maulvi enter the house. Heena had told me that he had pointedly told uncle and aunty to rid the *Kafirs* from their life. He persisted that they should not wear Western attire and believe more in '*Purdah*.' He had gotten to know about Mum's family in England. 'She has a Western influence.' He had pronounced, brimming with self-righteousness. 'So does her daughter.' "But this is so absurd," I cried in protest. With a pang, I realized how deeply the Qazmis cared for us.

Once again I was being called *Kafir*. In my own home this time. And slowly, the life-force of us idol worshippers was being washed away. There was a new dictionary in Kashmir, of limited words. *Jihad*, Kalashnikov and Separatist and there were talks of an Islamic Caliphate all over the world.

What is *Jihad*? I have often tried to understand the real meaning.

Jihad according to the Internet is an Islamic term referring to the religious duty of Muslims to maintain the religion.

What happens during *Jihad*? From the diary of Roshina kapoor. The internet does not state all this. But anyone be it Muslim, Hindu, Sikh or Buddhist who has been in Kashmir during the time insurgency started will vouch for what I fearlessly narrate.

The Muslim forgets the Hindu girl, his neighbour and childhood friend who has tied *Rakhi* around his wrist every year. He teases her on the road, makes lewd remarks and obscene gestures at her. She is a Hindu, his enemy. Wasn't it a Hindu Queen in our country who had sent a *Rakhi* to a Mughal Emperor asking him for brotherly protection? The Emperor honoured the delicate string and sent his troops led by himself. He had fortitude. But now we have *Jihad*.

What about the licensed mischief of Holi? When Muslims of Kashmir played the festival of colours with their Hindu friends and then went to their houses to taste the sweetmeats. But during Jihad, the Kalashnikov replaces the water gun and blood pours into the Dal Lake.

Jihad is when we erase the memory of Diwali at our Hindu friends' house, where we have lit and decorated little lamps.

And most of all *Jihad* is when we forget the part of Eid when our father would call on his Hindu friends and embrace them in a brotherly hug. That is the beauty of Islam.

Sick of these taints, the Hindu lashes out. He lynches, he torches. Children are orphaned, women are widowed. My Hindu head hangs in shame.

A lot of our Hindu friends left for Jammu or Delhi. Some under duress of the militants and some using the wisdom to leave before the situation became totally detrimental to their survival. December in Srinagar was always cold but this time it was cruel and dark. The sun remained eclipsed, and the gaiety of children played absenteeism. The Boulevard was stark, and not a single *shikara* or house boat could be seen on the Dal Lake. Hindus could be spotted pulling down the shutters over their shops. Their faces sad, their hearts bleeding. The premonition of a bleak tomorrow looming in front of them. Where would they go?

All one could see was Islamic fundamentalists. Those belonging to the 'Inquilaab Kashmir' had now started doing ridiculous marches across the city. As they announced that January the twentieth of next year would be the Republic Day of the Islamic Republic of Kashmir.

I also witnessed fear along with fanaticism on their faces. It intrigued me, and I realized puberty had barely set in while a rifle had been thrust into their hands. Some of the boys hardly looked a day above fourteen or fifteen. But this was no toy they were carrying. It was an assault weapon.

Secular and compassionate Muslims did have the courage to form Pro-Hindu unions insisting that the Hindus did not have to leave. But they would soon crumble as some family members would go missing. As for the Qazmis, they stood by us, through it all. Much to the annoyance of their many relatives who tried unsuccessfully to convince them otherwise.

Aafaq entered my room one evening. We looked at each other across the room. I was sitting at my study table. The curtains were drawn across. It was unheard of in these times for them, to be pulled back.

With all certainty, I knew our exodus from my land was inevitable.

Without saying a word he took me into his arms. I felt his hands tremble at the back of my neck. He was fastening the clasp of a slim, gold chain. It had a small pendant with the stark word 'Aafaq' carved out in Arabic. Time stood still as we stood in each other's arms for what seemed like eternity.

'Aafaq,' I whispered softly. He looked at me with love so right. "Please don't send me away." My voice was wavering now.

He remained unresponsive. I pushed further, knowing the memory of what I was about to ask, was the only thing, that would get me by.

"Aafaq, please kiss me before you send me away. Kiss me, like a man kisses the woman he loves." Our eyes locked as we recognized a similar sort of passion. He bent his head towards me and claimed my lips for the first time. He was shy, yet sure; tender, yet assertive and I yielded to him. What started as a feather gentle caress of my lips became a full exploration, as our tongues met. Somewhat awkwardly at first and then if they had always been entwined. With great reluctance he gently let go of me. We tiptoed up the stairs together, and watched the sun retire. My last sunset in Aafaq's arms.

For tomorrow we were leaving, running away from home. Noor Aunty had given us two *burqas*. We were to leave the land of my birth, as fugitives in black. The *burqas* were a farewell gift. My last memory of Kashmir will always be the frenzied mob which had gathered as we left, screaming *Kafir* at us and urging us to get lost.

How can I forget those awful slogans? *Pakistan se rishta kya?* (What is our relationship with Pakistan?)

'*La ilaha illallah.*' (There is no God but Allah.) '*Azaadi ka matlab kya?*' ('What is the meaning of independence?') '*La ilaha illallah.*' (There is no God but Allah.)

And today when I read the flag of ISIS. Right on the top. I can see the same words printed 'La ilaha illallah.' (There is no God but Allah)

My mind trails back to Srinagar. And those splendid years of my life. How did it go wrong?

□

9

It has now been quite some time since we left Srinagar. The days have stretched into weeks and the weeks into months. It is quite conclusive that return to Srinagar is not in the offing. We had barely made it to Jammu, when insurgency in Kashmir became so brutal that the entire Non-Muslim population of Kashmir emptied out of its habitat. The worst hit city to deal with the influx of migrants was Jammu, followed by New Delhi and other states of India.

Thanks to my grandfather's faithful servant, our ancestral house in Jammu, had been well taken care of. He did all within his means to welcome us, and we had a sturdy roof over our head. Otherwise we would have also boasted about living in one of the many canvas tents erected in the various camps for migrants around the city.

Despite all that was being provided to us, I did everything in my capacity to add to my parent's overflowing cup of woes. My dreams of being with my love had been cruelly shattered. This transformed me into someone who was forever whining and nitpicking with her parents and little brother at the slightest or even no pretext. I got to talk to Aafaq and Heena over the phone every couple of days. But the telephone in my grandfather's house did not have trunk dialling and I would have to wait for Aafaq to call. The phone lines would be subject to the weather and heavy blizzards that occurred in the valley. At the end of the day the news from Srinagar was always the same. The separatists or fundamentalists had achieved what they wanted. There were only a handful of Hindus left. It was now an Islamic state in a secular country. Kashmir belonged to radicals and hard liners who had distorted their wonderful religion for their own selfish needs, and were being played like puppets by neighbouring countries.

Heena told me that some factions would even barge into Muslim dwellings, and behave outrageously with family members. Their demands varied from ordering a round of mutton and other elaborate dishes, to complete evacuation of the house for them to hide and create permanent refuge. She went on in disgusted undertones that they would even try to force themselves on the women of the house. They were scared of no one as they had support from the ministers, bureaucrats and religious authorities. Militants would be smuggled indoors and hidden in basements, lofts and servant quarters of many houses. This was leading to a lot of civilians being injured or killed in the crossfire when the local Police or other Law Enforcement Officers would break in.

"What do you mean, Heena?" I was frantic now. Heena had called me and sounded very scared. "Can you hear me, Rosha? They came home with Maulvi Sallahudin. He was angry, and I even heard him shout at Abu. I can't tell you over the phone." The line crackled with static. "Try to understand, Rosha." Her voice was very faint. "Heena, I can't hear you. Where is Aafaq? Hello, hello."

I heard nothing after that. I sat down on the floor, the defunct receiver in my hand. Had some of those hard liners preaching intolerant Islam come home? Oh God, what would happen to Aafaq? I was petrified and annoyed that I was not there. Damn! the telephone lines. It was the usual scenario, whenever there would be a call from Srinagar. It could be days now before I would be able to speak to them again. What on earth did she mean by a Maulvi coming over? We the *Kafirs* were not there now, the assumedly corrupting influence. So the question of indecent attire could not arise. I was so confused. I banged the telephone angrily against the wall, and ran into my room. What had I done to deserve this? I thought in exasperation.

To say Jammu looked as packed as a can of sardines, would actually be putting it mildly. There were camps for Kashmiri migrants wherever you could look. It was actually tough to breathe. Just as the nose could smell sweat and grime, the mind could sense vulnerability and hopelessness. The government schools and university grounds had all been transformed into migrant camp areas. There were camps in bus stands, in railway stations, under flyovers and bridges. There were camps in places, where camps were not supposed to be like behind garbage disposal sites. When one city in a developing country like India has to accommodate nearly two hundred thousand more people, a lot will go wanting. It was a matter of survival and as Darwin correctly stated, centuries ago, only the fittest survive. Sometimes, when I would step out into the balcony, I could hear my grandfather's house being pointed out by colony association members and comments like 'Kashmiri migrants' would be levelled at us. We would be blamed for the outages of water and electricity in Jammu. We were a severe burden on the already beaten economy of the city. Rohan had summed it up in a few words, we were not the visitors from the mountains any more, we were the migrants from Kashmir. We were considered no better than lepers.

I boarded the bus to Muthi migrant camp. A lot of my school friends from Kashmir had been accommodated there with their families. It was nearly an hour's drive from Jammu city. As I entered the premises, the pungent odour of unclean human skin assailed my senses. There were armies of insects and all sorts of creepy crawlies.

I frantically hunted for tent number two hundred and four. That was the number provided by a profusely sweating Kashmiri Pandit, sitting at the camp's entrance. He had peered into a thick register and given me the number allotted to my friend, Surabhi Matto and her family. "It is near the latrines." He stated, trying to be helpful as he wiped his perspiring brow. My mind reeled in horror and dismay. Had God completely forsaken all these people over here? Surabhi's father had been the proud owner of massive showrooms of Kashmiri Pashminas and Silks on the Boulevard. If I had called her house near the Mughal Gardens anything other than palatial it would have been a blatant lie. That very house had been taken over by the militants, and she along with her family had left under the threat of the Kalashnikov. The militants had stormed into their house late at night after killing the guards posted outside. They had blazed down her father's showrooms earlier in the day and helped themselves to the cash counter. And now she was residing near a public convenience.

'Surabhi,' I screamed as I waved out to her. I spotted her face peering out from under the flap of a grey canvas tent.

"Roshina, I knew you would come." She ran towards me and we embraced each other for a long time. She took me into her camp where her mother and two sisters were busy cutting vegetables for dinner. My heart bled when I saw her sisters brewing, what suspiciously looked and smelt like turnip soup, over a makeshift stove.

"Oh Roshina! they were horrible, those last few months in Kashmir." Surabhi wailed and told me after the pleasantries were over. "You were wise to leave earlier." Her voice resonated the fear which would surely take years to take flight from her mind and soul.

"As soon as you left, nearly every day the militants would perform violent military-like marches on the roads screaming that this was not Kashmir but the Islamic Republic of Kashmir. There are so many radical outfits and Inquilaab Kashmir is just one of them. They have been literally brainwashed. Some of the Muslim population were on their side cheering them on and burning the Indian flag and posters of our famous leaders like Gandhi and Nehru. Our workers from the Showrooms, who were loyal to us, were almost beaten to death. The police were either powerless or are a part of this fanatical movement. It's as if they are possessed by a demon. Rosha, we have seen the uprisings before, there have always been issues regarding religion and creed in the valley but these militants are barbaric. I can't tell you how frightening it was when they broke into our house. They killed our servant's wife after raping her in front of him. Then they stabbed him several times and rejoiced as he bled. Papa was hit and kicked repeatedly. We were hiding in the attic with Mummy. Papa gave all Mummy's jewellery and valuables to them. They kept on calling him a vile Hindu dog and ordered him to flee.

Though most of these extremists were unschooled, one could tell that their commanders or chiefs were educated. It was apparent from the way they spoke. A few of them hadn't even covered their faces with scarves. They are not bothered about being identified and caught." But I wasn't paying much attention. I stood frozen in my tracks. I remembered Aafaq telling me about how he was sure that a whole of his friends from school and college had become radical. This was a nightmare. I was certain this was what Heena had been trying to tell me the other day. 'Surabhi,' her mother called. "How many times have I told you not to soak the coloured clothes with the whites? See this blue shirt of yours, has bled out all over your father's white shirt." "Sorry, Mummy, I will be more careful next time." Surabhi said good naturedly.

Surabhi Matto and washing clothes. If someone had said this a year ago I would have never believed them and would term the statement a figment of their imagination. Visions of the opulence of her life back in Kashmir kept appearing in front of my eyes. She had worn haute couture when people hadn't heard of the word. When I looked at her and her sisters closely, none of them had a single frown on their face. Nor could I hear a whimper or snivel leave their lips. I observed in Surabhi and her sisters the extreme gratitude for being alive. Each of the girls who in Srinagar were pampered-like princesses, was busy helping out. One with the cooking, the younger one was flattening the clothes so they could be worn as there was no scope for them to ironed. Surabhi's mother insisted that I stay for dinner and looked very crestfallen when I refused. It wasn't because I was horrified at the prospect of having turnip soup, it was because I was overwrought with guilt. I knew if I lingered on a single minute more, I would break down and cry. And I did not want them to think I was pitying them. Because I would have been sobbing out of shame, at my own smaller and ungrateful self. I assured aunty that I would be back at an earlier hour, after a couple of days. She hugged me and slipped some roasted almonds into my palm. "For the journey back home." She said lovingly when I had resisted. "And bring your mother next time, Rosha. I would love to catch up." I somehow managed to nod. While Surabhi escorted me back to the gate, she told me that her elder sister had been seeing a Muslim guy from college since the past couple of months. He had been one of the militants who had molested their servant's wife and killed her. "Bhumija is devastated," Surabhi whispered to me. "And can't even show her grief around our parents.

I feel it is God's way of revealing her boyfriend's true colours. We are pretty sure now, that his relationship with Bhumija was just a sham, a way to get intimate with us and find out about Papa's business. He was a devil in disguise. We didn't recognize him." This was so revolting, I thought. I hugged Surabhi and promised to come back soon. A group of men had gathered outside the camp and were erecting a banner. It read, '*Jis Kashmir par jaan lotayi hai voh Kashmir hamaara hai. Chalo Kashmir.*' (The Kashmir for which we gave our life is ours. Let's go back home.) It was wishful thinking.

I, Roshina Kapoor left Muthi Camp for displaced people of Armed conflict a new person. What had actually changed in my life? Precisely nothing. I was living in a house which could provide shelter for four families, but I was just getting used to cursing my lot. I had always wanted to leave Srinagar and study in New Delhi. And here was my friend who was washing clothes behind a lavatory. I was determined to change my whining attitude and help the ones less fortunate. At least I could start by behaving with my own family rather than treating them like dirt. I also carried back with me two sealed envelopes which were handed over to me by a little twelve-year-old girl. She had been playing with a group of children near the well. Her mother was standing in a mile long queue, for a bucket of water.

I had been about to leave the gates when I heard a voice crying out my name, "Rosha Didi, Rosha Didi, please wait." I turned around and saw it was Asha, the little girl who had lived with her family near our school bus stop. Her father had once worked as a driver for Abbas Uncle. Heena would always stop outside his house when we would alight from the bus and buy her an icecream. Heena's heart would melt with joy to see the delight on Asha's face.

"Bhai Jaan has sent this for you." She gushed breathlessly as she thrust a packet into my hands. And sped off before I could ask her anything. I grabbed the letters greedily and stuffed them into my bag.

Heena's letter was as usual affectionate. It was an echo of what she would say to me when we would speak over the phone. She missed us all but was at the same time relieved we were not there. It was dreadful, with the firing and bombs detonating at some place or the other. She had started her classes in the Medical College and would attend college covered in a *Burqa*. I feel 'safer' that way she had written. Some of our Muslim friends had acquired such extreme views on religion that she had disconnected from them. At the end she had written: Sometimes, to make myself feel better, I pretend I am not a part of this absolute mayhem, and I am just watching it on the television. I feel so happy for those few minutes that this is not Kashmir. She was relieved that the Army were being deployed to Kashmir. 'Probably, they will be able to handle this conflict before it escalates into a war.'

She had then enclosed the photograph of herself and Aafaq. The one I had clicked. The photo which will one day hang on the wall in my room. There was another one of hers, in her white Medical Apron. She looked every inch the budding, young doctor. The other letter was from Aafaq.

My Dearest Jaan,

Salaameleikum. May Allah provide peace to you and your family. I can't begin to describe how terribly I miss you. I imagine you everywhere, in every room, behind the Walnut tree and especially on the terrace. When I start studying it's your face that stares back at me from the pages of my book. And when I hear a knock at my door, I feel it's you with some fictitious doubt and that, too, in a subject like Math which you had given up years ago. I always saw through that make believe sum of yours. I would play along as it would give me a chance to be near you. I would actually be waiting for you to knock on my door.

I can't tell you how relieved I am that all of you are safe there. The situation doesn't seem to be improving at all. The propagation of hate and suspicion over here is uncontrollable. All our lives we used to hear the word 'Kashmiriyat' and now we know the names of different religious factions. One day they are going to be at loggerheads at each other. And probably all of this will stop. I have no idea how many are truly radical. Cash is a big factor for most of them. It is disturbing to see religion take an ugly turn. I have my last semester exams soon. Ammi and Abu want me to leave the city for some time as there is an enormous pressure on them. Abu says that I should go to the US and do my Masters, till the time things do not cool down here. However, I will not leave them in these circumstances of total lawlessness and anarchy. Somehow the respect that the United States and its distinguished universities used to inspire in me has vanished.

By the way I found my essay in your closet. I wasn't surprised. Never give up on this child-like quality of yours. It makes you so endearing. I think I was bowled over by you, the day you turned fifteen. It suddenly hit me, how crazy I was for you. I knew for sure that the familiarity I enjoyed with you would be impossible to find, with any other person. You, with your uncanny knack for getting into trouble. Sister Loyala had come home to meet us. She was very worried about all of you and calmed down once she got to know you are away from here and safe. After the amount you had bothered her, it was a very noble gesture. But she recognized you for the wonderful person you are. You can't blame me, for being crazy about you. The sisters of your Convent and the other missionaries are returning to their respective countries. I know that you are not of my faith, and you are more open minded. I respect you so much especially your strength of character. Allah has sent you here for a purpose. Because you are the sort of voice that can change the world. Never give up on your dreams. Use this time to find yourself, to grow. Challenge your mind to its maximum and never take the easy way out.

One day, we will be together, and the whole world will be ours. But I want a world which is free of self-interest and greed. Where people are peace loving and have never heard the word 'snatch.' Roshina, you can create that world. With your flair for words you can show everyone, how it was in Kashmir. Show the world, the purity of all religions. I went to Hazratbal shrine the other day, I glimpsed at the Dal Lake and remembered how beautiful you looked on the night I asked you to marry me. This is all for now.

With my sincere regards to aunty and uncle and love to Rohan.

Yours forever,
Aafaq

Aafaq's letter was a beautiful end to that day which had taught me a few of life's priceless lessons. I blushed while I remembered the desire with which he had kissed me.

If I ever have had a 'Coming of Age Day' in my life that was undisputedly one of them. Going to the camp and seeing with my own eyes, the plight of these 'Displaced victims' had awakened me to the luxury of my own fortunate situation. We had escaped unharmed from a conflict zone. My gutsy parents were fighting tooth and nail to establish themselves in a city where they had thought they would never return. We had a roof over our heads which could provide safe haven to a whole lane. Surabhi's fortitude and courage amidst the vermin around her had been an eye-opener. And now Aafaq in his letter was giving me accolades that I felt were undue my way. I had unnecessarily built a mountain of self-pity around me and was collapsing against its weight.

Aafaq was right, I had to make a change. No more sulking and no more blaming games. I was Roshina Kapoor. I was the girl who had climbed over the school wall and escaped to see a cricket match. I had faced a week of sermons on 'sinful behavior.' That did not discourage me in any way. I had left the Chapel, a house of God with a cheeky grin. It would take more than a couple of sparring fundamentalists wanting to flex their brawn to break my spirit.

"We are all going to New Delhi." Mum told a very surprised me the following week. I had come home after visiting Surabhi. I had started teaching the children in the camps till the time some arrangement for their schooling could be done. It was quite rewarding and to my amazement even Rohan volunteered to come along and help. He was really good with the little boys. I was quite proud of the way he won their trust and encouraged them to read and write.

Mum looked at my startled expression and went on. "Rosha, your father is slipping into a severe depression. I took him to a psychiatrist the other day. He has diagnosed it as post-traumatic stress disorder. That is the reason for his lack of sleep at night and subsequent fatigue and lethargy which occurs during the day. It is quite common in people who have had to flee war zones and have witnessed assault of any sort." "Mum, I hope it is nothing serious." My mother continued, "The doctor feels a change of place and a fresh start will do him a whole world of good. And personally your father and me were not very comfortable sending you away to a hostel in that metropolis, especially not now. I feel that, too, was giving him cause for more stress. We have been through too much and we want to hold on to the two of you for as long as possible. You can label it as insecurity however I don't possess any qualms in admitting it. We have lost our jobs, our friends and our belongings. But I will not be able to take it if anything happens to my family. Professionally, there are more opportunities over there for your father and me. I have my school friends and they have managed to arrange jobs for us in 'City Central University.' Things are still very unstable in Srinagar. God only knows when we will return, or if we ever will. Rudra was right. God bless him for insisting we leave when we did. It scares me to think of having to witness the terror that unfolded after we left." I found myself assaulted by a vortex of mixed emotions.

I was happy that my parents would be with me in New Delhi. But my parents leaving Jammu, too, spelt the impossibility of our return to Srinagar. I felt it was one step further away from Aafaq. Be reasonable, Rosha. I told myself. My parents were not in Srinagar that I would be denied the privilege of going back there during my college breaks. I was elated that they would be with me and I went into my mother's outstretched arms. We all needed each other. "Papa will be fine very soon." I declared passionately. I don't think I could have been happy in New Delhi without them any way. I pondered over what my mother had just said. Will we ever return to Srinagar? I didn't want to think on those lines at all. As it was, there was enough on my plate already.

□

10

The four of us arrived in New Delhi, in the month of August of nineteen-ninety. While our feet stepped onto the platform of New Delhi Railway Station, in the early hours of the morning, my uncle was one of the thousands of Army officers deployed to the Vale of Kashmir. The most beautiful state of India, now the most beautiful battlefield of the earth.

The boy behind me in the bus leaned forward and nudged me slightly below my waist. This was the second time in ten minutes. It was a tad too frequent to be classified a coincidence. After a month of travelling by the New Delhi Public Buses, one would think I would be attuned to such overtures. I was getting used to them but nevertheless they still revolted me. When I felt him move near me for what would be the third time, I deftly shifted step, and stamped on his foot, for all I was worth. He let out a howl and stood limping on one leg holding his injured foot in agony. I was no light weight. It was impossible to be, when you are five feet ten, unless you are what they these days have dubbed as 'size zero.' My stop had come and I flashed him a dirty look. Mum had cautioned me against such behaviour. Her word of advice was to ignore these advances. But it was tough to let your body be subjected to such conduct.

"I saw what you did," Jyoti remarked. She had gotten off the bus with me. "It was pretty brave of you." With a frank look her way I said, "I have had a good teacher."

Jyoti was my new friend in college. She lived a few blocks away from our house in R.K. Puram and made the to and fro journey to college and back fairly tolerable. Jyoti was the epitome of someone who had been born and brought up in the capital. She was smart and sassy. No one, irrespective of gender could mess with her including most of the varsity staff. Jyoti didn't have to curry favour with anyone. She had decided, that I with my Kashmiri background, was a sort of hillbilly who needed to be taken care of. Jyoti had taught me a thing or two about managing eve teasers. I witnessed her carefully as she would raise an alarm and draw attention of passersby. She would make sure the assailant would be subjected to sandals and slaps by a group of feminists. She would spew out dialogues varying from, "How dare you tease a girl?" to "Don't you have a sister of your own?" Or she would even run to the nearest cop and relay her story most dramatically. Nevertheless whatever Jyoti did narrate, would make them spring into action and force them to shake their pendulous abdomens as they tried to grab the offender.

Initially, it had surprised me that most of the people in New Delhi, at least my college students were unaware of the turmoil that was waging in Jammu and Kashmir. Majority didn't know the difference between Jammu and Srinagar city. They thought Jammu meant snow balls and skis. They were unaware that the temperature in Jammu was barely a couple of degrees less than that of Delhi. That Kashmiri Pandits in Jammu felt they were roasting in a furnace, and some had actually succumbed to heat strokes. New Delhi, too, had its fair share of camps for the Kashmiri migrants. But with a city this size the camps and their occupants were easily absorbed. Also life in a metropolis moved fast. People had an 'I give a damn attitude.' Jyoti was very aware of events happening not just in disturbed parts of India but the entire world. She came from a family of journalists and philanthropists. All had travelled over the world and had a gripping story to tell. She had an elder sister who was interning for National Geographic. I would sometimes catch her when she would have me believe to be oblivious. It was as if she was trying to amass all I had seen.

I found myself being drawn to her. And then I would think of Heena and immediately be remorseful. “Penny for your thoughts. You haven’t been listening to a word of what I said.” Jyoti scolded gently. “I’m sorry.” I offered as an apology. “No offense taken. Were you thinking of Kashmir?” She had an amazing quest for knowledge and one day would make a hard-nosed journalist, which was what she wanted to be. She also possessed an enviable glossary of words. But her every speech and argument would inevitably end with, “Sometimes you just have to say what the f....” Initially I would cringe inwards, as it was new to me. But now it was sort of rubbing on.

“Is it true about AFSPA and all. In Kashmir, I mean?” Jyoti was always forthright and her questions were without preamble. “Everyone is accusing the Army about a whole lot of atrocities on civilians in the name of the Act. They say our Indian Army is exploiting the power it gives.” AFSPA was the Armed Forces Special Powers Act which was an emergency law, providing immunity to armed forces from prosecution in disturbed areas of India.

“I can’t help you here.” I replied truthfully. “We left Kashmir before the Army was sent in. I am sure the Army is just doing its job. They are the only ones who can get Kashmir back for us.” Suddenly, I heard those slogans again. “*Ay Jabiron, Ay zalimon, Kashmir hamaara chhod do.*” (Hey oppressors and wicked ones, get out of our Kashmir.) We had heard all this for weeks before leaving. I heard the shots of Kalashnikovs. I remembered Surabhi’s tent behind the urinal. "What do you have to say?" Jyoti pounded mercilessly.

"What the f...?" I exclaimed loudly. It was quite comforting, I must admit.

"That's exactly what my Aunt Meena said, too, when my Dad mentioned it to her. This was after he read about the United Nations ruminate about the highhandedness and callousness of the Indian Army."

"Has your aunt lived in Kashmir?" I was curious. "No, but she knows a whole lot of people from there, you should meet her some day."

"Sounds nice." I said.

"Did I tell you that Kunal is interested in you?" Jyoti looked at my blank expression and shook her head in resignation. "I pretty much expected you to not know who I am talking about. The tall boy with glasses, in our grammar class. He said he would like to have coffee with you in the canteen one of these days."

She attentively observed my detatched response. "I guess the answer is no. Girl, either you have come from a nunnery or there is a gorgeous Kashmiri guy back home for you."

Jyoti in her astuteness had actually hit the nail on the head. I thought as I sipped on my coffee in the plane. She was nearly right on both accounts. I was Convent educated, if not really had taken the veil and Aafaq was gorgeous. "I will have to tell Kunal to take a flying f...," Jyoti said as she lit a cigarette. She offered me a drag which I accepted, and we walked into our gated colony. "Is that done on a flying saucer?" I asked her humorously. I ducked as she threw a fake punch my way.

But whoever wanted to have coffee with me would have to wait. As I belonged to Aafaq and Aafaq alone. And today was Friday and he would call me.

"Rosha, I have told you it is not safe for you to come here. Please be reasonable," he muttered. "Why on earth do I even tell you anything at all? I thought you would not overreact, but, Rosha, you haven't changed a bit." His voice sounded annoyed. "How can the Army take you for questioning, Aafaq? I am going to ask Chachu," I countered. I was getting very worked up. "Listen, Rosha, please stop all this foolhardiness. They are just doing their duty. Do you think life is a party for them over here, away from their families? The media and the West is trying its level best to brand them as the perpetrators. What are they supposed to do when they enter villages and unearth militants being sheltered by civilians? What on earth are civilians doing housing Militants in the first place? Why the uproar when they are injured in a confrontation? Think of it logically. I am proud of the Indian Army, Roshina, and I won't accept anyone saying anything to the contrary. I don't care at all what the Human Rights Watch or United Nations say about it. I am a computer engineer, and the Army knows that guys like me, with my technological skills are a Godsend to these radical outfits. Once the Internet comes to India, everything is going to change. The whole country is going to be connected to the outer world. Communication and correspondence is going to take a matter of minutes. You can't imagine how these outfits are going to profit. It will be so convenient to connect with their handlers across the borders. I was interrogated and that, too, in a very congenial way, if I had information about the guys from my college who have shunned their courses, and have disappeared. They did not accuse me of being antinational or anything like that at all."

"Are you sure, Aafaq? I hope they were not insinuating that you have an alliance with them." I wanted to get to the bottom of this.

"Roshina, stop it." He pleaded with me. "These are desperate times here in the city and desperate times call for desperate measures. Now tell me about college? I hope you have made some good friends?" He hurriedly changed the topic. Then Heena took over. I had to hear her nonstop chatter about how she had fainted in the dissection hall. "To think you have seen a nude man." I exclaimed, teasingly. "Rosha, I am going to kill you." I could visualize her blushing on the Afghan Rug which had occupied the wooden floor of the downstairs living room since years. 'Heena,' I murmur with all the softness I have. My voice is loving and my mind drifts back to nineteen ninety and what I found in the Hanuman temple.

□

11

There was a Migrant Camp in the compound of one of the temples near our house in R.K. Puram. Mum had started visiting the people there and with the help of a Non-governmental Organization (NGO), she had roped in a few doctors. They had started visiting the migrants and made sure the expectant women got their iron tablets and other medications as part of their antenatal check up. Vaccination drives were organized which were so essential to prevent epidemics from thriving.

The children of the camps were enrolled in government and private schools. Mum proved her gumption as she braved Papa's depression and calmly wrestled our crankiness together with the lows which came with living in a metropolis. I took a page out of her book and so did Rohan. We threw ourselves, single-mindedly in rehabilitating the camp migrants of our colony's temple. It started with Rohan and his friends, donating their old school books to the children in the camp out there. One of the boys from Rohan's class had a basement, which he emptied out. The boy's mother and her kitty party friends poured in their funds and converted the basement into a Coaching centre. Their noble intentions defied the scorn accompanying the word 'kitty.' The migrant children were taught English and Mathematics by anyone who could. Rohan appointed himself the colony treasurer and collected funds to purchase things like blackboards and stationery. Their energy and passion was contagious and soon our whole colony was involved in the 'Camp Rehabilitation Bug.' Whether it was financial or even shouldering the responsibility of a wholesome meal a day, it was a joint effort and everyone pitched in.

The Kashmiri migrants might have been forgotten by the government, but our colony did an exemplary task of extending its support in whatever way possible. In this very migrant camp, in the grounds of the Hanuman Temple, in Pocket B of R.K. Puram, Mum and I met a family from a small village near my beloved Sopore. What was unique about them was the their surname. It was Khan. They were Kashmiri Muslim.

"Can you please repeat what you said?" Mum requested them in perfect Kashmiri. Amidst the noise made by the ladies singing *bhajans* in the temple, and the children yelling, it was tough to figure out what was actually being said. In all fairness, we were unwilling to accept what Basheer Ahmed Khan of the tenement was saying, to be the truth. Basheer had worked as a Saffron Picker in Sopore and would commute by foot to his nearby village every day. His village had been completely taken over by the militants and every day his wife would have to cook for them and perform other chores. To her horror, one afternoon when she returned from collecting wood from the forest she saw the militants taking turns at Basheer's sister. She and her two daughters aged eight and six stood petrified as they witnessed the militants smothering the life out of the girl's sixteen-year-old body. They ran back into the forest in extreme fear. Basheer had taken up the matter with the Village Head. He was hand in glove with the militants as his son was Commander of that insurgent group. An '*avatar*' which inspired respect. The next day the militants had returned and in front of the entire village had stripped both Basheer and his wife. They had branded them with hot iron rods. It was a form of punishment for daring to be a whistleblower. Emboldened with their 'nouveau power,' the militants had sneeringly relayed to Basheer's wife that the fate of Basheer's sister awaits her and her daughters, if they ever cried foul again. Basheer and his family left their village that night, and headed to Srinagar by foot. They had been picked up by an Army jeep which had been patrolling the area and were escorted to the nearest migrant camp. There, they joined the Kashmiri Hindus, who welcomed them with a sensitivity they were in so much need of.

When the migrant Hindus were relocated to New Delhi, Basheeer and his family had marched along with them. For the first time in their lives, the Muslim family of Basheer Ahmed entered a Hindu temple. Where the idol of Lord Hanuman stood erected for all. The temple, where idol worshippers pray but make sure Basheer Ahmed's family gets three square meals. "Long live my Indian Army," he cried. "Otherwise we would have not survived that night." I glanced at his wife as she placed her hand protectively over her swollen belly. I saw Mum looking that way, too, and realized there was a new life growing inside that scared body.

"The militants have no religion," wept Basheer. "They just know how to loot and kill." He lifted his threadbare shirt and showed us the black ugly mark on his torso and arms made by the ignited iron rods. It was as if his flesh had been charred. I got hold of his two little girls, wanting to shield them from evidence of the brutality subjected to their parents. "The loud speakers from the mosque kept on blaring slogans like, 'long live Inquilaab Kashmir' and Pakistan Zindabad." The younger daughter told me calmly, her voice and eyes devoid of emotion. When you have looked at death in the face, I suppose you become zombie like yourself. Basheer managed a feeble smile when we told him about our association with Sopore.

We sat in his tenement, the *Kafirs* and the Muslims and cried for the lost Kashmir and the flower beds of saffron that were no longer ours.

□

12

Nineteen ninety ended and it became nineteen ninety-one. Though I made valiant efforts to learn about my foster city, it still didn't appeal to me. The Kashmir from where I hailed was a land of terrorist strikes, encounters, checkpoints and Army crackdowns. Things would be normal for a couple of days, and then there would be a mindless massacre in some part. India would not give up Kashmir for sure, but in the process it was losing a whole lot more. With the telephone in the living room and the phone booths on our street I managed to be in constant touch with Heena and Aafaq. The few letters that were smuggled in and out through human couriers were a bonus. As more and more troops were deployed, the religious outfits received exponential support from Pakistan and other countries. It was a viscous cycle. We knew how it had begun, but we did not know how it would stop.

"They are all perfectly fine, Kaju. Heena has sent you this." Chachu spoke gaily as he handed me a small velvet bag. My hands dived inside and rescued an envelope with my name written on it. I recognized Heena's handwriting. I felt a tug of disappointment that there wasn't a letter from Aafaq but then I assumed he was busy. My uncle had been waiting for me when I had arrived home from college. I now fully understood that we would forever be indebted to my uncle for getting us out, at the right time. "Now, there is another letter for someone called Roshina

Kapoor." Chachu announced waving an envelope in the air. I realized it must be the much yearned letter from Aafaq, and jumped upwards snatching it, out of my uncle's hands.

"Don't you want to know what Aafaq asked me to say?" Chachu drawled maddeningly. "Tell, Roshina, I love her. And I can't sta..." 'Chachu,' I shrieked, red faced with mortification. I didn't bother with privacy and ripped open the envelope and started reading the letter, right there in front of my uncle.

It took me a while to comprehend that all this time Chachu had been staring at me. It was as if he wanted me to mention something. He had an expectant air about him.

"Chachu, I know there is something weighing on your mind." I finally blurted as I saw him fidgeting around. In fact, I had never seen him so, what could I say, yes 'unsure' was the right word.

After a few moments of silence, he looked at me somewhat contritely. He told me he had been ordered by his Commanding Officer to read Aafaq's letters. "Why should anyone ask you to do that? What on earth does Aafaq's letter have to do with the Indian Army?" I couldn't for the love of God fathom an answer. "What is happening, Chachu? I thought this was a Democracy, not some nation under the tight leash of a military dictator. You have got to come clean with me. Have you read my letter?"

"Roshina, please stop jumping to conclusions. But tell me, are you not a true patriot?" "What a stupid thing to say, Chachu! Of course I am." I cried indignantly. My stomach was tied up in knots now. "We have gotten to know from a very reliable source that Aafaq and a few other of his friends are being sought out by Inquilaab Kashmir insurgents. To be precise by some handlers who are working for the Pakistan ISI." "So what?"

I immediately retorted. "Do you think I don't know? It has been happening since some time now. I must say, you guys are pretty slow on your surveillance front. No wonder we have had all those people slipping over our borders. Why don't you cast a wider net at the peripheries, instead of hurling insane accusations at innocent, young men? You have already questioned Aafaq. The only thing Aafaq Qazmi is guilty of being, is a computer professional. Chachu, why are you acting so silly?" I felt a familiar fury explode inside me. "Roshina, please relax. I am not pointing a finger at any one. I just wanted to know if he has mentioned it you. These insurgents have endless funds of money. There is backing from the West and the oil-rich nations of the world. According to Interpol, a whole lot of Pakistani youth in UK and Australia who have probably hardly seen their native countries are being radicalized in Birmingham and other cities across Europe. They are graduates in computers and even freshly passed out doctors. Maybe it's due to the racism they have experienced there, which has never let them fit in. But they visit Pakistan for a fortnight's holiday and never leave. They write letters home to their parents which we have intercepted. In these letters they blame their parents for making them live in the sinful lands of the West. They ruthlessly detach themselves from their families. And even have the gall to command their mothers and sisters to stop baring their faces to strange men.

Along with these young men comes the technical knowhow to establish ultra-sensitive computer networks. This is soon going to provide an easy route for money and ammunition to be transferred. So many missiles from the Soviet war with the Afghan Mujahideen have come in the hands of these *Jihadists* at our borders. There is pandemonium in your beloved Kashmir. With a family as well connected and wealthy as Aafaq's, they are clever enough to devise a new *modus operandi.* It scares me what it will be. Roshina, we as the Indian defence do not have to deal with merely the Inquilaab Kashmir. There are so many of these radical factions. I hope this makes them see the futility of their demands." I barely heard a word of what my uncle had to say. "I asked you a question, Chachu. Did you or did you not read Aafaq's letter?" I already knew the answer. But still in my heart I nurtured the hope that what I suspected, wouldn't be true. "Yes, I did." He said, looking a trifle regretful. Without a glance his way I stormed into my room and closed the door with a bang. I refused to come out till my uncle had left. Mum told me before going to bed that Chachu had gone straight back to Kashmir as the unrest in Sopore was making headway for disaster. "He got a call on his wireless that some militants had entered from Pakistan and had occupied a school building. They were firing indiscriminately from there."

Again there will be casualties and civilian ones, too. The United Nations and all those other bodies will be overjoyed. I felt a bit of remorse for sending Chachu to, what was now a war zone after such a display of animosity.

I went to bed without having my dinner. What a f...up life? And I wasn't using that offensive word as a joke but no other adjective was suitable to describe the misery tearing me apart. After every one had gone to bed, I went into the balcony and lit a cigarette. I had bought a pack with Jyoti. As soon as I carried it to my lips, a mighty gale of wind came and blew it out. I watched it being tossed into the grounds below. Through shut eyes, I pictured Aafaq carrying the cigarette to my mouth. "F...," I muttered and went inside.

The night in no way was any better as I had a horrible dream. Heena and me were little girls, in a scary looking hospital. I saw myself as a five year old wearing a black pinafore, enter an operation theatre. Heena was on the operation table looking deathly white. "Don't let them do this to me, Rosha Jaan." She begged. When I went near her she held out a bloodied organ of some sort. It was the same old familiar nightmare which had ravaged me since childhood and had been a harbinger of all things discreditable. It owed its roots to the day of our appendix operations.

College, the next day was a horror show. I suppose due to my constant dalliance with the migrant camps someone there had spilled the beans about Aafaq. Campus was abuzz with, "Roshina Kapoor, that girl from Srinagar, she was engaged to a Muslim. Can you believe it?" The fact that I wouldn't give any of the college guys the time of the day, had created a hate wave against me. I read 'Roshina Kapoor is a whore' scribbled over the classroom blackboard. Jyoti was up in arms and determined to get to the bottom of it. In my wretched state caused by the misery of the night, I was beyond caring.

"Any calls from Srinagar?" I asked Mum optimistically when I reached home that evening. "None at all," was her prompt response, though she did seem surprised to see my fretfulness. I sat besides our phone in the living room from six pm onwards, waiting for Aafaq to call. I checked the instrument several times to see if it were functional. It was soon ten pm. Rohan took pity on my worked up plight, and we sneaked out to the nearest phone booth. We tried to call Aafaq for nearly an hour but in vain. When we tried Zubeida's number, it was a similar story. "A faulty line," the sympathetic booth operator offered as an explanation. I prayed that all be well with the Qazmis. "You are being silly now," Rohan tried to reason as I spoke out loud. "They are Muslims. What can happen to them?" I was too restless to go to college the following day. And I still could not get through to Srinagar over the phone.

I camped on the living room floor the entire night, shivering in my sleeping bag as I was certain Aafaq would call. But I heard nothing except the clock tick. As dawn approached, I was about to go into my room when the phone rang.

'Rosha,' it was my uncle. He sounded extremely unnerved. "Get your mother on the line. It's urgent." I watched Mum as she spoke to Chachu and observed how distraught she had become. She signalled me to leave the room. I left reluctantly, but hovered at the doorway trying to figure out what was going on. Through her soft tones, I could make out that something was drastically wrong. She ended the call and looked at me, her lashes brimming with tears. I ran up to her. "Mum, what is the matter? Is it Aafaq?" She replied that Heena was down with a serious bout of jaundice and was desperate to see me. Chachu was back in the capital and would be escorting us to Srinagar. We were to fly to Srinagar the same afternoon itself. Chachu was waiting for us at the airport.

The flight from New Delhi to Srinagar was the longest journey of my life. It took all of my self-control to restrain myself from entering the cockpit and order the pilot to speed up. Chachu hadn't looked my way at all. My eyes closed flittingly, in intervals.

I dream that Heena is in the aeroplane by my side. I turn to her and smile. "I am going to the saffron garden without you, Rosha Jaan," she says. She pulls at my curly fringe and looks my way with her usual tenderness. I reach out to her but she is nowhere to be seen. I wake up with a startle. My hair has slipped out of its tight hair band, and has tumbled into my eyes. Has someone played with my locks?

□

13

Mum handed me a *burqa* as soon as we landed. I was coming back to my Motherland in circumstances I had never anticipated. I had fled with a *burqa* on, and I now returned wearing the same black cloth. Why? Because our leaders, irrespective of religion don't have the guts to snatch a rifle out of the hands of a fanatic. There are so many other lucrative scams to reckon with. Why bother with human mortalities?

Srinagar Airport was all about Army and security forces. We were immediately escorted into a massive military jeep. The mountains and landscape held no appeal for me. Overturned vehicles were lying on the sides of roads. The islands of Dal Lake looked decrepit. I saw the winding lane that had once lead to my school had been desecrated in a manner, most contemptuous. The reason being, it once had housed a Roman Catholic church.

And then it came, the sharp turn that went to Raj Bagh Road. The jeep zigzagged its way to my striking house. The front door was opened by an uncle of Heena's, and I walked inside feeling the tension in the air. There was a Maulvi sitting with Abbas Uncle in the living room. But I was in too much of a hurry to meet Heena that I didn't think why. Abbas Uncle stood up as Mum followed behind me. He started sobbing. Heena's room door was locked, and I pounded on it endlessly. After some time the door was opened by Ruhail's mother who looked ghastly. Noor Aunty sat on the floor and stared at me with a vacant expression. "Where is Heena?" I cried as the bed was bare. "Heena, Heena where are you? It is me. I have come to meet you." No sound came, but an eerie silence followed. She must be in the garden, hiding behind the walnut tree. I told myself. Oh Heena, when I find you I am going to punish you so badly for tormenting me like this. With this thought, I ran into the garden. "Heena, Heena," I scream. I dash behind the Walnut tree positive she is hiding there. In my panic I don't realize that I have run straight into Aafaq. "Where is Heena?" I ask him gasping for breath. Not in my wildest dreams had I imagined that my reunion with Aafaq would happen this way.

He remains quiet. "Aafaq, where is Heena? Where is she hiding?" He looks at me, still, without saying a word. 'Heena,' I scream again as I hurry to the bushes. There is no one. She must be at Zubeida's place. That's her and Zubeida, behind the curtain in Zubeida's room, laughing at my plight. I race back to the gate. Just wait and watch how I teach them a lesson. The Army officers stationed at the gate prevent me from leaving and I turn around to scream for Chachu to intervene. Aafaq is right behind me. "She is not at Zubeida's house. You cannot meet Heena." His voice is dull and lifeless. "She has left us all." "What do you mean?" I shout at him. "She is in a better place." He finally looks my way. I glare at him and in his eyes I see the *Darkness of Hell*. Suddenly, my head starts spinning and I fall on to the gravel pathway.

I have no memory of what happened after that. I was rushed to the Military Hospital. I had experienced what is medically classified as syncope. My blood pressure and heart rate fell way below normal, and I had lost consciousness. I was administered life-saving drugs through injections. My mother told me later when I came around that Heena had been raped by two men while coming home from college. Her car was flagged down, and the driver had been shot. The men had gagged and tied Heena and driven the car into the forest, where they had raped and beaten her. They had then thrown her a couple of streets away from her house. Ruhail's father had been tipped off by the press. She had been found bleeding on the road, by the police and a whole lot of reporters, for whom she was a sensational scoop. Mum's voice was muffled with sobs. "Who did it, Mummy?" In my anguish, I had resorted to what I used to address her as a child. "We don't know. The men were dressed in military fatigues. That's all we have been told." She replied, choking on the words. "She had been taken to the hospital." Mummy continued. "She had insisted to be taken home. Her family didn't leave her for a minute, and even told her they would send Aafaq to fetch you. But she would start to howl uncontrollably, at the mere mention of your name. Then on Thursday evening she managed to smuggle in her father's razor and had slashed her wrists, after she had locked her door. They found her lying in a pool of blood, on the cold bathroom tiles. The life so full of promise and love, violently destroyed. She had been buried amongst the flowers of saffron. She had left a letter to Aafaq saying she wanted to be buried in Rosha Jaan's saffron garden."

I cried, till there were no more tears left. Mummy cradled me in her arms, rocking me against her.

My delicate Heena. To think someone could have violated her body in such an inhuman way. Heena, how could you leave me? We had to rule the world together. You were going to be the world's best heart surgeon. Heena, whose translucent skin would get a bruise, even with a feather-like touch. I saw stars again, and heard Mummy frantically call for a nurse. I felt the sharp prick of a needle, and then felt nothing at all. Later in the evening I lay staring at the ceiling. I heard footsteps at the door and saw Aafaq looking at me. He turned around and left.

We remained in Srinagar for a whole week. We were given a room in Chachu's Mess. My uncle didn't leave our side for a single second. We went home every day. Noor Aunty would look at me and sob. She begged Mummy to take me back to New Delhi, that no harm should come my way, but my mother was insistent that we would stay.

Aafaq came and met me one day before we left for New Delhi. I was surprised as I had not expected him to come at all. I had not seen him whenever I had gone home as I would remain in the garden near the walnut tree. I had hung on to the foolish thought that somehow Heena would resurface out of somewhere. Zubeida had come over, but I had refused to meet her. It was too painful. She had understood and with a sorrowful look at me had gone back to her house.

We mourned in silence the loss of his loved one and mine. I looked straight ahead. There was so much of Heena in him. I wondered why I had never realized it before, their resemblance to one another. It was because both of them had fascinated me in their own unique way. What a painful reminder for his parents.

He handed me Heena's red bag, her prized possession. The bag had always been a bone of contention between the two of us. Probably, the one thing she had never been able to share with me.

"She begged me to hand it over to you when I see you next. I told her that I would go to New Delhi and bring you back. But she had maintained that she will call you herself and request you to come." His voice was thick with emotion, and I realized he needed to open up and talk. "She said she was very tired and asked me to give her some thing for the pain. I gave her the pain killers which the doctors had prescribed. The bastards had bitten her face and neck, like rabid dogs. She requested me to leave her room, saying she wanted to sleep. Why did I believe her?" He moaned, covering his face with his hands. I held him in my arms as he cried, unabashedly. I heard a slight movement, and I looked up. My uncle had entered my room. I gave him a cold look. My mind couldn't get over the fact that Heena's rapists had been wearing Army fatigues. He noiselessly retreated.

"Roshina, I will kill those animals with my own, bare hands." Though Aafaq's speech had been a little inarticulate, I knew I had heard him right. My mind went cold with fear. He mentioned a couple of other things, and then he got up abruptly and left. He didn't look back at me. It started that very moment. The void in my life that would last forever. And then I read the last letter, that Heena Qazmi would ever write to me.

Rosha Jaan, my sister, by blood,

I am sorry, my dearest friend. So sorry that I won't be there to dress you, on the day you marry my most precious brother. Sorry, I won't be there to pamper your children. I won't even be there when you become a famous novelist. But I will always be around you. I can't live like this as I am unclean. The disgrace is too much for me to bear with. I am not as strong as you.

Let the world know about our songs, our Pehalgam, your Saffron Garden and the beauty of our magnificent state. I want the people of India and the world to know how we lived in Kashmiriyat. This is not Kashmir any more. And I can't stay here. You have been made for a purpose, Rosha Jaan. You will go very far.

Please accept the *jhoomar* and promise me you will wear it the day you marry Aafaq. I will be there, watching you. Don't think bad of me, but I don't have a choice. Take care of my brother and let him know that he is the best brother, any one can have. Please spare my baby brother, Rohan, the horrible facts. I will be immensely saddened if he ever gets to know.

Will you find a nice girl for Ruhail? Someone like yourself. Silly me! For there can never be any one like you. Let me go now, Rosha Jaan. I am tired and want to rest forever, in your Saffron Garden as this way I will always belong to you.

Heena, your sister, by blood.

I carefully picked up the *jhoomar*. (Ornament worn on the head by Muslim girls at the time of their marriage.) Ruhail's family had gifted it to Heena many years ago as a token of her being their prospective daughter-in-law. It was a family heirloom. Then she had left me her yellow, velvet *firan*. I nestled it against my cheek and could feel her fragrance and the freshness of her skin. My hand touched something soft, and I realized it was the pink baby blanket with bunnies, the one I had always teased her about. I crawled into fetal position on the sofa, and cried like a trapped animal. We left for New Delhi the next day. I will never forget that horrible scene with Chachu which preceded our departure.

"Why haven't you caught Heena's killers?" I blasted my uncle. "It is a civilian matter." He replied icily. "Civilian, my foot! They were in a military jeep. They had military fatigues on. They called each other Captain and Major. They cut her face with a Swiss military knife. Aafaq told me." I took large gulps of air as I still was very weak, but there was no stopping me now. I wouldn't allow Chachu to get away with the martyr act. "Why aren't you doing anything? Why aren't you out looking for the culprits? Because she is Muslim. Or because her rape has gotten Army written all over it? Aafaq showed me a copy of the police report.

Your F… Army did this to my sister. Don't you dare patronize me. To think you actually had the nerve to read Aafaq's letters. How could you suggest that he was changing sides? It is true what the United Nations and

Human Rights Watch say about you. All those articles in the newspapers, full of condemnation. The Indian Army is being spat on all over the world. You are responsible for escalating this into a war. That's what everyone says. You are murderers and rapists. I hate you. You killed my sister." I screamed at the top of my voice. I had no regard for the fact that we were sitting in an Army Mess. "Soon the world will know the truth. I am going to expose you in New Delhi." I felt the flatness of my mother's palm against my cheek. My hand went to my face, nursing the welt on my flesh.

'Roshina,' she hurled in her most commandeering voice. "Don't you ever talk to your elders, especially your family members like that. We will not tolerate it." "Leave her alone, Bhabhi," Chachu protested. "She needs to grieve. We can't imagine what she is going through. And please, don't ever hit her.

Roshina, do you think the Army would ever have the stupidity to perform this monstrous deed in broad daylight when we are under the scrutiny of the reporters and press of the entire world? Would we use a military vehicle and wear an Army uniform? Credit the Army with some sense. Who do you think contacted the press and Ruhail's father? Can't you see how the militants, and these foreign mercenaries are trying to drag our name into utter squalor? Let me tell you with a hundred percent guarantee, it's not exactly that. I told you they are going to adopt a new approach to ensnare Aafaq and this is it. A great deal of his friends knew about you. With you gone, Heena became his Achilles. Most of those boys have gone the way rogue. They have him hook, line and sinker now. I know you can't believe me. But this is one allegation I will not have falling on the doorstep of the Indian Army." He left it at that as he stormed out of the Mess barking orders at his poor Major to drop us at our doorstep in New Delhi.

Papa and Rohan were at the airport to receive us. I hugged them both. It broke my heart when I remembered what Heena had written about not saying anything to Rohan.

Mummy came into my room in the night and handed me a mug of warm milk. As she was about to leave, she looked at me and said. "Take that stuff and nonsense out of your head regarding the Army being behind this tragedy. I think you are more mature than that." She observed my non-responsive attitude. "I know you don't actually believe the Army has any role to play in this. You just want an outlet for your grief. And your uncle is a punching bag for you. Goodnight. We will get through this I know we will, but we have to keep our wits about us."

□

14

At times like this, writers use words like pick up the pieces. But I had no pieces to pick up. It was over. There were no calls from Aafaq. There were no calls from his family. As Heena had requested, I never told Rohan about what happened to her. But he got to know from Mummy. And one night as I lay in bed missing my red haired sister, he entered my room and snuggled into my bed. He cried himself to sleep with his head lying on my shoulder. I cried, too, and my heart ached all over again. I missed Heena, and I missed her brother. When I would look at the fair, Kashmiri children in the camps I would think of my best friend. Is she here around me? I would ask myself. I would extend my arms forward and shut my eyes, hoping I would feel her.

Heena Qazmi was gone forever. It was the stark reality of my life. Out of the two little girls who had loved Kashmir with their life, only one was left. I picked up the blanket she had left me and placed it under my cheek, as I closed my eyes each night. In the morning, it would be soaked. As my sister, by blood, the girl with the burgundy flush was lost to me.

One afternoon over cold coffee in Connaught Place I disclosed my horrible ordeal to Jyoti. She had already realized that Aafaq was more than my best friend's brother. She had seen their photo when she had come home one day. And when I came back from Srinagar apathetic and listless, she had immediately smelt a rat. She offered me strength by letting me know she was there as a friend, without denying me the right to mourn. She was now dating the college president, Sachin and he was a reliable person. I started hanging out with them. One day while we were in the canteen she somewhat casually remarked. "Roshina, I was talking to my aunt who is a very talented writer. She runs her own magazine. According to her, the Indian Army has become the fall guy. It's so convenient for the Western media to point fingers at our Army. What on earth was the Gulf war regarding? It's all about oil. Why did the United States support the Afghan Mujahideen against the Soviets? Don't you find their holier than thou sermons about the wrongdoings of our Army hypocritical?" What Jyoti had to say was quite on the lines of what I was getting to hear from nearly everyone. I was being forced to use my common sense and reason. The awful argument I had gotten into with my uncle in Srinagar replayed in front of me. I missed Chachu and I was sure he, too, was hurting inside. He would phone my parents but I would refuse to talk to him. One day I came home from college and stopped in my tracks. Ruhail was there talking to Mummy.

"I have been in New Delhi since some time now. I work in the Jammu and Kashmir Guest House." He looked at me awkwardly, and I looked away. I couldn't glance at him without thinking of Heena and how he had shyly held her hand in the *shikara*. Then only to be fair, I told him about the *jhoomar*. After all, it had belonged to his family. "If Heena wanted you to have it then you shall." He said very softly.

"How is Aafaq? I haven't heard from him in a long time." I finally asked. "As good as anyone can be in the circumstances." He said as his eyes averted my gaze. "Is he working?" I carefully observed his evasive expression. "I think he is doing something of his own. Do you want to send a letter to Aafaq? I am going to Srinagar next week." But I didn't reply as I was observing the way his eyes had been darting. Why was he deflecting my questions?

"Tell me the truth, Ruhail. Where is Aafaq? I will not settle for anything but the right answer." "He is in Srinagar," was his prompt reply. "Don't bullshit me. I can tell when you are lying. What is he doing there?" Yes, I thought with a grimace. Roshina Kapoor is back.

"I just told you, Roshina. They say he does some computer work on contract basis, here and there." Who was this they? I thought in wonder. "Who does he do this contract work for, Ruhail? Inquilaab Kashmir. Is he helping those militants? Don't underestimate me just because I am a woman. If Aafaq Qazmi has turned his back on his country, to avenge his sister's death then I have every right to know." "Why, so you can get him arrested?" Ruhail's tone betrayed anger now. "Report on him. Go ahead, Rosha. It's not that simple in Kashmir. Nothing is black or white."

"It's not simple anywhere, Ruhail. But you always have a choice before making the final decision. And who are you to judge me? How dare you say I will rat on Aafaq? Because I am a Hindu? Or is it because I have an uncle in the Army? What do you know about love, Ruhail?" I clammed shut at once, feeling terrible as I saw his hurt look.

"I have read the report, Ruhail. According to Heena's statement, the assailants spoke grammatically incorrect English. How would officers speak poor English? A Major and a Captain hmm, that's what they called each other. Do you think they would reveal their actual rank if it were them or they would have actually addressed each other like that?" I found myself believing what I was telling Ruhail.

"Is he working for the insurgents? I just want a yes or no." But Ruhail's answers remained indistinct and he left. I knew for sure he had been hiding something. 'I will kill Heena's assailants.' I remembered Aafaq saying something like that in Kashmir. Please God, don't let him do anything stupid. What was I supposed to do?

Jyoti coaxed me into become member of the college debating society and literary circle. We had weekly workshops, where we were encouraged to think and speak 'Out of the box.' Little to my knowledge, Jyoti's writer Aunt, Meena Dhesi had heard me debating one evening in our college auditorium. I had been speaking on 'The Impact of Colonialism on Indian Literature.' Meena had found my argument very persuasive, and had asked Jyoti if I wanted a job as an Intern in her magazine, '*Ethos*.' It was the country's leading magazine, dealing with socio-political issues and the problems swarming the nation and our globe.

I obviously would be interviewed but Jyoti's secretive smile suggested that I was already part of the team. "Why don't you work for her?" I politely asked, not wanting to step on anyone's toes. "There is no nepotism in my family. Sachin and I want to start something with Sachin's brother. We have decided to begin a magazine over the Internet, it's what is called 'An Online' magazine."

It was just the sort of break I had been looking for. I had better call Heena right away, was my excited reaction. But then I came back to the present like a deflated balloon. It is such a hollow feeling to achieve even the tiniest of victories but not to have your loved ones around you. And that sensation has coexisted with me most of my adult life. At night I sat in the balcony and gazed at the black sky. Suddenly out of nowhere a star appeared, shining brightly. 'When we die we become stars.' I recalled Baba telling us, when we were little girls. "Is that you, Heena?" I asked aloud of the lone star.

Mum took me shopping, and I bought a pantsuit for my interview. It had been scheduled for Saturday afternoon. The office of *Ethos* was located in a quaint house, in a secluded and well-kept area of the capital. The atmosphere was pretty informal. And my prospective boss, was friendly without allowing anyone to undermine her position.

I sat across the table as Meena talked to someone on the phone. Her room was quite messy, I thought. There were files and journals lying in total disarray on her desk, but she had lovely paper weights which added to the luster of her office. She ended her call and looked my way frankly. "I really liked the way you spoke that day, Roshina. And the best part was, I could hear your sentiments, the depth of your passion. You granted a ripe flavour to a very sterile topic. And that is one of the finest qualities of a good writer. In this industry, a natural flair for words, and an impassioned way of writing are incomparable. And if one can manage not to compromise on Grammar and style then you have hooked the reader. You have all of these qualities." She smiled warmly seeing my surprised look. "But I will let Human Resources cut out a program for you, where you can attend college, graduate and work here for fixed hours over the weekend."

"Does that mean I have gotten the job?" I managed to say. She glanced at me through her glasses which were perched on the edge of her nose. "Are you kidding me, Honey? This office is your baby now. Let me give Human Resources a call. And Roshina, there is no need to dress formally in my office. I get too intimidated." She smiled amiably. "Jeans and any sort of top are sort of the dress code here. You have a natural panache which doesn't come from the pages of a glitzy magazine. Be yourself over here. That way you can concentrate better on the job at hand." She smiled again, this time dismissively.

□

15

Meena was a fabulous editor. She had graduated magna cum laude, from Wellesley College. She had brought in a lot of editors from American publishing houses, and American slang was used liberally. But there was no compromise on Grammar and tenses. Everyone conversed in flawless English. I may have acquired terms like 'cool' and 'period'; expressions like 'You look beat' and 'Holy crap'. However, I learnt not to sacrifice my limited dictionary of the Queen's English. Meena possessed an unrivalled ability to discern the truth. She would not get inhibited by the political honchos of the power capital, but made sure her columns ran the facts. And if the who's who of the city got ticked off, she couldn't care less. She consorted with the rich and famous and gained access to the murky details of company boardrooms and socialite bedrooms. She did rub some people the wrong way, but she never wanted to be in everyone's good books. It was all about a perfect story for her. Whether it was an article on 'Child Labor,' 'Women Trafficking,' or a scathing attack on our 'Country's Nuclear Policy.' Meena made sure people would pay attention with what she and her team had to say. She was very thoughtful, and would drop me home when it would get too late. My parents took an instant shine to her, and it seemed to be both ways. She had a whole lot of original one liners. Her favorite was for the fairer sex. "There are two ways a woman can get to the top. The first being on her back. That is the easiest but unsatisfactory way. The other is by crushing those balls, when they try to overpower her. And by balls, I don't mean eye balls." She was prepared to go out on a limb if she sensed potential. She was generous with praise, when praise was due and critiqued without being supercilious.

My father started going to work again and slowly regained his spirits. It was a very happy moment for us all when he started taking lectures in his college. Mum, Dad and Rohan attended my convocation as I graduated. I was grateful to God for each moment of joy, but I couldn't shrug off the pain. I smiled and went out for dinner with my parents. I wore the bangle, Aafaq's mother had given me and Heena's yellow firan. Only when you looked into my eyes could you see the misery that lay buried inside. There were still no news from Aafaq.

I enrolled in my Masters and opted for 'International Relations.' I worked for the magazine after college regularly and sometimes in the morning, when I didn't have class. When I would call Srinagar, I would be told by the servant that the family is praying and Aafaq is at work.

I left college early one afternoon and headed for the rickshaw stand, outside my college. I nearly jumped out of my skin when someone stepped out of the shadows and stood right in front of me.

"Hello, Roshina, how are you?" I looked up and was flabbergasted. It was Aafaq. I stared at him for a long time. The softness of his youth had been vanquished by a hardness, I was not familiar with. His body which had once been boyish was muscular. Had he been going to the gym? "Hi, Aafaq," I exclaimed feeling somewhat thrown off balance. "When did you come to New Delhi?" "Roshina, is there some place we can sit and talk?"

"Of course there is, Aafaq." I replied with a smile. "Let's go home. I was going to work but it's not a problem. I can go to my office later. My boss is very understanding."

He looked at me resolutely. "I have already been home and have met Rohan and your parents. They told me where to find you." His tone was neutral, giving nothing away.

"You left me for last." I stated, trying to be cheerful. But if I had expected him to laugh or at least smile, I was mistaken. From the corner of my eye, I saw my class mates look at him keenly. "There is a coffee shop at the end of the street. Come on, let's go." I got hold of his arm and started to cross the road.

"It is really wonderful that you are studying and working, too." Aafaq's voice did seem sincere enough. He had now bent his head and made an elaborate show of scanning the menu card. "What are you doing these days?" I asked him smoothly. He looked up and spoke, "I take assignments mostly, from telecommunication companies. I am in the process of starting a computer centre in Srinagar or Pampore. It is what they call a Cyber Café. I am going to England day after. There is a computer trade fair in London, which I plan to visit."

'One day, we will see your beautiful Lake District together,' he had promised. I thought of that moment on the Boulevard when he had whispered those words into my ear. He was giving a very fine impression of having forgotten that for sure. Had our relationship reached an impassé? Seemed unlikely, as our relationship if we had one, had barely reached the nascent stage. I realized that I was being very insensitive. I probably reminded him of Heena. I had been his sister's best friend. He was so used to seeing the two of us together.

'Roshina.' His look and tone were decided. It was as if he had made up his mind. There was no softness of his expression, and his eyes didn't crinkle at the corners.

I sucked in my breath. Why did I have a feeling that I wasn't going to like what he had to say? Without pausing further, he remarked. "It is very tough to say this, but I think it is in everyone's best interests that we break off our engagement." He stopped, waiting for me to react. Observing my stillness, he went on. "My parents are depressed and immensely frightened." He lay emphasis on each adjective, but I still made no sound nor movement. "I can't blame them, considering the circumstances. They have this fear which I say is quite founded that I might be targeted next. I cannot give them more sorrow." I continued to stir the sugar in my coffee cup and kept my gaze fastened on him.

I finally spoke. My voice dispassionate and objective. "Well-rehearsed speech, Aafaq, but I would like to know how does me being in your life endanger it?" "Don't be dense, Roshina. You are Hindu. I am Muslim." I laughed sarcastically. "It took you a long time to figure that out, didn't it? Your lot told us to get out, lest our women are taken as prostitutes and our men are shot in cold blood. Your creed is persecuting my creed and that, too, in my own state and you are acting as if it is our fault. Or does it come naturally to you, to play the wronged party? Let me tell you about being Hindu, in a state, where militants are trying to hunt you down. Let me tell you about being Hindu, yet an Indian and living in a migrant camp behind a bloody toilet. Don't give me this religion nonsense."

"I have lost my sister in a manner most sickening, to the Indian Army. Do you think that is easy to digest?" At least there was some feeling in his voice now. "How do you know for sure it was the Army? Okay, let's say it was the Army, how do you know they weren't Muslim?" I roared, as I became more daring. "I don't know the actual count but till what I knew last, there were a good many Muslims in the Indian Army."

"They were clean shaven, Roshina." "So what, Aafaq? You are clean shaven. Does that mean you are a Hindu? Well I must say, thank you, for actually making the effort to meet me in person and breaking it off. You could have sent me one of those f.... Dear Jane letters." I made a reference to those casual letters written usually by overseas soldiers to their girlfriends back home informing them of their change of heart.

He looked at me and remarked casually, "I must say your English vocabulary has surely expanded. This Dear Jane letter and all. I don't have the faintest idea what you are talking about. But I don't condone vulgar language, Rosha. It doesn't become you. We always had been close and physical attraction between two members of the opposite sex was going to happen." He made it sound like a Biology project.

"Since you are so sure, it is the Army. Do you think that officers would ever do it? And would they address each other as Major and Captain. That's just short of calling each other by their first name. Can't you see that they were deliberately misleading Heena to think it was the Army? Would they give away conclusive information that they have to get back to the Mess? How come she was found by the reporters? Do you think the Army would have dialled their number and told them to go and click some photos? It is the militants. They were aware of the self-recriminations that would come with rape, in a family like yours.

And now I, with my Hindu blood am a source of embarrassment to you, Aafaq. Is that what you are saying? What should we do to get even? Why don't you get me raped by the Inquilaab Kashmir, since you do seem to be their best pal these days. Do you know, I am called the Muslim whore in college? You don't feel bad that your fiancé is being branded a whore? Oh! but I'm not your fiancé, am I? And you are the only person who is living in purgatory hell, as you are the one who has lost his sister. I am the thick-skinned *Kafir* who lived on rent, on the first floor. What about my parents, Aafaq, who never thought about religion when I told them I love you? Imagine them allowing their only daughter to go ahead in a relationship, with a man whose religion would have probably demanded that I convert or will not be accepted. But they took that chance. Don't you think it was terrifying for them? Let me tell you one thing, Aafaq Qazmi, my parents are parents, too."

He looked at me contemplatively. "Don't overreact, Rosha, we are still going to be friends. Our lives are different now. And we have this distance to deal with. It is quite impractical to carry on this way. There is not a single guy in this room who wouldn't want to be in my place. You are so unaware of the appreciative looks that are coming your way. You will surely find someone nice and of your own religion."

My voice was scoffing as I yelled, "That is all that you think of, Aafaq, religion. Tell me, what do you think about my religion? Do you regret having us as tenants, and putting up lights in our house at Diwali? Do you ask yourself why you and your family took circumambulation of our temples, and why you celebrated Eid with us? Since you are determined to end it, then you can end it, period. But you have no right to come and suggest that what we had, was because of convenience, and neither will I hear anything wrong about my religion. It is better to be God fearing rather than religious." I said flatly. "You have no right to advise me on how to find the right guy. I am not a whore and even for you do not like being called one."

If Aafaq's red face was anything to go by then I was sure all heads had turned our way. "And let me tell you that what happened to your sister, was in no way a Hindu-Muslim thing. It was an atrocious ploy adopted by sick-minded individuals." I prided myself for not shedding a single tear. "You go your way, I will go mine. Good bye and good luck." I practically ran out on to the street and hauled myself into a waiting rickshaw.

I wiped the tears which poured down my cheeks, savagely. My best friend commits suicide and leaves me, now her brother, the love of my life suggests that somehow, I am accountable. The rickshaw stopped outside my office. I stepped out and heard a car door slam shut. Aafaq was heading my way. He had apparently followed me in his car. Why does he care? I thought heatedly. "Are you alright?" He was at my side and sounded quite disturbed. I smiled brightly at him. "Relax, Aafaq, it is not the end of the world for me. I will learn to get on with my life." He gave me a searching look. I stared back at him, unblinking. Whatever he was about to say went unheard as Meena sprung on us. 'Roshina,' her voice called out as she materialized out of her car. Meena had come to work in slim-fitting pants and a peasant neckline blouse. There was a bright scarf around her waist to emphasize its narrowness. "Now why are you having an obvious lover's tiff, right here on the road? You are always welcome to use the office." She looked at Aafaq with open appreciation as she addressed me. "Where on earth have you been hiding him all this while? No wonder you don't have eyes for any one here." She offered Aafaq her hand. "Hello, I am Meena." Aafaq shook hands with her politely and introduced himself. 'Qazmi,' she repeated as her eyes narrowed. Meena snapped her fingers excitedly in the air. "You must be the boy from the mountains. What brings you to town, Aafaq? And what are you doing monopolizing my office's latest asset in broad daylight?" She teased, "I have never seen her so worked up or so hot and bothered." Her voice was emphatic. Then as if struck by a brainwave, she announced with authority. "Roshina, now that you have an escort why don't you two come to my place after work? I have a small party going on at home. You will meet some very important people. I won't take no for an answer." She turned to Aafaq. "I have wanted to invite Roshina since a long time but would have to hold back because of the lateness of the hour the parties usually linger on to. On the contrary, you appear to know how to handle her." She said amusedly. "This brilliance in her cheeks and gleam in her eyes isn't because of our New Delhi sun. So do I take it, that the two of you will be there, latest by nine? Please understand, Aafaq Qazmi, my guests are very important to me. I need Roshina to be present so that she can do the columns, based on real first-hand impressions." Aafaq nodded respectfully. "I will make sure we are there by nine pm sharp." He looked my way and said, "Rosha, I will pick you up at eight o clock." He turned around and walked towards his car.

Meena put her arms around me protectively and we walked together into the building. "My dear child, aren't you going to tell me why with such a fine specimen of manhood and good manners in your life, you are crying your heart out?"

While she inhaled her nicotine through cigarettes mounted on a narrow holder. I told her about that land far away, where once upon a time, there had been paradise. And about my precious friend who was no longer with me, and her precious brother who no longer wanted me. Meena remained quiet and heard me till the very end, without letting anyone enter the room. She wiped my tears with kleenex. I could see her own eyes were moist.

"Jyoti had told me there was something going on between you and the guy back home." Meena said evenly. "I hadn't realized you were so deeply involved. You are strong minded and independent, without abusing the liberties your parents have given you. As for that boy from the mountains, Honey, if I had a man like him, I would be moping around for him, too. On a more serious note. I am really happy I have invited the two of you over. There is an American doctor friend of mine in town. He works for the Human Rights Watch, and has of late returned from Kashmir. It will be very informative for the two of you to hear his unbiased account of what is actually happening over there. Let me tell you one thing for sure, Aafaq Qazmi isn't coming to my place to meet me. But his look did say he found me a bit disreputable, and is concerned that you might be working for people rather unsavoury. That is the real reason why he has agreed to come tonight. It is tough for him to let go of you, no matter how mule headed he is trying to be. He still considers you as his. And you, Roshina Kapoor, are not helping yourself at all with this eternally miserable look. Get yourself a makeover." She said bluntly, giving me a critical look. "Go and buy some new clothes. I will elaborate. Get something downright sexy for yourself. Let our Kashmiri poster boy know what he is missing.

Allow me to make some calls and make sure those very important people I was talking about, are coming over tonight." I decided to take her advice. After all, I did possess a pair of racehorse legs.

□

16

That night was the first time I wore what is known to the world as, 'The little black dress.'

I geared it with sheer black tights. Though the dress fell to my knees, it had an interesting slit. And the sheer stockings displayed my slender legs in the best way possible. I sprayed perfume liberally, and gave myself a critical look. I hadn't experimented with makeup in fear of looking like a clown. I had just stuck to a light-coloured lipstick. My hair fell in curly waves, to my shoulders as I hadn't had a hair cut in over a year. I was ready before Aafaq came but let him wait and heard him talking to Rohan. The two of them were having an animated discussion regarding computers.

They both were dumbfounded as they looked up at me.

"I can't believe it's you, Didi. You look incredible." Rohan did the honours of breaking the silence.

"Aren't you wearing anything over that?" Aafaq asked me casually. Here he goes again. There was no plunging neckline or anything of the sort. On the contrary, the dress was quite high-necked and designed to lend a coy look. "Are you scared I might catch a chill? Or is this dress too daring for you?" Rohan realized that he was listening to what he should not be and bade us a hasty goodbye. "Aafaq, since you have set the ball in motion and have called off our engagement. I am not your fiancé anymore, and we have long established that you are not my brother." I stated vehemently as we sat inside his car. If I had discomfited him then it was intentional. "It's been very long since I have enjoyed myself, and today I fully intend to. So, no moral policing, please." He remained quiet and drove in silence.

Meena's house was very tastefully done. The interiors were eclectic as I had expected them to be. The party was in full swing. The music was light and mostly instrumental. There were a lot of well known of the Literati. They appeared to be a formidable bunch but I knew from prior encounters of the professional kind, they would be down to earth. Meena treated snobs and sycophants with the same minimal zeal. She had no time for them. I spotted her and she walked up to us. She gave us a warm welcome which included embracing Aafaq tightly. If Aafaq was a little taken aback, he didn't show it. She expertly maneuvered him away from me and led him to a small circle of friends.

I smiled inwards when I saw Aafaq talk to this danseuse who had recently received a national award. She was practically hanging on to every word he was saying. "Your Mughal Emperor has caused quite a riot, kid." Meena drawled as she handed me a long stemmed wine glass. I smiled at her and accepted my first glass of wine. Aafaq suddenly turned my way, and I lifted my glass to him. I noticed he was declining alcohol. Balls to you, Aafaq Qazmi. I will do, what I damn well please.

"My darling, Steven." I saw Meena blow kisses at a white-skinned guest who had come and stood right in front of us. Must be the doctor from Kashmir, I thought to myself. Meena nudged me forwards. "Roshina, this is Dr. Steven Cross. Steven is a doctor with Human Rights Watch. He has recently come back from Sopore. Steven, this is Roshina Kapoor, the young writer from Kashmir." "Hello, Roshina," drawled Dr. Cross. We shook hands. "Meena, you never mentioned how pretty this young writer from Kashmir is." He smiled appreciatively as he looked at me from top to toe. The accent was American and very friendly. I found his over familiarity a little disconcerting. And he still didn't loosen his grip on my hand. He gave me a very suggestive smile. I was a little unused to such overpowering, male attention. I didn't know a thing about how to deal with these big, bad wolves. Aafaq was looking at me with a scowl on his face. He headed our way. Had Meena been right? Was it really tough for him to say good bye? I hurriedly made the necessary introductions and skillfully withdrew my hand from the doctor's grasp.

"Human Rights Watch, did you say?" I recognized at once the scepticism in Aafaq's smooth tone. I hurriedly interjected. "Dr. Cross, what are you going to tell us about Kashmir that we don't already know? Is it about the atrocities performed by security personnel on civilians? Spare us the details. We also know about your native country's treatment of its detainees and suspected terrorists. Like your methods of water boarding, sleep deprivation and forced feeding through tubes. I even have a report in which detainees have complained that they were stripped and subjected to canine attacks. What do you have to say, Dr. Cross? It's okay when the United States of America tortures a suspected terrorist but not when India does?" I was quite surprised at my outspoken behaviour but I had felt it necessary.

Steven Cross had a serious expression on his face as he looked directly my way. His cheerful banter had dissipated. "I would say, Roshina Kapoor, that you are a hundred percent accurate. But with all the vast knowledge that you have amassed it's amazing that you have not read my report which I have submitted. And there I have condemned the United States Military for their extreme methods of torture."

His statement left me thunderstruck. I could tell by the similar expression on Aafaq's face, he thought so, too. "I am a doctor for the Human Rights Watch, but that doesn't mean that the 'Human Rights Watch' is a crooked body or the 'Human Rights Watch' has bought my silence.

I have examined women who claim to have been raped by Army personnel in Kashmir. Our team of medical experts always insists that gynecologists and that, too, female gynecologists be brought to tend to the ladies and perform a thorough internal examination." Dr. Cross continued in an eager voice. "Why do they refuse? The authorities ask these so-called victims of molestation to identify guilty soldiers, from line ups but they are unable to. I was the one who slammed the United Nations and the media who are hounding the Indian Army. There are so many contradictory statements. Most of these women are militant sympathizers. Some even their wives. And let me tell you that these very militants themselves have violated Hindu women, they have lived with as neighbours all their lives. Why?"

I answered instantly. "Because she is a *Kafir*." "That is very emotional reply, Roshina. Like all good writers you voice your heart. But it is only partially correct. The violent act of rape gives them so much of power. Most of the militants are from poor families in the villages. They have received no formal education and possess no intelligence quotient. They have never been employed as anything other than an errand boy, at a grocery store or as a labourer. They are sent to training camps in Pakistan. Then comes a supply of military uniform, armamentarium including the Kalashnikov their way. And a rank like chief or commander. For the first time in their lives, they feel good about themselves. People are scared of them now when they come back. And in their eyes it seems like respect."

"Dr. Cross, I really am enjoying your deep pride in our Defence system, but I am sure you are not aware of certain facts." Aafaq's tone was cold.

But Steven Cross wasn't one to be silenced. "I know one thing that in Kashmir, the easiest way to molest a woman and get away with it is by wearing military fatigues. The resentment towards the Army is so harsh that people are ready to believe anything. The unfortunate are the women who suffer and the Army which after all its painstaking efforts to provide security, has to defend itself from ludicrous accusations. Think of the time that is wasted in all these unnecessary backlashes. That is what the radicals want. They feel it's the way the Army will be forced to leave."

It was my turn now and I said, "Dr. Cross." "I won't answer, Roshina, if you call me Dr. Cross again. 'Steven' isn't that tough to pronounce." I felt immensely shy. Is this what they call healthy flirting? I darted a furtive glance at Aafaq and realized he was in a very pugnacious mood. He murmured something beneath his breath and walked away.

"I don't think, I am person of the month with your boyfriend." Steven said jovially. "He is not my boyfriend." I gulped my wine hastily. "He did a fine impression of behaving like one. I think you are going to be in need of this." He placed, what I saw was his visiting card in my hand. "Don't ever hesitate to call me. I will let you in on a secret. Nothing provides a much-needed spark to a relationship more than a little bit of old-fashioned jealousy. I think I have provided a catalyst to your boyfriend to reassert his claim on you." I looked at him in wonder. Had Meena told him about the sorry situation I was in? Was that the reason behind Steven's playful attitude? He winked at me and I relaxed.

"Should we leave, Roshina?" Aafaq enquired smoothly after some time as I was admiring one of the paintings dazzling the wall. "I think you have made your presence felt." After what was a large sip from my wine glass to provoke a scathing comment, I looked at him. He refrained from any remark.

We made our apologies to Meena. "It was really nice to get to know you, Aafaq. You should come more often. It is very nice to see Roshina elated." I gave her a warm embrace, and Aafaq shook hands with her. "I will be calling you for advice on our website." She kissed him on the cheek with a deft flourish.

Our shoulders brushed together as we walked towards the car. We sat in the car, and he turned to look at me. Old habits die hard as he leaned towards me and lovingly pushed away the fringe from my forehead. "I liked you better with short hair." "What difference does it make now, Aafaq?" We both sat there staring at the wind screen. He put the stereo on. An old Hindi number started playing. It had been Heena's favourite song. We wept for the sister who had left us, without so much as saying good bye. And also for our love which had been unable to withstand the test of time.

Aafaq walked me to my door. The light headedness caused by the wine was insufficient to provide a balm to my injured heart. "Like all love stories, our story, too, has a sad ending." I spoke faintly. He kissed me on the forehead and whispered in my ear. "I will never ever forget what we had. Stay away from the likes of that doctor. He would love to have you for dessert. I couldn't stand it when he held your hand." 'Aafaq,' I uttered, as my confidence grew on hearing the possessive quality of his voice. "I could see that you also realized what he said was quite logical. Think about it, Aafaq. I don't want you to be deluded that you can't see the facts." "Take care, Rosha Jaan." He kissed me, this time on the cheek and at the base of my neck. His hands trailed to the chain he had once placed there, and he closed his eyes. He walked back to the car. I ran after him. Aafaq was the only man I would ever love. Not in this lifetime but always. He heard me approach and turned around. He scooped me into his arms and held me close to him. My carefully manufactured defence cracked immediately. "I won't be able to live without you." Through closed eyes, I heard him say softly, "Don't make this tougher than it already is, Rosha Jaan." "It doesn't have to be tough, Aafaq. I am prepared to wait till you heal. But don't shut me out of your life." "I have made my decision, Rosha. It has been difficult because I have never known anyone like you. But there is no room in my life for love now." "We will work it out together, Aafaq, you and me." I looked at him solemnly.

"You don't have to beg, Rosha Jaan. It makes me feel awful." And then reluctantly as if it was against his better judgment. "I never thought you could grow any more beautiful, but you have." He held me close to him and kissed me, first on my cheeks, my forehead and then on my lips, without parting them. I rested my head on his shoulder. It seemed to be the natural thing to do. This is where I belong, I thought to myself. And then abruptly he broke contact and moved away from me. I stumbled and tried to regain my balance. He drove away, and I went indoors. As I undressed in my room, my fingers went to the slight mark he had left on my cheek, when he had kissed me. I felt cold and shut my window. The room became warmer. But what about the frost in my heart?

□

17

The Internet arrived in New Delhi by the end of the month and life revolutionized. It was all about websites and emails. Our magazine got its own website, and I felt a sense of achievement when my name was listed as one of the Junior Assistant Editors. Aafaq had neither called nor emailed me from England or wherever he was. I remembered him explaining to Heena and me, how computers were going to bring everyone closer. Ironically, that day had come but we had grown apart.

"Will the tallest girl in the city take pity on me and give me the pleasure of driving her home?" 'Chachu,' I yelled happily. As I saw his head emerge out from the rolled-down window of his car. He had pulled up right beside me as I was walking on the pavement. I ran to the passenger side, opened the door and hopped in. He said nothing but grinned like a school boy. "I have come in peace." Rudratej Kapoor remarked seriously, "The olive branch is in the back seat somewhere." This was my uncle who had loved me all my life. I will not lose him by acting reckless. The encounter with Dr. Cross the other night had been informative and had come at the right time. I found the Army's role more and more improbable. Chachu and I gave each other our customary high fives and we took the route home.

"By Jove, I can't believe my little niece who till yesterday was playing on my knee is now actually setting me up with her boss." We had been at home since an hour now and I had been talking nineteen to the dozen with my uncle. I told him all about Meena and what a compatible match she would be for him. "So, when are we having our blind date. Me and this boss lady of yours?" He drawled with a rakish grin and a lecherous twirl of an imaginary moustache. I laughed heartily. It was like old times. Chachu had bought a new computer for us. "Roshina, I am happy that you have found your way in the city and have learnt to live your life. I really admire your pluck. Both you and Rohan have been so accommodative to these different circumstances. And I am delighted to see that Rishabh is doing much better." He then looked at me straight in the eye and asked, "What happened between you and Aafaq? Your mother did mention something about a break up." Trust my uncle to come straight to the point. "Is the computer a bribe for me, to give the game away?" My voice was without feeling. No longer would I be the girl who wore her heart on her sleeve.

"I want to apologize to you, Chachu, for all the horrible things I said to you in Srinagar." "Apology not accepted, my dear child. As my daughter never has to apologize to me. I realized that you were in anguish at that period. And the circumstantial evidence that had been so amply provided did very little to persuade someone to think rationally. Especially for a family member or someone with a strong emotional connect as yours. But nevertheless, I am relieved that you have finally gotten rid of your distrust of the Army. It ripped my heart to witness what you were going through in Srinagar."

I then told my uncle about meeting Dr. Cross and how Aafaq had been there, too. "Chachu, I always did have misgivings about blaming the Army but now I am totally convinced of their innocence. The subterfuge of Heena's assailants was not fool proof. In fact, it had been too amateurish."

"Well, it wasn't that amateurish." My Uncle spoke dryly. "Because someone as intelligent and shrewd as Aafaq could actually fall for it and has been played for a fool. With all his brilliance in numbers and figures, he still couldn't do the Math. The dossier I have on Aafaq Qazmi is something you won't get anywhere. And yes, we are keeping tabs on him." That was my uncle's curt rejoinder to my admonishing look. "It's what we like to label as 'Military Surveillance.' It is routine when we suspect anti-national objective."

"Chachu, I think you had better start minding your own business." Chachu was busy connecting the computer to the mains supply. "Aafaq Qazmi is my business. Especially when he is my niece's fiancé. To be precise, he is business for the entire 'Anti-terrorism Wing' of the Army. I have not spent a single minute in peace, Rosha, ever since Heena...." Chachu's voice faltered with emotion. "We have performed crackdown after crackdown since then. And not left a stone unturned in the entire Kashmir to find the people responsible. We have cordoned off villages and searched them inside out. We ate, drank and Goddamn slept with militants, till we found moles. Moles, who were willing to talk for a price." Chachu mentioned harshly. "Heena is gone. May God, always take care of her. Her family is praying for her soul to enter heaven. In Islam, the doors of paradise are shut for those who end their own lives. But we are the Indian Army and are responsible for the security of each and every Indian citizen. We go into Kashmir and spend millions of the exchequers' money building bridges and roads for civilians, just to win their trust. Military crackdown operations occur when a village or house is being suspected of hiding a terrorist. An officer is always present at such an event. Do you think an officer will let any Indian soldier behave in such a way described by the media? What about when the Army wades through knee deep water, because the state is water logged? When we rescue the peasants and farmers, do we ask them their religion? No, we hoard them over our shoulders and carry them to safety. On the contrary when terrorists open fire in a bus full of civilians they segregate the Hindus from the Muslims. The Hindus face their bullets. We are the world's third largest Army. Why is it only in this country we don't think twice before condemning our military? Americans don't condemn their Army when they go and fight in the scorching deserts of Kuwait. Britons don't offer a bad word for their Army when they become part of the Allied Forces. But we love to lash out at those lads who sleep in bunkers, under tanks and get buried beneath forty feet of snow. While we wine and dine and adopt airs of intelligentsia.

I don't want to stray from the point. The point being that both you and I know that so many school and college friends of Aafaq had joined these outfits after attending madrassas in Pakistan. Now the next step from there is analysis of *Jihadist* potential. How many of them can be encouraged to engage in violence? The violence a psychopath possesses. The criminal intent of mind which makes him a bomb expert or an arson specialist. Ultimately, a suicide bomber. Aafaq confided in me the day I took him out for guy bonding in Srinagar. He told me about some of his friends who had bailed out from college. Some for the money, some genuinely had gone radical. It was when militancy in Kashmir was the tip of the ice berg. The common man was unaware of it. Aafaq Qazmi, aristocratic but modern Muslim with enormous wealth. The Qazmis could fund a *Jihad* of their own if they had wanted to. What lure could there be for him? He couldn't be sorted into any of the above categories. But he was required. To be precise he was required very urgently. His brilliance and flair for technology was well established in academic circles. And equally so were his secular thoughts. Keep in mind, some of these radicals have post-doctorates in Islamic studies and other subjects. They also knew how technological advancements would augment their cause." Chachu continued to look at me.

"The Indian Army devotes an entire section to counter insurgency called, 'Anti-terrorist Wing.' This wing constitutes fresh recruits with the adrenaline of youth, seasoned Generals and war veterans who have all been placed together. The Army's finest, determined to prevent any sort of a subversion. In retaliation, separatists and Pakistan sympathetic outfits in Kashmir receive funds from their wealthy benefactors all over the Arab world. Nevertheless, how to evict the Army from Kashmir? By rigorously murdering its reputation. So terms like human rights violation, exploitation of AFSPA, atrocities performed by security personnel on innocent civilians come into play. Do you know that the United States is the United Nations largest financial supporter, not only this year but ever since the formation of that body? It is so easy for the West and our media to create such an international uproar that it becomes tough for us to execute our duty. But everyone forgets that the first and foremost duty of the Indian Army is to secure India. What is the army going to do when a suspected militant is detained for interrogation? A militant who has killed innocent women and children because they are Hindu or even Muslim, but do not pledge allegiance to him. When the army was being maligned all over the valley, country and world, why not take advantage of its tarnished image. Let us make Heena Qazmi one more number, conspires Inquilaab Kashmir. This way the brother will surely get rid of his patriotic sentiments. They knew about Ruhail's father's political aspirations. That is the reason why he got a call after she was violated. Didn't you find that even a bit strange that her prospective in-laws were handed this piece of information first? The ordeal had to be made public. The Qazmi's misfortune was being broadcast to the whole of Kashmir. Your local daily in Srinagar, *Salaam Valley*. It was the first newspaper to run the story on Heena, and it left nothing to the reader's imagination. It is on the payroll of Inquilaab Kashmir. This is a well-established fact. And Heena, like the pure-hearted person she was, could not bear the shame associated with the word, rape." I heard my uncle's tirade till the end. And it made so much of sense to me.

"I want you to read this." He handed me a file. "It is classified information. But I want you to personally scrutinize the documents, and absorb the truth for yourself." I peered at the file and opened it.

"This vehicle was found two weeks after the rape, abandoned in the forests, thirty kilometers away from Srinagar." My uncle pointed at an enlarged photograph of a military Jeep. "What kind of vehicle does this seem to you?" 'A Jonga.' I answered taken aback. "It is something what you used to drive."

'No,' Chachu was harsh in his rejection. "This is a Russian military jeep made to look like a Jonga. Heena Qazmi had remembered the license number and had passed on the number to the doctor who had first tended to her. Would the officers ever molest someone in a vehicle registered to the Indian Army? And that, too, at a time when every news agency and United Nations is breathing down their back. She said the men were speaking in broken English and their speech was full of grammatical errors. Army officers are educated and hence proficient in English.

In their campaign to impersonate a military Jonga, they have given it a registration number of a different classification of vehicle."

My uncle then handed me another set of papers. It was a hard bound register of some sort. I read the report out loud.

"Military headquarters and each Officers' Mess all over J&K state were inspected. Commanding officers of each and every unit were able to account for each and every individual of each and every rank.

Naik Sukwinder Singh was on sick leave as he had fractured his leg. His leg was in a plaster and he was in the Base Hospital, Srinagar. He had undergone a surgery the day before.

Lt. colonel Ajay Malhotra, absent from duty. He was suffering from Herpes virus and admitted in an isolated ward in the Military Hospital, Anantnag.

Captain Javed Ali was on leave. Had gone to attend his sister's wedding. He was in Patna."

"Now look carefully at these records. See the entries. Rosha, please check the dates." I glanced at the documents. All dates were the same. It was the same time, day, date and year of Heena's horrible ordeal.

"These are copies of Javed Ali's Railway tickets. Now read this report carefully." My uncle went on.

I picked up the piece of paper which carried an attestation from Nissan, Japan. Nissan being the umbrella company of Jonga. Nissan had sent two of its Automobile Engineers to Srinagar, at the behest of the Indian Defence Minister. They had signed the following report.

On complete and thorough inspection of the above-mentioned vehicle, we to the best of our ability, affirm that the vehicle is made in the U.S.S.R. and has no bearing with Nissan, Japan. The document had been duly signed. But Chachu persisted. "Read the chassis number and engine number of the vehicle. With the help of these numbers we obtained the accurate registration number of the jeep. It was registered in the name of Abdul Kareem of Kabul. We didn't stop there. Look at this document, Roshina. Our senior officers were sent to Kabul, to the office of the Stolen Motors Department. I happened to be one of them. The jeep had been reported stolen in the month of May, 1987.

Rosha, I am risking my entire career so that you don't even have an iota of doubt that the Army had anything to do with this. We remained quiet and kept it under the wraps as we could not find the culprits. The kidnapping and molestation, of Heena Qazmi, in the records of the army has been attributed to a terrorist organization. The state was under too much of a political upheaval to reveal the name of the culprits. This has been done by some ruthless animals and not our Army.

Aafaq Qazmi is your new age terrorist, Rosha. Our intelligence wing and MI6 in England have been keeping close vigilance on Aafaq. His each and every movement in Birmingham has been closely monitored. He doesn't have to brandish a gun to instill fear and havoc. No, it is how he establishes a link, a network, how he improvises communication in the caves of the mountains."

I glanced at some papers which were in Urdu which I was very fluent in. There was a copy of a sale deed. "I don't understand, Chachu. What is this?" I gave my Uncle a bewildered look. "Except for the Saffron Garden, Aafaq has sold all his family land in Sopore. He has bought an old school building. That is going to be his new computer centre. And the rest of the money. It has been traced to a bank account in Islamabad. I am sure you know what it is going to be used for." I picked up some more photographs. They were of Aafaq in England. He was at London's underground tube train station. There were three men, undeniably Muslims with skull caps and clipped beards next to him. "Your country needs you, Roshina. Scotland Yard has found explosive materials like phenol, sand wires and trinitrotoluene at this address in Birmingham. It is right behind a mosque. Now this house was visited by Aafaq a couple of days ago. Check the dates on the photograph." There were photographs of Aafaq entering a house. The camera had zoomed in on the house number. It was the same house from where all the bomb materials and explosives had been found.

Chachu took out a computer disk from his bag and slid it into the computer. A man's face appeared on the screen of the monitor. His face was covered behind a chequered scarf. But I could make out he was bespectacled. "Your Muslim brothers all around the world are suffering." He said in deeply-accented Urdu. It was the Urdu spoken in Pakistan. "Is this why you have believed in the Prophet for so long?" There were images of anti-Muslim riots in various countries of the world like Sri Lanka, Myanmar and France. There were clippings of the military detention centers in Srinagar where terror suspects were being held. "The United States of America flatters itself and claims to be the land of the free. It is a country of hatred. A country which had made slaves out of the Blacks who now fetch them their medals. They are hypocrites. We will have an Islamic state and we will also have an Islamic Caliphate. There is no room for *Kafirs*. Kashmir will not be part of a *Kafir* nation. We need our freedom. The West has coined the word Nigger. And they dare take offense at the word *Kafir*. They make fun of Black skin and denigrate our Muslim Arab brothers by calling them 'Sand Niggers.' The West will pay. We will show them what Muslims can do."

The video ended showing a madrassa where little boys had rifles and were being taught to kill the *Kafir*.

"Kill your parents if they stop you from *Jihad*." The teacher was shouting at them. They, in the innocence of their youth were repeating the slogan with gusto. "These are the videos that are going to go viral on the hundred computers that Aafaq Qazmi is going to operate in Sopore. And then they will be online for thousands if not millions to get unduly influenced." Uncle exclaimed bitterly.

I looked at Chachu and the sheaf of papers in my hand. My uncle was taking out another bundle of enlarged photographs. "I don't want to see them. But I do know who should see them. Ruhail Geelani." I announced firmly.

"Be a man, Ruhail. Stop protecting him. You are his worst enemy right now. You do know that under the 'Anti-terrorist Act' I can have you arrested and detained." Chachu said authoritatively. My uncle and I had immediately set out to meet Ruhail. We were sure he could help us in some way. "Ruhail, what happened with Heena was never about her, it was all about Aafaq. Look at these photographs carefully." Chachu ordered him.

I, too, peered at the photograph of Aafaq. He had grown a beard and was wearing a skull cap. He was with another sinister looking man. "This man is Ibrahim Khan. Nationality Afghan. He is the ousted commander of the orthodox Taliban. He now lives in exile, in Yemen as his methods of punishment were too cruel, even for Afghanistan. And he can be seen fraternizing with Aafaq in Birmingham." The picture showed the two of them in what seemed to be a disreputable alley.

"This is Salim Ahmadi. Wanted Arson specialist. A Chemical engineer who turned radical in 1980. Nationality Pakistani. Responsible for blasts in Indian and American embassies in Australia in 1985." Aafaq was standing next to this person in the photograph.

"Are you trying to say that Aafaq is ignorant to the true identity of these criminals?" Chachu spoke caustically.

Ruhail remained quiet for several moments and then spoke. "I really don't know, Roshina, but I have heard that Aafaq and other computer professionals are being approached by the radicals." Chachu gave him an eagle-eyed glance. But Ruhail's eyes were tough to read.

"We are aware of that, Ruhail. That's old news. Give us some facts." Ruhail seemed to be contemplating for several seconds and then spoke. "Aafaq has not told me anything, but I could overhear him when he was talking on the phone. I feel there is an extensive plan to sabotage 'The International Peace Summit,' in December this year."

The International Peace Summit. I thought staggeringly. I couldn't believe it. Meena had told me to do a background research on all the dignitaries who were to attend. It was scheduled for five days from the fifteenth to the nineteenth of December in New Delhi. The lectures and seminars were going to be conducted in different venues all over the capital. The dignitaries would be commuting each day from their lodgings to the different centres. Oh my God! we had to prevent this from turning into a debacle. India would face severe repercussions if anything happened to any of the guests and speakers. The delegates and guest speakers were Nobel laureates, think-tank executives and philanthropists.

There was such a lot of publicity and Indian authorities were spending billions on hospitality, which included security of these eminent people. We were trying to wipe away the country's tarnished image as a terrorist nation. Our diplomatic relations with these countries would be damaged forever.

"And where is Aafaq now?" Chachu asked Ruhail as he watched him closely.

"He is back in Srinagar since the past several days." He answered smoothly. "But he has a ticket for the day after from London to New Delhi." Chachu contradicted. "He didn't fly back directly." Ruhail looked at me. "He boarded a cruise liner from Bali to Bombay and caught a Modi Luft flight from Bombay to Srinagar. He had left London for Bali last week."

"Thanks, Ruhail. I hereby strictly instruct you that if you ever hide information pertaining to the security of India you will face the consequences. If in future I need your help, I might not be refined with my modes of extracting information. Be grateful that Roshina was with me." Uncle stormed out abruptly. I could see that he was very enraged. With a final, entreating look at Ruhail, I followed my uncle to our waiting car.

"You are to accompany me to Kashmir." Chachu stated not wasting a single moment, in beating about the bush. We were on our way back home. "We will head out straight to Sopore. If there is one person Aafaq is going to trust, it is you. He knows for sure that you would never lie to him regarding the identity of Heena's rapists." I nodded in understanding. My mind had already been made before my uncle had mentioned it.

"You will be doing both Aafaq and your nation a great favour."

"I have no problem, Chachu." Was my firm and honest answer. "I was certain you would say that. But I am not that sure about your parents. I don't want to say anything to antagonize them, especially Rishabh. Only when he has so recently recovered." He dropped me outside our complex gates. "Go and spend some time with your family now. I will come over later and talk to them."

"Chachu, I will never squeal on Aafaq though. Not even for my country."

He stared at me. "That is a very incongruous remark, Roshina." His mouth curled upwards in a smile. "I know, Kaju. I also am pretty sure it is going to take a lot more than a computer to bribe you." With a tender pat on my cheek, he drove away. The tires of his car screeched nosily in protest, as he drove away at breakneck speed.

□

18

My uncle returned to our house later that evening but he wasn't alone. There were two other gentlemen with him who were Generals, in the Anti-terrorist Wing of the Army. I recognized one of them from the newspapers. He had been decorated with a Medal of Honour by our President a couple of days ago

They left after talking to my parents for a good couple of hours. Chachu stayed back, and I rushed into the living room, my frayed nerves making me anxious.

I could tell that my father was dead against it. His, "If only you had children of your own, Rudra, you would know what we are feeling right now." Was clearly indicative about what he thought. That was the first part. It continued as, "What made you think I would let you use my daughter as bait?"

My uncle was looking at the floor. Mum had been quiet for a while, and she was massaging her forehead with her fingers. The indication that she was facing the onslaught of one of her terrible migraines. When she spoke, the finality in her tone left little room for argument. My heart was weighed down with anticipation. "I don't understand, all this is very scary. First we face ethnic cleansing in Kashmir and are forced to leave without a thing to our name. We try to make a small life for ourselves. But we still are not spared calamity after calamity. Heena was like my daughter." Her voice broke. "And it's not only us.

It seems to be a sort of uncontrollable hate wave. I, too, Rishabh, am an Army officer's daughter. I love my country, as much as the men who risk their lives to give us a fuller existence. Today I watched a video so horrifying where Christians, Jews, Hindus were all termed as enemies of Allah. I heard names like 'Muslim Brotherhood.' They are practically endorsing the worst form of bigotry. It is a fact now that the Pakistani ISI is training them to become radical. And those Mujahideen have been aiding them. I am Roshina's mother and no one can want her welfare more than me. But I trust Rudra and know that he will safeguard our daughter's life better than either of us. We owe those Qazmis a lot, Rishabh. They have lost one child. We have to help prevent them lose another. It is our duty to get their son out of this web of lies and bloodshed. I won't allow them to fall into decrepitude. If anything happens to Aafaq, will you be able to live with your conscience? Rudra is not hatching a diabolical plot. This is the Army. It is all about well-planned and executed military strategies, which stem from our men of nerve. And Rudra knows that if a single hair of my daughter's head will be harmed, I will personally make a minced meat out of him." Chachu gave Mum a mock salute and hurriedly drained his whiskey glass. He looked at my mother gravely. I gave my mother a grateful look. She smiled at me and I realized she was very emotional. Papa's eyes registered defeat.

But it was settled. The next morning saw me sitting in a military aircraft as we soared through the skies towards Srinagar.

"You know what, Chachu?" I said breathlessly trying to match my pace with his long strides. "I think I could somewhat get used to it." "Used to what?" Chachu asked me, though his tone was preoccupied. "All these salutes and flags, this yes, Sir thing." "Oh my child! it is hard work being in the Army, let me tell you that." We had landed in Srinagar a couple of hours ago. Moreover, now we had embarked on our journey towards Sopore in a military jeep. There was a young officer called Sharma along with the driver. Sharma held a Captain's rank and was visibly terrified of Chachu. The institute was a couple of kilometers before Sopore. My mind could recall memories so bittersweet. This was the quintessence of Kashmir. The village children chased us and called out to us playfully. Their morning dew innocence, an epitome of what Kashmir had exemplified. I took a deep breath and braced myself for what I were about to spot. Spread before me were the pastures of saffron. There were no flowers in bloom. But I couldn't believe what I heard. 'Rosha Jaan, Rosha Jaan,' the breeze around me sighed. Astonished and disturbed, I leaned out of the open window. Was I hearing things? The wind blew my hair, and I thought of Heena and her long red hair flying behind her in these very fields. All of a sudden the jeep slammed to a halt and we were lunged forwards. Captain Sharma jumped out of the jeep, and Chachu's hands went to his revolver at once. "It was a deer, Sir," Sharma explained as he returned to us. The deer could be seen running back gracefully into the forest. He looked back at me. Our eyes locked for several seconds. With a poised bow of his head, he sprinted away. Fortunately, he wasn't limping.

Aafaq's institute was large and impressive. There was a mosque inside the gated complex. I remembered it had once been a residential school. What sort of learning was being offered here, now, I thought ruefully. "Rosha, this is not going to be easy for you. But it determines the shape of your country. And will hence determine the shape of the globe. Pakistan cannot take Kashmir as India will never give it." Chachu told me firmly as we walked to the building with determined steps. I nodded my head in earnest.

The receptionist was an elderly male who I recognized at once as Yusuf Baba. He had been the caretaker of Aafaq's grandfather's farmhouse. He had always battled crippling rheumatism but was a loyal worker.

Though he was quite happy to see me, I could tell that our arrival had immediately made him nervous. More because of my uniformed uncle, was my assumption.

The door of one of the classrooms opened and Aafaq stepped into the reception.

I knew him well enough to accept that he wasn't nonplussed to see us. It was as if he had been expecting company. "Salaameleikum, Chachaji. It is quite a surprise to see you here. I wish you hadn't brought Roshina though." Chachu responded quite amiably. "It is very noble of you to think of Roshina, but I think that you should leave her well-being to her family." A muscle twitched in Aafaq's jaw. "This is an official visit. I don't come to you as Roshina's uncle but I have a message for you, from, 'The Supreme Commander of the Indian Armed Forces,' the President of India. So can you please request your valet to leave as what I have to say has to be said in private. As for Rosha, she has clearance from the top most level."

At the same moment a religious *Maulvi* entered the reception. His eyes grew malicious as they narrowed on Chachu and disapproving as they rested on me. After flashing Aafaq a pointed look, he walked into the other room. Sheer fury blazed in his eyes.

Aafaq opened a door and ushered us inside. It seemed to be a classroom with rows of computers and tables placed, side by side.

"I want you to read this, Aafaq." My uncle's voice was terse as he handed over the Army report. Aafaq read it very carefully, still and emotionless. He then took out the photographs from a Manila envelope. My uncle repeated all the information he had shared with me in

New Delhi. He detailed the attendance of the officers and soldiers. And shared the grammatical errors made by Heena's assailants, the report from Nissan and the stolen vehicle report.

"Think of it, Aafaq. You are an Indian." My uncle took advantage of Aafaq's silence. "You took pride in the nation's Defence. You wanted to do your country proud. Your idol was Rakesh Sharma." My uncle was referring to the first Indian to go to space. "You have such a logical mind. Who could have informed the press? Only the culprits. Would security personnel give themselves away like that?" Aafaq stood motionless as my uncle reasoned with him. I looked at Aafaq and realized that he was battling with his own self, that instant. 'Aafaq,' I said quietly. I placed my hand on his elbow and forced him to look at me. "Do you think what Heena and I shared was just a normal friendship? Do you think, I don't hurt inside? Can you be true to yourself if you claim she was your sister and a mere friend to me?" I paused to catch my breath.

"What is the difference in your loss and mine? The difference is the divide caused by ethnic cleansing. I was away after her death, away from you, your family and away from Srinagar.

As a consequence, I didn't see the mourn and grief that you witnessed. And that's how you were exploited. They made sure that they catch you when everything around you was crashing. You are being pitted against your country. Do not go against your wonderful religion, Aafaq. The people you are fraternizing with have set you up."

"Aafaq, our Intelligence Division have been able to access your emails and trace IP addresses." Chachu handed him some more documents. "These are records of your telephone calls. We know who you are connected to, Aafaq. They are your sister's perpetrators." Chachu spread all the documents and pictures on the table in sequence. I looked at a blueprint of London's famous underground maze of tube trains. Various stations had been circled in red. It was evident that terrorist strikes were being planned at these places. "We have unearthed all this evidence from a disembodied loft of a flat in Birmingham. We have complete details about the hijacking plans that are being formulated. Look at the prisoners they are going to demand to be released in exchange. All of them are hardened criminals. They kill innocent people and children irrespective of religion. And now see the sum of money which has been wired into their accounts through Hawala. Do you think we are unaware of the terror plot which has been formulated to interfere with the World Peace Summit and transform it into a bloody spectacle for the entire world?"

Aafaq looked at us. I could infer that his uncertainty was piling up. It took him about several minutes to find his voice. "I have been so blind and foolish." He moaned. "Oh God! why did I not realize what sinister people I have established a rapport with? I will tell you whatever I know. There is definitely a proposal to disrupt the Peace Summit. To think that I have actually been hand in glove with my sister's violators." His hands went to his face as his body was wracked with sobs. "I will do anything in my means to help you. I have intel on the master plan, and a whole assortment of paper work in a basement in Srinagar. I will hand it over to you. I do not care for my life. I am responsible for creating a world class computer information system for the wrong people. I don't mind being behind bars for the rest of my life." Turning towards me, he admitted. "Rosha Jaan, I did nurture doubts regarding the extent of the Army's role. But when I would remember the sight of Heena's dead body covered in blood, it would prevent me from thinking rationally.

I will tell you everything. I don't care about myself any more. I will not offer any resistance whatsoever."

"But you are not going behind bars. Chachu, please tell him that you have spoken to your superiors. Let him know about the Presidential Pardon that can be managed for him." I firmly protested. My uncle had promised that Aafaq would not be badgered by the law if he surrendered.

"Roshina, I need to talk to him in private for some time as this is strictly confidential. Please trust me. I am on your side. On both of your side. But I have to adhere to some rules and regulations of my trade. We have to discuss provisions for his parents' safety." Chachu was categorical. I am so selfish I thought to myself. In the '*joie de vivre*' of clearing the air with Aafaq, the plight of his parents had totally escaped my mind. "Is there any room Rosha can remain in for a while?"

Aafaq rang a bell and Yusuf Baba hovered inside. "Baba, take Roshina to my office and stay there with her." I followed Yusuf Baba out of the classroom. I turned back and realized my uncle and Aafaq were engrossed in deep conversation. "Rosha Jaan, you have to protect Aafaq *Sahib*." I peered at Yusuf Baba's lined face questioningly. He placed his fingers on his lips as if suggesting be quiet and urged me to follow him. There was a voice speaking, in chaste Urdu to a classroom of young boys, barely in their teens.

"*Jihad*, cannot be accomplished without blood. All *Kafirs* are enemies of *Jihad*."Said the voice. I did not possess the courage to peep inside and identify the owner. But the voice did ring a bell. I just couldn't place it at that moment.

"All *Jihadists* go the kingdom of heaven.

Allah commands you to kill enemies of *Jihad*. Kill your parents if they prevent you from joining *Jihad*. Kill your brother or sister if either of them prevent you from performing *Jihad*."

"*Jihad, Jihad*!" The boys screamed in unison. It was horrible. I heard them for several minutes and went back to Aafaq's room with Baba.

My uncle and Aafaq looked at me when I entered. The undercurrents in the air were tangible. Was it me, being too sensitive, or did I actually feel that both of them were a little upset to see me return? Stop reading too much into things. I warned myself. But the way my life had become a roller-coaster ride, I could be pardoned for my misgivings.

"This is my cellular number." Aafaq told Chachu. "I will come to Srinagar tomorrow and hand over everything to you."

"Very well, I will consult Headquarters and brief you about the venue accordingly. I think we should leave immediately. I don't want to raise any suspicions."

Aafaq helped me up the step of the jeep. "I had this notion you would come. Like I could always sense you were about to make your way into my room. No matter what it takes, I will get you out of this mess." I closed my eyes as I felt a strange feeling in the pit of my stomach. "Rosha, we have to go." Chachu urged softly.

The jeep started and I waved at Aafaq. I wondered if our farewells will ever end. It still wasn't going to be easy for us. But at least he is free from the chains of evil. The institute diminished as the jeep ventured further away. Aafaq was still in my line of vision. As well as was the *Maulvi*. I spotted him clearly punching numbers into his mobile phone. The only one who doesn't have a cellular is me. I thought dryly.

We had been in the vehicle for hardly five minutes when I looked at my uncle. He understood at once and gave instructions to Captain Sharma. It was time to say goodbye to, 'My sister, by blood.'

'My Saffron Garden,' was weather beaten. No seeds, no flowers, no butterflies. My mind tussled with images of two little girls chasing rabbits and scattering petals on the porch. And now one of those little girls lay buried under its unkind soils.

Islamic graves are supposed to have no headstones. I received direction from the 'All Powerful' as a compelling force coerced me to a grove eliciting a wondrous light.

I knelt down alongside Heena's resting place. My hands went to the hood of my *parka*, and I slipped it over my head. Then as Heena had taught me those many years ago, in the mosque at Eid, I prayed. 'Allah,' I pleaded, "Please allow my friend to enter the kingdom of heaven." Then I prayed, like Sister Loyala taught us to pray for those who had left us. Ironically, I prayed as a Muslim and I prayed as a Christian. But not as a Hindu.

Suddenly, I felt that an enormous load had been removed from my heart. I discovered the power of prayer through the power of love. The beauty of religion is to respect all other faiths. God has already gifted you one theology when you set foot on this earth. And then he provides you an opportunity to learn about other philosophies through friends who are devoted to convictions so worthy. If we all believe in one God then that makes us brothers and sisters. So why do we indulge in transgressions?

It became cold all of a sudden, and I dug my hands in the pockets of my new *parka*. My finger tips brushed against a silken fiber. I peered at it in shock. It was a saffron flower that flickered in the wind. I had been blessed by a beautiful angel called Heena Qazmi, my Guardian Angel, with a heart of gold. I felt a few minutes of peace. Just like in the mosque at Eid.

□

19

I was exhausted when we had arrived back in the Army Mess in Srinagar. I went to my room and fell into a deep sleep. I woke up to the sound of knocking on the door. My uncle stepped inside, "I have finalized the project with Aafaq. He will meet us on Prabhat Lank, the small island in Nagin Lake tomorrow afternoon at fifteen hundred hours. My men have briefed his parents. Aafaq has conveyed as much as he can at this moment. In fact, they were able to meet him. The senior Qazmis are already on a plane to the nearest international airport. We have deliberately chosen Nagin Lake as it is less crowded than the Dal. And tomorrow there is a houseboat staff union strike. Hopefully, the lake will be clear of houseboats. Everything is going according to plan." Yet, my mind was twitchy. Something was not right. I just couldn't put my finger on it. "You still haven't given me the details of what will happen to Aafaq. His protection and security." I reminded Chachu.

"I am sorry. I have been busy in making sure that nothing goes wrong tomorrow. Aafaq has agreed to hand over to us the complete particulars of the World Peace Summit. He is giving evidence which will help us put behind bars notorious terrorists who have somehow till now, evaded being nabbed. Aafaq will have to leave India for some time. He will enter a witness protection programme and will return with a new identity in a couple of years, maybe more. It is for his benefit. Once the insurgents realize he has double crossed them they are going to hound him unless all these precautions are taken." It took me a few minutes to digest all this. "Where will he be taken, may I ask?" "I don't know that at all. In fact, I never will. There can be no breach in his security. I am sure you want the best for him, don't you?" Chachu stated abruptly.

Of course, I do, I thought to myself but what about me? I never knew that I would ever pay such a high price for *Jihad*. "This is the protocol the Army follows in situations of this sort." I heard Chachu say with finality in his tone.

"When will he be leaving?" I tremulously asked. But my uncle was busy on his mobile again. I decided to go over some articles to take my mind off things. Meena had given me some printouts. She had wanted me to draft a brief summary of an article called, 'The Carter Doctrines.' I read the pages and found them so unbelievable. The article stated that when Jimmy Carter was the President of the United States, American Intelligence Services began to aid the Mujahideen of Afghanistan a good six months before the Soviet Army invaded Afghanistan. And then these Afghan Mujahideen eventually with the ISI of Pakistan, started conflict in Kashmir. It was awful. Couldn't superpowers think beyond themselves?

I excused myself after an early dinner. Chachu was very busy talking to his juniors, and his phone didn't stop ringing for a moment. I wanted everything to go according to plan. This was Aafaq's life we were talking about. I would only be at ease when I saw for myself Aafaq being escorted to a safe destination. The next morning I went outdoors, onto the sprawling lawn and had a cup of tea with my uncle who was awake. He appeared worse for the wear. "Have you heard from Aafaq?" I asked him. He shook his head in refusal. It was clear that a lot was playing on his mind.

My own mind was working overtime and nothing could occupy me, such was its restless state. "Miss Roshina, there is a call for you." Sharma came and told me after a while.

'Hello,' I practically shouted into the phone, positive it was Aafaq. But the line went dead in a split second.

"Roshina, who was it?" Chachu had marched into the room and directed the question to me. He looked even more harassed than the morning. "I don't know. It just got disconnected." "Sharma, who had called for Roshina?" Chachu enquired loudly. Sharma was now trembling with fear, sensing the anger boiling in my uncle's voice.

"It was a young lady for Roshina, I mean Miss Roshina, Sir." "Did she state her age?" Chachu was relentless in his interrogation. "I don't understand, Sir," stammered Sharma.

"I said did the lady inform you, how old she was?" "No, Sir, she did not give her age." "Then how do you know if she is young, old or even middle aged." Sharma looked very embarrassed. "You admitted there was a young lady for Roshina. But don't know for certain. But let me tell you one thing for sure, Sharma. You are an idiot." My uncle growled.

"Yes, Sir." Sharma saluted.

"You have just about revealed to whoever that lady was, that Roshina Kapoor is here.

I told you that any phone call for Roshina, even from her parents is going to go through me. You have announced her location to a person beyond these four walls." Then looking at me, he ordered, "Roshina, pack at once. We are not coming back here."

I found it very strange that my Chachu had gotten so agitated nevertheless I didn't say a word. It did baffle me to think who could be calling, as except my parents no one knew where I was. Mum had called my office and informed them I was down with fever and would require a week off to recuperate.

"Rosha, I want you to wear this." Chachu handed me a bullet proof vest. "Is it necessary?" "Yes, Roshina, it is. Do not worry. This is routine procedure in Special Operations. We have to be prepared for attack from all quarters. That stupid Sharma! Please cover your head with a scarf."

There were four more officers, Sharma, Chachu and me. "The rest of our team is already on the lake," briefed Chachu. "Aafaq will be escorted by two of my men, by boat to the island." Chachu was matter of fact. "Aafaq just called me. He has retrieved whatever papers he could and will meet us there." I was relieved that there had been some communication from him. Chachu finally managed a smile my way. "Nothing will happen to Aafaq."

Prabhat Lank was a beautiful island in the Nagin. The first rays of the sun at dawn were believed to strike this little piece of land before any other place in Srinagar. Astronomers had revealed that it had something to do with the air above the island. The island would give an impression of being illuminated as it would take on a golden hue.

We stepped on to the island soil precisely one hour before our scheduled time. The Chinar trees were laden with bronze leaves. There were exotic birds in unbelievable colours. There was a massive building, what more the correct word to describe it, would be edifice, as so imposing was its architecture. "It was erected by the British." Chachu explained. "The officers of the Raj would have their meetings here. In the evenings, they would have their gala balls and picnics by moonlight. Their wives would be resplendent with their furs and finery. Champagne would flow, and *hors d oeuvres* would be served." The Army officers entered the building and reached the terrace. Suddenly, an acorn fell at my feet. I picked it up. A souvenir for Rohan, I mused.

Chachu was looking at the lake through his binoculars. "Aafaq is approaching," he stated and then spoke into his wireless. I looked out and watched Aafaq as he sat in a boat with two more officers who I had spotted in the Mess the previous night. Aafaq had covered his eyes with sunglasses. The boat anchored and all men stepped onto the island. They were followed, by another boat ferrying four more officers. I realized they had been waiting for Aafaq and had followed him all the way up to here.

Aafaq nodded at uncle and handed him a large rucksack and a leather case. "It's all here." He then walked straight up to me.

"Rosha Jaan. Thank you for loving me the way you do. Without you, nothing would have been possible." I remained silent and looked at him. He had removed his glasses, and I stared into his eyes with yearning. "Take me with you, Aafaq." I was at my genuine most. "You know I can't, Jaan, but remember I will always love you."

His eyes reveal a sheen incomparable to what I have ever experienced. Must be due to the brightness of the skies. He gathers me in his arms and right here in front of everyone kisses me fully on the lips. It is unbelievable. Sharma, the poor chap, has the gall to grin my way which earns him a spiteful glance from my uncle. Aafaq lets me go with enormous reluctance. He twists the strands of my hair which have escaped from under my scarf and whispers the single word 'Jamila' (the feminine form of

Jamil) into my ear. Out of awkwardness I move away from him, and I hear another thud noise.

An acorn again, I think. But what has rolled at my feet is definitely not an acorn. I look at it carefully. Oh my God! It is a tear gas canister. I recognize it at once from all the riots, I have witnessed at the time of Ethnic Cleansing here, in this very city. I scream, but my voice is silenced by the deafening sound made by the outburst of bullets. Aafaq falls to the ground. My mind falls prey to an agonizing pain, a pain so intense, I feel I have been torn apart. My eyes start to burn and I can't see a thing clearly. Every breath I take is laboured. I turn around and watch the hazy silhouette of Chachu's men firing their weapons. I realize, there were militants lying in wait on the building's terrace. Nearly sightless now, I cough my way to where Aafaq lies. Nothing can happen to him. What will I tell Heena? Aafaq, I can't live without you. From out of nowhere, someone grabs hold of me and slips something over my head. For several minutes, I see nothing but pitch blackness and feel a constriction tighten at my neck. There is another gunshot at my side and my darkness is over. "Are you okay, Roshina?" It is Sharma. He has come to my rescue after shooting my captor and removing the hood which had been placed over my head. My eyes feel on fire but somehow I wobble towards Aafaq.

A loud-pitched scream finally escapes my mouth as I peer down in agony at the gruesome sight that greets me. Where had once been a beautiful face is a mass of bloodied flesh. I fall down on my knees beside him and place my ears on his chest, which is a gaping wound. But there is no movement. I prod open his eyes. Why are they lifeless, I lament? I want to see the brown fleck in the right eye. Chachu sits beside me and gently closes Aafaq's eyes. I look fiercely at him. How can my uncle be so cruel? Helplessly,

I try to nudge them open. "Let him be in peace, Rosha." Chachu holds me close to him as the sobs hollow out my soul. The birds flying over us sense my wretchedness and they scuttle their wings. Their screeching noises ricochet in the skies. "A travesty of justice," they seem to exclaim. On this fine afternoon, under a clear blue sky, Aafaq Qazmi has said farewell to me for the last time in his life.

Aafaq's body is carefully zipped into a plastic bag. In my mind engulfed by pain, I see the four of us as children racing through the wind in Pehalgam. I see Aafaq smile at me as I wade through the Lidder. "You are as beautiful as the Farishtey, Rosha Jaan." I hear him say. And what had he called me when he had held me in his arms for the last time, 'Jamila.'

"Please take him to my Saffron Garden." My voice sounds incoherent. Yet another burial which the Kafir will not attend.

I hear the buzz of a chopper in the sky. But nothing affects me now. It performs an aerial reconnaissance and makes an expert landing on the little isle. My head spins like the blades of its rotor.

It is the General in Command, Northern Command who alights from the chopper. Chachu stands ramrod straight and salutes smartly, his heels clicking.

Why is everything going on normally? I despair.

"Roshina Kapoor?" The General demands. How does he know my name? I wonder as hysteria bubbles inside me.

"No grievous harm, Sir. But needs medical aid."

"And the militants?"

"All dead, Sir."

"Documents and proof?"

"All obtained. In our possession, Sir." Chachu replies.

"Aafaq Qazmi?" Is the next enquiry.

Chachu looks my way.

"Aafaq Qazmi has died as a true martyr of India, Sir." I find my voice so strange.

"Operation Saffron, a success, Sir." Chachu continues.

"Start all crackdowns with effect from now." The General announces loudly.

"Yes, Sir."

"Give Aafaq Qazmi a funeral everyone will remember. Bury him with honors provided to a patriot of India."

General Ibrahim Qureshi looks at me sympathetically.

□

20

The story goes that the *Maulvi* in Aafaq's institute had realized that Aafaq was going to defect and had contacted his superiors in Inquilaab Kashmir. News of Aafaq's impending deception had enraged the radicals. Aafaq had been pursued by them. The militants had entered the island, hours before us, and had hidden in the building. They had been determined to kill Aafaq. It was not just about the crucial information he would supply us. It was also about defying 'omerta.' They were unaware that the evening Chachu and me had returned from Sopore, Aafaq had also come to Srinagar at night. He had immediately reported to Military Headquarters and supplied the Army with all the documents they had needed. Aafaq had managed to handover the rest of the information to Chachu on the island.

When the militant had covered me with the hood, he had been trying to kidnap me. Sharma had emerged as quite the hero and had shot him. Because of the houseboat union strike, it had been very easy for the terrorists to reach the island unobserved. The Army had proved to be a spanner to their getaway and ultimately foiled many of their plans. Yes, indeed in military records 'Operation Saffron' was a success.

Aafaq had died with his name cleared. He would not be remembered as a radicalist, separatist or jihadist.

But Aafaq Qazmi, the Kashmiri Muslim who offered the supreme sacrifice of life for his country. A true Indian patriot. He was buried in the Saffron Garden next to his beloved sister. I didn't attend his funeral as I was flown out of Srinagar within the next couple of hours. I was taken by chopper to Jammu with Commandos and spent the night at the Governor's house. I was whisked out of Jammu at the crack of dawn and back with my family, my strength, in my period of grief.

Aafaq's documents led the Army to another hideout in Srinagar where finely crafted plans to target airports, railway stations and public offices of the country were discovered. All had been listed for terrorist strikes. Arrests were made all over the country. Army and security forces were beefed up at borders and information was extracted in the way it is supposed to be at military detention centers. My uncle was promoted to Brigadier. The International Peace Summit happened as schedule, without any hitches and disruptions. At least by means of terror strikes. It was an inspiring confluence of like-minded people. India won back its reputation of conviviality, and a country where all religions reside in harmony. Meena had taken me to attend one of the seminars in the Summit. I strive for a world free from arms and religious intolerance through my words.

I never heard from Aafaq's parents after that. Mum got to know through their relatives that they are somewhere in the Middle East. They have donated their enviable wealth to charity. I will never meet them again. I have lost my Muslim family. My Muslim family which loved us family of idol worshippers. The family which had loved a Hindu girl as a daughter and would have loved the same *'Kafir'* even more as a daughter-in-law.

For those who say it is unheard of. I do not blame them as we live in a world deflowered by greed and hatred.

Let me explain to them that love knows no religion. And once upon a time in Kashmir, Hindus and Muslims were friends first, foremost and forever. Diversity of doctrines added to the riches of life. Let me show them the papers of my saffron garden. A garden which belongs to a Hindu *Kafir,* in a town, which is proclaimed to be Muslim dominated.

I aimed to be the writer my wonderful friends thought I was capable of becoming. Academics and Meena kept me occupied during the day. At night, I would lie awake in my bed or stand in my porch and gaze at the stars.

Rohan became a software engineer and conquered Silicon valley. According to him, Aafaq was the only person who could beat him at computers. He is married to a white American girl called Kathryn. She is a lovely person and like all foreigners is in love with Kashmir. Rohan has taken her there several times. Kathryn claims that mine and Aafaq's love story can save the world.

My parents eventually migrated to the United States. They live next door to Rohan and are doting grandparents to his children. I completed my Masters and continued at Meena's office for more than a decade. I am so grateful to her for giving me the advantage of flexi hours and work at home arrangements when Zohaib was a young boy. She was a pillar of strength and arranged low interest loans for me and practically held my hand, when I started my own magazine. I did my doctorate in International Relations. My thesis topic, believe it or not was, 'The Carter Doctrines.' I did manage to set up my uncle and Meena on a blind date. They both got on like a house on fire. Meena did come late to work the next day, and I could swear that there was a hickey (In Meena's words) on her neck. But that's all. They are good friends. I wrote my first book three years ago. It was quite successful, and I dedicated all the royalties to the rehabilitation of rape victims. No girl will suffer like Heena, and feel unclean or impure. I made sure of that.

As for Zohaib, I became a mother to a four-year-old son. A readymade mother to the sweetest child on earth.

When I saw Zohaib at the Kashmiri Migrant Camp in West Delhi, my maternal instincts surfaced instantly. His grubby hands, his bare feet, and his wide-eyed innocence tugged at my heart. His parents had been stripped of their little walnut farm in Anantnag by the militants. In the sense that the fields had been razed to the ground as his family had refused to support *Jihad*. His mother had perished in child birth when they had to flee to New Delhi. So had his baby sister. His father succumbed to cholera in the migrant camp, and he was found by the authorities, crying over his father's dead body. I knew there was a reason he had come into my life. With Meena's contacts, I was able to cut through all the red tape and permitted to legally adopt him. He has brought the Holy Quran back into my life. We read the Holy Quran and Bhagawad Gita together. When people ask me about my Muslim son, I say he belongs to the most beautiful religion in the world. When people ask him about his *Kafir* mother. He soberly answers that I am not a Mother but a Hindu Goddess.

I have been to the United States several times. It is a beautiful country. There is wealth, there are immense resources. Everyone is busy and progressive. When I visited Boston and saw MIT, obviously I thought of Aafaq. It was once his dream to study there. I was in New York when the World Trade Centre incurred terrorist strikes of the deadliest type in history. I got out of my cab as the Magnificent Twin Towers burnt to the ground, altering the Manhattan Skyline forever. The fear and panic on people's faces as their loved ones roasted. It was awful and reminiscent of what I had seen in Srinagar. The masked men brandishing Kalashnikovs, ordering Hindu women to become sex slaves, threatening Hindu men with death. Similar fear, similar panic. How many gallons of blood and tears will be shed in exchange for oil? Places might be different, people may be dissimilar, colour of their skin may be distinct. But there are so many similarities like fear, bereavement and displacement. Today there are more than ten million refugees from Syria and Iraq. I remember the young village boys in Kashmir forced to pick up arms. Their bellies were empty, and their clothes, nothing but rags. My friends in Kuwait have narrated similar incidents about the Iraqi Army during the Gulf War. ISIS rebels share the same story.

Last year I went to Greece and Turkey along with my senior editorial staff, and young journalists who were interning with us. The way these countries are grappling with problems of water, first aid and prevention of epidemics is admirable. We documented stories of the refugees from Syria who had been evicted from their homes. I felt I was back at the Muthi Camp in Jammu. Zohaib and his friends worked alongside, 'Doctors without borders' doing their best to save people from wasting away. I want our articles and columns to be read by statesmen and policy makers. If only we all took one common stand throughout the globe and didn't have vested interests in our hearts. We read about boats capsizing, dinghies collapsing and sigh as pictures of drowning children go viral. We all have our needs, but every penny we send their way can prevent a mortality. We don't realize that one day it can be us.

Chachu, lives in New Delhi. He retired as a General and was given a farewell party that rocked the whole town. Accordingly, the 'Jolly good fellow' of the Armed Forces hung his uniform for the last time. My uncle has been an excellent grandparent to Zohaib. He would come and babysit when we would be stranded without a nanny. It would be quite a sight to see my strapping uncle crawling over the floor on his fours with Zohaib saddled on his back, ordering him to 'giddy up.'

Ruhail is my friend. He has never found a substitute for his first love and has steered clear of marriage. And somehow that elevates his position in my eyes. Ruhail guided Zohaib with religion and taught him to read the Holy Quran. My house is full of food on Eid and brightly lit with *Diyas* on Diwali. I wouldn't have had it any other way. As I look out of the window, I realize we are approaching Srinagar.

The Captain announces that we should get ready for landing. The baby is bundled up by his mother, and a feeding bottle placed in his mouth. After some time the wheels of the aircraft finally touch the airstrip. I open my eyes. The baby restlessly removes his bottle from his mouth, looks my way, burps rudely and laughs at his shocking display of bad manners. I laugh along with him.

"Are you finally going to tell me what possessed you to haul your rusty old handle of a mother all the way up here?" I asked Zohaib with a mock scowl. We were sitting in a taxi and I could see that we were heading towards the Boulevard. "Mum, you certainly don't look like a rusty old handle. Everyone in college thought you were my elder sister. When I used to hear you talk about Kashmir, your face would light up. But when I would ever suggest a trip you would go blank. I thought as soon as I graduate I want to visit Kashmir with my mother and see what it is all about. Mum, I know your story. I want to feel it. And feel it from my heart."

"Zohaib, you are all I have." I exposed to my son my hidden insecurities. "Sometimes I feel that you will be snatched away, too." "Mum, you took me in years ago, gave me a chance at life when there was nothing or no one there for me. I was snotty nosed and ridden with lice. Neither was I related to you, nor was I your responsibility. Why would I ever leave you? And where would I go?" We looked at each other and I kissed him on the forehead. He held my hand. "Let me show you, your favourite place." I smiled at his undertaking.

Our taxi stopped on the Boulevard besides the Dal Lake. We stepped outside and then I saw *the floating market*. It was as if time had stood still. It was just like before. Nothing had changed. The exotic flowers and fruits, the priceless spices. Boats full of saffron blazing a fiery red in the morning sun. Tourists laughed and reclined in *shikaras*, sipping tea as their hands slipped through the fine Cashmere wool. They were all here, people from all over the country, some from different areas of the world, on a lake by the mountains.

This was not my Kashmir, your Kashmir but it was our Kashmir. The Kashmir that contained all the religions of the world A 'Guldasta'. I had come 'home' at the bidding of my Muslim son. "Let them know what it was, Rosha Jaan." I heard Heena's voice trail over the rippling waters of the Dal. "Tell the world our story."

At night we had dinner in our houseboat. We had gone over the entire city and visited Hazratbal shrine, Shankaracharya Temple and the Mughal Gardens. We were thoroughly exhausted when we had returned. We sat in the balcony after dinner and gazed at the night sky. It was, as I had expected, splashed with stars. They twinkled merrily, and if I closed my eyes I could be taken back to the night Aafaq had told me he loved me. Zohaib looked my way and held my hand. 'Mum,' he said softly. 'Yes dear,' I sighed. "Mum, with no offense to Van Gogh, but our starry night is far more becoming. You were right." I smiled at him. I had taken him to the New York Museum and we saw Van Gogh's Starry Night there. We had stared at the painting in rapt fascination. "Yes, Zohaib, this is far more captivating."

"Mummy, I would like you to take me to *your Saffron Garden* tomorrow. Are you comfortable? If not, then forget about it."

"I am fine, Zohaib, and I am glad you mentioned it as I wanted to go." I told him truthfully. He came up behind me and put his hands on my shoulders. "Mum, I am so proud of you."

□

21

The following morning we waited at the Boulevard for our taxi to take us to Sopore. It had snowed all night long. I was talking to my office from my mobile phone. I looked up and saw Ruhail walking our way. Ruhail who had been in my life, providing support without ever expecting anything in return. So you can't blame me for the jolt I experienced when I received a text message, with his marriage proposal. It had made me question my feelings for him, from the inner most core of my heart. And I felt the need to examine the reason for him asking me, in the sweetest of ways, for my hand in marriage. Had I ever led him on, had been my first question. I was definitely sure the answer was no.

"Hello, Roshina." He said as he hugged me sideways. He had started doing that only a couple of years ago. Otherwise he had always maintained a distance and had never given me reason to take offense at any sort of over-familiarity.

"Did you set him up to this?" I gave Zohaib an accusatory glare. But Ruhail intervened. "I had come to meet my parents and bumped into him, at Adoos." He mentioned the name of the city's most reputed patisserie.

"Yes, but I am guilty of calling him today and letting him know about our plans to visit Sopore." Zohaib truthfully admitted. Ruhail looked at me. "Do you mind if I come, too, Roshina? I have never been able to visit.

I remained quiet but smiled at him in invitation. Our taxi had arrived and I gestured him to step inside.

So we journeyed to 'My Saffron Garden in Sopore'. The Hindu woman, her Muslim son and her Muslim friend. This is why India is secular and always will be. Sopore, which had been all but ruined with floods last year and because of our Army had been handed back to civilization.

And now, 'My Saffron Garden' gifted to me by the purest soul on earth. A soul so chaste that it could not accept the ugly blow handed to her. Flanked by mountains and enclosed by snow, the garden beckoned me to enter.

Hence, I visited the graves of the brother and sister who had given meaning to my life.

Zohaib slipped his hand into mine as we trampled across the ice. The garden was covered with snow. The farmhouse had shut down decades ago. The porch where we had done cartwheels, was snowed in. We kneeled down at the grave area, and I took in deep breaths.

We all folded our hands, and we prayed. Strangely enough, I wasn't at a low ebb, and I didn't shed a single tear. I felt at peace. I had finally put the past behind me. Thanks to this wonderful child of mine. Zohaib, belonged to a different faith than mine. But an enchanting one. Like Heena and Aafaq he had gifted me abundant riches. Love knows no religion. Love is sublime. My son will never leave me. And this is all that matters.

Zohaib held my hand as we walked back to the taxi. "Would you like to go to Anantnag? I have the name of your father's relatives. They are your family after all."

"My home is New Delhi and I have no family but you and your family. Mum, this trip was for you, not me. I wanted to give you closure. This is what I was trying to say over the phone."

"Are you playing the shrink with me?" I asked him playfully. "I thought you wanted to specialize in Pediatrics."

His lips curled in a smile. And then he softly remarked, "Mum, get Ruhail Uncle out of his misery." We both looked at Ruhail who was busy talking to one of the gardeners. Out of loyalty to Heena's family, he would come and feed the soil and make sure the grave area was clean.

"Don't worry, Zohaib. I have already thought of that."

"Have you really thought about it?" He peered at me dubiously. "Yes, my dear son, I have." I tweaked the tip of his nose and gave him a lopsided grin. "I can bet you have written him off like all the others." "Zohaib, you make it sound like I have had a long list of suitors all making a beeline for me."

Zohaib coloured, "Mum, you don't know how much I was ragged because of you. Some of the seniors actually would threaten to beat the crap out of me for not passing on your mobile number. You made quite an impression on Orientation day. It was horrible to hear guys gushing about you." It was one of our precious mother son moments and we both laughed loudly. I will always have Zohaib. I thought with joy.

I dealt with Ruhail when we were back in Srinagar.

"I am sorry, Ruhail. It's just that I am still in love with Aafaq. There is no room in my life for another person. I will always be looking back. You need someone who takes you ahead." "I can't be accused of not trying or not making my feelings clear." 'Yes,' I said, "You did the right thing." Mum's voice from many years ago surfaced advising me to disclose my feelings to Aafaq. In my eyes, you will always belong to Heena. And one sister cannot break the heart of another. But I didn't say that to him.

"Is this the part when I say I will walk out of your life as I cannot have this friendship any more?" He gave an exaggerated wave of his hands.

"No, this is the part where we do something more interesting." I exclaimed.

I looked at his confused look and smiled at him. We were in the houseboat and I walked him to the porch. Zohaib was waiting there, and next to him was a small table piled up with the most exotic of Kashmiri food. "We have come a long way, Ruhail." I looked at him. He smiled genuinely. For me he was and always would be a substitute brother.

It was an evening devoted to family and friends. But now one thing was left and that was visiting my house on Raj Bagh. Tomorrow Zohaib and I would go to Pehalgam for two nights and then fly back to Delhi.

I stood in the lawn of my house. My glorious house which had been the cynosure of all eyes had been reduced to a rubble. The room which I had once claimed to be my boudoir was nothing better than a wreckage. There was no first floor as there was no ground floor. The garden was like a wild forest with grass that climbed up around my waist. And the walnut tree had been felled and stood like a humble stump.

"Rosha Jaan." I heard a familiar voice. It was Zubeida. We hugged each other as we smiled through our tears. "I saw you from my window. I couldn't believe it was you." "What happened to the house?" I asked her. "My uncle has never mentioned anything to me." "After Heena...passed away." Her voice faltered. "The rest of the family gave up. Aafaq Bhai Jaan, too, was killed. I am sure you know that aunty and uncle disappeared. The house was taken over by fundamentalists. They would come here and unleash terror on the whole street. We would hear them at night, high on drugs as they would scream and make merry. Then one night they set fire to the house." "And Heena's tree?" I asked. "It was burnt, too, Rosha Jaan. After a couple of days, I requested my gardener to prune it properly and let it remain as it was. I still come here and pray Heena will emerge out, from behind and scare me." There were so many who loved you, Heena. I thought as I wiped away my tears.

Zubeida took me to her house. She lived there with her husband and two daughters. Her parents were no more, and she had lost her brothers to *Jihad* a long time ago. Her elder daughter had read my novel and was delighted to meet me. I duly signed the book and handed it to her with a smile.

"When Ammi used to tell me you used to live next door I wouldn't believe her. She says you and Heena Aunty were her best friends. We hardly have any Hindu girls in our school now. It must have been so nice living in those days." "It was not nice, it was wonderful." I gave her a wistful look. These children have seen nothing but hatred and violence in Kashmir. Their mother's tales must sound so farfetched and untrue. Zubeida was a link to my glorious past. We exchanged numbers and promised to stay in touch. With a final glance at Heena's tree I took leave from Raj Bagh Road. But I will definitely come back soon, was my silent promise.

□

22

A month has lapsed since we have returned from Kashmir. I feel a buoyancy which I have not felt in years and there is a spring in my step. The courage and determination which 'Time' stole, is back with me, its rightful owner. The draft of my second book is progressing in my mind. Undoubtedly, the book will be about Kashmir, but right now my only child is undergoing the highs and lows of first love. And that feeling, I honestly know very well. It is cute to see him besotted, but then why is something sending me shivers down my spine? My son will never leave me. I repeat that to myself nearly a dozen times a day. Am I heading towards Alzheimer's?

"She is very sweet person, Mum. Her name is Nagma. She is a French citizen, though a person of Indian Origin." Zohaib had told me over dinner last week. He had paused ever so slight but I had detected a note of anxiety. He had further mentioned that she had been born and brought up in France and had studied there. She had now joined their hospital and was six months junior to Zohaib in their mandatory internship. Nagma didn't know which part of India she hailed from as her mother, who was widowed had never divulged such tales. "The mother is quite orthodox." Zohaib had announced. His look had faltered. I smiled at him reassuringly. But the seed had been sown. The seed of doubt. Sometimes the word orthodox could transform into extreme and extreme into radical. I was sure I couldn't go through all that now. I will never forgive myself for the soft 'Oh!' which had left my mouth. Zohaib looked devastated. So I had flashed him a broad smile. "What about Nagma?" I queried evenly. "Mum, Nagma is conservative but she is not orthodox. She is after all a person of Indian origin. You are going to love Nagma. She has read your book, so has her mother." I had not wanted to be a dampener on Zohaib's fresh enthusiasm and I reprimanded myself for being so nagging.

My uncle had just come back from a World Cruise and had invited me for lunch at the Defence Officers' Club. He had met up with my parents and Rohan in California. After he shared the latest snippets from their lives. I told him of my own adventure. He was flabbergasted to say the least. "Mind boggling news, I say, Rosha, dear girl. This was one fence which you had to mend. But I do wish you had let me know." He frowned at me. "Would you have flown in from the Caribbean or some destination equally exotic and accompanied me?" "Okay, I got your point, but this accomplishment of yours positively calls for bubbly. The best bottle of champagne, young chap." He instructed the nearest waiter. "My daughter has conquered Everest."

It was in between lunch I told my uncle about Zohaib's love interest. At first Chachu gave out a loud guffaw. "Our little boy has finally become a man." And then he looked at me speculatively as he saw my uneasy air. "And what might I ask is troubling you?" "No, it's just the word orthodox, that Zohaib used to describe the mother." Chachu was thoughtful. "Lived all their life in France have they? Ask Zohaib to give me the mother's name." 'Chachu,' I squealed throwing my table napkin at him. "You are incorrigible. Stop thinking of women all the time."

Chachu smiled at me. But he looked a little concerned. "Can you put that away?" I asked him sternly as he started loading his pipe. "Ahh! woman you are becoming a shrew." And to my horror he puffed in the club right there in the 'No Smoking Zone.'

My Chachu had one puff too many, so it seems. The Military Hospital called me the following evening. My uncle had experienced a heart attack. I was listed as his next of kin. I raced to my car and nearly banged into my neighbour's brand new Jag while reversing. "Get yourself together, old girl." I told myself sternly. I sounded so much like my uncle. When I called Zohaib, I was directed to his voice mail.

"He has had a massive myocardial infarction." The cardiologist informed me. Which in medical jargon meant heart attack. "Years of smoking have permanently damaged his heart muscles and narrowed his arteries with plaques. There is a hundred percent blockage in his aorta. He is breathing with a ventilator."

My uncle was in the Intensive Care Unit and no visitors were allowed. I waited outside and was so grateful when in half an hour Zohaib arrived. "I saw your message and sat in my car." I nodded at him. "What did the doctor say?" He saw my ashen face, ushered me to a couch and went and spoke to the doctor. Zohaib had a special bond with Chachu. My Uncle had been a grandfather, father, uncle and brother. Chachu had taught him how to shave, how to guzzle beer and how to drive. It is strange, in this country where we fight over temples, mosques and religious places, there exist people who believe in love, irrespective of religion. Why couldn't there be more families like mine? "But there are. The Qazmis and Ruhail's family." A voice said from inside.

We spent the entire night on the couch in the reception, sipping coffee from a Styrofoam cup. "He is awake and has been asking for you incessantly." The doctor told me as he left my uncle's room in the morning. "How is he?" "Like all Army men here he is a fighter, but the damage to his heart is irreversible. Things don't look good." Seeing my shattered look, he added. "Let me tell you, the nurses are practically fighting over who gets to administer his medication. Everyone has suddenly turned into a regular Florence Nightingale." That was Chachu, a charmer right till the end.

My uncle lay still on his bed strapped to a ventilator, with countless tubes piercing him. Something told me he was not going to be around for long. I rebuked myself as the tears welled in my eyes. "I will be strong, just like my uncle." I repeated to myself.

I went up to him and he gripped my hand firmly. The moment I sat down on the chair beside him he removed the oxygen mask from his face.

"Chachu, you are not supposed to do that." I urged in fear. "I am not going to meet my only child looking like an alien from Mars." He said feebly. The way my uncle winced while talking, I knew what an effort it was costing him. "My Dearest, Kaju." He managed, "You have given me immense joy, my child."

"Chachu, please rest." I implored. "That's just about what I will be doing from now onwards, Kaju, rest." "I won't have you talking like that, Chachu," I warned him. Nonetheless I moved nearer to him. I could see that he was fretting over something.

'Aafaq,' he said in a broken voice. I gazed at him in wonder. What was possessing him to talk about Aafaq when he was drawing his last breath? Must be the effect of the medication. His grip on my wrist strengthened and became vice-like.

"Rosha, listen to me." "Chachu, it's okay. I am listening." 'Rosha,' he struggled to take a breath. 'Aafaq.' Oh God his mind is wandering. I thought. And then again. "Aafaq is…." He fell back against his pillows as his eyes shut. The machine beeped making a piercing sound while the line went flat.

Chachu had left me forever.

□

23

The bullets were fired from the rifle under the order of the commanding officer. I trembled each time the rounds went off in the air. The sound of bullets being fired always ignites panic in me. It brings back the picture of those bullets piercing into Aafaq's chest and face. Now they signal the end of the Indian Army's greatest General ever. I had requested Rohan and my parents not to fly down for the funeral. Papa had not been keeping well. And I had Zohaib. Sheetal had been managing the office with flair, so things were being taken care of. Meena was in Europe and would be back by the end of the week.

I saw a young girl in the crowd of mourners. She had come with Zohaib's friends. I had never seen her before and presumed she must be Nagma. I could tell that she was from Kashmir. She possessed the typical beauty of the Kashmiri Muslim. Our eyes met and I smiled at her. She smiled back, but I realized she was genuinely shy. I could also see that Zohaib had observed our exchange of pleasantries and was quite relieved. I also spotted Sharma. He nodded at me, respectfully. He was a Brigadier now. I smiled back at him. He had saved my life once. There was a very elegant woman on his arm. Sharma had always been a sweetheart. Nagma strode up to me. "Zohaib will never leave me." I kept on reaffirming. I cursed myself at the same time for behaving like an over-possessive lunatic.

"I am so sorry for your loss." She came and told me in heavily-accented English. Probably, because of the fact that she was Kashmiri, there was a sense of familiarity about her. It was as if I had seen her somewhere before. Which was quite absurd. "Thank you for coming, Nagma. It was extremely thoughtful of you." "My pleasure, Ms. Kapoor. Mummy will be coming to see you soon. She really enjoyed your book." Just one book, dear. I thought to myself. Why am I acting so waspishly? What on earth had gotten into me? "I would be extremely pleased to meet her." I replied as genuinely as possible and made a mental note to find a good therapist, before Zohaib, kicked me out of his life. I wondered if Zohaib had been completely honest with her regarding my marital status? He had used the word orthodox hadn't he?

"Your uncle was a great man and an excellent mentor, Ms. Roshina." Sharma alleged sincerely as he came and stood next to me with his wife. "In fact, we all idolized him. Please don't hesitate to call me if you ever need my help in any way whatsoever."

"Thank you," I graciously replied. We made small talk for several minutes, and then I politely excused myself.

Subsequently, I got a call from the office of Komal Kohli. She identified herself as my late uncle's lawyer. So weird to think of him as 'late.' She requested my presence during the hearing of his will.

Komal Kohli was a remarkably attractive woman, and I wondered if she had been one of my uncle's many lady friends.

"You are the major beneficiary of your uncle's will, Roshina. To your brother, Rohan Kapoor, your uncle has left his cherished 'Gun collection.' Your uncle was a very fair man and found Rohan Kapoor to be a man of more than moderate means. To your son, Zohaib Ali, your uncle has left a two bedroom flat in Noida. You have inherited your uncle's share in your ancestral property in Jammu and his flat in New Delhi. He has also left you and your brother jointly a cottage in Cochin. His liquid cash which is quite a tidy sum is to be sent to the 'Kashmiri Migrants Fund'. He requested me to see that I personally deliver you this." It was a sealed envelope with my name in his digital handwriting marked 'PRIVATE AND CONFIDENTIAL. FOR ROSHINA KAPOOR ONLY.' There was a small package, which I placed in my bag.

"Any problems or queries, Roshina, please feel free to call me and avail my services. Your Chachu loved you more than anyone else on this earth. And now after meeting you, I understand why. You are an exceptionally wonderful person. He was immensely proud of you." "And what about you?" I asked her directly. She was deterred by the frankness of my query but nevertheless looked at me while replying. "Rudratej and I fell madly in love with each other in college, but my father did not approve of him as he had registered for the Army. I even suggested we elope but Rudra wouldn't hear it. He thought my stubborn father would eventually come around. As for asking Rudra not to join the Army, that was like killing the person inside him. He had the making of a fine general, even then. My father developed pancreatic cancer. With him on his death bed, I married my husband, and your uncle went around breaking hearts all over the country. We bumped into each other when my husband being a Civil Servant, was working in Nagaland. Your uncle was posted as a Colonel over there. I have no secrets from my husband, and he was large hearted enough to include Rudratej in the wonderful world, we had created for ourselves. You see, I have a very happy marriage. Rudra was back in my life and heart as a friend and it has been like that since then. I was stunned that Rudra hadn't settled down with someone whereas I was living a fairly decent life with a very decent man. A man who was broad minded enough to let me maintain a platonic relationship with someone I had once been willing to throw caution to the wind and run away with. To be honest, Vijay, my husband liked Rudratej, a feeling which Rudra reciprocated. They developed a mutual respect for one another." I looked at the charming Komal Kohli and thought of my handsome Chachu. What an amazingly good looking couple they would have made. My poor uncle who had tried to nurture his broken heart with an endless list of mindless affairs. And never once had he mentioned Komal. Did my parents know? I thought. Surely, Papa must have. No wonder Chachu had done so much for Aafaq and me. He knew what it is to be madly in love. Rudratej Kapoor, an officer and a gentleman forever. I love you with all my heart.

I reached home and opened the envelope with trembling hands. How many more skeletons were going to tumble out of the closet?

My dearest Rosha, my darling child,

By now you must have attended my funeral. Please throw my remains off any cliff, my dear child as every part of me is a part of this glorious nation.

I have had a fantastic life. My biggest asset has been my only child, Roshina Kapoor. You have provided me the pride and joy of being a parent without the pain that children give. When you were a little girl I used to feel so envious of my brother. You were a doll, Rosha, and you possessed the goodness of both your parents. By the way, how did you like Komal?

Yes, I was crazy about her. Destiny it seems had other plans for us both. I was amazed when I met her after all those years. Again, she entered my life. Not in the way I had ever thought, but I had her friendship once more. You were correct when you said that love stories never have a happy ending. But in the end I was happy with the way things turned out. As no woman would ever be able to compete with the love I had for India.

It always used to surprise me how a person as intelligent as Aafaq could have fallen for the atrocious, yet so transparent plot, hatched by the Inquilaab Kashmir? How could he think that the Army was in any way connected? He did, but only for a couple of weeks and then he thought like the level-headed person he was. He realized the Army was totally innocent and so then the needle of suspicion fell on 'Inquilaab Kashmir.' But they, too, were blameless.

Remember when we went to Sopore, to talk to Aafaq. We asked you to step outside our room. Aafaq told me the shocking conspiracy that he had unearthed.

I will have to take you to that time in Srinagar when Aafaq Qazmi's family was sent a marriage proposal by the family of Saira Hyder Ali. A proposal which was rejected outrightedly by Aafaq. Though it was made little known, Saira eventually married Feroze Ansari. He was the Commander of the religious outfit 'Kashmere Mujahid.' They were supporters of Pakistan. It sprouted in the early eighties but gave way to internal strife. All this is speculation. We have never been able to actually verify Feroze's whereabouts. Saira got married to Feroze and became radical. His violent ideologies and Pro-Taliban thoughts held great appeal to her. Most of Feroze's family were in Pakistan. They were lying low key while insurgency erupted in Kashmir. Saira changed her name to Ruksana. Saira was obsessed with Aafaq and never forgot him. Rather she was undoubtedly a psychiatric patient. She felt a lot more than 'slighted' when he got engaged to you. A Hindu girl, belonging to the religion she loathed. She was enraged that he had chosen a *Kafir*. She was consumed with revenge and could go to any lengths to keep the two of you apart. How to hurt Aafaq

Qazmi? How to hurt the Hindu *Kafir*? How to separate the two of you? These thoughts tormented her. So when insurgency raised its ugly head, her brain so polluted by hate and retribution, planned all that wrong doing for our dear Heena. Aafaq Qazmi would instantly break off with you and hate his country and all *Kafirs*, especially Hindus. And if he ever saw through the plot, every trace of evidence would point at 'Inquilaab Kashmir.' As the 'Kashmere Mujahid' had been out of the scene since a long time. There was no trace of them. Rumor was the outfit had disbanded as the Commander Feroze had succumbed to a suicide bombing. Some said Feroze and Ruksana had sought asylum in Pakistan. Others swore it to be Afghanistan.

Saira or Ruksana was killing two birds with one stone. 1. She would get to hurt Aafaq and his family by getting Heena molested. 2. The two of you would be separated.

But she hadn't reckoned for his sharp mind and his friends in 'Inquilaab Kashmir' who assured him of their innocence. Aafaq even met the leader of the organization who offered Aafaq his life if he or his men had ever looked at his sister. They gave him irrefutable evidence with regards to Saira and Feroze's involvement. It was crystal clear how the Army and subsequently the 'Inquilaab Kashmir' had been set up. With their help, Aafaq put the pieces of the jigsaw puzzle together. He realized the gravity of the situation, and his concern was just for you. He deliberately left incriminating evidence for the Army to link his involvement with 'Inquilaab Kashmir' and knew you would be approached by me. Aafaq was scared that you would be next on that insane woman's list. He could not let anything happen to you. He needed our help. He revealed all this to me. Though Saira Hyder and Feroze had disappeared, from the face of this earth and had been off the radar, Aafaq was positive it was nothing but a smokescreen. He was certain Saira would never let the two of you live together in peace. And he knew that if he told you the truth you would never give him up and endanger your own life. 'Operation Saffron' was a high level military operation to flush out militants from Sopore. But those militants were not 'Inquilaab Kashmir.' It was some foreign faction which we wanted to annihilate, who were sending in *Jihadist* after *Jihadist* in swarms from the border. And all those documents were their execution plans. 'Inquilaab Kashmir' helped us as a mark of respect for Aafaq and because of his personal tragedy. It is so true that in Kashmir it is one radical group fighting the other.

Aafaq gave us all this information on one condition. In exchange he wanted you out of harm's way. He knew by simply disappearing from your life you would leave no stone unturned in finding him. So you had to consider him to be dead. And that way Saira Hyder would be satisfied that since he is no more, her efforts to keep you apart were successful. She would hence leave you alone. That was his prime concern. He loved you more than you ever knew. He could not take any more chances with your life. He gave up his family, his country for you to lead a normal existence. He had not indulged in any anti-national activities at all. Not via a computer and assuredly not via a Kalashnikov. Aafaq Qazmi is a patriot of India. He was not a Jihadist.

When there was that blank call for you in the afternoon before we left for Prabhat Lank I got suspicious. I couldn't take any chances, not with a cold-blooded sociopath harboring a serious vendetta against you. I was frantic that you leave Srinagar at once and have never encouraged you to go back. I was with Aafaq that evening after you left for Jammu. When I called you at the Governor's house, he was sitting next to me and could hear your voice over the speaker. I promised him that you will be protected till the moment you die. Aafaq asked me to do everything in my power to avenge Heena's death. That was the last time I saw him, and then I had to sever all ties with him. The following morning he was flown out of the country. I don't think he ever communicated with his parents either. After a couple of months I went to Kandahar on a top secret assignment and shot Heena's assailants. I did it out of love for the hapless child who had suffered in the most unimaginable way. Heena's assailants were mercenaries, high on opium and on Saira's upkeep. Interpol claims Saira and her husband are dead. But like I said there is no evidence to support that theory. Today during lunch something made me want to give you your last chance at love. You looked so lonely. And now Zohaib has grown up. I got this number from an old friend of mine who lives in Kuwait. *Aafaq is alive.* There was a twelve digit number written on the side of the page.

On Prabhat Lank that day, there were no militants and no casualties. Aafaq handed us the necessary documents which his friends had supplied. Those photographs of his were all innocent and some morphed. Those men in the ruins were Army officers. While that hood was placed over your head, Aafaq was sneaked into the building on the isle. The person you thought to be Aafaq was a dead militant of Aafaq's height and build. His face had been severely blown off in a bomb blast so we used him as a dummy. The bullets that were fired were all blank, and the blood you saw, was a chemical used in warfare and espionage. We all had a special protective gel in our eyes so the tear gas wouldn't affect us. Besides, most of us were wearing protective glasses. We had all been given an antidote to prevent the breathing difficulties which you felt. You were given a very meager dose of the chemical through tear gas. That is why we had to hood you to make sure that you could not see what we were doing. Inquilaab Kashmir were guilty of lot of things but they had nothing to do with what happened to Heena. I had my doubts from the beginning.

Try to forgive your uncle. But I thought as a father, and no father can let his daughter come in harm's way. Unknown to you, I have provided you military security and protection. You will be safeguarded by the Indian Army till the day you die. I made that promise to Aafaq. I knew you had gone to Kashmir. My men were there. I am happy you could visit your Saffron Garden. Only Heena rests there. Aafaq is waiting for you to find him. But I still urge you to be careful.

Sharma can be completely trusted.

Farewell my child,
Rudratej Kapoor.

I read the letter again and pinch myself several times. This can't be happening. *Aafaq is alive*. I remember looking desperately into his eyes when he had been shot on Prabhat island. I had recklessly tried to search for the brown fleck in his right eye. But that had not been Aafaq and those eyes were not Aafaq's eyes. I pick up my phone. I look at the contact number which uncle had left and memorize it at once. With one hand I try to dial the number, and with my other hand I open the packet my uncle has left me. But the phone rings, startling me. 'Zohaib Calling' flashes on the screen. "Mum, I am downstairs in our building's reception. Nagma is with me." He sounds bothered. "That's very nice, bring her upstairs. Zohaib, I have brilliant news." But Zohaib doesn't listen to what I have to say. "Her mother is with us. She has flown in from Paris and wants to convey her condolences." "It's okay, Zohaib. Please bring her along." In my new found happiness, my social etiquettes soar sky rocketing. I examine the content of Uncle's packet thoughtfully and carefully place it back in my bag.

I hurriedly plump up the cushions on the sofa and put the kettle on in the kitchen. What an auspicious day, Aafaq is alive, and my son is bringing his girl friend home. Nagma is our good luck charm.

I hear the bell ring and I rush to open the door.

Zohaib and Nagma smile at me. It is evident, how jumpy they both are. Behind them is a woman in a Burqa. I remember Zohaib describing Nagma's mother as orthodox. But nothing can spoil my good mood today. I welcome my guests inside. A tall gentleman, not facing me as he is busy on his phone, stands in the foyer a couple of feet away from my door. He is certainly not with my guests. I close my front door. And in all the excitement I forget to latch it.

Zohaib immediately escorts Nagma to the porch. He mumbles something about her having a green thumb and wanting to see my plants. It had been on the tip of my tongue to tell him about this amazing revelation but I realize now is not the time. Nagma's mother sits down on the sofa in front of me. Her face is fully veiled. I smile at her. Now whether she returns the smile, is an enigma for obvious reasons. Anyhow I do start feeling uncomfortable. The kettle starts whistling. "I will fetch our tea." I say brightly. Is this what they mean when they say, 'Saved By The Bell?' I walk back carefully with a tray loaded with tea and muffins. And hopefully a bit of composure. If only I could get two minutes alone with Zohaib to tell him what has happened. I guess I will have to wait.

I bend down to offer Nagma's mother a cup of tea.

The veil has been lifted.

I look into the face of Saira Hyder Ali.

"I told you, Roshina, that Aafaq will never be yours." She lets out a peel of laughter. I swerve backwards.

I hear soft footsteps behind me. I am panting hard as

I turn around and almost bump into someone.

Apparently, the tall gentleman from our landing had found my door open and had taken the liberty of stepping inside. This is all I need now. Does he know his life is at risk in this room with a killer on the loose? At present the entire room resounds with Saira's insane merriment.

"Sorry, but your door was open." He has a foreign accent. Definitely Middle Eastern.

It is unbelievable.

He is tall, taller than me. Fair, fairer than me, just like most men from Kashmir. He has a broken nose.

But his eyes, they are like emeralds. Like what a Maharaja covets to gift his favourite concubine.

I hunt for the brown fleck. It can't be possible. It won't be there. But it is. Like it always has been, there in his right eye.

The tray slips out of my hands and crashes to the floor.

The noise is deafening.

My mind races to my last lunch with Chachu in the club.

"What are you doing, Chachu?" My uncle had picked up my phone and was punching some numbers. "I am feeding Sharma's number in your phone. He is a very efficient Brigadier. It always comes in handy to know a guy in uniform." "But I have you, Chachu." I had interjected.

"I have one foot in the grave, Kaju. Look here, girl. I have put him in speed dialling."

And now I keep my gaze on Saira. She is laughing maniacally. I move out of earshot and rescue my mobile phone from the pocket of my jeans. My fingers sprint to speed dialling. "Come on, come on," I tell myself. I press the key and 'Calling Sharma' shows up on my screen. I dare a glance at Aafaq. He, too, has seen Saira and has put his glasses on. "We are outside your building. Keep the enemies engaged in conversation." Is Sharma's reassuring command.

As the phone disconnects the thought accosts me, what did he mean by enemies?

I remember praying in My Saffron Garden.

What had been my thoughts?

Zohaib will never leave me.

And today when Komal Kohli had handed me a package, she had insisted.

"Your uncle left this for you. But he wanted you to open it only after you read his letter."

I had opened it after reading the letter, just as Zohaib had called.

It was a revolver sealed in a thick envelope.

There was a small note attached to it.

The weapon I used to kill Heena's violators. It is loaded. Always keep it this way.

I had hurriedly put the weapon back in the bag. Where is my bag?

Oh my God! What is Aafaq doing? The laughter finally diminishes.

I do remember mentioning that the sound of bullets being fired has always ignited panic inside me.

□

Epilogue

I stare at the green eyes. The green eyes with the brown fleck. "Rosha, meri jaan." I hear the most delightful endearment.

We will have Kashmiriyat once again. All over the world.

My nocturnal foes none other than the demons. In all likelihood they have finally bid me adieu.

I am Roshina Kapoor and nothing can break my spirit.

YOU IN YOUR HAND

by Drora Shirai

YOU IN YOUR HAND

by Drora Shirai

Translation From Hebrew: Ethel Broido

Typesetting: Marzel A.S. - Jerusalem

Cover Design: Shlomit Reshef

ISBN 965-229-137-4

Edition 9 8 7 6 5 4 3 2 1

Gefen Publishing House Ltd.
POB 6056, Jerusalem
91060 Israel

Gefen Books
12 New St., Hewlett
N.Y., U.S.A. 11557

Printed in Israel

How this book differs from others on a similar subject

1. Firstly, I have analyzed the hands of both famous and lesser known individuals in this country and through the medium of this analysis, have shown how different incidents and events in their lives are reflected in the basic characteristics as evidenced by the potential seen in their hands. These analyses are accompanied by prints of these personalities' hands together with the graphic explanation which indicates how I arrived at these conclusions.
2. The book is written in a readable and easily understandable style. The information it contains can be grasped by any level of the public. All the explanations and models are accompanied by clear diagrams and illustrations which enable the reader to grasp the information on both an intellectual and visual level.

Dedication

This book is dedicated to the memory of Dr. Erwin Kaplan, with whose help this book was published.

Dr. Kaplan was an excellent surgeon, and an extraordinary person. Many of those wounded in the Six Day war owe their lives to him. I met him by chance, when I began my search for interesting personalities for my book. At first, he was very skeptical toward the reading of the palm. Little by little, he began to change his mind after I read his palm. I told him about his self and I saw a number of events in his life which he had actually experienced. He was so impressed with my diagnosis, that he began to consult with me about his patients, using photocopies of their hands. At a certain point, he felt I should put all of my knowledge in writing. He persisted until I finished writing this book.

To my great sorrow, he did not live to see the publication of my book. He died at the age of 65, shortly before this book was published.

May his memory be blessed.

Contents

FOREWORD

How did I arrive at chirology?

At the age of twenty I worked as a handicrafts teacher in Beersheba, in Israel, where I had a friend who was interested in parapsychology and related subjects. One day, he said to me: "Let me see your hand and we shall see how many years you have to live. The subject held no interest for me whatsoever and I treated it with considerable sceptism and a certain degree of contempt. However, I held out my palm, and after considering it for some time, he exclaimed with utter seriousness: "You have only three more years to live." From that moment and for the following three years, I lived in constant fear of the inevitable. I refrained from driving and hesitated to go anywhere by car. I was reluctant to go up or down stairs lest I slip and break my neck. I had become a pronounced hypochondriac, bearing in mind that my father had died of a heart disease at the age of 39 and that I had also lost an aunt from the same illness. I was convinced that this was what fate had in store for me as well.

Three years went by and another twenty followed. The angel of death evidently had no intention of keeping this alleged appointment. Many years later when attending a lecture on chirology and the study of hands, my curiosity was aroused. My friend's forecast of many years earlier came to mind. I spoke to the lecturer about it and wondered what prompted such a startling prediction. As his reaction also reflected my own opinion, I am quoting what he said at the time: "Not everyone who reads a book on chirology can become a chirologist. The subject calls for profound and extensive study, and more than anything else, one must know how to advise people."

Although most people frankly declare that they do not believe in supernatural phenomena, there are still many who do believe in some aspect of the metaphysical. For instance, most people are undoubtedly aware of their astrological signs and their significance, and many follow the astrological columns in the press. As to predictions regarding the future, I personally believe in fate. In the lines of the palm it is possible to foretell future events, including a fatal occurence, but at the same time, I believe that people are masters of their own fate and that they have the power to influence and even to change the course of their lives once they are aware of their own capacities and inclinations. The chirologists task is to work in a positive manner and guide the individual towards optimistic and positive channels, helping him or her to act accordingly. Naturally, there is an element of self-suggestion in predicting the future, as 'predictions tend to fulfil themselves'. When I tell someone that at a certain age they are liable to be involved in an accident, they will subconsciously switch their minds to a mental state in which an accident is a possibility. On the other hand, if I act positively and offer soothing advice which encourages and strengthens the person while helping him or her to understand the various possibilities inherent in the situation, it may release the positive energies needed in the circumstances and the prediction may not take place at all, or if it does, may not be very effective.

The advantage that a chirologist has over a psychologist is in the former's ability to actually foresee the future problem and to supply the guidance needed to deal with it before rather than after its has occurred. In business matters, for instance, I can often predict the possibility of a serious loss and warn my client in advance and thus provide him with an opportunity to reconsider his plans. A friend once discussed with me the possibility of selling his apartment and using the sum he received in order to start a business. In his palm, I saw that he was liable to suffer a substantial loss of capital. I advised him not to go ahead with his plans but he did not take my advice. Within a year, he had lost both his apartment and the business. Another client with a similar problem took my advice. Some time later, I noticed a dynamic change in my client's palm and the possible losses were avoided.

Hence my message is as follows: if you are getting advice through such channels, make certain you are receiving advice from a professional and not an amateur who has read a number of books on the subject. You should be aware of the fact that your prosperity or ruin may depend on one hour of consultation. Take my own experience as proof of this message. After that devastating forecast, I decided to study the subject thoroughly and penetrate its very core before trying to advise anyone and I have made it my life's work to help people to realize their potential and achieve a better and happier life.

FOREWORD TO CHIROLOGY

Man's earnest desire to understand the meaning of existence and the secret of the future is as ancient as the world itself. Standing before the forces of nature – those tremendous elements which utterly dominated his life – he sought some assurance in his ability to anticipate what lay ahead and in trying to understand the meaning of things. The ancients spent long periods contemplating the world around them, trying to fathom its secrets and attempting to find the key to its natural order.

This prolonged inquiry produced various and strange ways of predicting the future. Some of these methods of divining the future were based on signs which were understood only by a few chosen "priests", who passed on their knowledge to later generations and peoples, such as the Babylonians, the ancient Persians and Egyptians, the Aztecs and Incas of Central America. They would interpret 'the words of the gods' in slaughtered animals' guts, in the shapes of clouds and the waves of the sea, in the direction of the winds and the flickering flames of the sacred fire. The Greeks and the Romans appealed to their oracles or clairvoyants in order to learn the wishes and pleasure of their gods but they also resorted to such strange media as onions, eggs and cheeses, in order to foretell the future. Astrology was developed and functioned in the East (both the Near and Far East) and in the West, at a very high level, frequently resulting in the decisions of kings and heads of states being ruled by their astrologers' advice and admonitions.

Other methods of prediction found that man and his body was the source of signs which could serve to indicate the future. These methods were mainly developed in ancient India, where a civilization and culture had flourished thousands of years before that of Europe. In this culture, man was the focus of interest and center of study as the possible key to the understanding of the gods, much as the microcosm is the epitome of and reveals the macrocosm.

Based on this philosophy, the ancient Indians developed the 'Smodrika' (a gift to humankind from the sea god Smodra), a unique study of the significance of body signs, which became the source of various predictive theories which were based on the different part of the body:

- Phrenology – the study of the conformation of the skull
- Physiognomy – the study of the facial features
- Podiology – the study of the conformation of the feet
- Iridology – the study of the iris
- and Chirology (Cheirology) – the study of the conformation of the palms of the hands

Hands play an important role in the ritual and ceremonies of all known religions. Man's suppliance to God or his gods, involves gestures of the hands. Benediction is usually rendered by raised hands and by the priest's touch. An official nomination or swearing-in of an official generally involves some hand gesture, as do ceremonies relating to judicial or legal processes. In the ancient world and still today, the conclusion of business deals or historic agreements is marked by the shaking of hands. In these instances, the hand serves as a symbol of validity and the handshake signifies the confirmation and strengthening of a promise or an oath.

Hands also have an extremely important function in the performance of magic. In the East, the hand is believed to have the power to get rid of harmful elements by waving it around the head or in front of the body, or through the medium of hand-shaped amulets (Hamsah) or the print of the palm over a door or entrance-way. Belief in the protective nature of the hand has been current since the Stone Age, as is evident from the frescos found in pre-historic caves in the Pyrenees. It was commonly supposed that the hand was capable of getting rid of evil spirits by painting it (hence the use of henna hinna), as well as by the wearing of rings and bracelets which had originally served as talismen or lucky amulets. In magical terms, the clasping of one hand in the other is considered an action which deters harmful intentions, while the Romans believed that clasped hands had the power to delay the birth process and they also forbade the clasping of hands during prayer, sacrificial rites, or the assemblies of royal institutions. The outstretched hand, on the other hand, symbolized the healing properties ascribed to saints and prophets in particular (such as Jesus, Muhammad, and others.) Certain expressive hand gestures are used as sex symbols (in the form of "rude gestures"). In Hebrew, the word for hand (yad) is also used for a memorial or gravestone and many gravestones are indeed embellished with carved hands.

Because of the extensive use of the hands, they may consciously or unconsciously come into contact with various elements of pollution and even serve as the medium for spreading disease. This is why such emphasis is placed on the cleanliness of hands in religious ceremonies as well as in daily life. The precepts dealing with the washing of hands before a meal or a religious ritual was one of the most important in Judaic law (with an entire book of the Mishnah devoted to the subject) and in Islamic tradition, as well as an accepted ritual in most cultures. Symbolically, it expressed purity of heart and a rejection of sin. Among most individuals, it is a physiological fact that the right hand is the dominant one and this undoubtedly engendered the widespread belief in its superiority. In the Bible, the right hand always takes priority. The Biblical text speaks of 'The right hand of the Lord is exalted: the right hand of the Lord doeth valiantly" (Ps.118: 16) and "If I forget thee, O Jerusalem, let my right hand forget her cunning" (Ps. 137: 5) is used as a form of oath. The right hand is always used in religious rituals – for blessing (in most religions), for bearing the Grace cup and the palm branch, and for touching the Mezuza on the doorpost. Again, it is the right hand which is used for providing validity to the swearing process, the transfer of property, and simply for greeting. The left hand, on the contrary, is considered less important (a fact which is expressed for instance in its Roman version Sinistra, i.e.'bad luck', and similarly in its Arabic version), and is generally not used in purifying rites. At the same time, there are instances in which preference is given to the left hand: phyllacteries are laid on the left hand, and the Romans believed that it is the lucky hand with regard to omens and the telling of fortunes. In chirology, it is generally accepted that the right hand indicates the development of character and personality in one's adult years, while the left hand points to the inherited factors and the influences of childhood. Some of the chirological experts prefer to read the left hand on the assumption that its format and linear impressions have been less affected by a persons' work and physical actions and also by the fact that the left hand is nearer to the heart and plays an important role in the performance of magic.

Chirology is a discipline which enables us to get to know a person's character and foresee his or her future by means of the shape of his hand and the network of its lines and structure. An understanding of the hand is based on the belief that the human body is not an accidental construction, but is conditioned by its spiritual attributes and the outer forces which determine the individual's fate. The factual reasoning behind the theory is based on the nature of the link between the hand and the brain. The hands, or more precisely, the tips of our fingers, are the 'antenna' of our bodies in which our tactile sense is centered. An infant learns the nature of objects and their textures by direct contact with them, the blind person is capable of finding his way (and even reading) by touching objects and feeling his way by means of his outstretched hands. A study of the anatomical atlas reveals that the palms of the hands, and especially the tips of the fingers, have the greatest number of tactile nerves extending from the brain. They are more abundant here than in any other part of the body. As the brain is the functional center of the body as well as its sensual and intellectual center, the developed sensual and conscious neural link between the brain and the palms of the hands indicate the extent to which information is transferred in two directions: from the brain to the hands and vice versa. It is therefore natural that the transferred information should be etched on the outer surface of the sensory area as it is on the folds of the brain, and the skin, the nervous system, and the brain, develop from the outer layer (ectoderm) of the three layers of the of the embryo. The lines of the hand should therefore reflect the impressions registered by the brain via the nervous system, and hence reflect our personalities as well.

The source of the word "chirology" is the Greek word KHEIR, which means hand, but the roots of its teachings lie in ancient India, some five thousand years back. It was developed from the "Smodrika", with the aim of finding definitive criteria which would enable us to understand the nature of man by observing his body. The basis of this approach are borne out by the most ancient books to be found in Indian temples, and it seems that they were a remnant of even more ancient times, before people knew how to write. Some are written in an ancient Tamil language, others in an early Sanskrit, and there are others which cannot be deciphered. One of these ancient texts, written in poetic form, contains hundreds of stanzas, each of which defines a line of the palm, and is ascribed to Walamika Maharishi – a legendary literary figure supposed to have existed some five thousand years ago. Cheiro tells that he himself saw a very old volume on the subject of chirology in one of the Brahmin temples which was made of human skin and had a text written in indelible red ink. The book contained hundreds of illustrations and captions relating to the signs and drawings on the palms of the hands, and its most ancient part (one of three) was dated to an earlier era. In addition, he claims that there is a rich ancient literature to be found in the temples of Hindustan, which is zealously kept secret by the Brahmin monks. All of which is evidence of the fact that the reading and study of the palm enjoyed considerable status in ancient Indian culture and was studied and researched in a thorough and systematic manner.

From ancient India, study of the hand was introduced throughout the East – to Persia, Babylon, and Egypt on the one hand, and to Tibet and China on the other. The Chinese version of this study differs from that of India, and relates to different areas and signs. Until the present, a foretelling system is accepted in China which is based on fingerprints, according to the principles of the Chinese book "I Ching", in which the hand is divided into eight major sections ("palaces") related to the opposing forces (Yin and Yang).

In ancient East, this study was the province of the seers of Babylon and the magicians of Egypt (Exodus vii: 7,11) and in addition to their knowledge of Astrology, served as one of their sources of power. From many passages in the Bible, one can conclude that the practice of reading palms was known in other circles as well: for instance:

1) 'And he said, "Wherefore doth my lord thus pursue after his servant for what have I done? or what evil is in mind hand?' (I Samuel, xxvi:18).
2) 'Length of days is in her right hand; and in her left hand riches and honour.' (Prov.iii:16)
3) 'He sealeth up the hand of every man ; that all men may know his work (Job xxxvii: 7).

These passages were understood in the Middle Ages as an allusion to chirology, and there are also claims that they were intentionally translated in this manner in order not to appear to be lending support to teachings opposed to by the church.

The use of the study and discipline of chirology was common among the Jews for many generations, but its manifestation in Judaic literature is not continuous. It is only after the Biblical period that we find specific references in the Qumran scrolls, where we encounter character analyses based on the shape of the various organs of the body. The first detailed Hebrew text on chirology is Facial Expression and Features, an esoteric and mystical work from the Talmudic period, and in the Responsa of the Babylonian gaons, one can gauge the extent of their understanding of the subject within the context of their studies of the supernatural and mystical: "And the first would examine the lines of the hands until they could differentiate between them... and we heard from the elders that they say that there is within the lines, a section of the hand to be used for blessing" (responsum of Rav Hay Gaon). In the twelfth and thirteenth centuries, the seers of Ashkenaz (Germany) were preoccupied with the teachings of chirology without linking it to their religious studies or mysticism, and from the same period, we still have various texts which were found partially in books of remedies and incantations to ward off evil. In the Kabbalah, there are many notable references to the study of chirology and an entire chapter of the Zohar is devoted to the subject. In later generations, the cabbalists made widespread use of this knowledge and works on the subject continued to appear (such as the History of Man a study of the face and the hand by Moses ben Elihu from the fifteenth century).

The Greeks inherited the discipline of hand-reading from the Egyptians, and the greatest of their philosophers and scientists made extensive use of it. It is known that Pythagoras, Hippocrates, Plinius, Pericles and Aristotles employed their knowledge of this discipline with the utmost seriousness, and were of the opinion that Aristotle (according to Hispanius) sent his pupil Alexander the Great, an ancient book on the theory of hand-reading, which he claimed to have found on the altar of Hermes (or perhaps wrote himself), and ordered him to study it. Another book entitled Secretum Secretorum ascribed to Aristotle and well-known during the Middle Ages and the Renaissance has even been translated into Hebrew. The Romans were also knowledgeable on the subject, as one can see from the letters of the poet Juvenal (60-130 A.D.), Plautus (254-148 B.C.), and Virgil (70-19 B.C.). According to the historian Josephus Flavius, the Emperor Augustus was very familiar with this discipline and used it to test the loyalty of his courtiers, even using his knowledge to expose a man who pretended to be Herod's son.

The Romans introduced chirology to Europe, but with the decline of the Roman empire and its culture, this discipline also subsided, as it was considered the work of the devil and forbidden by the Church. The Christian Church fought ceaselessly to put an end to all occult studies and anyone who dabbled in such studies as astrology, hypnosis, or chirology, was burned at the stake. As a result, most of the knowledge related to these subjects as well as the fact that they were labelled as suspect and 'vain beliefs', produced attitudes of derision and ridicule as well as prejudices from which they suffer until the present day. This was also the period during which chirology became the province of the gypsies and other groups on the fringes of society, who exploited their knowledge in order to dupe the more simple members of the public and and did a great deal of harm to the pursuit and knowledge of chirology.

It was only during the Renaissance that the individual began to free himself from the restricting burden of the church and become the renewed focus of interest. Once again, the older teachings came into their own and enjoyed serious and critical attention as well as original and constructive thought, in which the most qualitative change was the move from predicting the future to purely character analysis. In 1475, the first book dealing with chirology was printed in Germany – one of the first to be printed – and in 1490, another book was published on the same subject. In the fifteenth and sixteenth centuries, the science of chirology was very popular in England, and Queen Elizabeth I would regularly consult the chirologist Dr. John-Day (this was also Napoleon's wont). Until the eighteenth century, chirology was accepted as a branch of medicine and even studied in a number of European universities, but with the advent of the age of reason and scientific thinking which called for experimentation and proof, the onset of the nineteenth century once again witnessed the decline of interest in the study of chirology.

At the beginning of the nineteenth century, the Frenchmen D'Arpentigny and Desbarrolles, placed the study of chirology on a scientific basis, each in his own fashion. D'Arpentigny focused his attention on physiognomy -the the hand's outward form, based on an analysis and sifting of information gathered in the course of years of scientific and methodical research. He was the first to categorize the shape of the hand into types and actually revolutionized thinking on the subject. The results of his work rendered chirology its present-day character.

In the nineteenth century, interest in chirology as a medium of fortune-telling was aroused and hundreds of books were published on the subject. Among them, it is worth noting the work of the Duke of St. Germain, published in the United States in 1897 which centers on the discovery of early intimations of disasters and insanity. Towards the end of the nineteenth century, there were two scholars dealing with chirology who left their mark on the development of the discipline to this very day. The better-known of the two is Cheiro, i.e. Louis Hamon (1866-1936), who had a considerable reputation for discerning the character and future of some of the central figures of his generation. He was extremely knowledgable in a wide range of various aspects of mysticism, which he researched thoroughly and spent a number of years in India delving into ancient texts. The many books he published on the subject turned chirology into an accepted and useful science, although there are those who claim that his forecasts of the future were founded on his outstanding abilities rather than a genuine forecasting element inherent in the study. His colleague William Bonham, who researched the subject for decades and amassed findings in a systematic and scientific manner, directed the study of chirology into the psychological field, dealing with occupational and marriage guidance and in this way succeeded in changing the "entertainment" image of chirology.

THE RIGHT HAND AND THE LEFT HAND

Cheiro writes in his book that the left hand is the one we are born with, and that perhaps the right hand is the one we create. If this is so, the left hand must be the one which manifests our heredity – that is, all those characteristics, talents and illnesses which our parents have bequeathed to us. The right hand, however, reflects our own personality, that is the extent to which we have realized and fulfilled ourselves and if we were sufficiently aware of the family's hereditary illnesses in order to act to prevent their occurrence.

In many instances I see indications of promising intellectual development in a client's hand, but the right hand reveals that this individual has done nothing to exploit this inherent potential. The reasons for this may have been environmental, such as insufficient parental support in childhood, or disturbing and offensive social surroundings which create a lack of security and self-confidence. As a chirologist, this is the point at which I must encourage, support, and offer guidance as to the direction the client should take, what studies to pursue, and similar matters. Moreover, in a number of instances, I have discovered hereditary illnesses which appear both in the left and the right hand (for instance, it is possible to discover the possibility of such diseases as angina pectoris in the lines of the hand). In which case I would proceed to caution the person and warn him or her against smoking, while at the same time, suggest intensive physical activity – and then it would be likely that a change in the lines of the right hand would change and the problem would not actually be present or at least, far less imminent.

Cheiro claims that even in those individuals who are left-handed, the diagnosis should be made on the basis of the right hand. I am not convinced that this is indeed the case because in left-handed people, the right half of the brain (and body) is dominant and hence the lines of the hand are stronger and more firmly set. Therefore, when I examine the hands of someone sitting opposite me, I firstly clarify whether the person is right-handed or left-handed. After that, I examine both hands and make my diagnosis on the basis of both hands. Every sign which appears in both the left and the right hand is of greater importance because it confirms and increases the likelihood that these things will take place or have taken place. If I discern, for instance, that there is an indication that points to the danger of an accident and this appears on both hands at the same age, then the likelihood that this will happen (or has happened in the past) is much greater and this is a tested and trustworthy indicator. If the warning sign only appears on the left hand, it is merely a possibility (a likelihood of 50%) and is not certain to occur. In my experience, this working- principle has always proved to be correct.

TYPICAL HAND SHAPES

The lines of the palm, its shape and that of the fingers, are the most telling characteristics of hand-analysis. Typical combinations of these consistent characteristics are the prototype – or the original model or pattern for defining purposes (which could be roughly or generally attributed to various peoples or ethnic groups with specific "national characteristics").

Each of these characteristics or traits of the palm carry some weight in analyzing the personality of the individual and his or her qualities. On the basis of all its details, the lines of the palm reveal the person's potential and whether or not these have been fully realized. According to the form of the hand, it is also possible to determine and indicate what type of occupation would suit the owner of the hand. However, the lines may support or deny this. Sometimes the significance of the lines contradict the basic chacteristics manifested by the shape of the hand and therefore it is important not to determine personality traits merely on the basis of the hand type but to take into consideration all the details of the entire hand.

The lines of the palm are more important, in principle, than the information conveyed by the shape of the hand, since few hand shapes conform to their prototype, that is, when all the characteristics belong to the same type, as we shall see below). Mostly, they are a mixture of two or more types, such as a square palm with conical or philosophical fingers. The palm type is classified by its internal side while the fingers are classified by their external side.

Hand types are usually categorized according to the following seven prototypes:

1) The Primitive hand
2) The Square hand
3) The Large (flat) hand
4) The philosophical hand
5) The Conical hand
6) The Emotional hand
7) The Mixed hand

THE PRIMITIVE HAND

DESCRIPTION

This type of hand appears in its classic form among the Eskimos and primitive Indian tribes. Owners of this type of hand have the lowest natural intellectual capacity. The hand is coarse and crude; the palm is large, thick and heavy. The fingers are short and stubby, including the thumb. There are few lines in the palm apart from the three basic lines: the Life line, the Head line and the Heart line, which is usually very short in this instance.

The characteristic Head Line is straight and short.

The primitive hand indicates a low intelligence, a fairly inadequate thinking capacity and most skills are at an animal level. Possessors of this type of hand find it difficult to control their passions, enjoy eating and drinking and have almost no control over their sexual drives. Their emotions are rarely expressed and they are aggressive individuals with marked destructive tendencies.

Classification of such a palm as the Primitive type may point to a suitable occupation for someone with this type of hand. They have a close kinship with nature and the earth, hence agricultural work, work on a nature-reserve, working with earth-related materials, or any manual work which does not require a developed mind, would suit them. Such people are not ambitious and are therefore not interested in advancing their careers beyond their present state. In most situations, their emotions take precedence over their common sense or logic.

The Primitive Hand

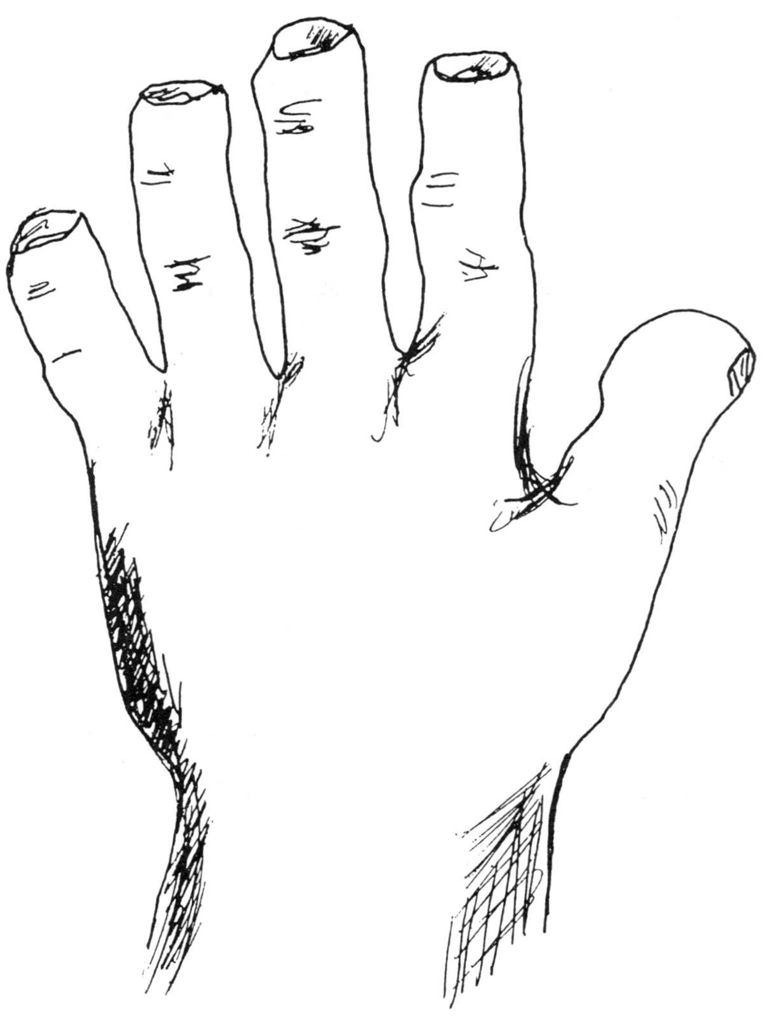

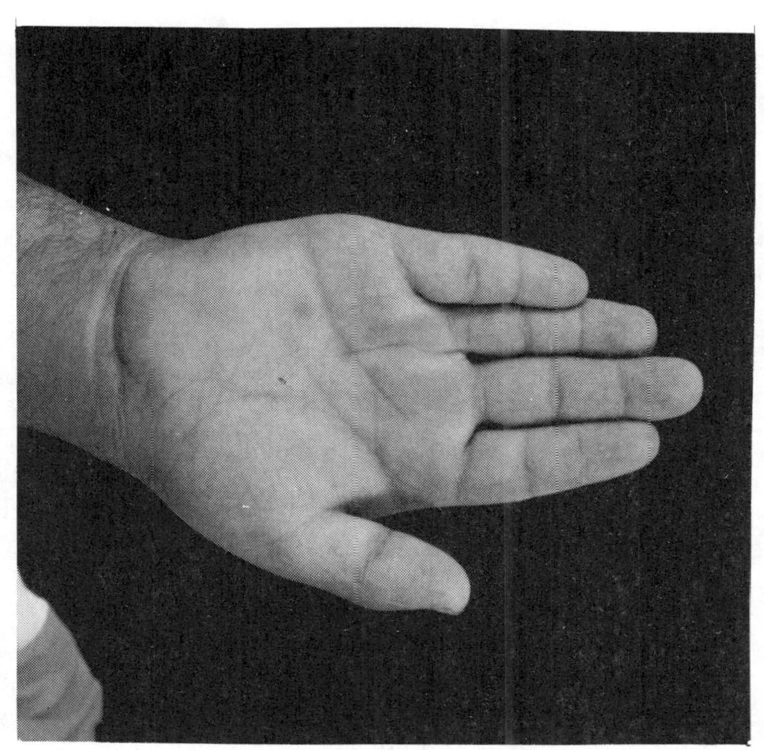

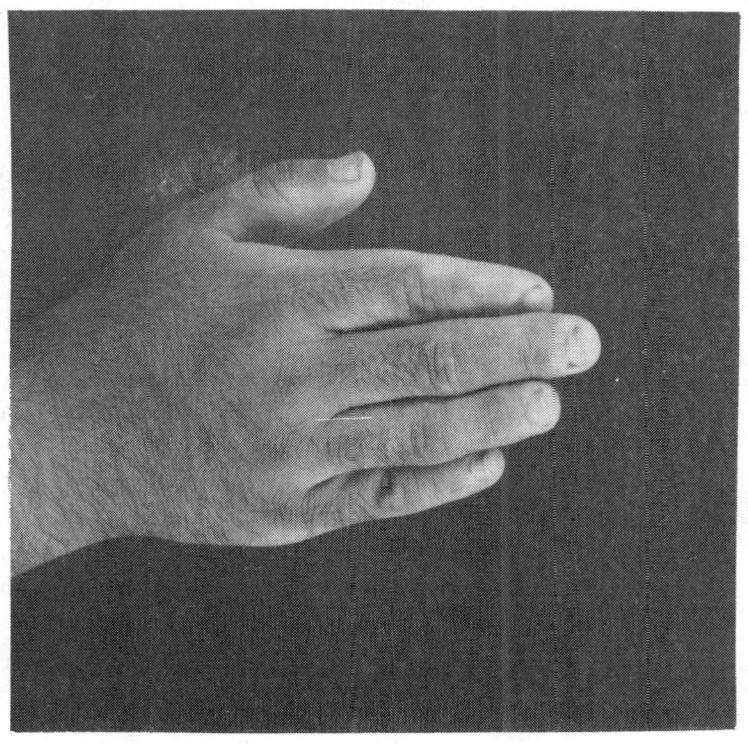

THE SQUARE HAND

The Square hand in its classic form appears in people belonging to an Aryan race, namely the British, Germans, Scandinavians, Swiss, etc.

DESCRIPTION

The palm is square at its base and similarly square at the roots of the fingers, as well as square at the tips of the fingers, which are smooth without extending or widening at the joints. The finger-nails are square as well. The thumb is usually well-developed, with a square top-joint (will-joint) which includes the nail.

Characteristic Head Line of the Square hand – a straight or diagonal line extending across the palm.

The owner of the Square hand is generally the useful or practical type, and blessed with the skills and the ability to use them. They are punctual, accurate and efficient people, who prefer order, rules, and discipline. They lead their lives according to a schedule, with a time and a place for everything, including their households or hobbies.

They are intelligent people with the capacity for rational thinking as far as their decisions are concerned but they are also stubborn and persevering. They do lack vision and originality, however, and tend to be as 'square' as their palms. They seek and are interested in the material and practial aspects of existence. The basic dominating characteristics of their personality are logic and practicality, and they therefore tend to look for the material basis of their pursuits. They are attracted to banking, business or similar occupations which involve dealing with money. If they have analytical qualities (a straight Head line) they are likely to succeed in occupations dealing with the natural sciences, mathematics and physics.

People with Square hands have a developed sense of responsibility and can usually be trusted. The governing characteristic of their personalities is one of practicality and decisiveness.

The Square Hand

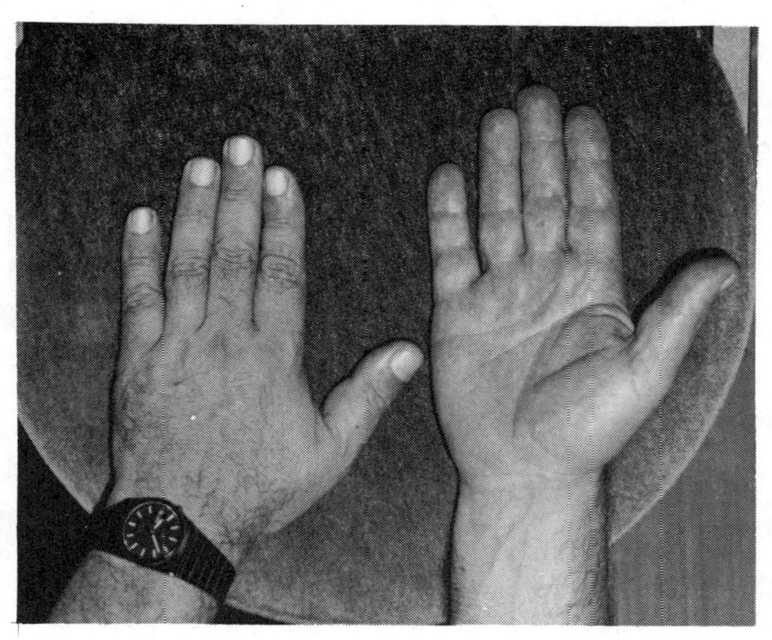

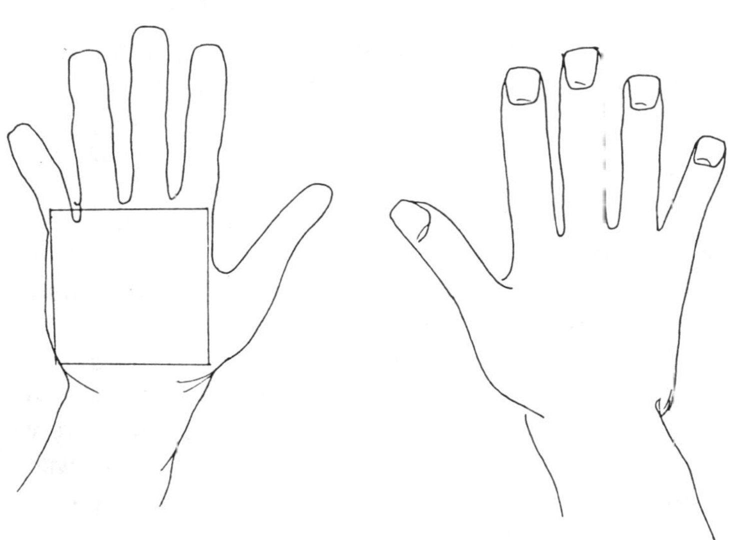

THE LARGE HAND (or FLAT HAND)

The large hand is wide at the base and narrower towards the fingers, or the contrary- narrow at the base and wider towards the fingers, forming a sort of inverted trapeze. The fingers widen towards the tips, and resemble a leaf. The nails resemble a shell, and the thumb also widens at the will joint while its lower part is narrow.

The Typical Head line of the Large Hand is the Arched Headline which touches the Moon Mount.

The special traits of the wide hand is the love of action, energy and independence – with the most marked characteristic being a freedom of spirit and imagination. Hence, one can find this type of hand among outstanding scientists and explorers, and also among engineers and those who engage in manual labour. They are full of curiosity, constantly seeking after the unknown and in the main, generally make a name for themselves through their inventions and discoveries. Frequently, the wide hand is soft and relaxed which is an indication of a restless and irritable personality. Such people are subject to changing moods and cannot concentrate on a specific task for any length of time. Vision and independent thinking enable them become extremely creative. One of the typical elements of their personalities is their individualism, which is accompanied by a strong inner drive to act independently without being fettered by routine or conventions. They look for the unique in all their activities, and especially in their careers. This latter element causes them to be frequently misunderstood by society and become argumentative in social situations. At any rate, this side of their personality focuses on the constant need to create something new (build a unique and original building, to perfect advanced inventions, develop theories, etc.) They can pursue such careers as medicine, teaching, music and acting, and will always be distinctive in whatever they undertake. The wide hand always points to very gifted people and indeed owners of such hands are people who contribute a great deal to society and their fellow man. They are also people of considerable courage and daring.

The Large Hand

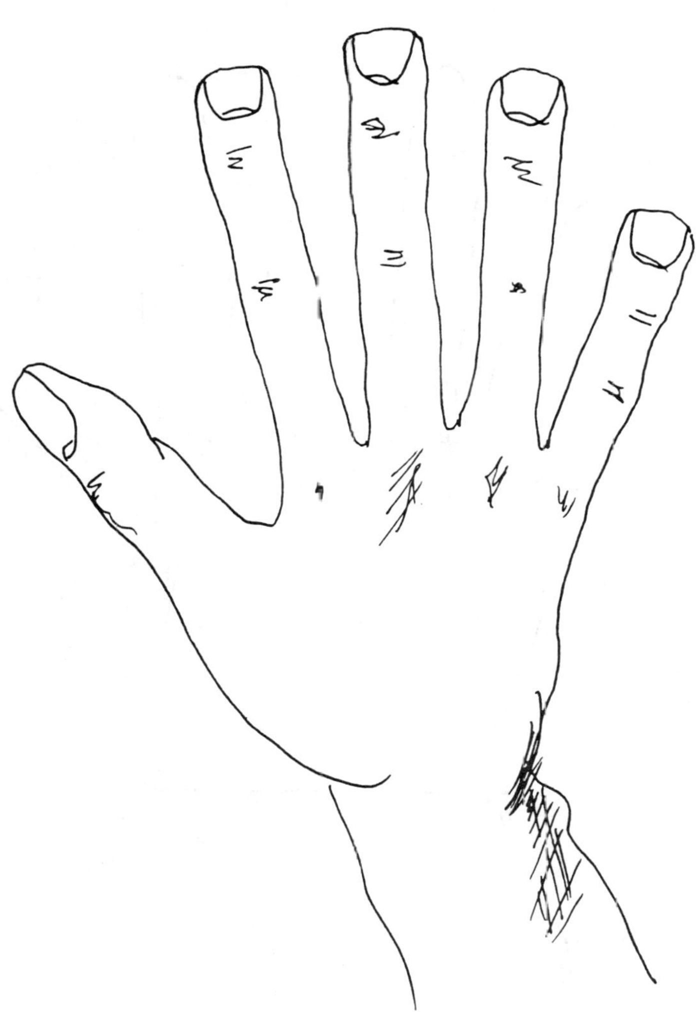

The Large Idealistic Hand

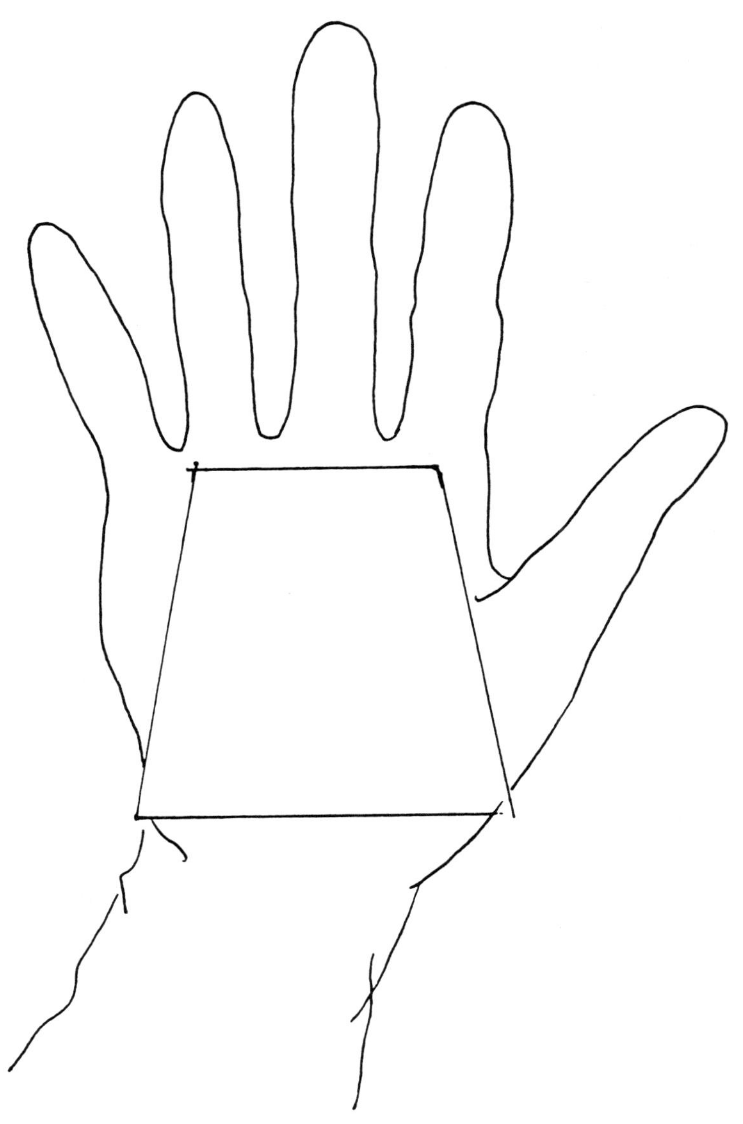

The Large Practical Hand

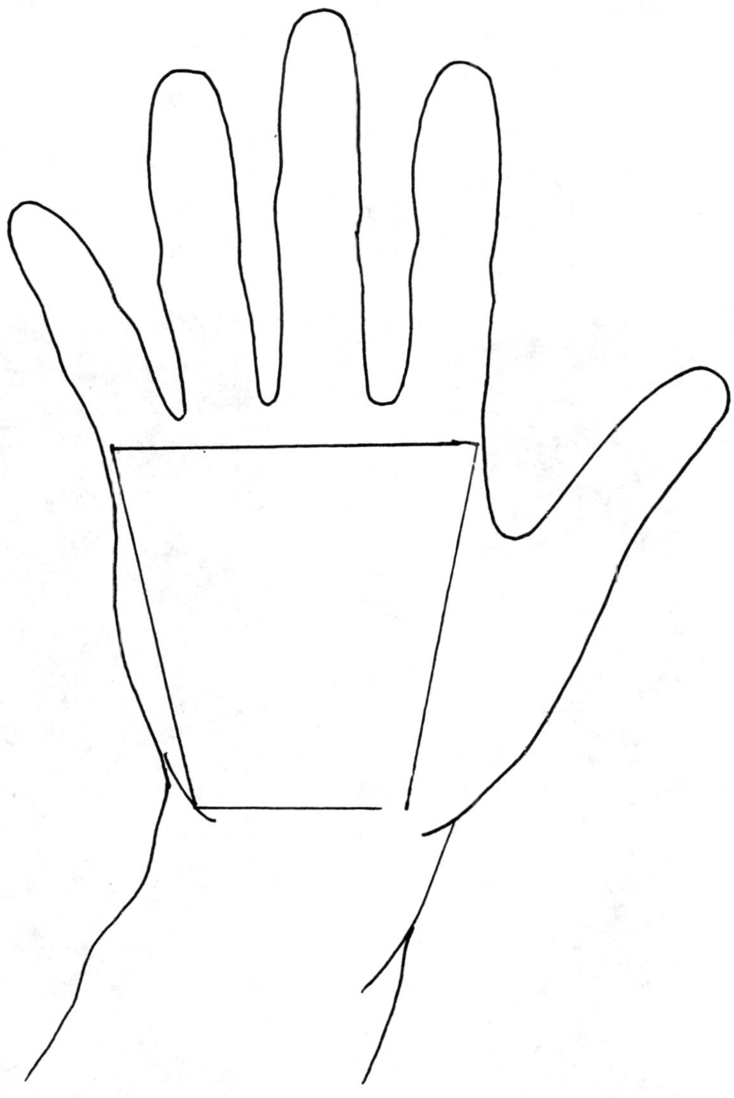

The large hand can be divided into two types, according to their shape:

1) When the hand is wider at the base of the fingers, and becomes narrower toward the wrist, it is the more practical of the two types; if the owner of this hand is an inventor, he will use his talents for building engines, ships, railways, etc. Such individuals are rational and very practical.
2) When the hand is wider at the base of the palm and narrow at the base of the fingers. This is the hand of an idealist, and is generally termed "the wider idealistic hand". Owners of such a hand have an inclination and strong motivations to work for society as a whole and are prompted by intellectual and spiritual ideas.

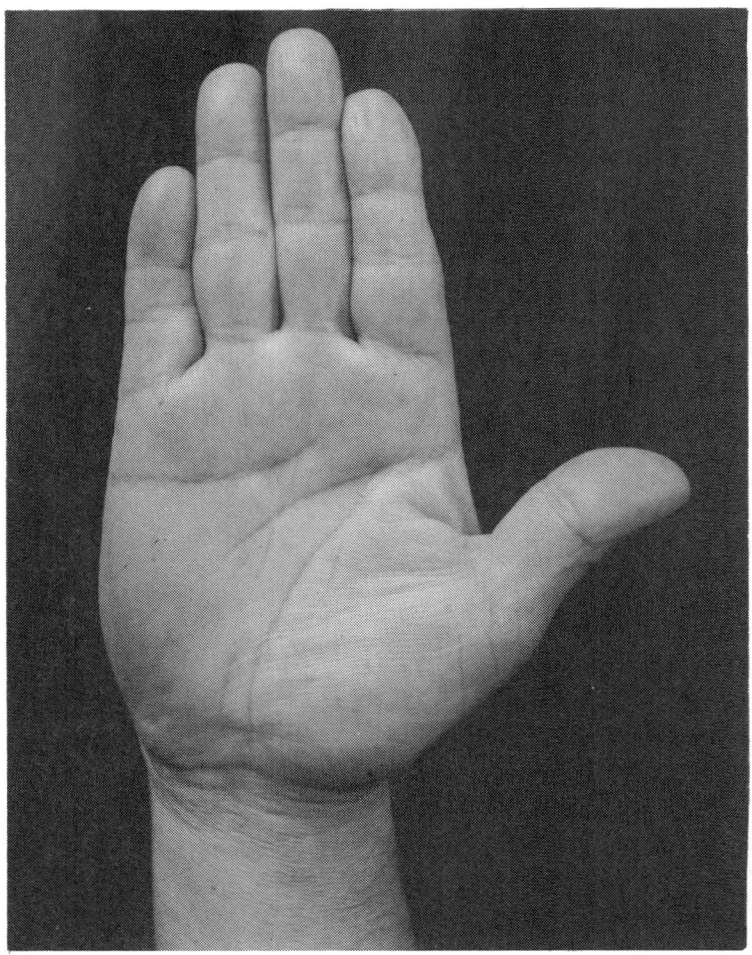

THE PHILOSOPHICAL HAND

DESCRIPTION

The hand is generally long and the fingers are also long and slim, and are characterised by bulging joints which appear to have very little flesh on them. The fingernails are especially large or almond- shaped.

Typical Head line of the philosophical hand – arched and connected with the life-line to a large extent

The philosophical hand bears evidence of a high degree of spirituality and humanism. As the name philosophical denotes, it derives from a combination of the Greek "philo", meaning 'lover of', and "sophia" – wisdom. This is the hand of someone who is deeply interested in wisdom but this does not apply to material success, which is not its owner's strong point. Such hands are frequently to be found among the Eastern peoples, especially in India, where mystical ideas are particularly advanced. As to their characteristics, these people are very sensitive, unusually intuitive and secretive, who weigh their opinions and express themselves with care, who are blessed with serenity and who generally approach their actions in a basic and thorough manner.

The philosophic hand is that of the student and the teacher: they are people who love to study and are inclined to completely submerge themselves in their studies, and are keen on researching and the intellectual development of ideas. At the same time, they are rather unworldly and impractical and frequently encounter problems in dealing with material and economic concerns and can be easily led astray in money matters (especially when the Head line is arched and the heart-line is long.)

The owners of this hand are the most humane and are generally engaged in occupations dealing with an understanding of and aid to their fellow members of society. It can be found among doctors, psychologists, teachers and is particularly prevalent among people who occupy key positions within the context of their religion. As stated, their owners are blessed with a marked intuitive sense and would therefore succeed in such pursuits.

The Philosophical Hand

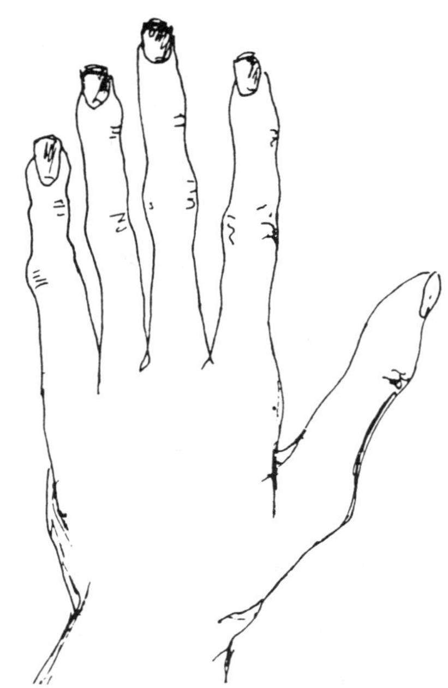

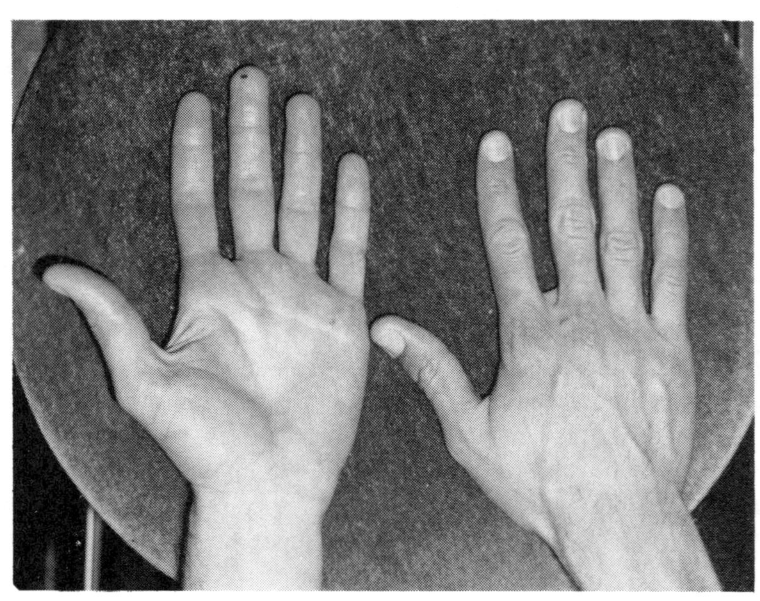

THE CONICAL HAND

DESCRIPTION

the palm is rectangular and the fingers become pointed towards the tips. The joints are smooth and the nails generally narrow and long.

Typical Head line in a conical hand is arched to a limited degree.

Characteristics of the Conical Hand

The most typical trait of the bearer of this hand is the love of art in all its guises. This strong feeling is directed in particular to music and painting. The owners of this hand generally possess good taste and are sensitive to color and beauty. This type of hand is common among the Italians, the Greeks, and the people of the Levant.

The singular qualities of this hand are impulsiveness and desire. Possessors of this type of hand are entirely lacking in patience and tire easily. They are sensitive and tend to display such characteristics as laziness and pleasure-seeking. They are both clever and quick-witted and are generally considered very intelligent. One of their weaknesses, however, is that they are unable to probe deeply into any field and their knowledge is superficial and acquired mainly with the intention of impressing others. They also frequently judge things too impulsively. Despite the fact that they are thought of as good conversationalists and are often the center of any social gathering, the negative side of their characters (impulsiveness and desire) can make people keep their distance.

In social contacts, the owners of the conical hand are quick to lose their tempers as well as to take offense, while being proud-spirited and shallow in their relationship to friendship and love. There are elements of egoism and egocentricity in their personalities and are inclined to place too much emphasis on themselves and their personal needs.

This type of hand is rightly called the "artistic type" but only in rare cases are the owners of this type of hand capable of fulfilling their artistic ideas in practice. More than others, they are quick to react to music, the subtlety of colors, tears, joy, and the surrounding atmosphere in general, but they are also extremely sentimental and easily reach the peak of enthusiasm, which is immediately followed by the depths of sadness and despair.

One frequently finds conical hands among public figures, such as actors, singers, orators, and anyone whose career is based on arousing emotions. In order to be able to express their talents in a practical fashion, it is helpful if elements of the sqare hand are also present. The Head line, when it is emphasized at its beginning and its end, can also lend support to this type of personality or supply it with the ambition which will move and drive it forward.

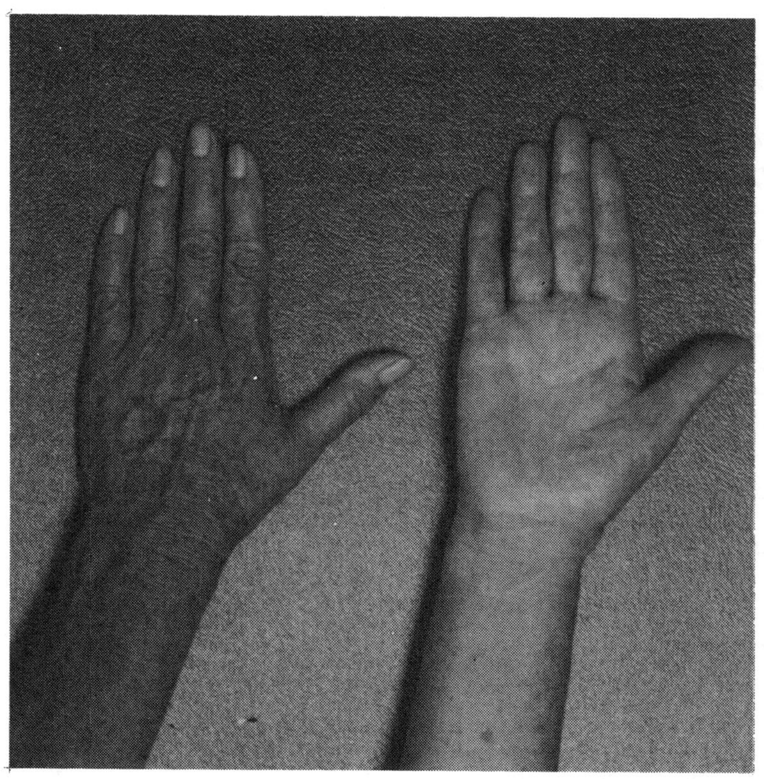

Note that the fingers become narrow towards the tips

The Conical Hand

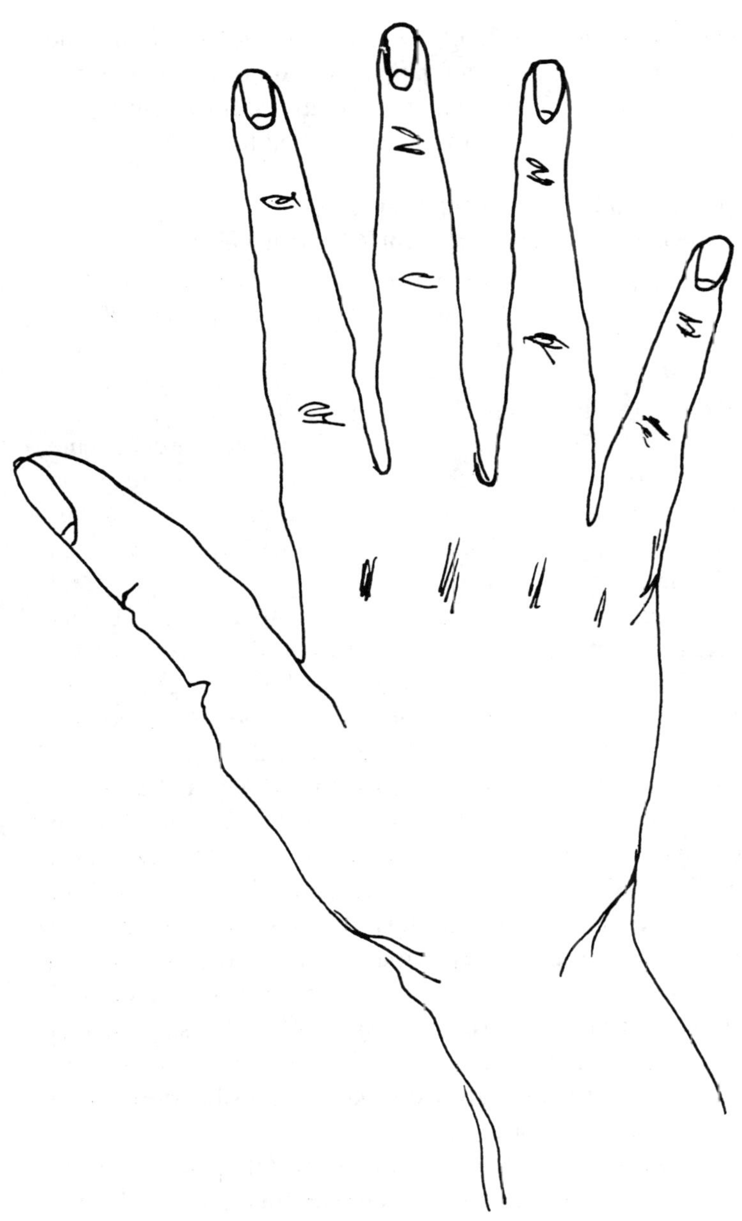

THE EMOTIONAL HAND

DESCRIPTION

The palm is rectangular, long, narrow, and fragile-looking. The fingers are delicate and graceful, pointed and long, with almond-shaped fingernails. The hand is generally soft and weak on contact. This hand is the most attractive of all hands.

The typical Head line of the emotional hand – a sharp and arched line moving down to the Moon Mount

This hand expresses sensitivity and sentimentality, at times to a degree which arouses pity. Such individuals have very delicate personalities and cannot cope with life's problems (particularly in the material sense). The possessors of this type of hand are extremely impractical, and devote their lives to improving society and helping their fellow-beings. Naturally, such people contribute immensely to society and their environment. They are of an idealistic nature and tend to thrive on dreams and illusions, "afloat". They appreciate beauty in any form, with a developed sense for art. They are delicate, quiet, know how to keep a secret and are given to trusting almost everyone. As a result, they are ofter the target of foul behaviour on the part of those they have trusted. They are completely unaware of how one goes about being practical, and thus it is clear that this is not the hand of a business-man or an accountant. Variety appeals to them; music, happiness and sorrow, is expressed with subtlety and in many forms. Owners of the emotional hand are basically religious and feel intensely the mystery of existence. They are blessed with a highly developed intuition and display considerable sensitivity and can serve as excellent mediums. At the same time, they are extremely intelligent, very capable of serious study and understanding. Their nervous systems are sensitive and vulnerable, which may explain their tendency to succumb to various psychosomatic illnesses (such as migraine, ulcers and asthma). They should be advised to keep a sensible diet and to indulge in intensive sporting activities.

In other words, one can define the owners of these lovely hands as people who love all humankind – but they themselves will have to suffer in our materialistic world.

Note: If there is also a Head line denoting mathematical ability in this emotional hand, it may help its owners by giving them a greater sense of practicality.

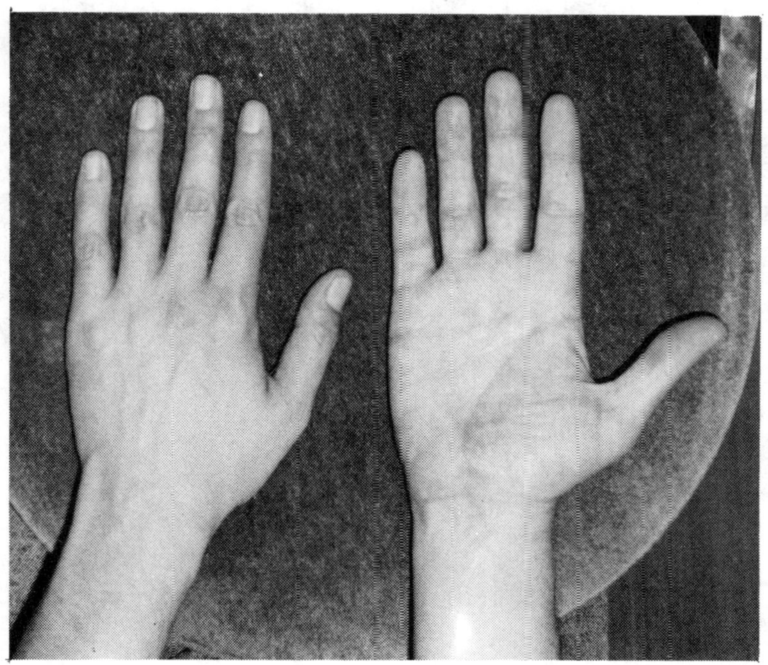

The Emotional Hand

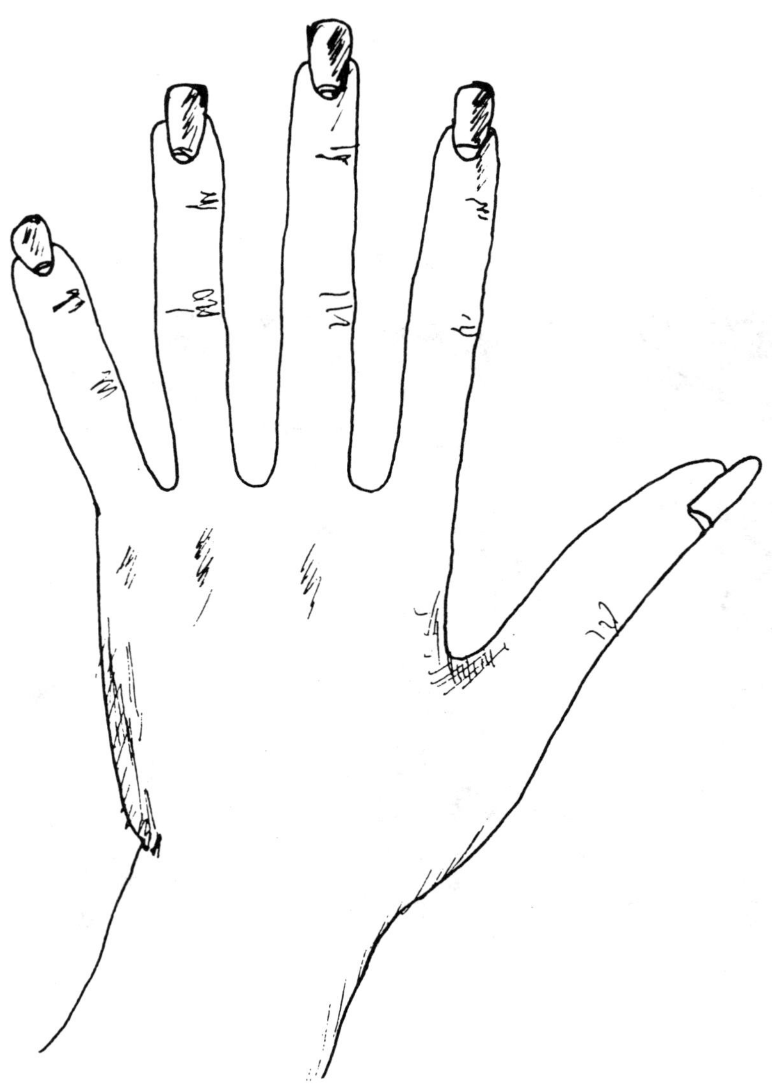

THE MIXED HAND

DESCRIPTION

This is a difficult hand to describe, as elements from other types of hands are likely to appear here. For instance, one can find an element from the philosophical hand in the finger joints while at the same time, one of the fingers may be conical and another square, while the palm itself may belong to still another category. What actually places it in the mixed category is its owner's variety of ideas, many-sided personality, and a lack of perseverence or ability to focus on one specific area. Hence, the possessors of this hand are inclined to devote themselves to a number of occupations at the same time – all in a rather superficial manner. They are brilliant conversationalists and interesting individuals and make an outward impression of being very intelligent, but the absence of staying power and their many interests leads to a lack of depth in their knowledge and ways of thinking.

As the possessors of the mixed hand are blessed with a talent for expressing themselves and the ability to see and judge people and situations from various angles, they can be good diplomats, successful members of the media (television and newspaper correspondents, for instance) and the moderators or chairmen of large social events. As mentioned, they have many aspects to their personalities and can get along well with all types of people.

The most singular element in their personalties is their ability to adjust to circumstances. They are restless and change their minds and needs incessantly, and due to their lack of stability, will infrequently succeed in their pursuits. However, if we find in the mixed hand an element of the square hand plus a straight, long, and emphatic Head line, which is not attached to the Life line, this will afford them the possibility of succeeding and add to their staying power in their work and career.

The Mixed Hand

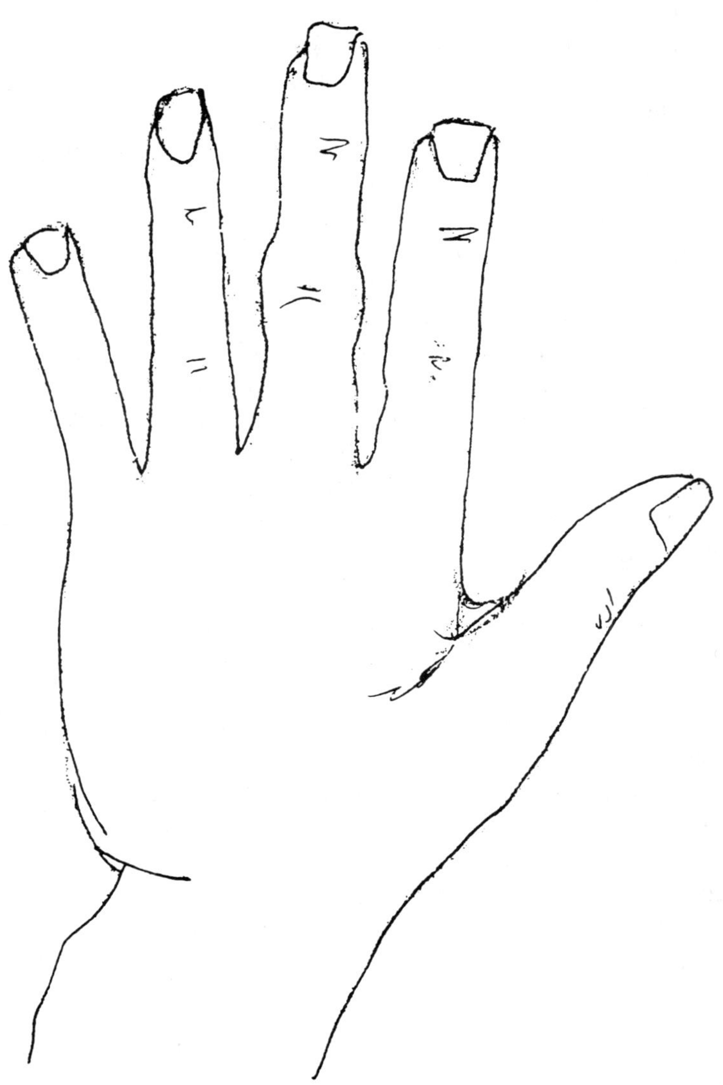

The Mixed Hand

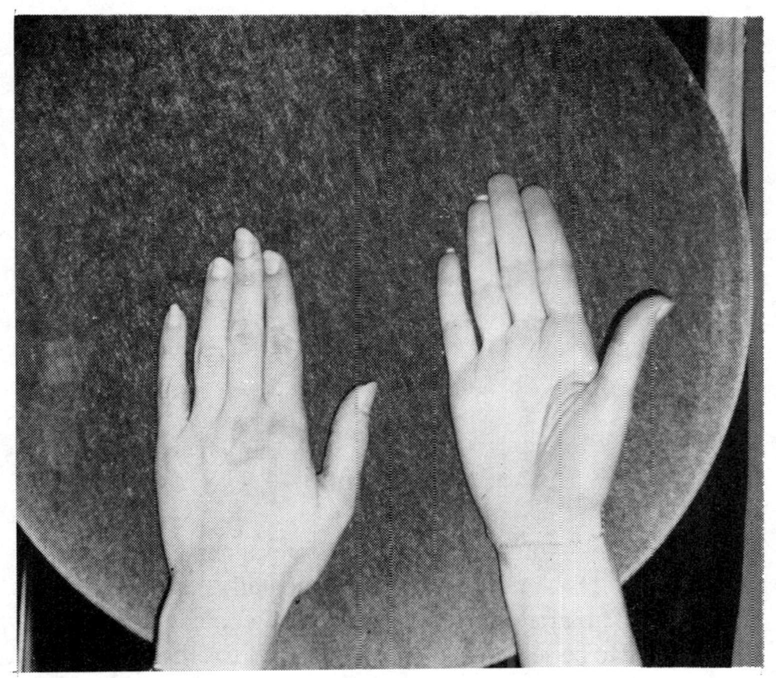

FLEXIBILITY OF THE PALM

A Stiff Palm

A palm which is stiff to the touch points to a difficult and unbending person, with an anxious and nervous personality. Such an individual hesitates to express his emotions and therefore has problems relating to society.

An Elastic Palm

This palm is soft and spongy, rather like cotton wool to the touch. It denotes a naturally optimistic individual, capable of coping with health and other of life's problems. The owner of this hand is blessed with the ability to deal well with stressful situations, and is very industrious and the owner of a sensual nature. (In the course of my work, I have learned that the survivors of the Holocaust generally had elastic palms, which evidently denotes an abiding capacity to survive).

A Soft Palm

A palm which is soft to the touch indicates a person who seeks a life of ease. This individual is fundamentally lazy, appreciates comfort and luxuries, and is very sensual. People with soft hands are inclined to be selfish and even insensitive to others (obviously one should take note of the length and quality of the Heart line).

The Concave Hand

The concave palm is defined as a hand that sinks at its center, a state which indicates a lack of sensitivity to its surroundings and marked egoism. Cheiro claims that this state can be deducted from the quality of the remainder of the lines of the palm and brings bad luck.

THE FINGERS

The shape of the fingers, their size and thickness (in relation to the size of the entire palm and to the rest of the fingers) tell us a great deal about the personality of their owner. Finger length can be compared both from the inner side of the palm or from the back of the palm

Long fingers

Long fingers express love and attention to details, a characteristic which can apply equally to the decor of a room or the management of an office. Owners of such fingers have good taste in matters of dress, in the presentation of food, and in anything which has to do with the aesthetic aspect of life. They have marked artistic leanings and appreciate art in many forms and levels. At the same time, long fingers also indicate a developed intellectual capacity. Their owners are intellectuals capable of prolonged thought but are frequently inadequate in practical matters.

Short Fingers

Short fingers indicate a fickle and impulsive individual. People with (relatively) short fingers are given to hasty reactions and conclusions and quick thinking. They are extremely practical but do not have a great deal of patience.

Short and Thick Fingers

Indicate Egoism.

Flexibility

When the fingers are rigid and bend upward (towards the palm) when extended, indicate the careful and suspicious nature of a closed and introverted person. When the fingers are elastic and bend backward in an arc, their owner possesses considerable charm, has an easy-going personality who tends to compromise easily and is a sociable and popular member of society.

Flexibility Of Fingers

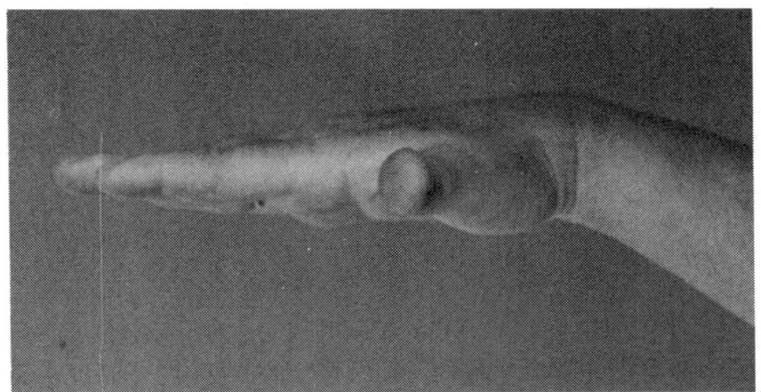

1. Normal stiff fingers

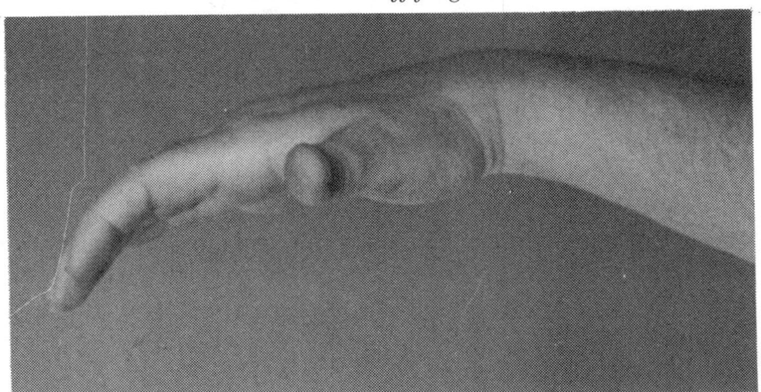

2. Arching towards the palm

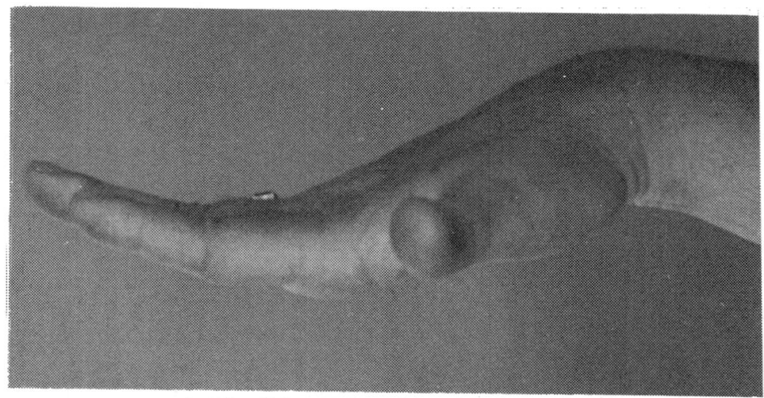

3. Flexible and arching backwards

FINGER RELATIONSHIPS

The Forefinger – Jupiter

The characteristics of the forefinger (Jupiter) are ambition, the desire to dominate, self-respect and the pursuit of justice. The Jupiter finger (also known as the finger of justice or the teacher) indicates the extent of a persons'competitiveness, ambition and leadership qualities.

A Long Jupiter Finger

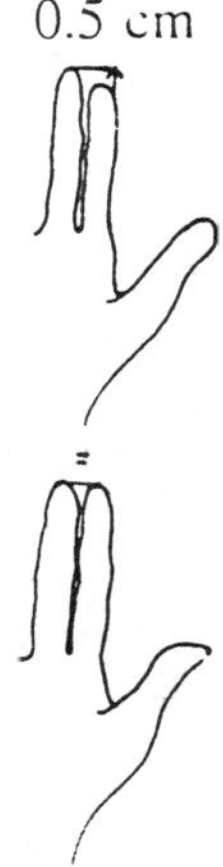

Shorter than its neighbor Saturn by at least 0.5 cm, this length indicates a tendency towards arrogance and haughtiness. This person will be presumptous, extremely ambitious, with aspirations to become a leader and the person who always has to have the final word.

A Jupiter Finger of the same length as Saturn

This phenomena indicates an unusual power-drive. The owner believes himself to be a law unto himself – in other words, a dictator.

A Short Jupiter Finger

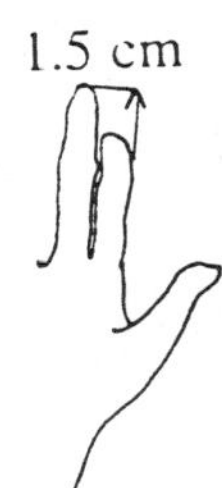

A Jupiter finger which is about 1.5 cm shorter than the Saturn finger indicates a person who is reluctant to take responsibility and will therefore refrain from accepting an executive role or a senior position. The owner of such a finger will overreact to his or her surroundings and is excessively influenced by his peers. This is frequently a sign of an inferiority complex.

Note: An active Jupiter Mount may conteract and balance the negative tendencies of a Jupiter finger which is too short.

A Bent Jupiter Finger

A Jupiter finger bent towards the Saturn finger indicates a strong attachment to one's family. The owner of such a finger is keenly aware of his family obligations and shows a consistent willingness to abide by them.

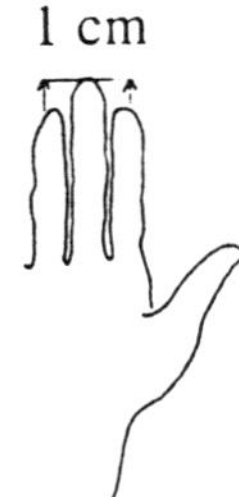

Saturn Finger

The finger known as the Saturn is the middle finger, which is strongly and stably rooted in the palm. This rootedness stands for the person's role as founder of the family and reveals a willingness to maintain the stability of family life.

Saturn symbolizes seriousness, intellectual depth, as well as isolation and a tendency to depression. This finger is considered long if it extends beyond the two fingers on its either side by 1 cm. It is evidence of a ponderous and serious personality and its possessor would be a careful and somewhat isolated person with a writing talent and an inclination towards such subjects as philosophy, sociology and psychology, and at times, also agriculture or botany.

A very long Saturn finger

This finger is considered extremely long when it is 1 cm. longer than its neighbors. Such fingers reveal a personality with mental problems, moodiness, and a strong leaning towards depression, seclusion and bouts of self-pity.

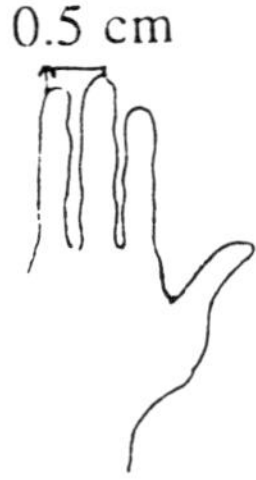

Sun Finger

The Sun finger signifies wealth, happiness and a general state of well-being. It generally indicates the ability to create positive relationships with the surrounding environment and an ability to enjoy life.

A Sun finger which is shorter than Saturn by 0.5 cm is considered a long finger. It indicates strong artistic tendencies, the desire for fame and publicity and hence the ability to work with the public (teaching, social work, welfare, etc.) Other more specific and suitable occupations can be inferred from the palm lines.

A very long Sun finger

This finger, when it is almost the same length as the Saturn finger, indicates a tendency to gamble and a certain lack of responsibility. Such individuals are likely to play with their own and with other peoples' lives. They are usually smooth talkers and enjoy misleading others. They are obsessive about gambling of all kinds and can be seen frequenting casinos as well as the Stock Exchange.

A very short Sun Finger

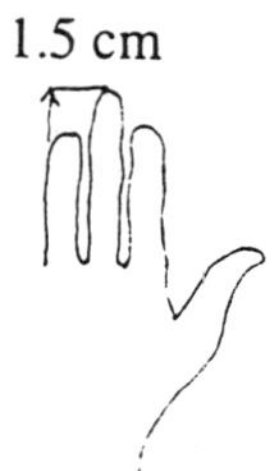

(i.e,. 1.5 cm shorter than the Saturn finger)

While the long Sun finger indicates sociability, the short one is characteristic of the opposite qualities: lack of communication, problematic personal relationships and a complete absence of self-confidence. This type of finger is indicative of someone who is hesitant and finds it very hard to take risks. Hardly someone to be found in a casino, for instance.

A bent Sun Finger (Bent towards Saturn)

Such a phenomena signifies that the owner is conservative and strongly attached to his home and surroundings.

Mercury Finger

The Mercury finger is the small, last finger of the hand. It is related to self-expression – in writing or in speech, and also signifies astuteness in business affairs.

A Long Mercury Finger

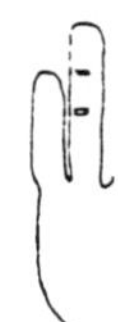

When the Mercury finger reaches the last joint of the Sun finger, it is considered long and indicates a writer or someone who is extremely articulate. Its owner would be an interesting conversation partner, an impressive lecturer or a convincing talker on a large range of subjects. A long and stubby finger is evidence of materialistic motives and greediness.

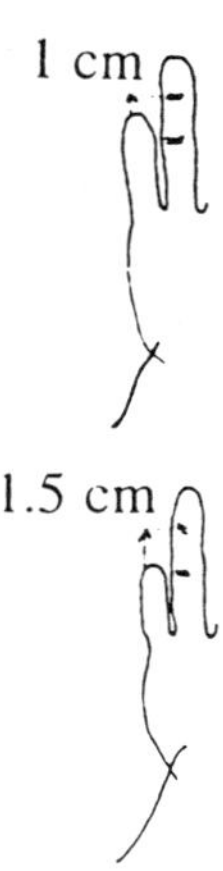

A Short Mercury Finger

The Mercury Finger is considered short when it is less that 1 cm. from the upper joint of the Sun Finger. If the finger is short and thin in relation to the remainder of the fingers – the ability to express oneself is inadequate. Material consideration is also faulty. There may be problems with regard to money matters as a result of careless spending and an inability to look after the family's finances properly.

When the Mercury Finger is thick, this may be a sign that this individual is generous and giving.

Note: When an active mount appears below a short finger, this mount is there to compensate for the lack implied by the short finger.

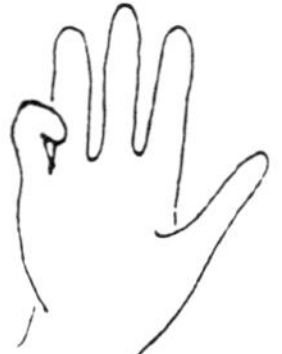

A deformed or bent Mercury Finger turning inward

This is a sign of an inability to communicate with other people (even with the individual's own family) as well as serious problems connected with money.

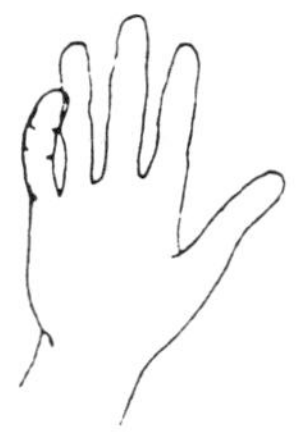

Mercury Finger markedly bent towards the Sun finger

This indicates dishonesty. This person frequently does not recognize the difference between reality and illusion and tends to tell himself accounts of events that never took place, and convinces himself that his inventions are true.

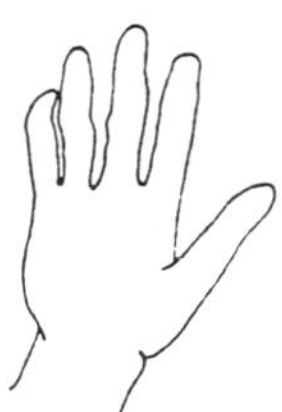

A slightly bent Mercury Finger

This is a sign that there is a deep need for independence and a conflict between this need and the individual's obligations, especially those of the the person's family. This also indicates shrewdness, slyness, as well as sensuality and erotic trains of thought.

THE MOUNTS

A great deal of significance is ascribed to the mounts of the palm with regard to discerning character, and they are of no less importance than the lines themselves. The mounts are protruding folds of skin situated in various parts of the hand. They assume three different sizes: very protruding bumps (swollen), which are defined as active; less protruding bumps, of ordinary dimensions; and a state in which one cannot notice any protrusion at all – that is, flatness. We find seven protrusions of this kind, which are called according to the fingers above them:

1) Jupiter Mount – signifying ambition and the desire to dominate
2) Saturn Mount – signifying seriousness, depression and self-control
3) Sun Mount – signifying acuity, and success in social positions: a sense of humor and a feeling for art
4) Mercury Mount – signifying wisdom, an ability to express oneself in writing and speech, talent for commerce and science
5) Mars Mount – signifying courage, vitality, a fighting spirit and a sense of discretion
6) Venus Mount – signifying love, sensuality and desire
7) Moon Mount – signifying imagination and desire

JUPITER Mount

This mount lies at the base of the first finger (Jupiter finger). If it is active, it indicates a strong desire to dominate, to be a leader and to organize, and also denotes excessive ambition, a great deal of self- respect and concern with reaching one's goal. When this mount is not active, these characteristics will not come to the fore unless the palm displays other signs which bolster up these characteristics.

SATURN Mount

This mount lies at the base of the second finger. If it is active, it indicates seriousness, perseverance, loneliness, and a leaning towards literature and philosophy. When this mount is especially active (huge) this is a presage of depression, a pessimistic attitude, melancholy, egocentricity, isolation and withdrawal from society.

Mounts Of The Palm

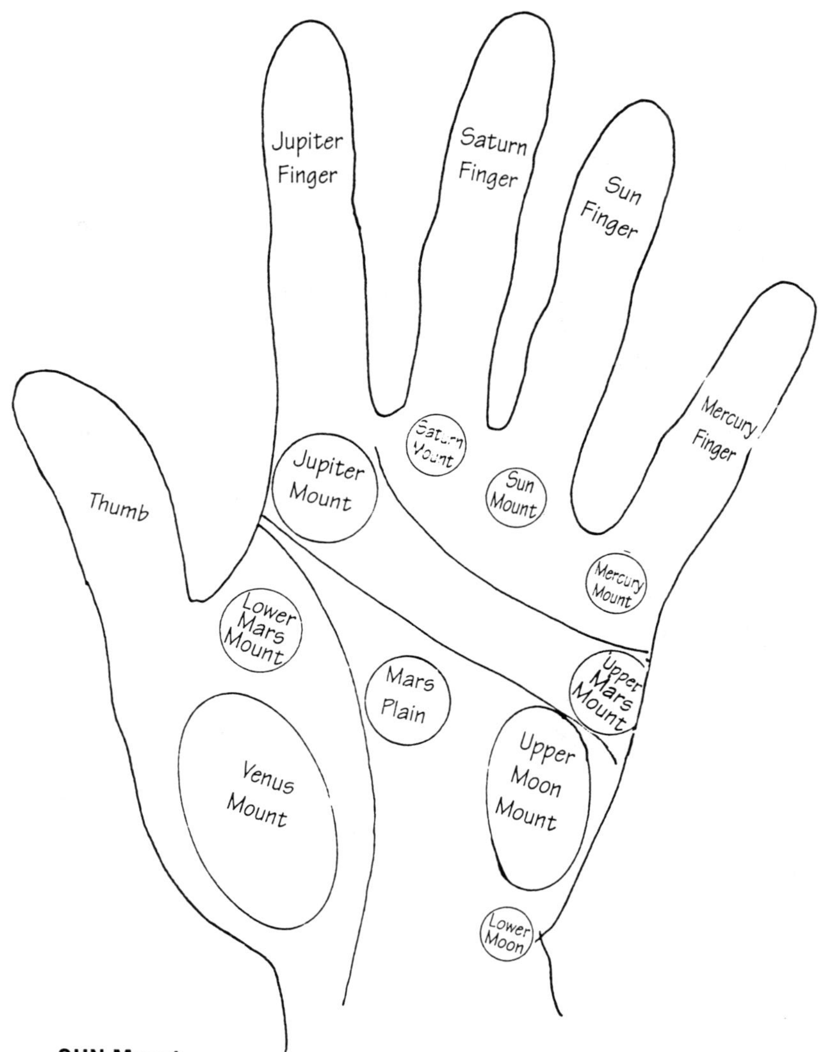

SUN Mount

This mount lies at the base of the third finger. If it is active and well-shaped, it shows an interest in art and an enthusiasm for all forms of beauty. Possessors of hands distinguished by this mount will have an open and generous personality together with a strength of character, a sense of humor and a generally easy-going nature. They are drawn to public activities and society as a whole.

When this mount is unpronounced, it is a negagive sign and produces excessive earnestness and a lack of sufficient flexibility.

MERCURY Mount

This mount is to be found at the base of the fourth finger. If it is protruding, it indicates quick-wittedness, acuity and a well-developed ability to express oneself in writing and speaking. This mount is connected with logic as well as considerable activity, and in those hands in which this mount is developed, it may reveal a talent for sciences, research and/or commerce.

VENUS Mount

This mount is to be found at the base of the thumb, in the area around the Life line. If it is protruding and well-shaped, it denotes an ability to express love and and warmth towards one's life-partner as well as an emotional and artistic nature. People with an active Venus Mount are blessed with much charm and the power to attract the opposite sex, as well as with creativeness and vitality. They are individuals with an open and generous character, conversationally at ease but temperamental.

MARS Mount

The name Mars Mount is actually applied to two different mounts which are to be found in two different areas of the palm: one situated between the upper part of the Life line and the thumb, while the second is to be found in the area stretching from the Heart line to the end of the Head line. The first is called "the lower Mars Mount" and relates mainly to physical characteristics; the second is called the "upper Mars Mount" and relates primarily to intellectual traits.

The Lower MARS Mount

If it is active, this denotes both courage and discretion. Individuals with this mount boast of the ability to make decisions and an adherence to their aims. They do not accept criticism gracefully and hold confirmed and decisive opinions. They are independent thinkers and generally do not tend to consult other people. The major character defects of these "doers" are their impulsive reactions and their lack of self-control. They have a tendency to land in dangerous situations of various kinds, particularly if there is a large gap (more than 5 mm.) between the Head line and the life- line, which is a sign of recklessness or haste. This mount is typical of military personel and those who are involved in all kinds of secret activities.

UPPER MARS Mount

A protruding upper Mars Mount indicates on the part of its owner the capacity for independent thinking as well as to express views and ideas without hesitation, even if they are provocative opinions. People with a developed upper Mars Mount are considered courageous, critical and frequently even agressive. If the lower Mars Mount is also active, this may bring about an excessive degree of antagonism (physical or verbal).

MOON Mount

The Moon Mount stretches from one end of the Head Line until the base of the palm on its outer side, and actually divides it in two: the mount situated beneath the end of the Head Line and called the "Upper Moon Mount", and part of the mount situated beneath it, until the base of the palm – the "Lower Moon Mount". The Moon Mount is considered the source of imagination, romantic inclinations, marked creativity, idealism and travel, the latter mainly at sea. We find prominent and developed moon mounts among many poets and writers, for instance. Individuals with active Moon Mounts are fortunate in having a talent for invention and unique ideas in whatever field they undertake and are attracted to everything which is novel and original. In general, they are also the possessors of a highly- developed intuition. When the Moon Mount is too active, this is a sign that the sexual drive is stressed and that the imagination is unhibitedly linked to this drive. An individual possessing such a mount will be restless and subject to frequent changes of mood, as well as impulsive reactions.

Note: When the Moon Mount and the Venus Mount are large and active to the same extent, the sexual impulses will be particularly strong. When the Moon Mount is active – particularly the lower mount towards the base of the palm – the imagination will be almost impossible to restrain, a situation which can lead to mental confusion. Possessors of huge lower mounts suffer more than most individuals from bouts of anxiety and fear, which may possibly be expressed in the form of hysterical moods and hypochondria.

PROTRUSIONS AT THE TIPS OF THE FINGERS

These are the cushions at the tops of the fingers, as well as midway along the fingers. Their shape has considerable relevance to the indiviual's qualities and traits, to the quality of sensitivity to one's surroundings, to the individual's creativity and inclination towards artistic endeavors.

- ROUND CUSHION – denotes a talent for graphics, delicate handicrafts and an advanced technical sense.
- POINTED CUSHION – is evidence of an pronouced feeling for one's surroundings and a highly developed intuitive sense towards other people. When such an individual is in an alien surrounding, he or she is immediately aware of whether the atmosphere is friendly or otherwise. The spiritual and intellectual contact with others is very developed in people with pointed cushions at the tips of their fingers.

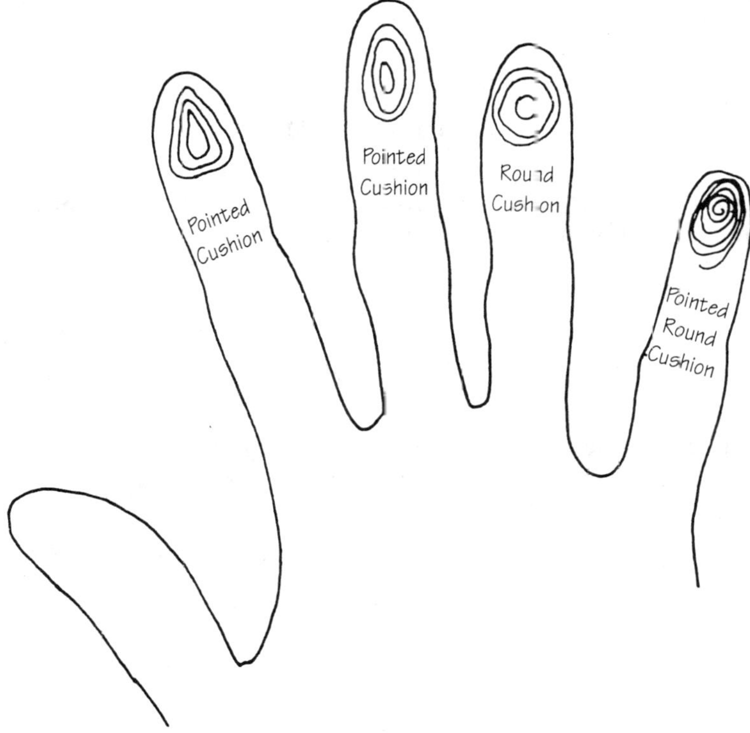

COLOR OF THE PALM

The color of the palm is determined by the inner side of the hand and not by the outer side.

A WHITE AND PALE HAND

indicates someone who is self-centered and shows little interest in others. Healthwise, this person is tendency towards anaemia.

A YELLOW HAND

indicates someone subject to moodiness and depression, sickly, and a particular tendency to suffer from liver and gall problems.

A PINK HAND

indicates an optimistic and exceedingly hopeful personality. Such an individual will be contented and pleased with life.

A REDDISH HAND

can be found among people who are healthy both mentally and physically, with strong desires and a warm personality.

SMOOTH HANDS

Smooth palms, that is, palms with few lines apart from the basic ones, are characteristic of people who are calm and contented with their lot. It would be a mistake to assume that they are unfeeling, for this is not the case. In the main, these individuals are in full control of their feelings and are seldom worried or anxious. But if they are fearful and anxious – there is evidently a good reason for this. Only when the hand is soft is there some justification for considering the person indifferent.

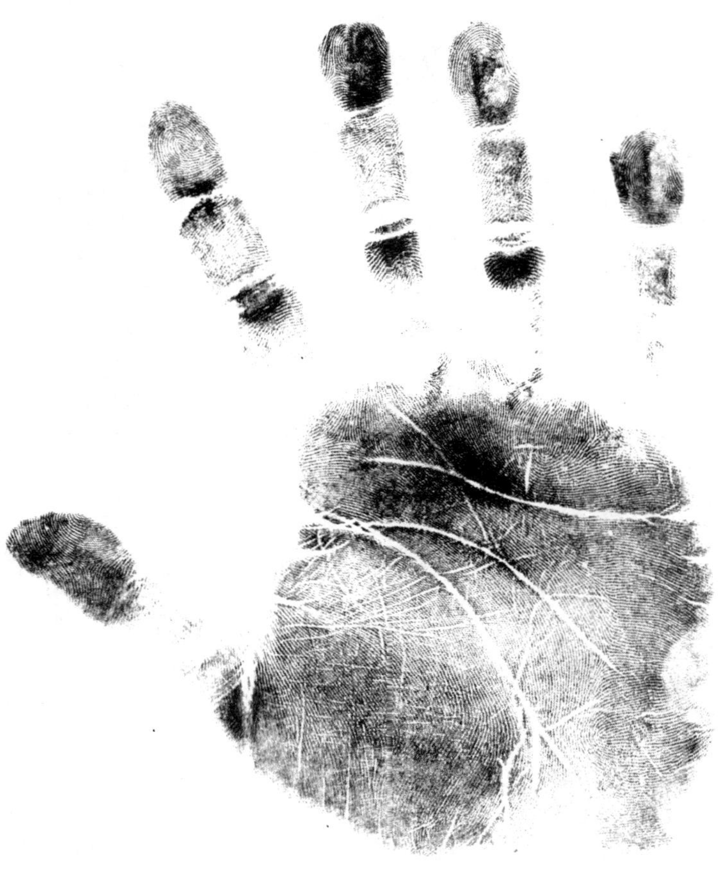

A HEAVILY-LINED PALM

A heavily lined palm is one with many thin lines covering the palm in both horizontal and vertical directions, giving the impression of a network. Such a palm points to a nervous character and an inclination to indulge in excessive anxiety over unimportant matters – particularly in the case of a soft palm. Possessors of such hands are inclined to worry about a variety of imaginary illnesses and other non-existent troubles (this problem is intensified when the lower Moon Mount is huge). If the hand is stiff or elastic, the network of lines indicates a stormy and energetic personality.

THE THUMB

The thumb plays a very important and even decisive role in reading and understanding the palm. The gypsies used the thumb as a primary authoritative source in determining character. They based their judgments and decisions on the angle formed by the thumb and by its general appearance. In India the thumb served as the foundation of an entire study. In Christianity as well, the thumb is accorded considerable importance as it serves as a symbol of the deity, while in the Anglican Church, it is common practice during prayer to make the sign of the cross with the thumb.

It is interesting to note that already in ancient times, the midwives observed that when the new-born baby's fingers closed around the thumb for a number of days after birth, it was a sign that the infant was a weakling. If this continued for some time afterwards, it was generally an indication that the child was feeble-minded, an assumption that was generally borne out at a later stage. It has been proven that all those who were retarded from birth had weak and puny thumbs and some had thumbs which were so weak that they could not assume their proper shape at all. At any rate, almost all feeble-minded people have weak thumbs.

If we examine a chimpanzee's hands, we find that the thumb does not reach the first joint of the Jupiter finger, that is to say that it is very short. The conclusion to be derived from this is that the individual's intellectual capacity will be developed in accordance with the extent to which the thumb is erect and its proportions large. In other words, a person whose thumb is thickly set in its base, short and stubby, will belong to someone who will be crude and of a cruel disposition and brutish instincts, while someone with a long and elegant thumb will be intellectually aware and discriminating, and capable of fulfilling his aspirations.

A well-shaped thumb, leaning downwards and bent towards the fingers, indicates an extremely careful character, closed and fearful, who is difficult to draw out of his shell; that is, someone who is suspicious of others and buttoned up. If the thumb is long – its owner will use his intelligence to get the better of his enemies; if the thumb is short and stubby – its owner may use violence in order to overcome his opponents.

An interesting note involves those who hide their thumbs within their fists, revealing an absence of self-confidence.

To sum up, one can say that a long and well-shaped thumb points to elevated intellectual aspirations while the short and thick thumb indicates a stubborn and brutal quality, and a weak thumb is indicative of an ineffective will-power.

In ancient times, the knowledgeable chirologists were already aware that the thumb is divided into specific areas, representing the three forces dominating our world: **love, reason and will-power**.

- Will-power is represented by the first joint, or the "nail joint",
- Reason is represented by the second joint,
- Love is represented by the third joint.

THE FIRST JOINT: WILL-POWER

When the joint of the first vertebra is large and well-developed or longer than the other joints, this points to a strong will-power (particularly in the mental sphere). The possesssor of this type of thumb-joint, will have ample self-confidence and the capacity to make decisions and carry them out. Note: When the Head line is long, well-defined, smooth and separated from the Life line, the will-power will be able to prove its effectiveness.

THE SECOND JOINT: REASON

To the extent that this joint (the second joint) is longer, it is considered the most developed and indicates a firm and constructive intellect. People whose second joint is long will be capable of intelligent reasoning and deliberation, self-control and given to well- based logical analyses (especially when the Head line is mathematical or straight).

THE THIRD JOINT: LOVE

When the lower knuckle bone protrudes and the joint extending to the base of the palm is long, it can be considered developed. People with this type of developed love-joint can express their feelings in the most genuine and convincing fashion. They have a profound need to express their affection and share their feelings with their mate. If this joint is not well- developed, their sexual relationship will lack emotional content and the relationship will only be successful if the sexual contact is good (one should naturally take the heart-line into account, as well as everything it implies).

THE RELATIONSHIP BETWEEN THE THUMB-JOINTS

If the first joint is unusually developed in relationship to the second and third, then the will-power is unevenly matched both with regard to its force and its size, and a person with this kind of thumb will attempt to achieve things that are beyond his powers or go in for impractical and unrealistic projects.

The Thumb Joints

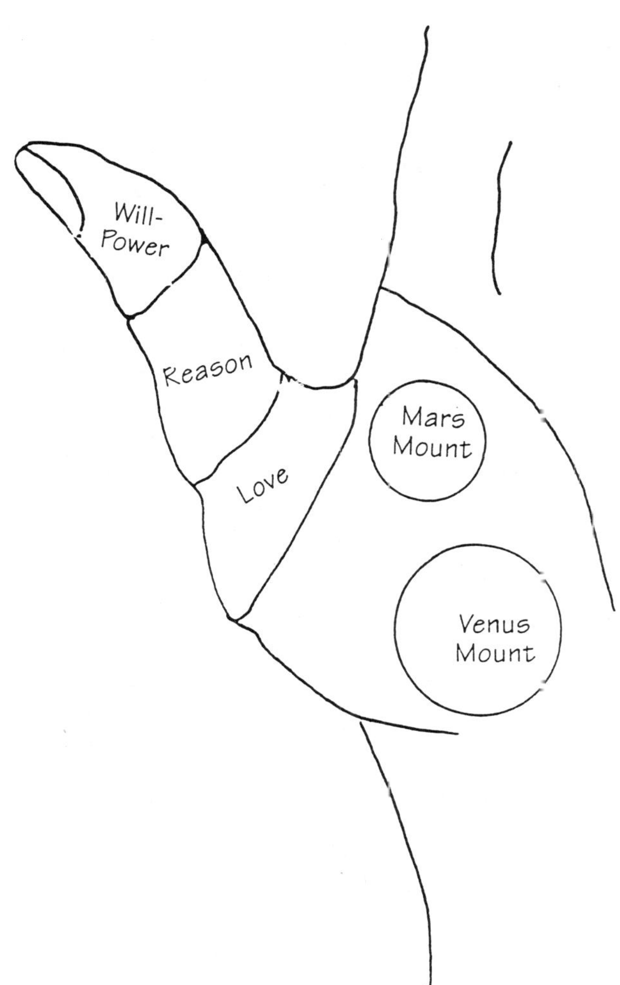

A person possessing a second joint (reason) which is long in relationship to the first joint, will tend to spend more time and effort on consideration and thought and will go in for more planning than in the execution of his ideas.

When the two first joints are equally developed and emphasized to the same degree, then there is a balance between the person's thinking and will- power. Such a person is blessed with the ability to judge matters intelligently and execute his plans in practice. However, the same person also needs an intensive sensitivity to his or her surroundings for his well-laid plans to come to fruition.

When the third joint (the love joint) is more active than the other joints, a person possessing this type of joint will need a great deal of enthusiasm and emotional support in order to enable his will-power express itself in practical terms. He, too, is in need of an intimate emotional contact with his surroundings in order to execute his plans successfully.

A THUMB WITH A FLEXIBLE WILL-POWER JOINT

A flexible thumb which bends backwards indicates a flexible character, and someone who is willing to compromise and is quick to suppress his own desires for the sake of someone else. The owner of such a thumb is inclined to accomodate himself to others' needs and to situations with comparative ease and feels well in whatever type of company he finds himself in. Such an individual will be warm-hearted, loving, very humane and good-humored. He adapts well and quickly to new working conditions and surroundings. His main fault would be the inclination to waste both time and money. (See figure 1.)

A THUMB WITH AN INFLEXIBLE WILL-POWER JOINT

A stiff thumb points to an inflexible and stubborn person, at times quite dogmatic (especially if the hand is also stiff). People with stiff thumbs are very ambitious, determined to succeed and achieve their aspirations. At the same time, they are very responsible individuals who can be relied on in every respect. When they set themselves a particular goal, there is no doubt that they will reach it – or in other words, they follow through on whatever they set out to do, whether it is in the context of their work or their family. They have a marked sense of justice and a considerable capacity for self-control, and it is very difficult to stand up to them. These are the characteristics which go to make up the officers and soldiers who function best at their duties. (See figure 2.)

Note: The inflexible thumb is mainly to be found among politicians or other leaders.

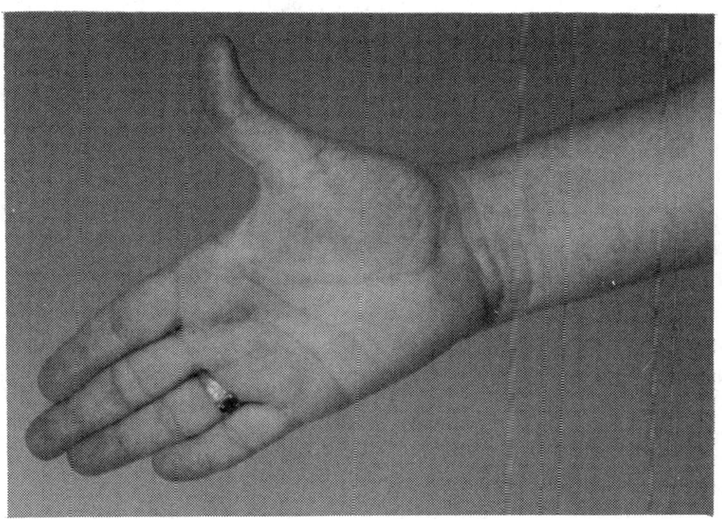

Figure 1. Flexible Thumb

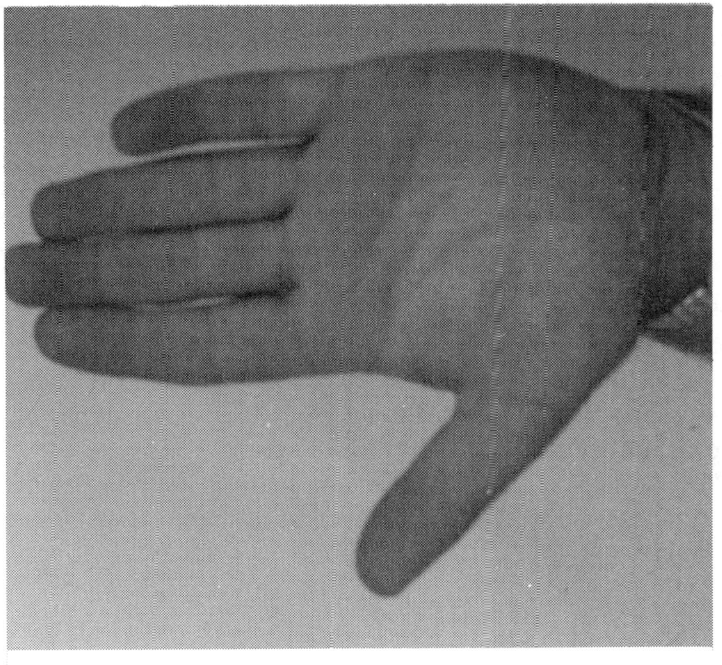

Figure 2. Inflexible Thumb

THUMB WITH WILL-POWER JOINT BENDING INWARDS

When the will-power joint bends inwards, it is a sign that the person whose joint this is, is a difficult and suspicious individual who does not trust a soul, not even those nearest to this person, who is also a closed and stubborn person. It also denotes that the person is stingy with regard to money matters. (See Figure 1. p. 63)

THUMB WITH VARIOUS TYPES OF REASON-JOINT

When the reason-joint is indented, it indicates a sensitive and tactful person who would refrain from offending others. When this joint is full and straight-sided, it implies that its owner is a logical and egoistic individual. A full and awkward, sloping, joint infers a crude and tactless individual of a quarrelsome nature. This type does not take anyone else into consideration and is insistent only on his own needs. There are many elements here of sexual passion. (See Figure 2, pg. 63)

A LONG THUMB

How does one determine whether a thumb is long?

1) If the thumb is as long as or longer than the other fingers, it is considered long:
2) The more the thumb gets nearer the length of the middle joint of the Jupiter finger, it is considered long (one can test this by placing one finger over the other). A long thumb indicates high intelligence, and a strong personality with considerable will-power and self-control. Such an individual knows how to struggle for and reach whatever goal he or she have set for themselves in the most effective manner. (See Figure 2, p. 64).

A SHORT THUMB

A short thumb is a sign of a low degree of intelligence. The shorter the thumb, the more primitive the owner. A short thumb indicates a lesser capacity to cope with life and points to a passionate person who cannot adequately control his instincts.

Note: A long and distinct Head line counters, to some extent, the deficiencies associated with this type of thumb. (See Figure 1, pg. 65).

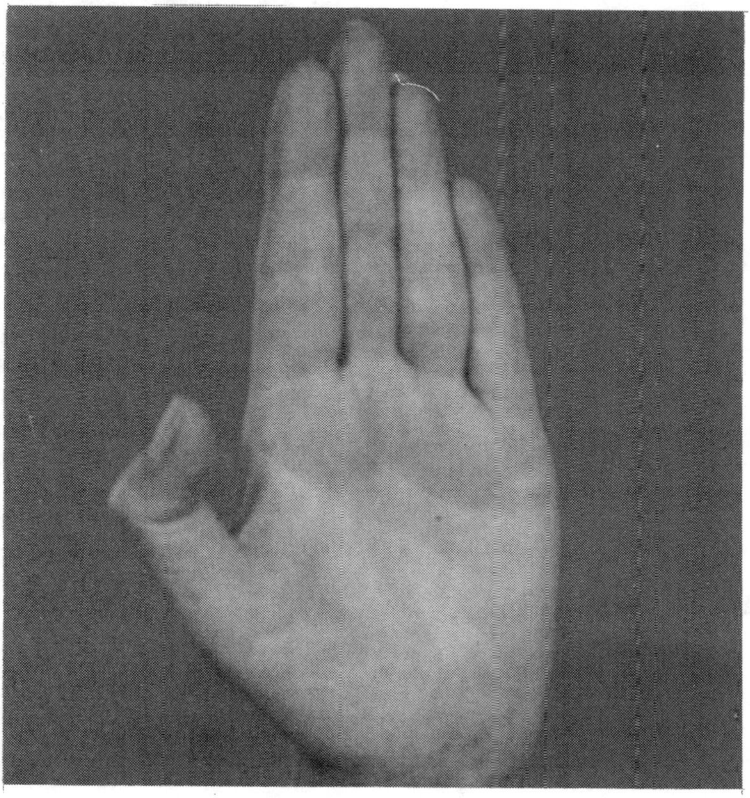

Figure 1.

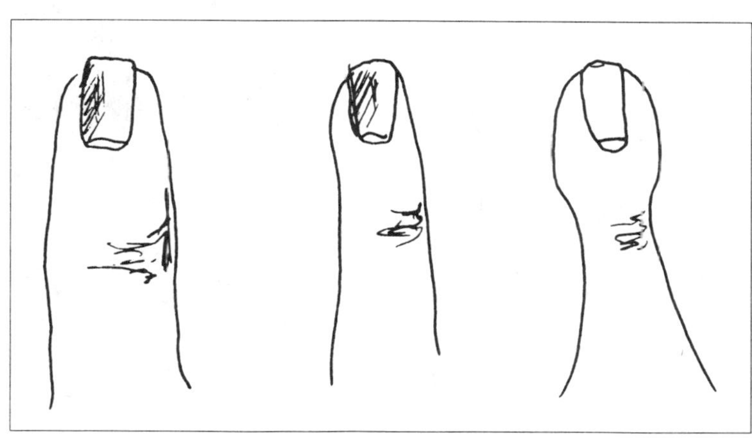

Sloping *Straight* *Waist-like*

Figure 2.

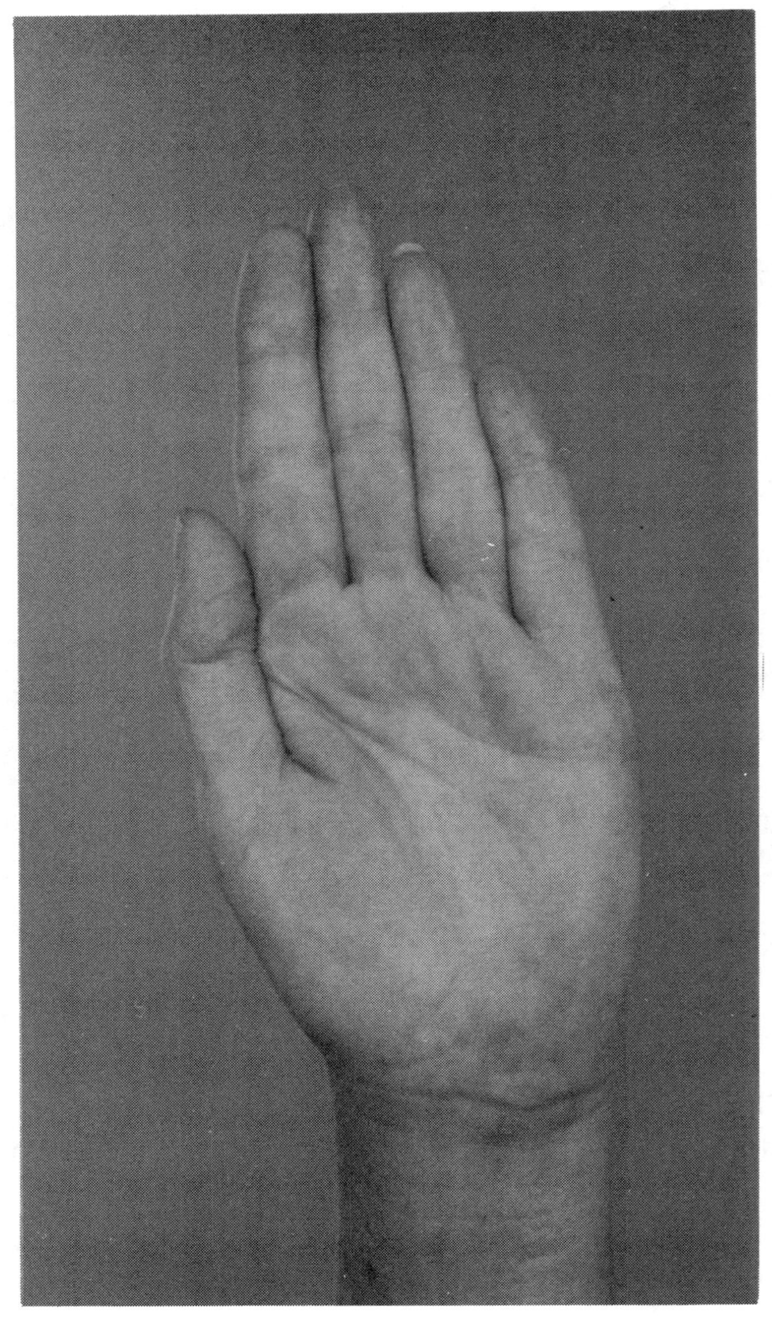

Figure 2: Long Thumb

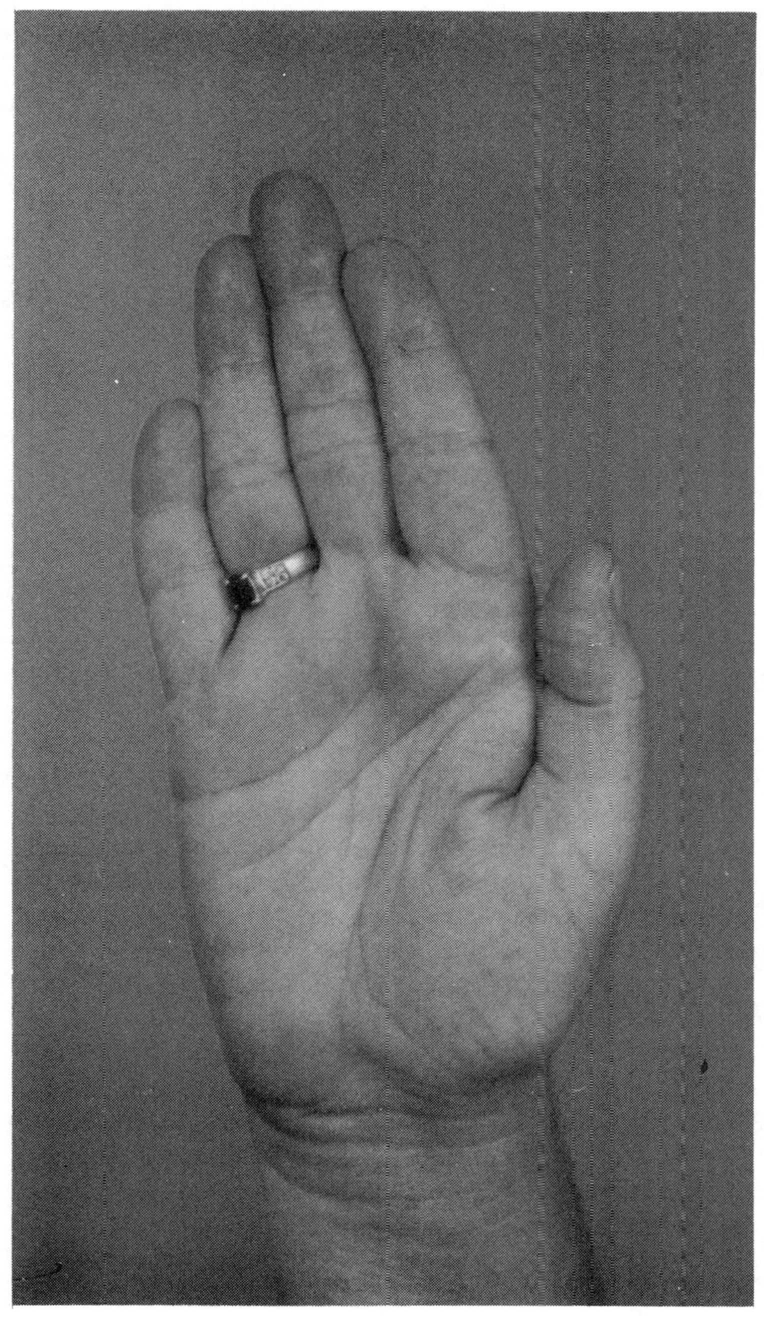

Figure 1: Short Thumb

A LEAF-LIKE THUMB (CLUB)

With this type of thumb, the will-power joint (the first joint) is like a knob: the joint is thick and ungraceful, with a short nail. People with this type of thumb are lacking inhibitions, incline towards extreme nervousness and have no self-control. In most cases, the first joint is stiff, a characteristic which implies perseverence in fulfilling one's goal, which may even drive them to acts of violence and crime when they lose control or when they need to fulfill their desires. They suffer from restlessness and display an element of cruelty in their make-up. Such individuals are usually prone to changing moods (the chirologist Cheiro points out that many murderers have such thumbs). It is worth noting that a good Head line is a restraining factor on the faulty characteristics indicated by the Club thumb.

Note: There is no reason to ascribe all the above deficiencies to this thumb, unless there are also other indications of violence in the hand. (See Figure 1,).

THE ANGLE OF THE THUMB IN RELATIONSHIP TO THE JUPITER FINGER

A 90-DEGREE ANGLE

This will indicate a person who feels comfortable in society, capable of establishing satisfactory social contacts. This individual will react spontaneously and has few inhibitions and little restraint. People with this type of thumb generally say what they think and are not capable of keeping secrets.

A 30-DEGREE ANGLE

This will indicate a person who is utterly different from someone with a 90-degree angle. This would be a very closed and suspicious individual, afraid of exposure, lacking spontaneity and enduring considerable difficulties in trying to establish social contacts. This person would also be excessively careful in everything pertaining to money matters, and could be called miserly.

A 45-DEGREE ANGLE

Many of the characteristics of the possessor of such a thumb is similar to the 30 degree angle, but much less prominent. On the whole, individuals with this type of thumb prefer deeper relationships rather than superficial ones. This diagnosis is not evidence of stinginess, but certainly points to reticence and a certain selectivity in choosing friends, and in every revelation of feeling towards others.

(See Figure 2 – Angles of the thumb)

Figure 1: A Leaf-like Thumb (Club)

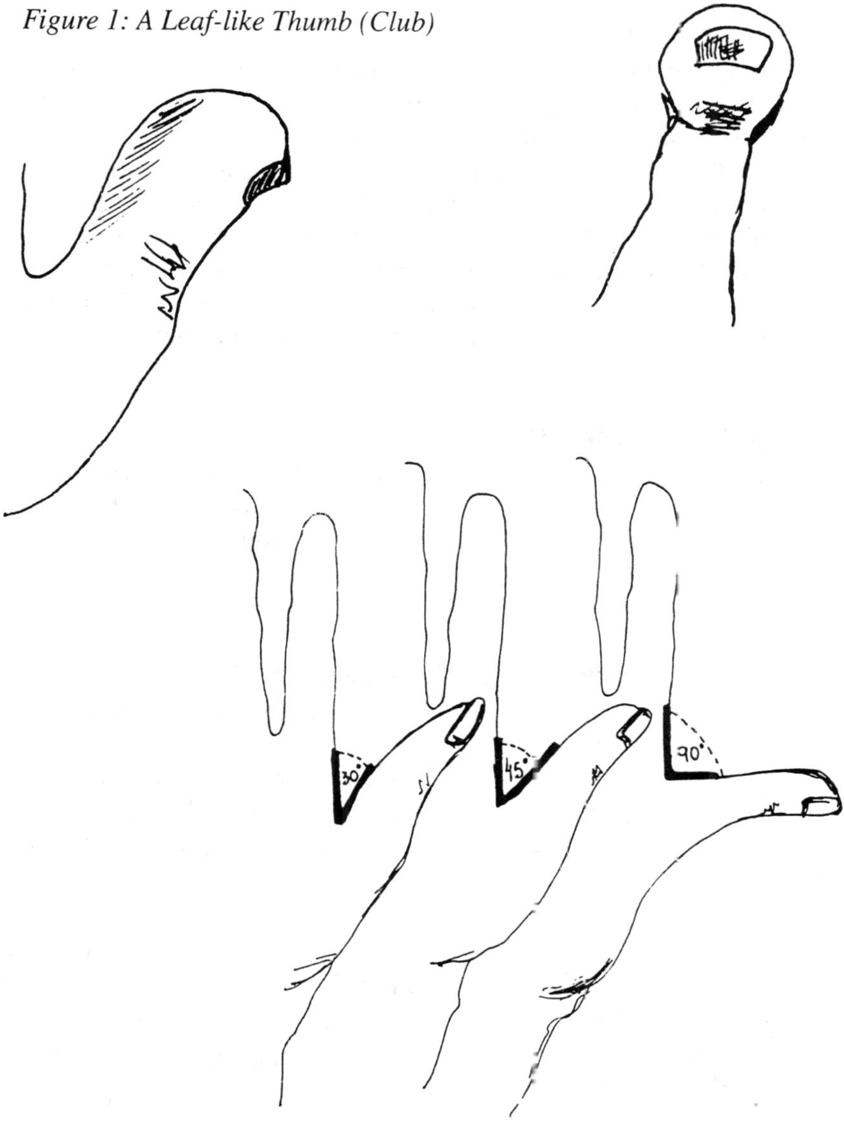

Figure 2: Angles of the Thumb

FINGERNAILS

Determining illnesses on the basis of the conditions and shape of the nails.

The nails are a clear guide to every aspect of the individual's health and illnesses; they also supply considerable information about the character of the individual and hence one can discern personality traits with some degree of certainty.

On the whole, short fingernails generally indicate a leaning towards heart diseases. People with such fingernails are also likely to suffer from problems in the lower parts of their bodies, and also internal organs. People with long fingernails, on the other hand, are inclined to suffer from medical problems in the upper parts of their bodies (the head, the lungs and the chest).

LONG NAILS

Generally an indication of illnesses relating to eye-sight and the chest. The situation will be more severe when the nails are soft and ribbed.

LARGE AND BROAD NAILS (SQUARE)

Indicate a tendency to throat pains and infections, ailments of the bronchial tubes, a possibility of asthma, and spastic brochitis. When the nails are long and broad at the tips, and bluish in appearance, this condition points to some disorder of the circulatory system and a weakness of the heart.

NARROW AND LONG NAILS

If one notices horizontal ridges on the surface of the nail, this may be evidence of general weakness and fragility. A narrow and long nail may also point to spinal problems.

SHORT NAILS

SHORT NAILS, THIN AND FLAT AT THE BASE

If there are no crescents at the base of the nail, this implies a weak circulatory system (while large crescents indicate a satisfactory circulatory system).

SHORT AND FLAT NAILS, DEEPLY EMBEDDED IN THE FLESH AT ITS BASE

This indicates disorders of the nervous system.

SHORT AND FLAT NAILS CURVING OUTWARDS (Shell-shaped)

Indicates the possibility of a stroke (deriving from a temporary neurotic state).

CRESCENTS AT THE BASE OF THE NAILS

When the crescents are very large, this is an indication that the circulation is too active owing to an accelerated heart beat. When there are no crescents, this points to a weak heart and a tendency to heart attacks or other disorders of the heart.

WHITE SPOTS ON THE NAILS

Such marks are evidence of a weak nervous system or are due to excessive stress. As a rule, if the nail is strong and pink and does not break frequently – this is an indication of good health. On the other hand, if the nail is fragile and bluish, this is a warning sign of failing health.

HORIZONTAL RIDGES ACROSS THE NAIL

Horizontal ridges on the surface of the nail are a negative sign indicating a weak nervous system and a general decline in the person's state of health. The time-span of this decline is measured from the base of the nail upwards. From the base of the nail – the assumed time-span is a month. When these ridges appear from the middle of the nail upwards, the time indicated is four months, and when they appear at the edge of the nail, the decline is thought to have taken nine months (the growth of an entire nail takes nine months).

DIAGNOSING CHARACTER FROM THE NAILS

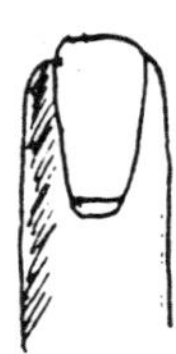

LONG NAILS

People with long nails are more easy-going and polite than those with short nails. They refrain from expressing criticism, are considerate, humane and possess both patience and tolerance. They have a marked tendency to occupy positions dealing with social welfare, such as medicine, teaching, and the care of children and the elderly.

LONG AND NARROW NAILS

Nails of this type are evidence of an artistic and sensitive nature. They are generally fond of poetry, painting, and the fine arts. They are blessed with a highly developed aesthetic sense and consider beauty as the highest of ideals. However, at the same time, they are inclined to indulge in day-dreams and are generally not very realistic, preferring not to face the facts of life directly.

SHORT NAILS

Short nails are typical of people who are extremely critical, even towards themselves. They are quick-witted and swiftly grasp the essence of situations.

They are shrewd, clever, and capable of serious judgment. Their thought processes are generally speedy, and before one can finish a sentence, they are aware of what one intended to say. They enjoy argumentation and are difficult to down in a verbal contest. They are inwardly restless and not very patient – a combination which leads to an overly aggressive character.

SHORT NAILS – WIDER THAN THEIR LENGTH

People with this type of nails are quarrelsome and tend to interfere in other people's affairs.

Note: Toe-nails which grow into the flesh of the toe are indications of an anxious and nervous individual.

SQUARE NAILS (OF EQUAL LENGTH AND BREADTH)

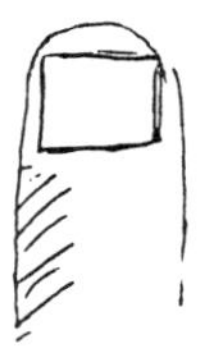

These nails are typical of the square hand and hence all the characteristics of the square hand also apply to the owners of square nails: logic, practicality, considered judgment and an inclination towards pragmatic occupations.

SHELL-SHAPED NAILS

Nails in the form of shells are indicative of a person with a talent for the various applied arts (handicrafts, painting, graphic art, design, etc.) Possessors of this type of nail are individualists and original in the way they think and work. They are also rebellious and do not accept domination from any source, preferring to work according to their own individual concepts.

The Palm Lines

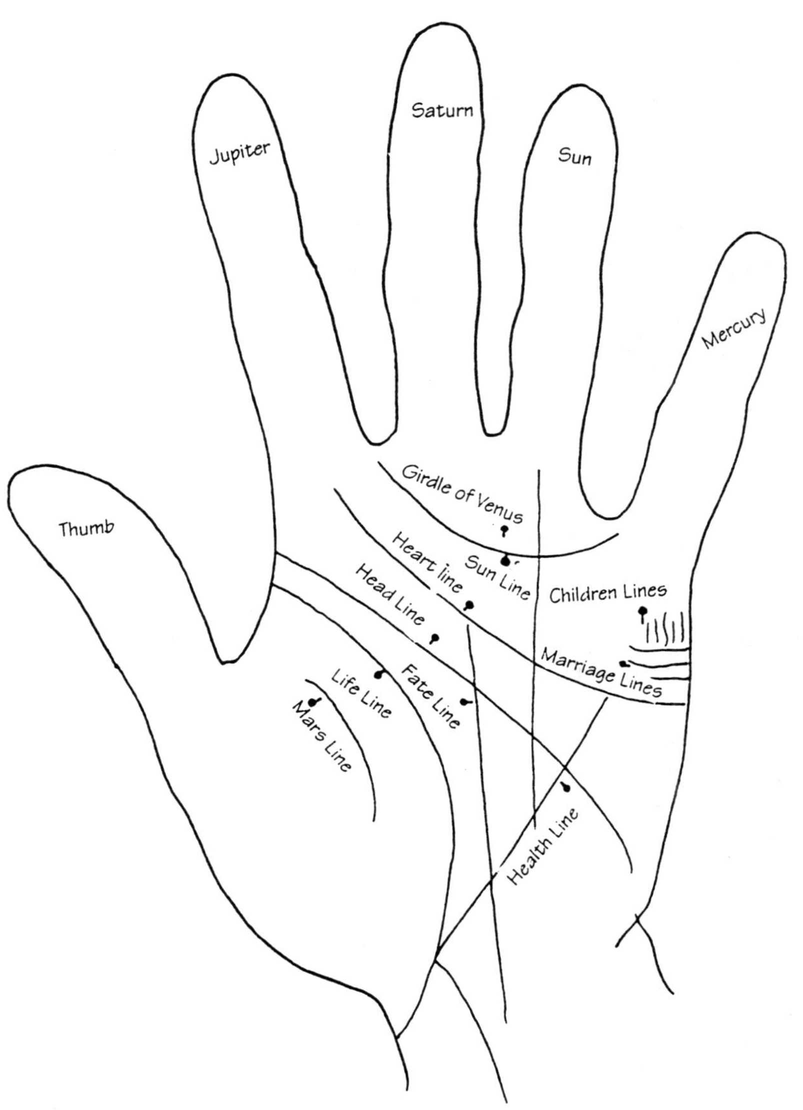

LIFE LINE

The Life line reflects the state of our physical and mental energies. A good Life line should be a clear, sharp, deeply set line. without any breaks, islands or irregularities in the line itself. (This is a true characteristic of all the major palm lines)

However, it is normal in the course of a life to have had occasional mishaps, such as the breaking of a leg or hand in childhood, minor or major accidents, sickness, etc. These events leave their mark on your Life line in the shape of small islands or continuity breaks. A serious occurrence is predictable as it appears in the line well before it occurs.

THE NATURAL COURSE OF THE LIFE LINE

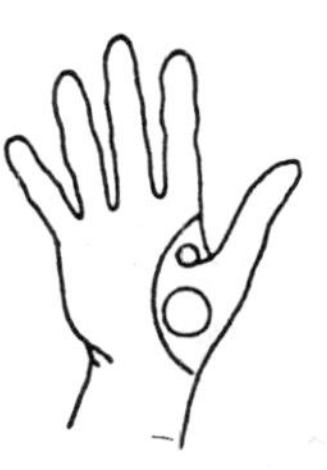

The classic Life line starts under Jupiter Mount, between the thumb and forefinger, draws an arc around Venus Mount and continues until the wrist.

It is usually accepted that the longer the line, the longer life will go on, and the shorter the line, the shorter the life of its owner. I have learned from my own experience that if the line is long, it is usually not sharply defined and there are fewer supporting lines (Mars lines) or outer lines (Fate lines), and hence this assumption of a longer life is not warranted.

In order that the body's energies should be kept working effectively for years, there must be a supporting line, particularly in one's more advanced years. If, on the other hand, the life-line is short and there are no inner supporting lines and the life-line ends abruptly on both hands at the same age, then it is most likely that death will occur at the age indicated by the cutting off of the life-line. This occurs very rarely, and in most cases, there will be an inner or outer supporting line which points to the fact that despite the impending danger, life will continue and the problem will pass. In this case, the supporting line becomes the life-line and is decisive in setting the moment of dying.

When the line is deep and is not irregular or shaggy, it indicates great vitality, energy and fitness.

A Thick Life line

All the characteristics ascribed to the good life-line are also applicable to the thick life-line. It is worth adding that this line is evidence of a great deal of physical stamina which provides its owner with vitality and considerable energy. However, it also suggests a low threshold of physical suffering and a tendency to be strongly affected by the most minor ailments.

Note: The depth of the lines generally derives from physical labor.

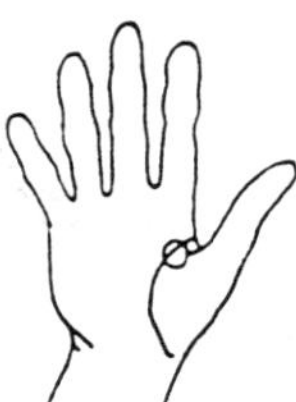

Life line Starting Close to the Thumb

When emerging very near the thumb (from the lower Mars Mount), the life-line indicates a selfish, lazy person, lacking energy and spirit. This person will most likely have problems expressing his feelings even to his life companion or his children. Such an individual is not likely to have many children.

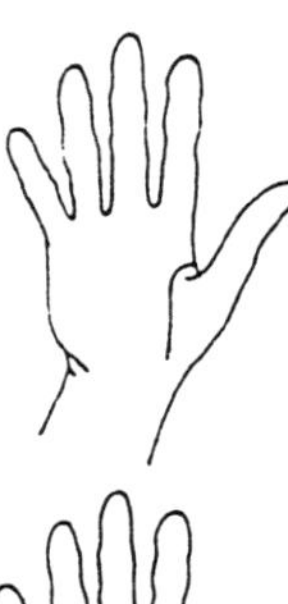

Vertical Life Line

The vertical Life line crosses Venus Mount and descends vertically. Everything mentioned with regard to the life-line beginning near the thumb, also applies to the vertical line, but in addition, also indicates a short life-span and an inferior physical condition.

Chain-shaped Life line

This line resembles a chain made of little ring-like lines and indicates a serious lack of inner energy and strength. People with such lines are physically and mentally vulnerable. They tend to be sickly and have problems functioning in any stressful situation.

An Interrupted Life line

This line, made up of mainly interrupted segments, indicates a strong tendency towards nervous breakdowns and health problems. The general state of health is poor but the emphasis here is on psychological and other problems linked to the nervous system, which leads to the individual's inability to cope with life adequately.

A Life line resembling a network

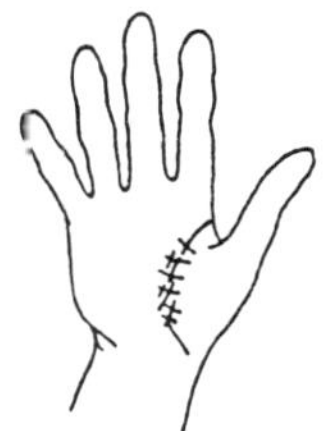

A life-line of this nature is that of a neurotic person. Obviously, this state weakens the body's energy and the appearance of this network can serve as a warning of a possible nervous breakdown.

INTERRUPTIONS IN THE LIFE LINE

Overlapping Interruptions

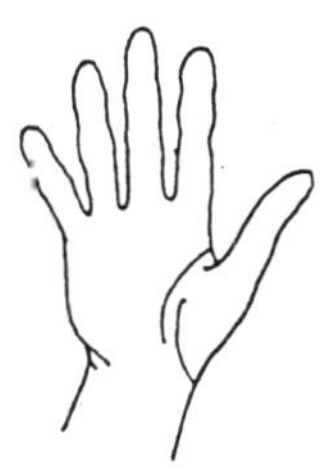

This type of life-line is one that has been cut off at a certain point and its continuation overlaps the original line. Such a break in the line is a sign that an accident or an illnes has occurred at the age indicated by the interruption (according to the life-line's calendar of events). At that age, there is the danger of real physical harm; for instance, if someone overturned in his car and emerged unharmed from the incident, this person would, at the same time, still be in danger. If the interruption appears in both hands at the same age point, the possible danger would be more imminent.

A simple break in the Life line

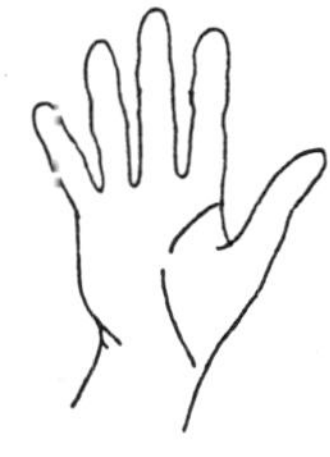

This type of interruption, where the Life line continues after a certain break, is more dangerous than an overlapping Life line. It's significance lies in a fatality indicated by the age point of the break. Note: The size of the interruption, whether it is an overlapping or a simple break, indicates the extent of the danger involved.

Types of Islands in the Life line

An island appearing on the Life line means that during that particular period, the individual is in a poor state of health, psychologically or physically, resulting from an operation or illness (an island of this sort may also appear after an accident or a nervous breakdown). A hair-like island (the inner side of the island being as thin as a hair) signifies that there is no physical danger but that there is considerable stress during that period.

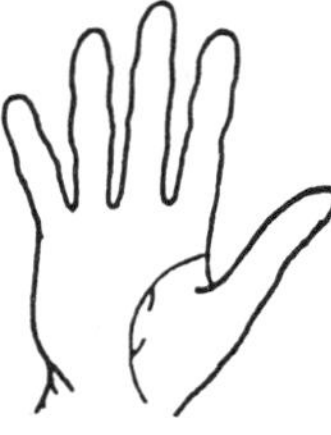

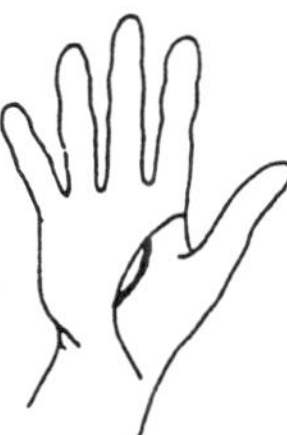

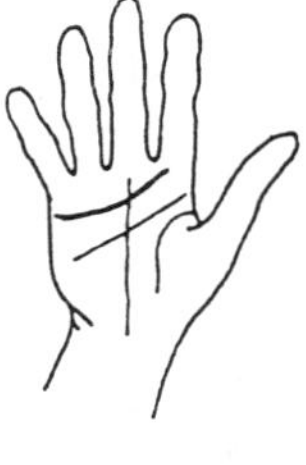

A Short Life line

Theoretically, one can say that if the Life line is a short one, the individual's life is also a short one. However, if the Fate line appears alongside the life-line, it acts as the continuation of the life-line, and one must view this as an overlapping life-line. The same applies to the Mars Line.

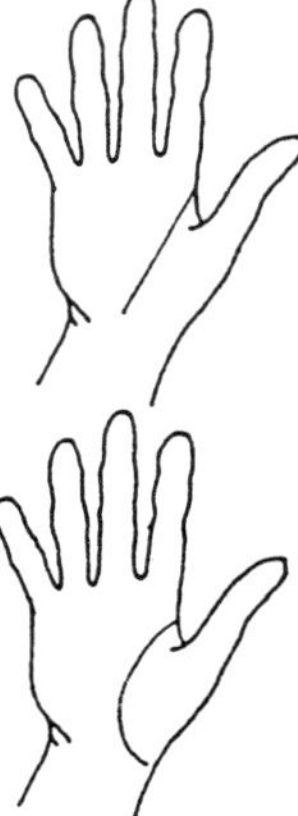

A Diagonal life-Line

This Life line moves toward the lower Moon Mount. At times, at the end, it moves back to its original course at the base of the hand. In general, this type of Life line points to an adventurous personality, who needs endless change and new and interesting challenges. This individual finds the daily and ordinary routine unbearable.

Note: If this type of line appears in addition to a long sun-finger and a protruding sun-hill, this may be evidence of a marked disposition for gambling.

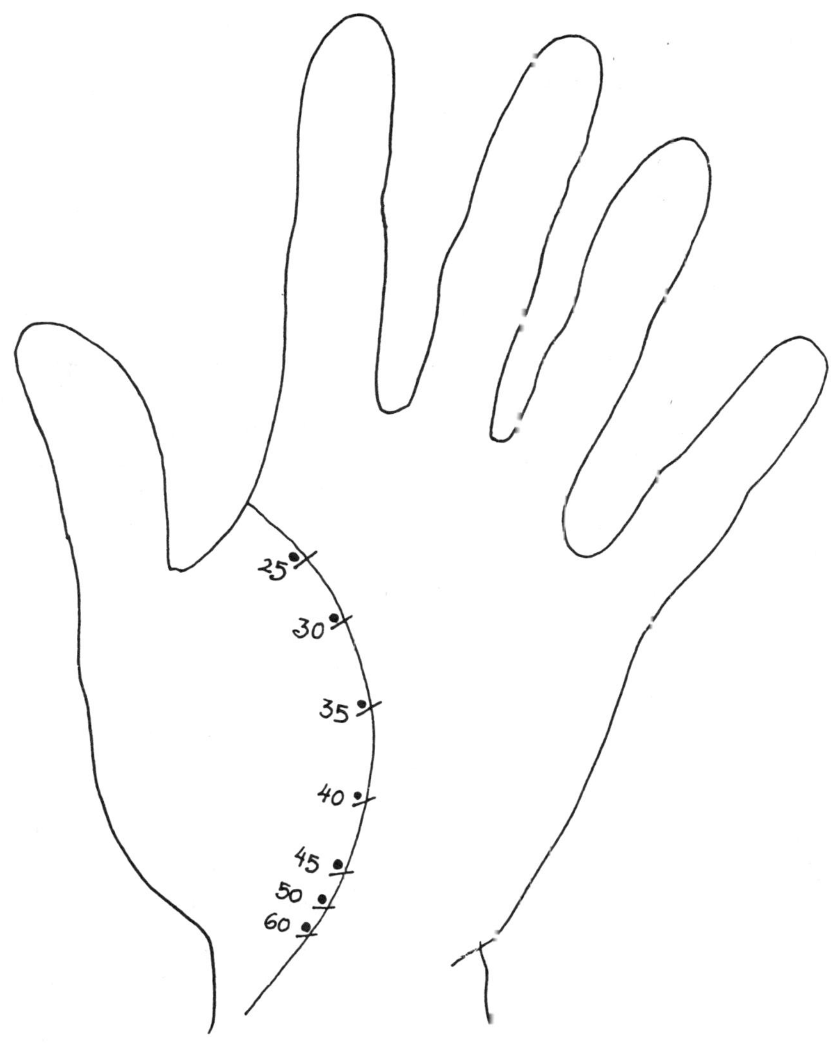

CALENDAR OF EVENTS, WHICH AT CERTAIN AGES HAVE LEFT OR WILL LEAVE THEIR MARK ON THE ***LIFE LINE***

(See the age-marks along the Life line)

MARS LINE

The Mars Line is the line which supports the Life Line and appears on the inner side of the Life line, generally parallel to it. At times, it appears on the Venus Mount.

The following significance is ascribed to the Mars Line:

- Energy and Vitality.
- Protection from disease, accidents, and various other crises
- Strengthening the Life line

Moreover, this line indicates a vigorous and belligerent type and a certain degree of aggressiveness.

This line may appear in an interrupted fashion or at the end of the Life line. If the line appears parallel to a break or island on the Life line, this is a sign that the individual will overcome the problem despite its severity.

The Mars line is one of the lines which may appear on the hand in the course of one's life-time. Even if it is comparatively small, it may eventually become longer.

This line is specifically a **protective** line, which strengthens the Life line, and adds a great deal of energy and physical and psychological strength. When the Life line is weak (unclear or insufficiently defined) the Mars line will strengthen it and even sometimes serve as a substitute of the Life line. When the Life line is clear and strong, there is no need for a Mars line and it serves as a sort of "bonus".

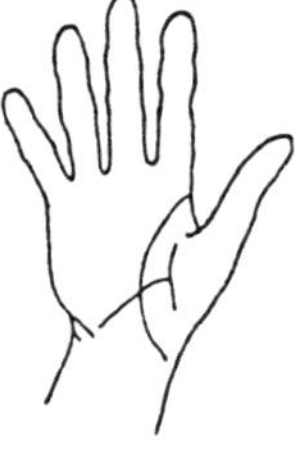

An extension from the Mars line which crosses the Life line indicates carelessness or an unconsidered act which may endanger the individual's life at the age-mark on which the line crosses the Life Line. The intention here mainly applies to a person who takes his life and health lightly (such as an alcoholic, a heavy smoker or drug addict).

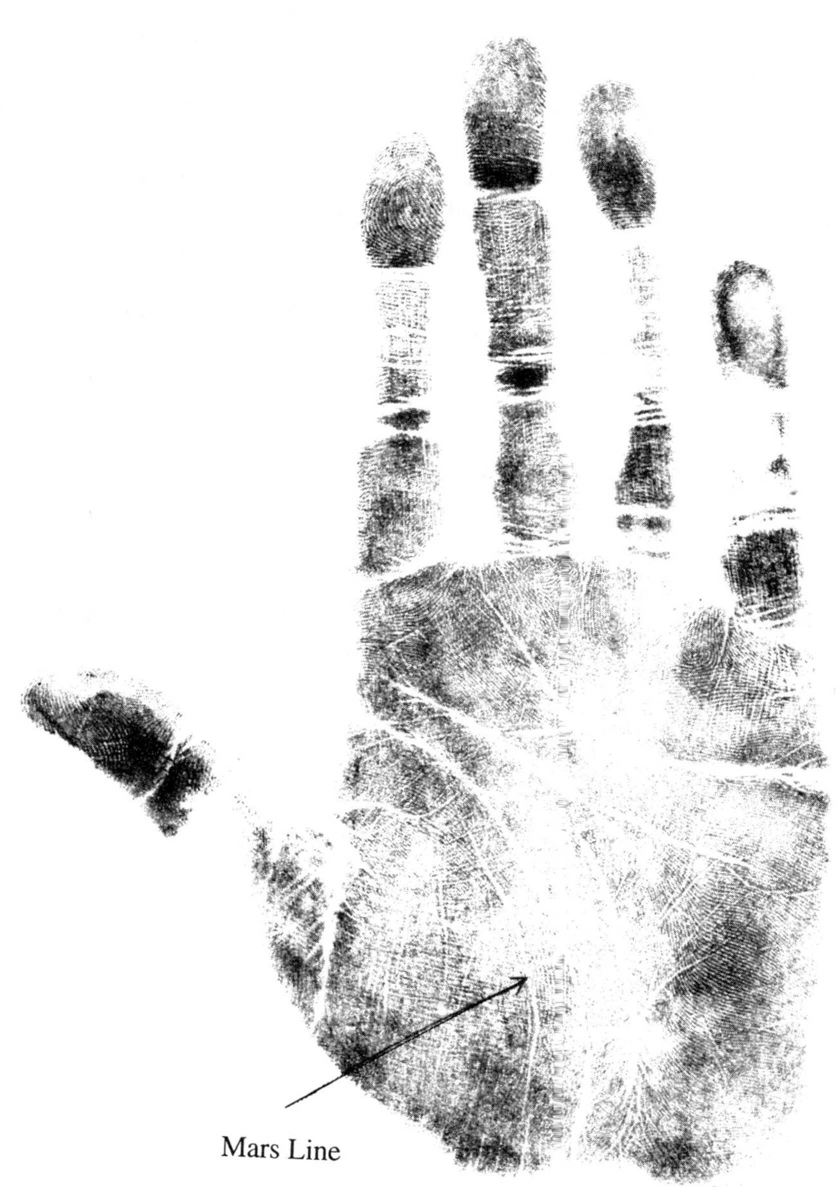
Mars Line

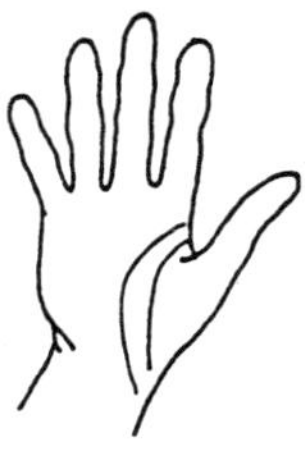

DOUBLE LIFE LINE (Very Long Mars Line)

When the Mars Line is parallel to the Life line and it is almost the same length, or at least three-quarters the length, it is considered as a double of the Life line. It generally affords bodily energy and considerable power.

Note: There are chirologists who claim that the Double Life line also supplies a great deal of mental energy in addition to the physical. From my own experience, I have learned that this is not quite the case. Most the individuals with double Life lines that I have encountered have suffered from an inner restlessness, tension and difficult periods of stress, and uncontrolled outbursts of anger which created difficult psychological problems, all of which was due to the fact that they had no outlet for their excessive energy (mean·ng a lack of physical activity).

In the event that the Life line is weak, a long Mars line will strengthen it and frequently take its place.

TRAVEL LINES

These are lines which extend from the lower part of the Life line towards the base of the hand, creating branches or ramifications.

These travel lines indicate journeys outside of one's homeland. When the lines are conspicuous, these journeys can be meaningful for a number of years. If these lines are faint in relation to the Life line, the journeys would be short (limited to a few months). It is impossible to know the date of the journey on the basis of the travel lines on the palm, but it is possible to venture a guess on the basis of the substantial changes of the Fate line and the Sun line.

Note: At times, the travel line appears as a continuation of the Life line and it then merits twice the importance because it then becomes a diagonal Life line and all that this implies, in addition to its role as a travel line. It is worth noting that most of the people on whose hands such a line appeared, left their homeland to live elsewhere.

When the Life line and the Travel line are of the same thickness, the journeys abroad will be frequent and significant.

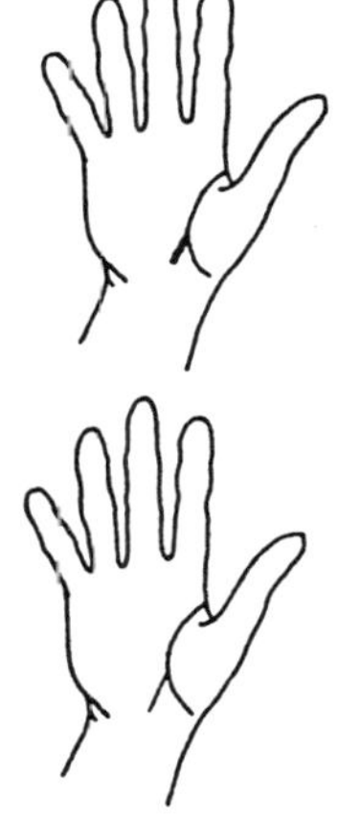

When the Travel Line is thick and deeply engraved in relation to the Life line, this indicates long journeys (for a number of years) and the possibility of emigration.

When the Travel line is thin and lacks depth in relation to the Life line, the journeys will be short and unimportant.

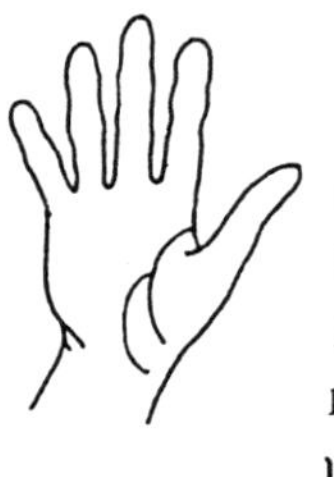

Vhen the Travel line forms an arc and moves ownward towards the base of the hand, it indicates iat the person will go on a large number of journeys mainly of short duration) and will always return to iis or her homeland.

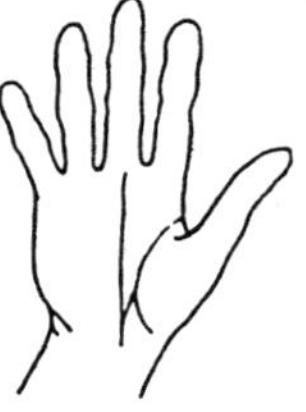

A Travel line which joins the Fate line, points to important and significant journeys related to the person's occupation and income.

THE HEAD LINE

The Head Line is the most important element of the palm, reflecting our intellectual and mental capacities. This line reveals our thinking ability, powers of concentration and alertness, as well as our perseverence, occupational or professional leanings, logical sense, idealistic and romantic inclinations, and our creativity and imaginative gifts. Similar to the Life line, we would prefer that this line be clearly defined and deep, so that the traits indicated should actually materialize. When this line is long and clearly defined, and reaches almost to the end of the hand or even the end, this is an indication of a highly developed intellect and a complex and capable personality. If, on the other hand, the line is short and does not extend beyond 2.5 cm., it is evidence of a rather poor intelligence. This does not mean that someone with a short Head line is not capable of excelling at a specific line of work, but that this individual has mental limitations with regard to other spheres of activity.

When the Head line is altogether weak, all the other qualities attributed to this individual are reduced. An island or break in the Head line points to a problem which results in a decline in the persons ability to concentrate and leads to absent-mindedness, confusion and proper functioning of the personality – including the physical aspect. For instance, a substantial island will appear on the head line of someone who was at the peak of his or her academic studies and about to be divorced, would not be capable of pursuing their studies. When the crisis indicated by the island had passed, the student would successfully return to his or her studies. An island or break in the Head line can also indicate a blow to the head incurred during a fall or accident, or an illness connected with the brain or the head and this can be finally determined on the basis of the Life line.

Note: To determine the persons' gifts and abilities, it is necessary to refer to other elements of the hand, such as the shape of the palm, the fingers and the nails, the nature of the hills, etc.

A Good Head Line

What is a good Head line? When it is sharp, smooth, clear and deep, and extends across at least three-quarters of the palm. Such a line is a clear indication of a high degree of intelligence. Note that the quality of the line is more significant than it's length. The beginning of the line indicates the quality of intelligence and strength of character. A good beginning of the line is an indication of self-confidence, even when the Life line and the Head line are joined.

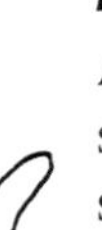

A Straight Head Line

A line drawn across the palm with no more than 2 cm space from the Heart line above, indicates common sense and practicality, a realistic person who tends towards mathematics and the exact sciences and relates to practical subjects rather than to spiritual matters. Logic is the more dominant factor of this person's personality. A smaller than 2 cm space between the Heart and the Head lines suggests a stubborn, critical person who over-emphasizes his logical approach.

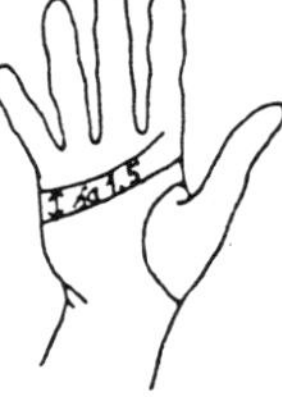

A straight Head line is evidence of a brilliant mind. (Every long Head line, even when it is not straight, indicates a high level of intelligence).

A Head line starting from the Jupiter Mount

A Head line starting from the Jupiter Mount and touching on the Life line, lends the greatest force to the characteristics of the Head line. It suggests talent and ability in various fields, as well as considerable energy, the capacity to make decisions and courage. People with this type of Head line will be extremely ambitious, particularly when the Jupiter Mount is very evident. Such individuals possess an element of discretion and the desire to dominate and lead, and can boast of extraordinary organizational powers. One can also claim that they are given to careful deliberations (characteristics suited to good army officers or government administrators).

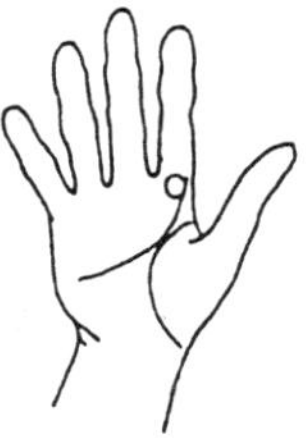

A Short Head line

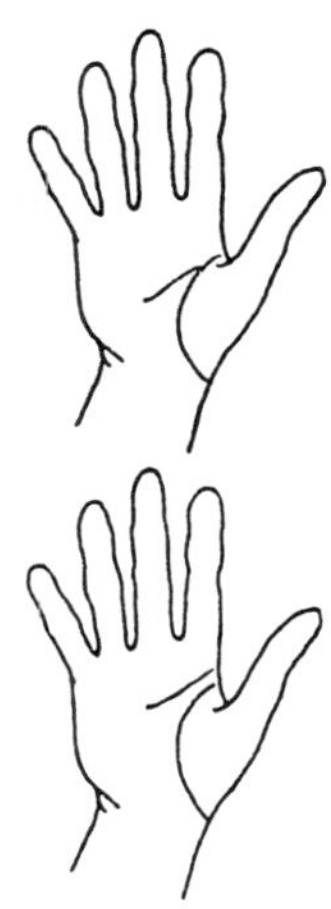

A Head line considered short is one that is not longer than 2.5 cm. It is an indication of a low degree of intelligence, a limited learning ability and a simple personality. This does not mean that an individual with such a line is not capable of succeeding in specific spheres but they would be likely to encounter difficulties when they are obliged to cope with problems arising during the course of their work. A person with a short Head line is materialistic by nature and lacks a creative imagination.

Note: If the Head line and the Life line are connected, the length of the Head line is measured from the point at which it separates from the Life line (taking into account the significance of the connection).

A Diagonal Head line

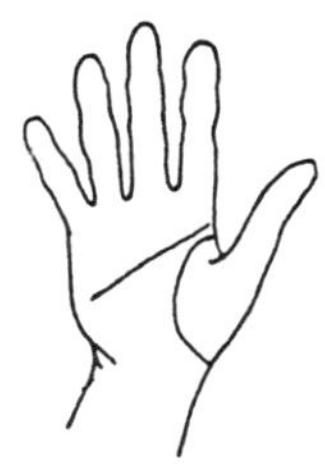

This line takes into account a gap of more than 2 cm.between the end of the Head line and that of the Heart line. All the characteristics ascribed to the straight Head line, also apply here and this also includes most of the characterists of the arched Head line. A person with such a line can be both realistic and humane in his or her professional lives, although the humanistic approach will be foremost.

An Arched Head Line

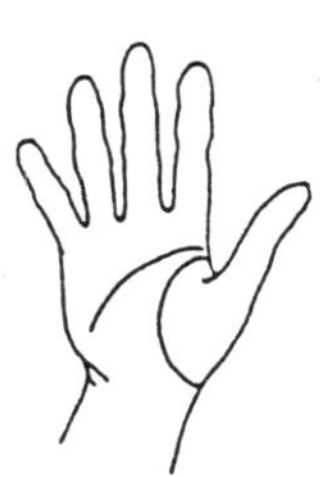

When the Head Line is arched, this indicates that there is a creative imagination present, and an inclination towards art and the humanistic professions, or such applied arts as graphics or mechanical inventiveness (technicians and engineers frequently have this type of line). This line is also evidence of a romantic and idealistic temperament. An arched line reaching the Moon hill, is a sign of a literary talent. The more steeply the line slopes down, the more pronounced these characteristics will be in evidence. The arched Head line also reveals a tendency to indulge in changing moods and experience excessive sensitivity and vulnerability.

Note: In order to understand in which sphere this individual is gifted, it is important to recognize the type of palm on which this Head line appears.

A Sharply Descending Arched Head Line

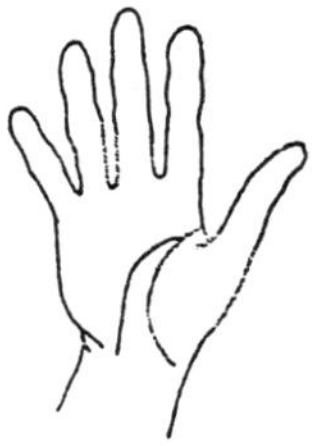

A Head line descending in a sharp slope is a sign of over-sensitivity and a strong disposition towards changing moods, as well as a constant and conscious use of the imagination (when both the lower and the upper Moon Mount are active and protruding, these tendencies will be most felt). People with such a head line are under constant emotional pressure and tend to be very vulnerable. A Head line descending sharply stresses all those characteristics indicated in the case of an ordinary arched Head line.

Note: When the Head line curves severely, this may be a sign of mental imbalance and a suicidal tendency.

A Double Head Line

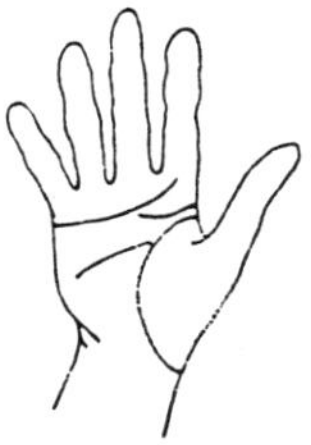

A double Head line indicates the presence of recognized intellectual capacities: marked talent in many diverse fields, a good memory, a talent for languages, literature, and the ability to deal with different spheres at the same time. People with double Head lines are indeed generally involved in at least two areas at the same time.

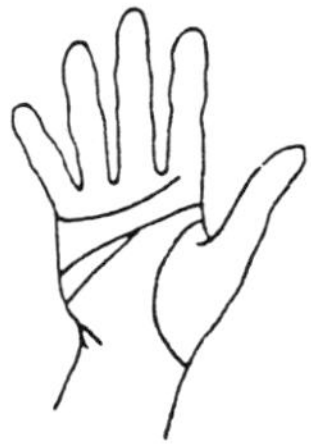

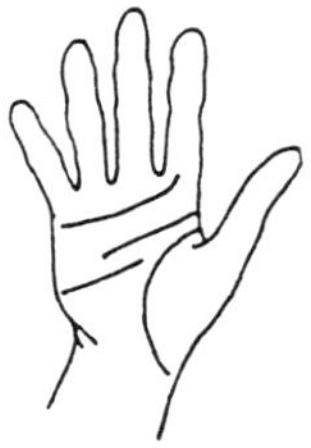

There is no question but that the double Head line is evidence of a well-developed intellect, an serious capacity for study and an excellent mind – all of which on condition that the two Head lines are clearly defined, for if this is not the case, this may be evidence of psychological problems and a complex personality. People with double Head lines are also individuals with “dual personalities’. If one of the Head lines is straight and the second arched or diagonal, one aspect of their personality will be sensitive and delicate while the other aspect will be cold and rationalistic. These individuals have a special gift for “playing about” with human nature and amusing themselves by experimenting with the fate of others for their own benefit, particularly if the Sun finger is especially long.

Problematic Double Head line

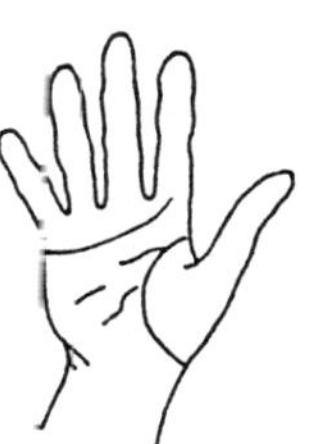

Here we have a situation in which there are a number of Head Lines – three or four lines – which are disorderly (that is, chain- like or lacking depth and a uniform aspect, or simply very weak). This phenomena indicates an unstable and complex personality, inconsistent and with an inability to concentrate. At times, when there are a great many problematic Head lines present, this may be an intimation of a psychopathic personality.

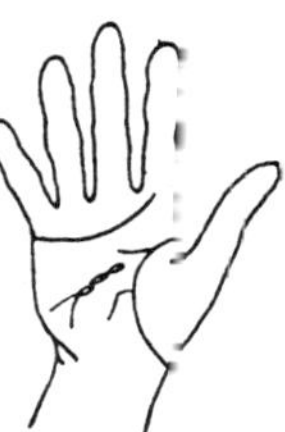

A Break in the Head Line

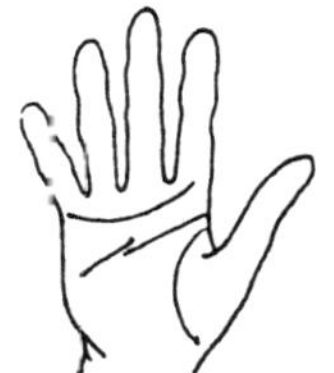

Indicates a physical injury of the head resulting from an accident or some physical violence.

An Island on the Head Line

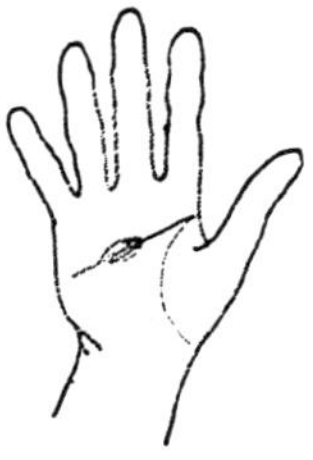

An island on the Head Line is a sign of a period of extreme emotional tension (which may come from divorce proceedings, the loss of a loved one, the loss of a large amount of money, etc.). As a result of this stress, a person would not be able to concentrate or function properly. The period of stress is indicated by the size of the island. A complete and thick island can be a sign of a blow to the head or even some brain disease.

A Faulty and Unclear Head Line

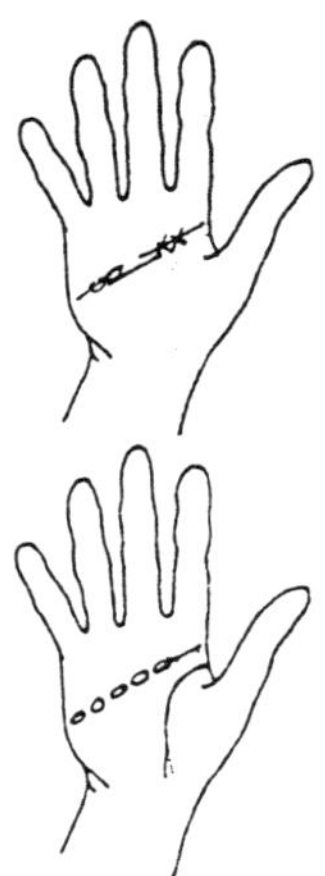

A faulty Head Line is one with the Head line in the form of many islands or a weak and superficial line, or an interrupted one. People with Head lines of this kind are incapable of functioning properly in their daily lives. They have a problem concentrating and they generally suffer from absent-mindedness. One frequently finds such lines in the hands of respectable people who occupy high administrative positions but if we examine them more closely, we find that the saying "do not look at the jug, but what is inside it" seems to suit them well. They are impressive conversationalists and seem to be quite uninhibited as far as speaking is concerned but they actually say very little, for they are superficial as far as their thinking and actions are concerned. They do, however know how to make an impression which is completely misleading.

A Head Line which ascends beyond the Heart Line

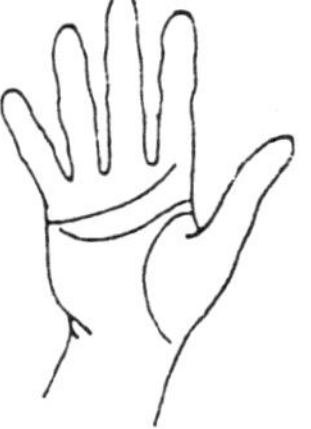

This type of Head Line may be the sign of a difficult and stubborn person (in money matters, to the point of miserliness),as well as of aggressive elements, rigidity, vindictiveness and egoism. Here the intelligence gets the better of the emotion, especially if the Head Line is very near the Heart Line and the latter is short and unclear. In this case, all these elements will be expressed in a particularly sharp and extreme manner.

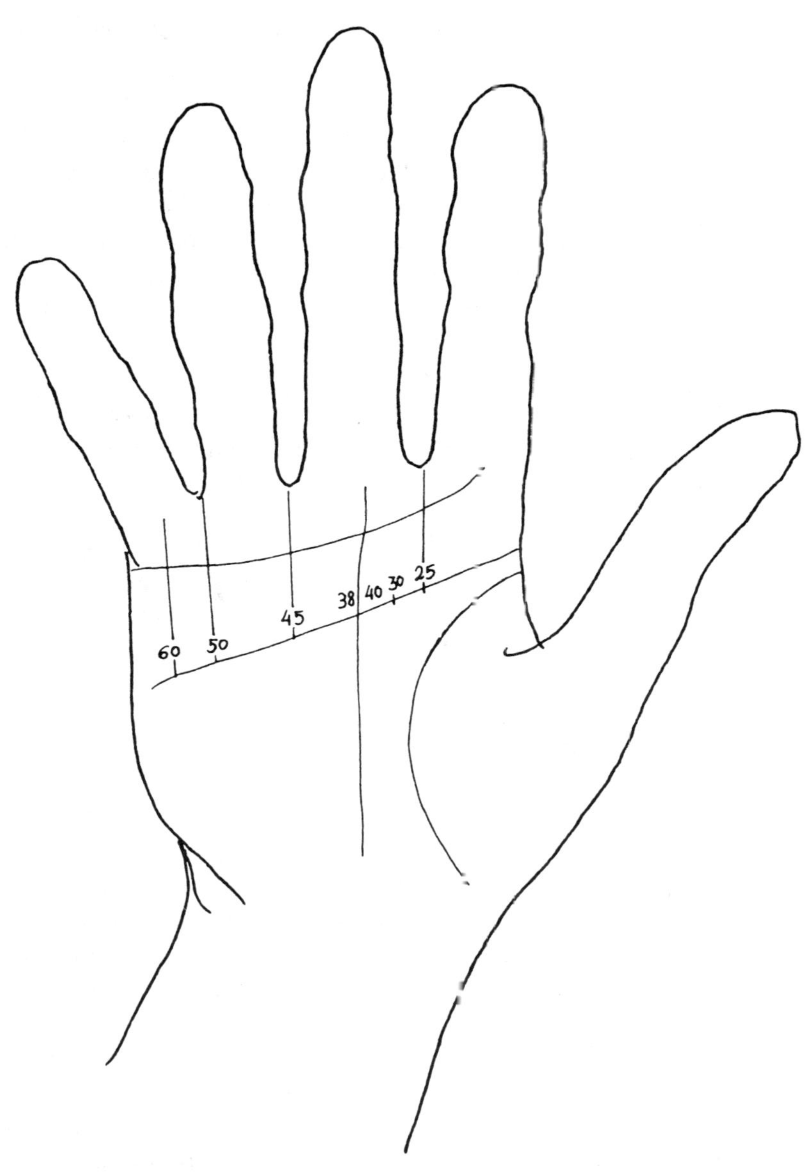

CALENDAR OF EVENTS, WHICH HAVE OR WILL LEAVE THEIR MARK ON THE ***HEAD LINE***
(See the Age Marks along the Line)

A Head Line that ascends from its outset towards the Heart Line

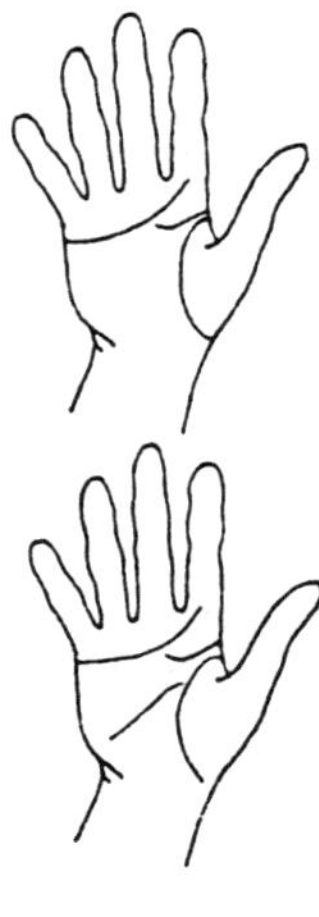

This instance is far more serious than the previous diagnosis. In this case where the Head Line begins its ascent towards the Heart Line and stops there, the emotions are suppressed by the intelligence. The individual, here, is motivated by cold and dry considerations and his or her attitude to life is logical and barren. This type of person has no means of expressing feelings. Under certain circumstances, this individual may be involved in embezzlement, dishonest, and mercenary behavior. There is also the possibility that people with this type of Head Line will display abnormal and criminal tendencies, to the point where nothing will stop them from achieving their aims and the smallest provocation may trigger off an outburst and the open expression of these tendencies. These indications are much more serious if they do not form part of the double Head Line.

Combination "Apish Line"

The Combination Line is one line intertwined with the Head Line or the Heart Line. It is straight as an arrow and stretched across the entire width of the palm. Towards its end, there are tiny lines resembling ears of corn, a typical sign of the Heart Line. As various disorders in the form of islands, interruptions, and ramifications generally appear along the Heart Line, one finds similar phenomena on the Combination Line.

People with this type of line are very sensitive and are easily offended, although this is not very obvious as they are very reticent and egocentric. They have great emotional potential but have difficulty in expressing their feelings towards the people surrounding them. These hidden emotional assets will find their outlet in unlimited devotion and loyalty towards their families and close friends. As they are egocentric and inclined to isolate themselves, they create the feeling that they are difficult to understand and somewhat eccentric. They are generally defined as extremists, as they are radical both as to feelings and opinions.

Palm With Combination Line

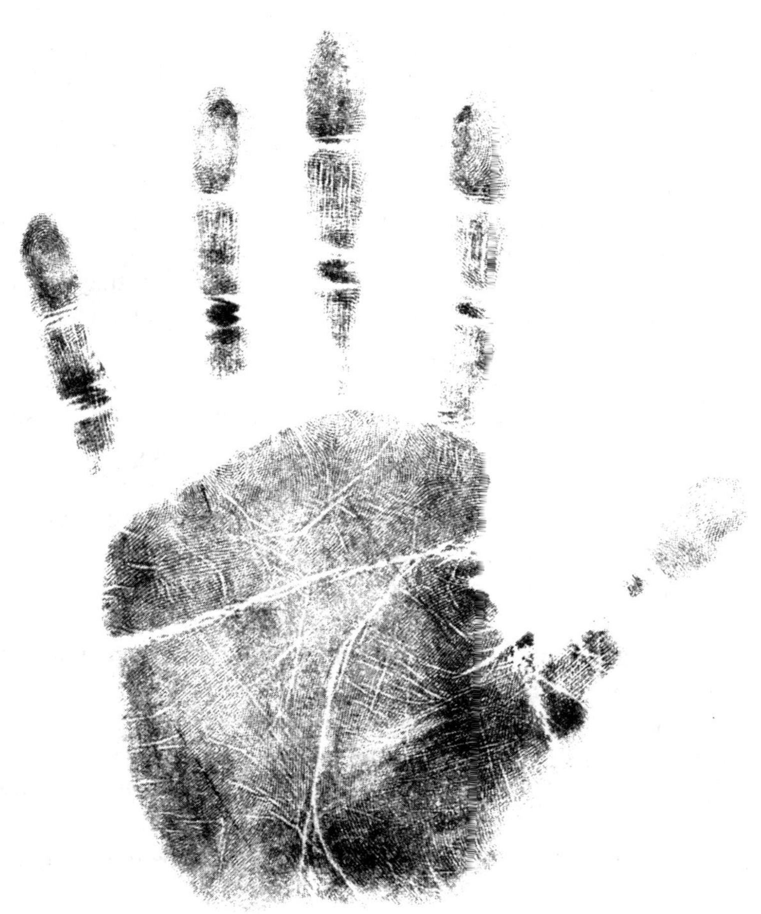

There is no middle way, as far as they are concerned: they either love or hate, they either approve of a certain political party, or are uncompro- mi singly opposed to it.

Their thinking capacity is the dominant factor in their make-up. Most of them can boast of a highly developed intellect and an excellent level of achievement. Their ability to concentrate is noteworthy and they are both quick-witted and independent in their ways of thinking and are thus able to solve problems quickly and carry out projects in the most effective manner. Individuals with this type of line are very talented in various fields, and it is therefore difficult to advise them with regard to their professional pursuits. They are able to bear a high level of suffering, have a strong will- power and devote themselves to whatever they set out to do. In other words, they are blessed with strong characters.

It is odd that this type of palm line also exists among mongoloids (that is, mentally retarded people), and is one of the typical signs of this kind of disturbance. No one knows the reason for this. At any rate, when an infant is born with a Combination Line which is well- developed after three months, one can expect that this child will be very talented as an adult and that all the traits mentioned above will develop in a positive fashion (when the line has the desired quality and is not disorderly).

The Combination Line can be found among five to ten percent of the population. It appears in either the left or the right hand. In any case, when this line only appears on the left hand – we use this line to analyse the bearer's character. If the line lies near the usual course of the Head Line, it means that reasoning and intelligence will be more dominant than the emotions. On the other hand, if the Combination Line appears too close to the usual course of the Heart Line, then the emotions will be the dominant factor.

HOW THE PALM REVEALS THE EXTENT OF AN INDIVIDUAL'S SELF-CONFIDENCE

What is Self-confidence? A person's self-confidence is measured by his or her ability to fulfil their desires and urges without fear or inhibitions. It is the successful expression of one's personality; it implies an ability to weigh up situations accurately, to act with discretion, and carry out one's tasks with the maximum efficiency, when the surrounding conditions do not hamper or inhibit the execution of one's ideas.

Head line and Life line connected for 1.5 cm.

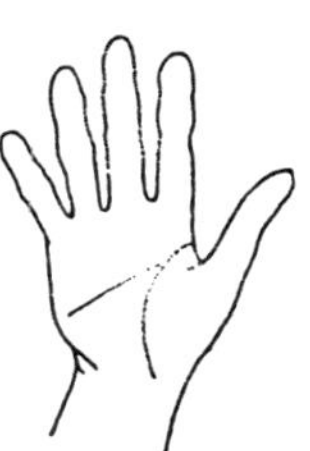

The connection between the Head line and the Life line indicates lack of self-confidence and the longer the connection, the greater the lack. People with 1.5 cm. of connected lines have great difficulty in taking decisions and carrying them out. They are constantly in a state of tension and emotional stress and are therefore unable to fulfill their desires and needs and their abilities remain unrealized. A good part of their emotional energy is directed towards inner struggles, and hence reduces their ability to carry out their day-to-day functions.

Head line and Life Line connected for 2.0 cm or more

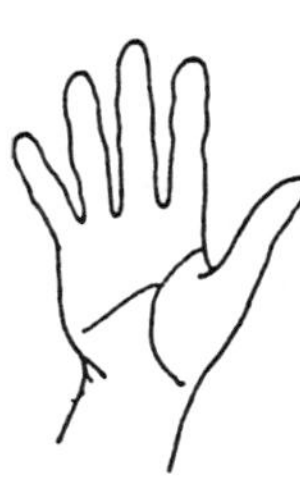

This long connection indicates a complete lack of self- confidence, nervousness and excessive anxiety. Such individuals are inclined to lie to themselves and delude themselves into believing their illusions. They frequently postpone the execution of their duties, and are incapable of coping with stressful states. When the lines are weak and lacking depth, this is a sign that they tend to be affected by various psychosomatic illnesses (head-aches, ulcer, asthma, etc.).

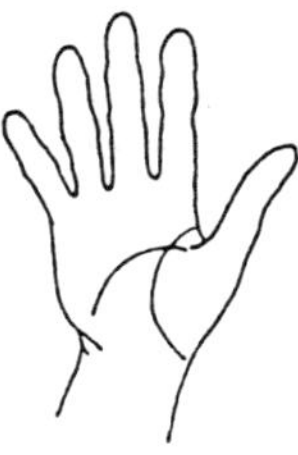

Head Line starting from the Life line and crossing it

When the Head-Line begins within the Life line and crosses it on the way, this is a sign of a very negative and problematic aspect of the personality. People with such a line, are subject to an extreme lack of self-confidence – which can be expressed in over-aggressiveness towards their surroundings. They are very sensitive and tend to be easily offended by trivial things, and their reactions will be quick, thoughtless and unreasonable, affecting their judgment and in the long run, doing themselves harm.

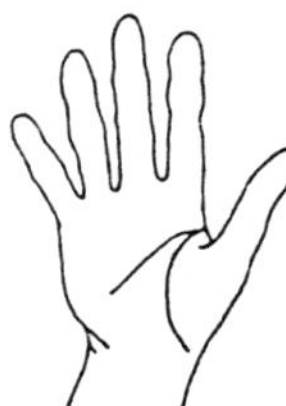

Head Line and Life line touching at one point

This is a positive state which indicates a satisfactory self-confidence, a reasonable amount of sensitivity, good judgment and caution.

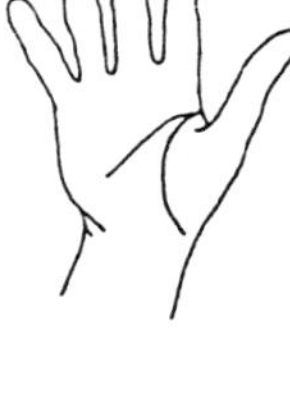

Space between the Head Line and the Life line – up to 5 mm.

This is one of the most positive signs appearing on the palm. It is an indication of an optimal amount of self-confidence. People with such lines are free of inhibitions, are able to judge and consider matters sensibly, and can execute their wishes and needs. They are quick-witted and constructive, think independently and can take decisions and carry them out in the best possible way (this is one of the classic signs of leadership quality).

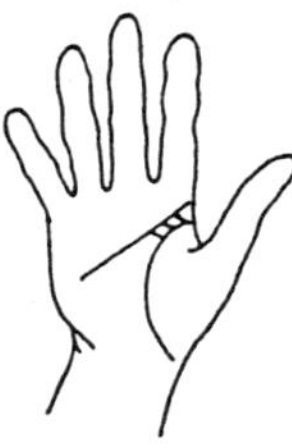

Separated Head line and Life line, with small connecting lines

The tiny lines connecting the Head line and the Life line which fill the gap between them are anxiety lines. They reduce and weaken the person's self-confidence indicated by the division between these lines. This situation points to excessive anxiety, inner tension and a disposition towards hysteria (especially if the lower Moon Mount is stressed).

Space between the Head line and the Life line – over 5mm.

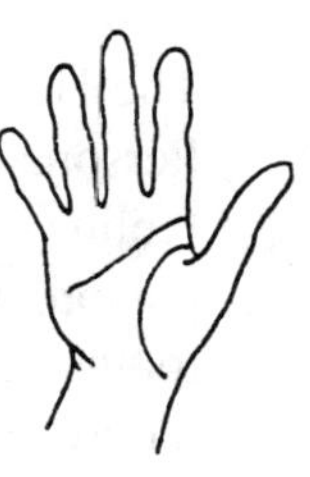

This situation is also positive, but to a lesser degree in comparison with the smaller gap, because this element is a sign of an exaggerated self-confidence, which can cause carelessness, hasty judgments, and impulsive reactions (such as careless driving, unwise slips of the tongue, etc.) Such individuals have little patience or tolerance of their surroundings, and may have problems concentrating. All these characteristics make for a boastful and superficial person. And indeed, people with such a space are inclined to quarrel more easily than others.

THE HEART LINE

The Heart line is one of the most important lines on the palm. Personally, I love to deal with it as it relates to the world of our feelings. It shows to what extent we are able to feel with another person, whether we are capable of offering warmth and love, and to what extent. The Heart line also indicates generosity, a giving nature and the ability to care for and help another human being. Obviously, negative characteristics in the line, such as disorders, lack of depth or a disorderly form, or even a line which is too short, may be a sign of an absence of feeling, wickedness and an inability to express feelings adequately and appropriately – in other words, selfishness. The Heart line should be clear, sharply defined, with extensions no greater than 0.5 cm., if it is to be an expression of the good traits it embodies.

The Heart line's natural course begins below the Jupiter Mount, and stretches from that point across the palm, ending below the Mercury Mount. It can start out from the middle of the Jupiter Mount, or between the Jupiter and Saturn fingers, or from the center of the Saturn Mount. Appearing at the end of the line are tiny lines resembling ears of corn, which is a characteristic sign of this line.

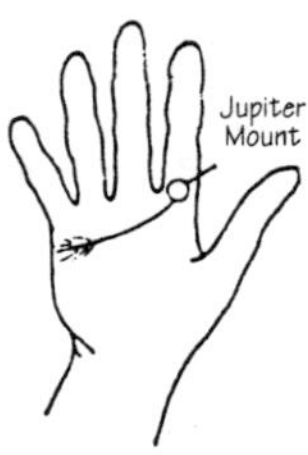

Heart line beginning at Jupiter Mount

Such a line is a sign of the highest form of love. Its owner is emotionally stable, knows how to love and is able to express his feelings but at the same time he also wants his love retaliated. This is the line of a kind and caring person who is generous and helpful.

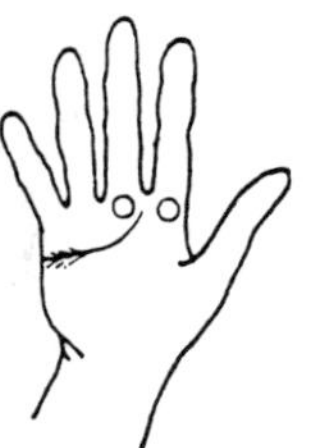

Heart line starting between the Jupiter and Saturn Fingers

Such a long line indicates a person with great emotional depth. This person does not need the revelation of expressions of love and is not given to demonstrating his or her feelings. Being certain of his own feelings, he frequently does not understand why his wife complains that he does not love her, for his love is an inward feeling which he takes for granted.

People with such lines are quiet and stable, and contribute considerably to the family unit.

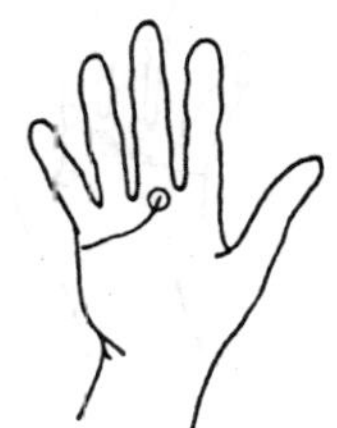

Heart line starting from the Saturn Mount

Indicates a lusty, sensual person who can control his feelings and may prove extremely selfish in a love relationship.

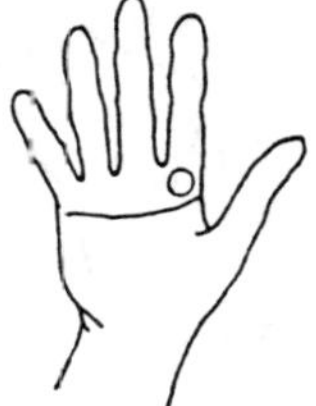

Heart line which by-passes the Jupiter Mount

This long line is evidence of an abundance of caring and loving feelings – but also a marked inclination to be jealous. It also indicates loyalty and honesty as well as a tendency to love blindly and an incapacity to see the beloved's faults.

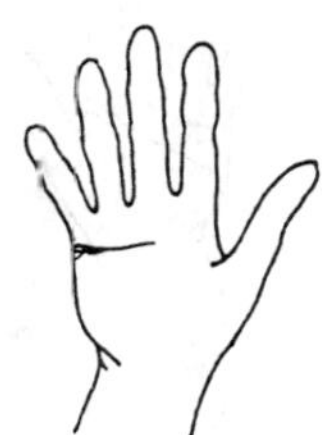

Heart line beginning below Saturn Mount

A Heart line starting some distance beneath the Saturn Mount is considered a short line. It is evidence of an egoist who has complete control of his or her feelings, or lack of feelings. People with such a short line are vengeful by nature, and incline to bear resentment and unable to forgive. They are very sensual and their love relationships are more sexual than emotional (particularly if the Venus and Moon Mounts are very active).

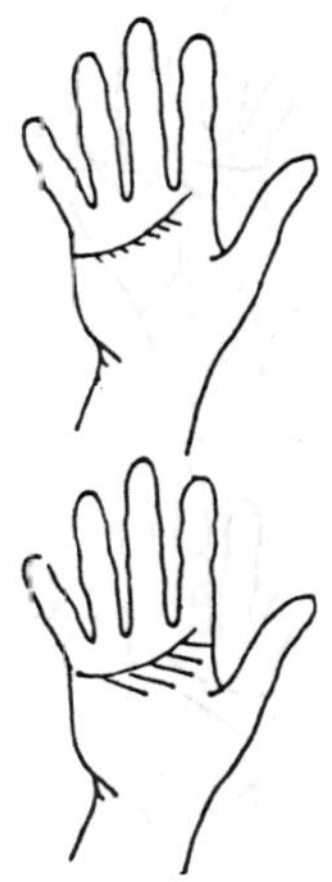

Little lines extending from the Heart line

Indicate many love affairs of a romantic nature but also of short duration. This is the line of a person who cannot maintain a stable love relationship and who is unstable emotionally and has few moral values.

Lines or ramifications longer than 5mm indicate serious disappointments in the person's love life.

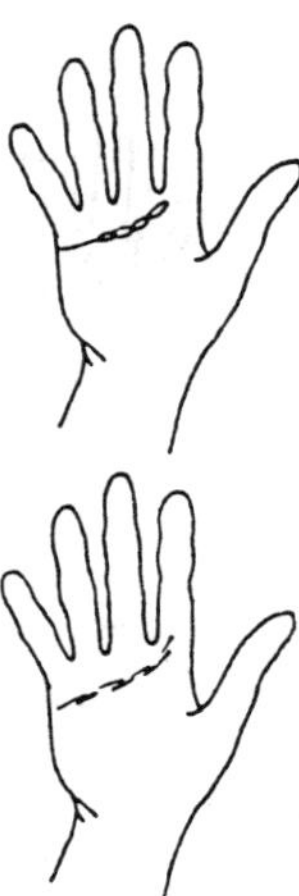

Unclear or chain-like Heart line

When the line is not uniform and contains many little islands, or there are little lines on at least three-quarters of its length, this is a sign of a person who has experienced many emotional disappointments in his or her life, particularly in their childhood and as a result, cannot adequately express their feelings. This may be interpreted as an absence of feelings. Such individuals are inclined to display indifference, contempt and even cynicism towards the opposite sex and are unable to establish genuinely warm and loving relationships (this situation may even lead to sexual deviation).

Note: One can include in this category a Heart line with tiny lines.

A shorter Heart line than Head line

The emotional life of a person with such a line is dominated by his or her intellect, with logic occupying the leading role. Such a person would refrain from devoting all their attentions to a spouse or life-companion. Considerations such as money, a career, and the love of comfort and luxuries, would be at the fore of their interests and if there were a "danger" of an emotional involvement which could affect the persons status, there would be no hesitation in cutting off such a relationship.

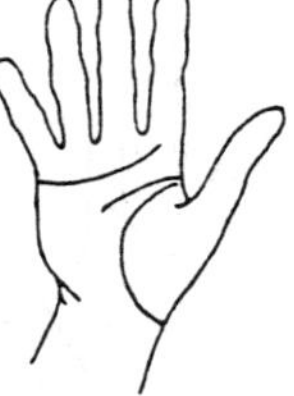

A longer Heart line than Head line

Here, the emotions rule without restrictions, and there is no suitable balance between the emotions and the intellect. Decisions are dictated by the feelings and this tends to affect one's ability to judge wisely. This line also indicates someone who would be generous and inclined to make sacrifices for their beloved.

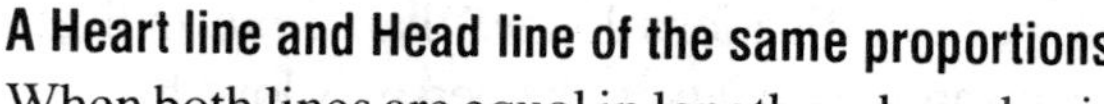

A Heart line and Head line of the same proportions

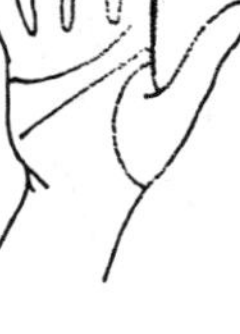

When both lines are equal in length and emphasis, this is a sign of an inclination to act on behalf of one's beloved in both practical and considered ways. There exists a good balance between the emotions and the intellect. This person is basically good-natured at heart.

A red Heart line

A person with such a line would have violent lusts and express his desires in very bestial terms. Such an individual is in need of intensive sexual activity without emotional involvement.

A distance of 0.5 cm. between the Heart line and the Head line

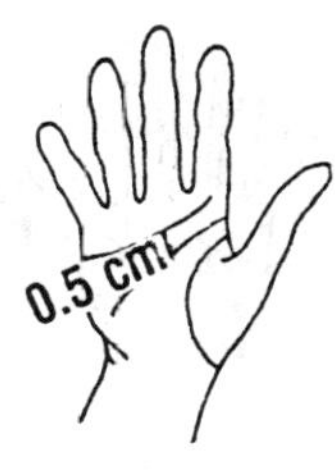

This small space between the two lines indicates that the intellect dominates the emotions. Such a person will act on the basis of logical considerations in all aspects of his life.

Note: The length of the Heart line and its tiny ramifications restrict this diagnosis to a certain extent.

A distance of 1.0 cm. between the Heart line and the Head line

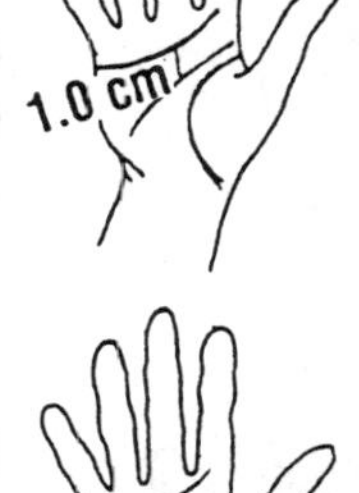

Here there is a good balance between the emotions and the intellect, which enables the individual to judge and view situations in their proper proportions.

A distance of more than 1.0 cm. between the Heart line and the Head line

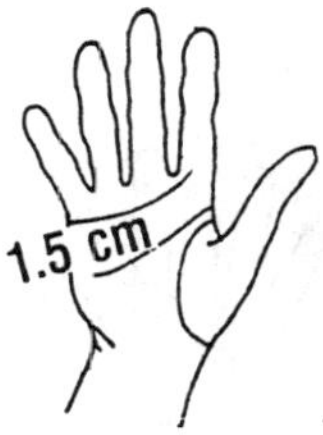

Here the emotions reign over the intellect. This hand describes an emotional person, sensitive and vulnerable, who is inclined to act on the basis of his feelings.

1.5 cm

A broken Heart line

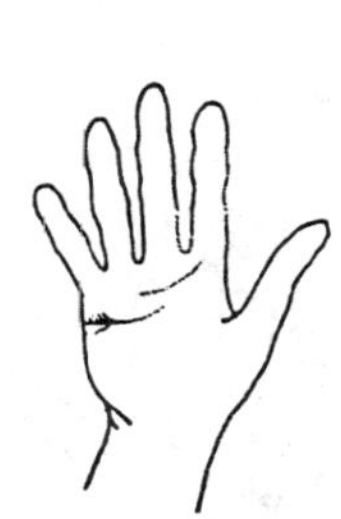

A broken Heart line points to disappointment in love or a severe emotional crisis whose cause it is not always possible to define. If the break is beneath the Saturn Mount – the disappointment occurred as a result of someone's death. If it is beneath the Sun Mount, then the source of the blighted hopes lay in a slighted pride, while if it is beneath the Mercury Mount, then the cause would be the result of madness or capriciousness.

A break in the Heart line would always be an indication of frustrated emotional attachment, generally between a man and a woman.

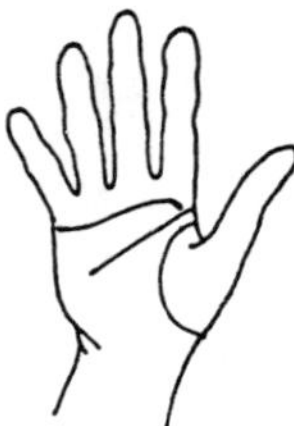

A very low Heart line which descends toward the Head line at the outset.

This is a distinct sign of unhappiness in an emotional relationship during childhood.

Branches extending from the Heart line

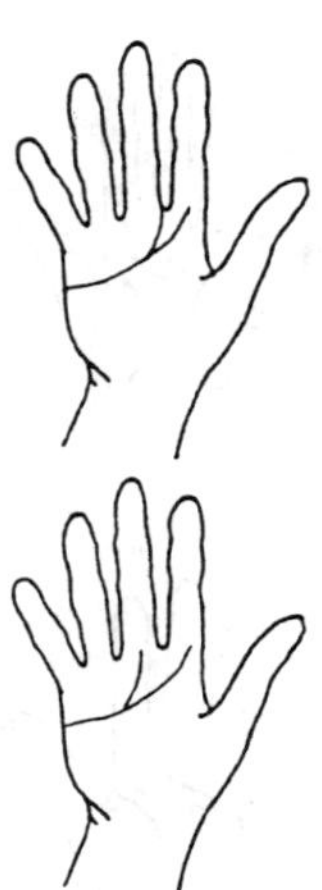

When the Heart line branches off in fork-like lines, with one branch leaning on the Jupiter Mount and the other between the first and second finger, this is an indication that the peron is happy and lucky in love, with a capacity to give and take in a stable emotional relationship. On the other hand, when the lines are wide apart and one is on the Jupiter Mount and the other on Saturn Mount, this points to a hesitant person who is generally unable to build a happy marriage because of his fickle temperament (little branches extending from the Heart line restrain this negative characteristic).

Note: The noted chirologue Cheiro claims that if the Heart line is thin and lacks any ramifications, this is evidence of emotional frigidity.

An island on the Heart line

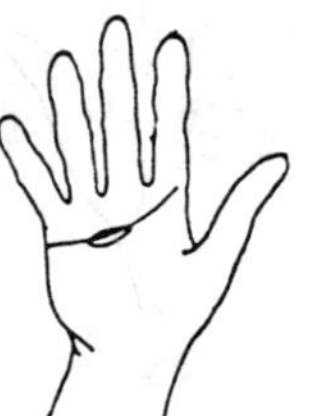

The existence of an island on the Heart line may be a sign of a possible heart attack, of problems of the circulatory system or the eyesight (problems which may exist or grow worse as a result of an emotional blow, even though one cannot pinpoint the exact source of these afflictions). The larger the island, the greater the problem. The age at which the island appears can be determined according to the calendar of events of the Heart- Line.

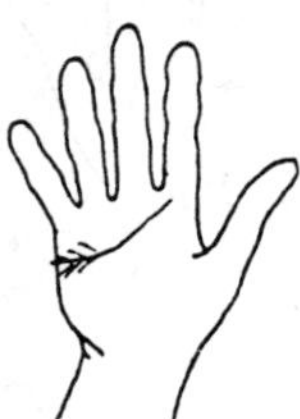

The "ear of corn"

The "ear of corn" or those little lines branching out from the end of the Heart line are a sign of fertility (birth-giving). The absence of these tiny lines may indicate biological barrenness (which may have emotional origins).

A double Heart-Line

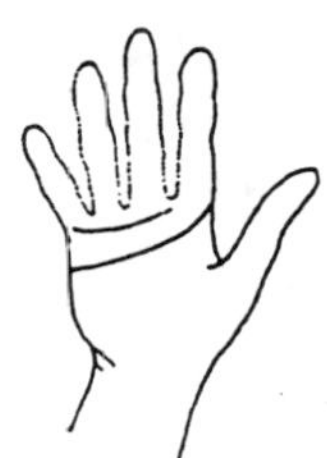

A quite unusual situation which points to an abundance of feelings, unlimited kindness, the desire and need to relate to and help one's mate – sometimes at the expense of the person's own private life. Such an individual would be advised to work at a caring profession, so that he or she would be able to properly direct and unburden himself of his excessive emotional baggage.

A Heart line, Head line and Life line connected at their outset

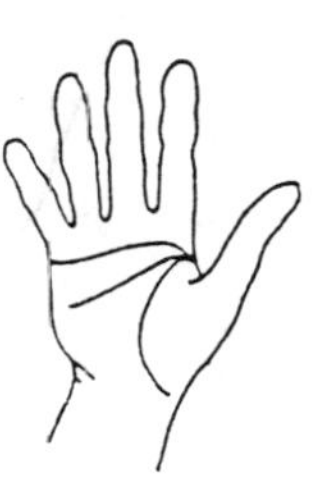

When all three lines are attached at the beginning of their course, this indicates a serious personality problem. People with this type of palm lines have no control over their drives and instincts and may behave in an unexpected and destructive fashion as a result of uncontrolled urges and the use of violence. In many cases, these reactions have their source in a difficult childhood caused by the parents' unhappy relationship which tend to be expressed in outbursts of jealousy towards one's spouse.

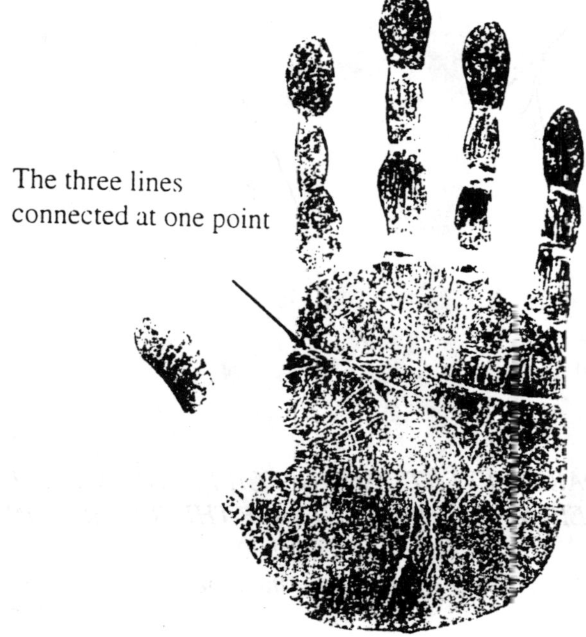

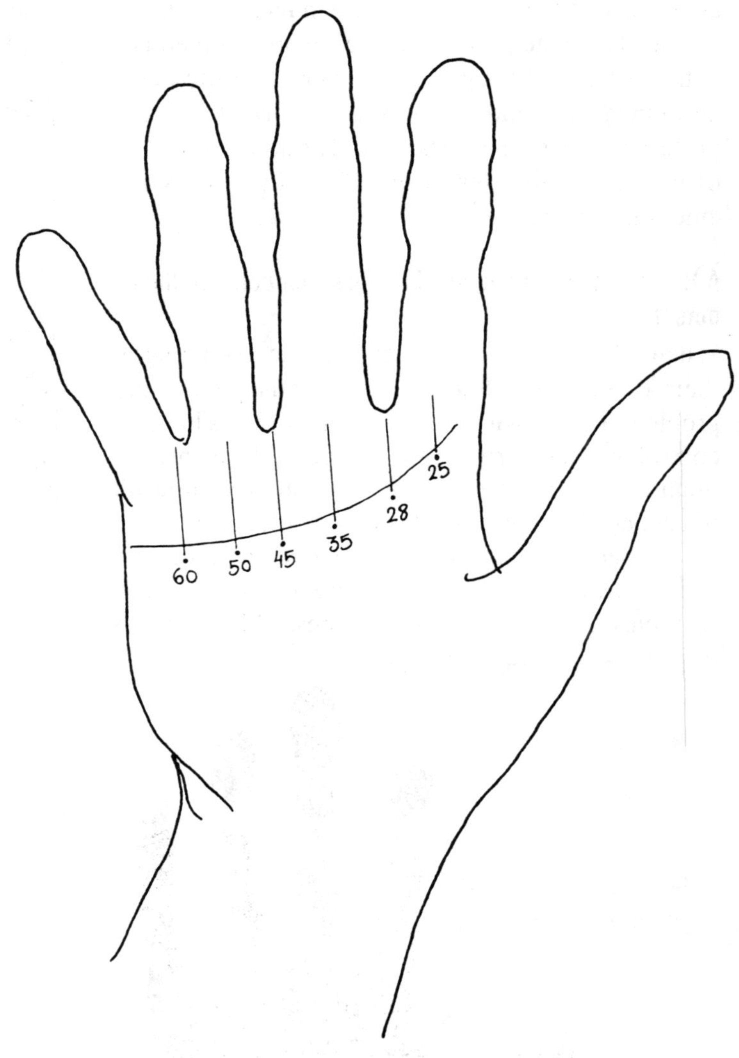

CALENDAR OF EVENTS, AND SPECIFIC AGES WHICH LEFT THEIR MARK (OR WILL LEAVE THEIR MARK) ON THE HEART LINE
(See the Ages along the Line)

THE GIRDLE OF VENUS

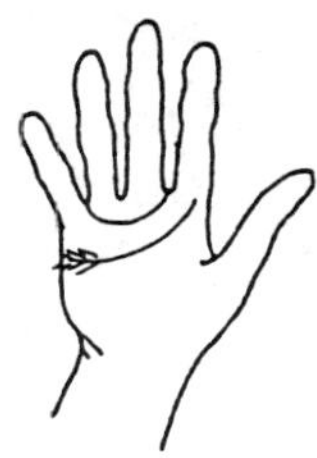

The Girdle of Venus is a line (continuous or interrupted), starting from between the first and second fingers and ending between the third and fourth fingers in the form of a semi-circle above the Heart line. There are two different interpretations of the significance attached to the Girdle of Venus:

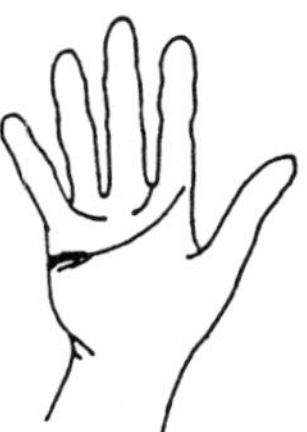

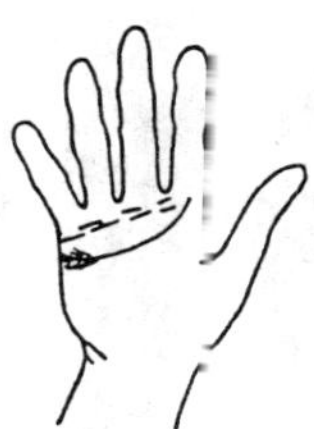

a) The first is that it indicates a high degree of intelligence and a profoundly intuitive nature,
b) The second indicates quickly changing moods, excessive sensitivity, evident inner anxiety and a tendency towards hysteria and depression.

Note: In order to properly understand the negative influences of the Girdle of Venus, one must examine the remainder of the lines of the palm as well as the shape of the hand: a square or primitivae hand will be less influenced by the Girdle of Venus.

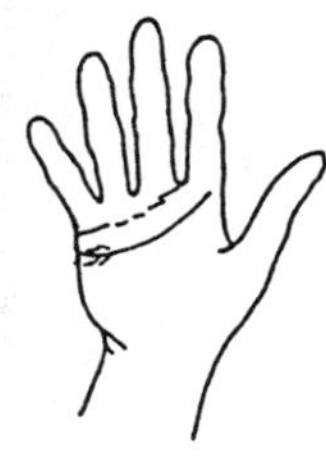

- The Girdle of Venus which continues to the end of the hand and touches the marriage line is a sign of serious problems within the marriage relationship, stemming from the difficult temperaments of the marriage partners. It is generally characterized by very demanding people with unrealistic and exacting expectations, that is, people who are hard to live with.

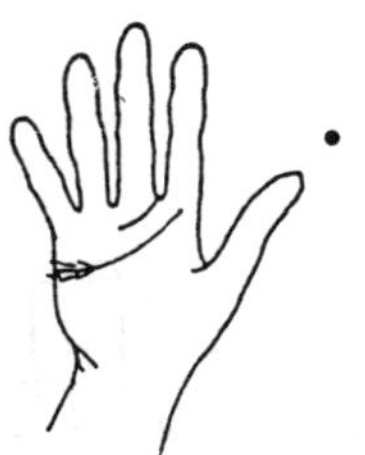

- When half the Girdle of Venus (a short horizontal line) appears on the palm, this points to a lack of perseverance and pessimism.

The Girdle Of Venus

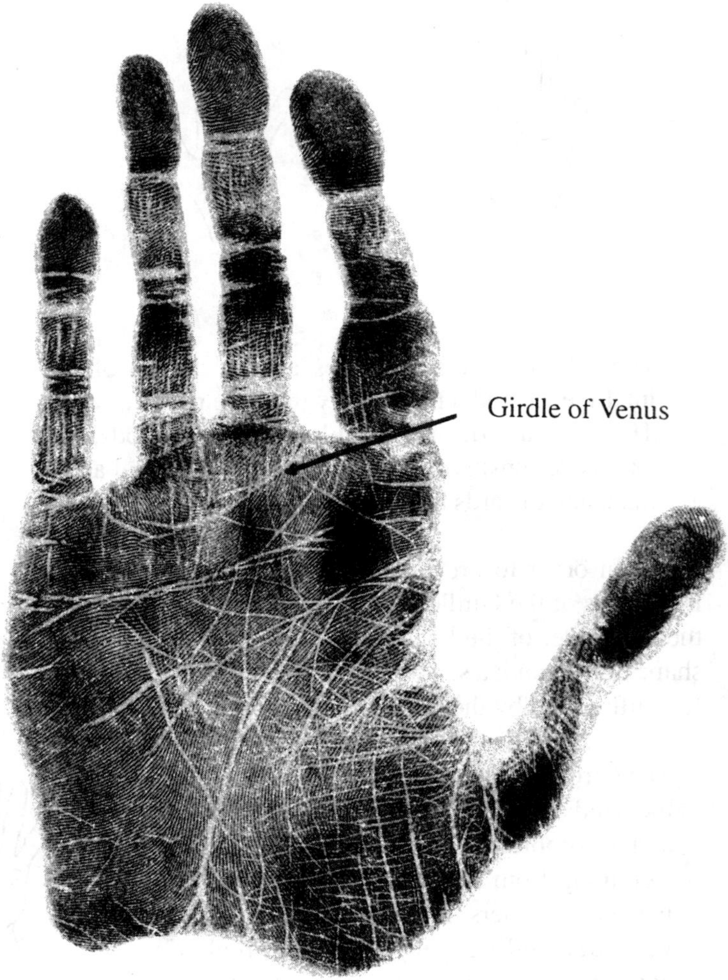

Girdle of Venus

THE LINE OF FATE

This line relates to all our worldly affairs: the practical and material occupations and professional aspects of our lives, the accomplishments and failures in these areas and especially to our careers and the extent to which we have learned to fulfil our potentials. The Fate Line also indicates the strength of character, and how much approval we may expect from other people. We frequently find evidence here of personal crises, changes in our careers, success in business, or unhappily, losses.

It is generally accepted that we ascribe to the Fate line the various events in our lives over which we have no control, but I am of the opinion that everyone is in control of his or her fate and that its successful outcome or failure lies in the individual's direction.

When we refer to the Fate Line, we are ascribing considerable importance to this type of hand. For instance, when a good Fate Line appears on a square, primitive or broad hand, we give it more weight than to a similar line appearing on the Philosophic, Conical, or the Emotional hand, particularly when we are dealing with material success. This is not surprising, as these people are inclined to believe in the power of fate, and it is quite common for the Fate Line to appear on their hands. The owners of the Square or Broad hands, on the other hand, are much more rational and generally do not believe in Fate, and hence the appearance of the Fate Line on their hands will merely strengthen them and give them greater drive to succeed in their careers.

A Rigid Fate Line, Straight and Long

A straight Fate Line, which begins at the base of the hand and continues upward in an uninterrupted line is quite uncommon. Such a line indicates that the person always knows what he or she wants and is aware of their aim in life. This type of line indicates a very strong personality and the likelihood of material stability (that is, when the line is not faulty).

A Fate Line attached to the Life Line or rising from it

A Fate Line which is partly connected or attached to the Life Line (also if it starts out separately) points to the possibility that at a certain period, particularly in one's youth, the person was under the influence of his parents or other family members, who prevented the individual from developing and maturing as a result of his or her obligations towards them (for instance, a person whose parents were in need of financial support or whose marriage was problematic and unsatisfactory). The age at which the Fate Line branches out from the Life Line (according to the calendar of events of the Fate Line) marks the point at which the person managed to free himself from these obligations and burdens.

A Fate Line extending from the Girdle of Venus

The meaning of such a line is that the connection with one's spouse or parents is more problematic than the former case (when the line extends from the Life Line), and the family or romantic reality is very complex.

(Not very long ago, a business man asked for my advice regarding some business matters. When I looked at his hand, I discovered such a line. It seems that his wife went out of her mind after the birth of their first child and many years of hospitalization in an institution for the mentally ill. In view of the circumstances, the individual was obliged to devote himself entirely to family affairs and his business ventures suffered and did not succeed).

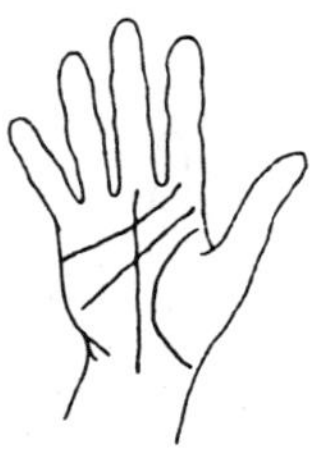

A Fate line rising from the base of the hand and continuing until the Saturn Mount.

Such a line is a sign of outstanding success. This person has unusual possibilities of developing both in the direction of his career and intellectually.

A Fate Line extending from the Moon Mount

In this instance, the success of the person will depend on appreciation from his surroundings. In general, such a line indicates the capacity to succeed in an artistic career, or is a sign of a person who has social ambitions of a high order which are likely to succeed when connected with the public, such as social work, education and teaching, or any type of occupation dealing with the public. It is possible to be more precise about the type of work by taking into consideration the type of hand and other lines of the palm.

A Fate Line branching off in various directions

In principle, when the Fate Line branches out towards the Saturn Mount or in the direction of other mounts, this indicates that the qualities attributed to that mount will influence the life of the hand's owner, particularly as far as his career is concerned.

If the line turns in the direction of the Jupiter Mount, this indicates the presence of marked boastfulness and a person with strong motivation to further his career or to control the careers of others (this is one of the signs of leadership qualities). At any rate, this person will always strive to direct or issue directions to others, but will not suffer other people's control over his own activities. A Fate Line branching towards Jupiter is very common among public officials, heads of institutions and enterprises, city leaders, etc.

A Fate Line which continues on its usual course to the Saturn Mount

This type of Fate Line is very common, and generally indicates that the owner will achieve all his wishes in the professional sphere, especially if there are no faults in the line. As the Saturn Mount is considered the symbol of fatalism (fate's control over our lives) then man has little control over his fate and he will encounter situations in which he cannot control the fateful events in his life (and not only as far as his career is concerned).

This sign takes on more weight if the Fate Line actually reaches the beginning of the Saturn finger.

A Fate Line moving towards the Sun Mount

A certain sign of fame and luck; the possibility of material, professional, and social success. This type of line is typical of artists and well-known public figures.

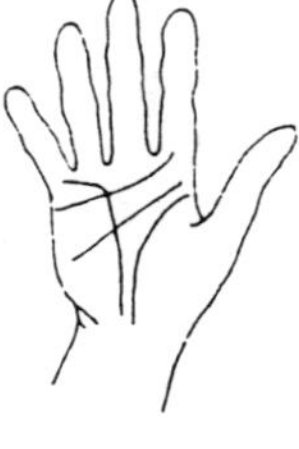

A Fate Line facing the Mercury Mount

In such an instance, the person with this hand can become an outstanding success in commercial affairs or science.

A Fate Line which begins from the center of the palm (Mars Plain)

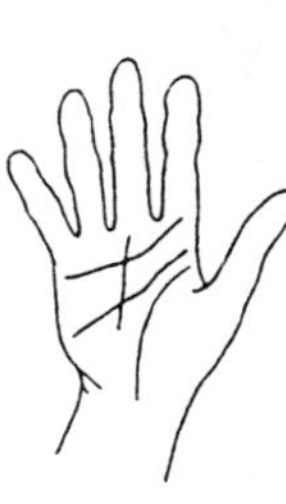

A Fate Line which begins at the center of the palm points to a person who has not found his or her way early in life, and only at the age of thirty or thereabouts do they find themselves as a result of their personal ambition and drive. One can assume that until this age, these peoples' lives were difficult, or grey and dull, until they found the means of expressing their true personalities.

An example of this is that of a person who was obliged to work for a living at something that did not interest him, as was the case of a production engineer whom I knew, who worked on a machine in an enterprise until the age of 28. At that point, he decided to return to his studies in order to further his professional knowledge, and at the age of 30-32 became an engineer. His life then became infinitely more interesting and his financial situation also changed beyond recognition – all of which was indicated by the Fate Line which began to grow and develop from the concave area in the center of the palm.

A Fate Line which begins to appear at the age of 35 – above the Head Line

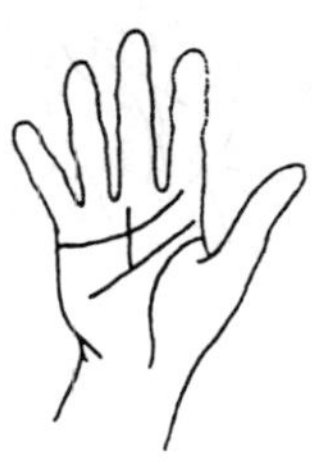

A Fate Line which begins comparatively late, above the Head-Line indicates – like its predecessor – a late career development or self- realization. There are no lucky elements in this persons life and all his or her achievements will be the fruit of the persons deliberation and will-power. It is important to examine the type of hand on which this line appears: it will be more meaningful if it appears on a square hand, and less so, on a conical or emotional hand.

A Fate Line which begins on the Heart Line

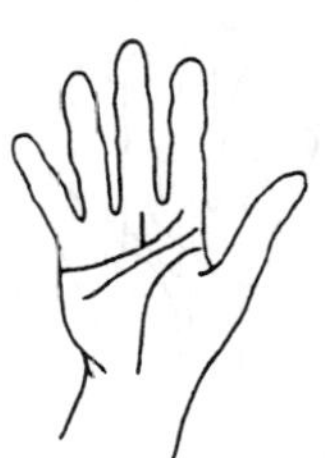

This is a very rare state. We do not ascribe much significance to this type of line with regard to the person's career or luck in life, owing to the very late stage at which it appears.

A Fate-Line cut off by the Head Line

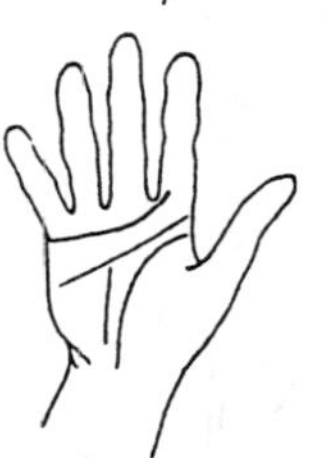

A successful career will be cut short by some foolish act or mistaken consideration, that is, a rational but unwise decision or not properly thought out, can bring a career to an end.

A Fate-Line which stops suddenly at the Heart Line

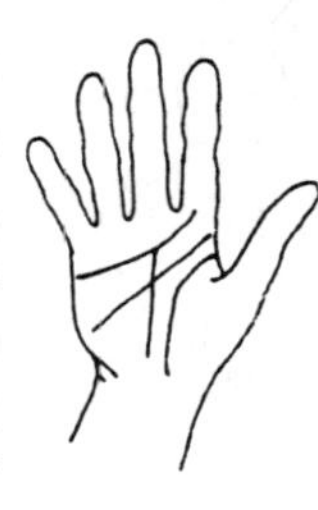

The achievements of this person will be cut short as the result of an error in making a decision in connection with his or her emotional life (that is an emotional rather than a rational decision). If the Fate-Line joings the Heart LIne and together they rise twoards the Jupiter Mount, this person would then fulfil his or her aspirations owing to the influence of this Mount.

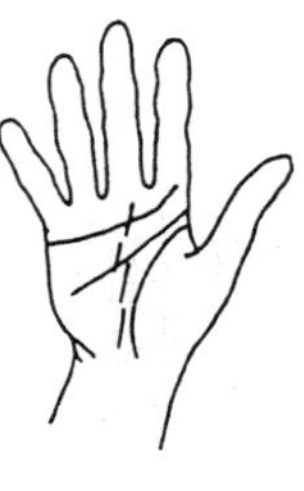

An interrupted Fate-Line lacking uniformity

Every interrupted line is evidence that the matters which should be under control are not running smoothly. When the Fate-Line is disconnected and irregular in shape, this is a sign that the person's career will be neither peaceful, certain, nor stable. This person's life may be subject to ups and downs. Many crises may arise in either the professional area or psychologically. If the Fate Line is cut off suddenly (an open break) this is a certain sign of bad luck and loss. If the break is overlapping, this is a sign of a change in the course of the person's life – whether career-wise or the person's place of work or residence.

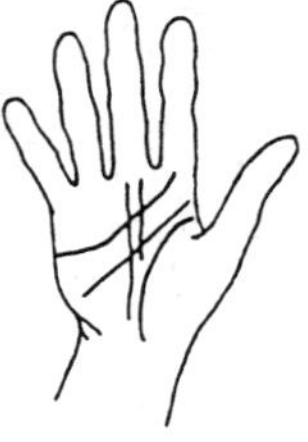

A Double Fate-Line

This is an excellent sign. It points to two separate careers which the owner of this hand pursues simultaneously, or work and studies in different spheres. This is a sign of luck and success in life.

An Island on the Fate-Line

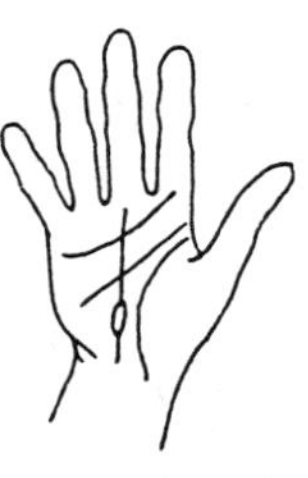

Sign of an absence of luck and a loss of money or work at the age it appears (according to the calendar of events). In certain instances, this may point to an emotional or psychological problem at the time (the category of problem can be pin-pointed on the basis of the additional signs on the palm). An island on the Fate Line may also appear during a crisis caused by divorce proceedings.

A Palm without a Fate-Line

The complete absence of a Fate-Line constitutes a negative sign for the palm. People without a Fate-Line are likely to succeed in their careers. However, they will not be happy because they are not capable of experiencing strong feelings: they do not feel happiness or sadness, there are neither smiles nor tears in their lives. They can be described as insensitive and dull – they eat, drink and sleep, but actually live like a plant, without feelings.

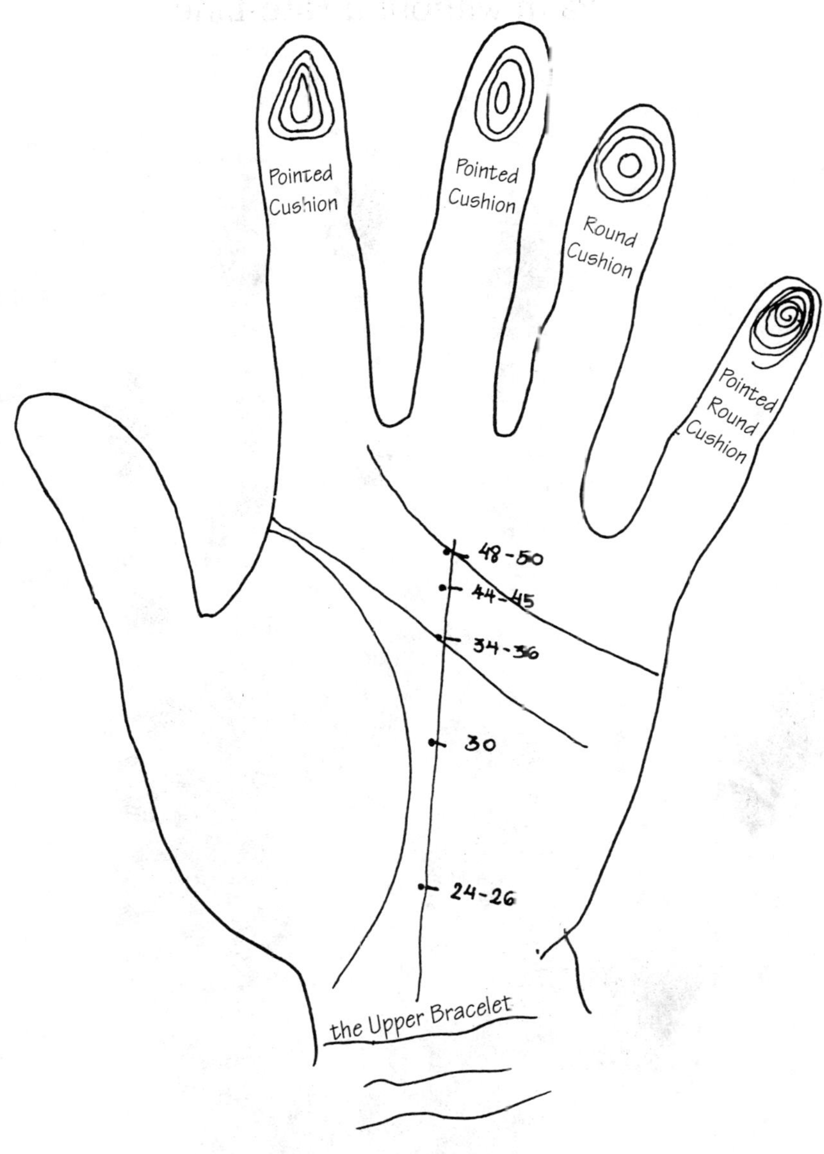

Calendar of Events, which at a certain age left its mark (or will leave their mark) on the ***FATE LINE***
(Note the ages along the Line)

Palm without a Fate-Line

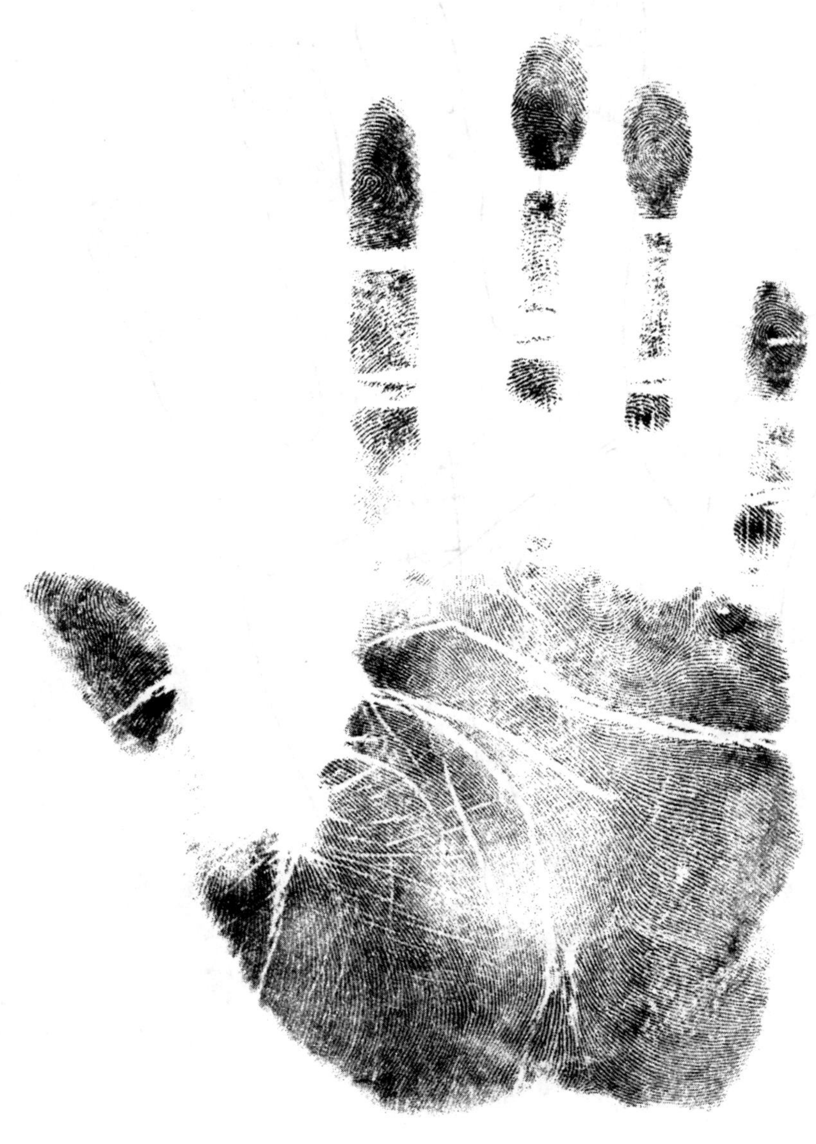

Palm with a continuous and good Fate Line

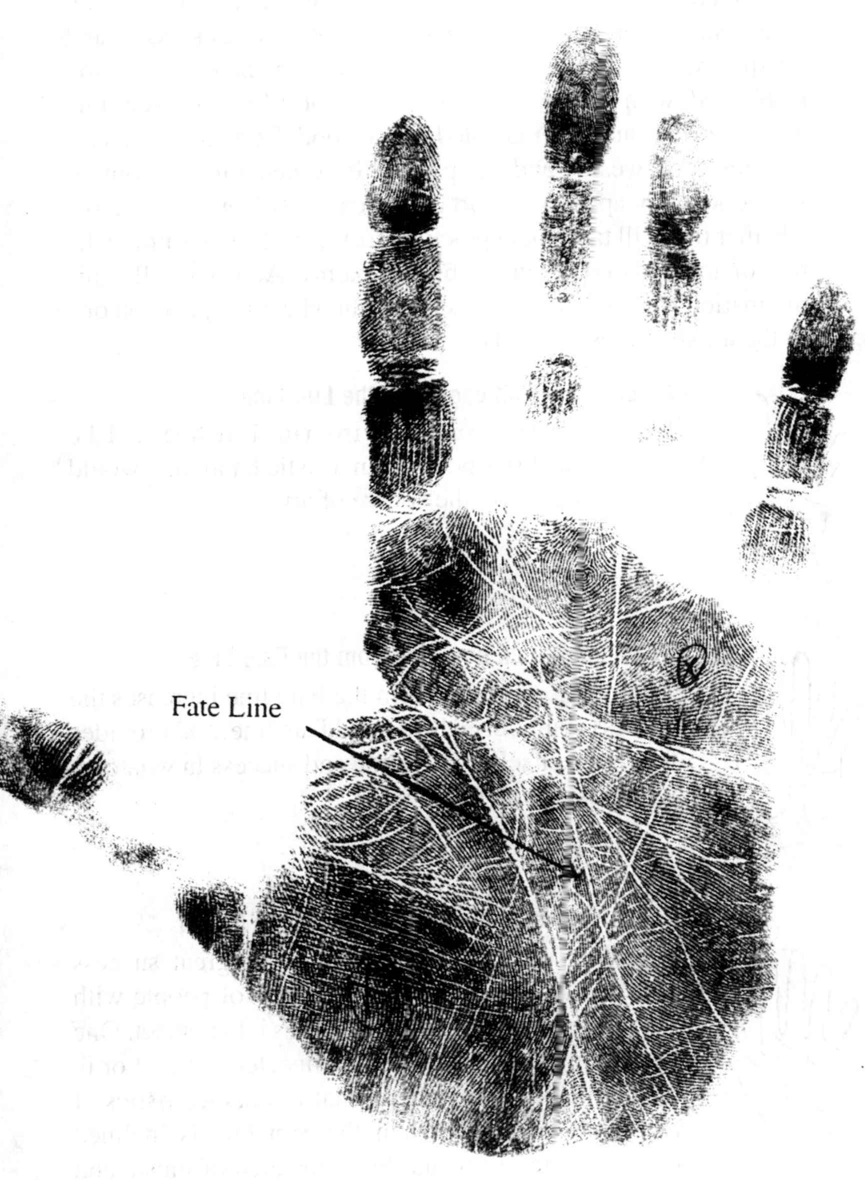

THE SUN LINE

The Sun line is the line of success. As the Sun relates to the Earth, so the Sun line relates to our lives – and it denotes success and prosperity. From whatever age it appears on the hand, the person is blessed with happiness and the joy of life. The Sun line increases the success indicated by a good Fate line and is a guarantee of wealth and happiness. It is generally a sign of someone who appreciates art and beauty (in order to know whether this will take some practical form, one must examine the rest of information provided by the palm). And naturally this inclination will be much more significant when it appears on one of the artistic types of hands.

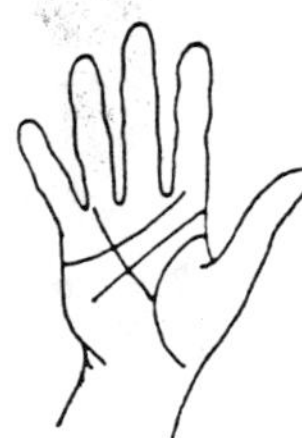

A Sun line which begins on the Life Line

When the Sun line emerges from the Life line, and the other indications point to an artistic hand, this would ensure success in the sphere of art.

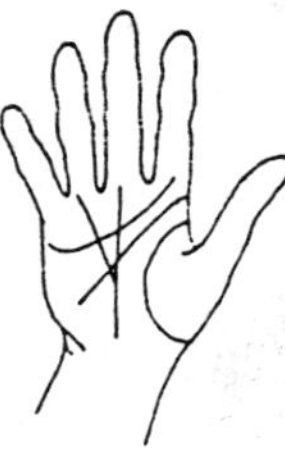

A Sun line which emerges from the Fate Line

A Sun line emerging from the Fate line increases the success symbolized by a good Fate line, and provides for a greater self- realization and success in whatever field this person is occupied.

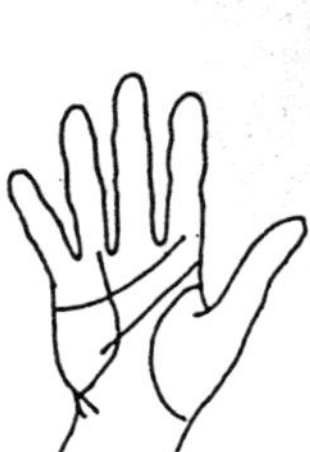

A Sun line which begins from the Moon Mount

The significance of this Sun line is great success which is dependent on the influence of people with whom the owner of this hand comes into contact. One is referring here to activities connected with art or in the public or social sphere (that is, characteristics of the Moon Mount). When the Sun line is inclined upwards, success would be in the area of music and singing, writing or any artistic medium which calls for imagination.

If the Head line is straight, then success in this case would generally be found in the public domain.

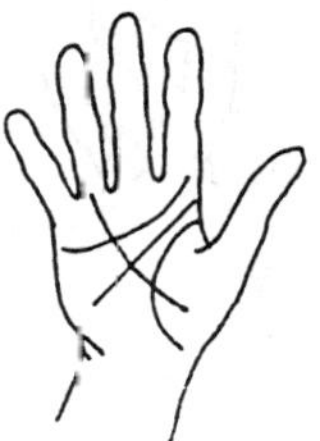

Sun line emerging from the Girdle of Venus

Wealth and happiness will be the lot of this person owing to his or her marriage to someone both rich and famous.

A Very Long Sun line starting from the base of the hand and reaching the lower edge of the Sun Finger

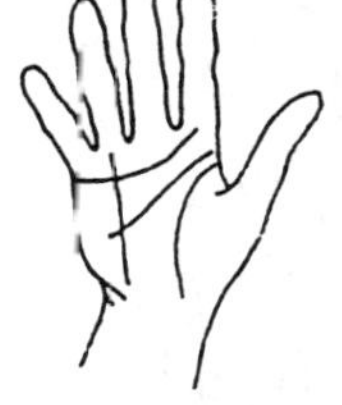

Such a long and firm Sun Line is a sign of success and fame from a comparatively early age and is quite rare. We find such hands among famous people, especially actors and others engaged in the sphere of entertainment although it can appear in the hands of political figures or successful officers of the higher ranks.

[Not very long ago, one of the wardens of the Ramle prison visited me. There was such a line on the print of his hand, accompanied by a very good Fate line. On further examination of the lines of the palm it occured to me that most of his life, he had occupied roles of authority within a government framework. Obviously, he had enjoyed both repute and success in most of these positions...(see hand print on page).

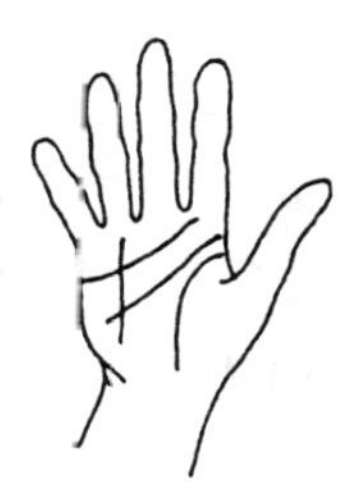

Sun line emerging from the Plain of Mars

A Sun line starting from the Plain of Mars (like the Fate line) is a sign of success from approximately the age of thirty. This state would come only after many years of difficulties and hard work.

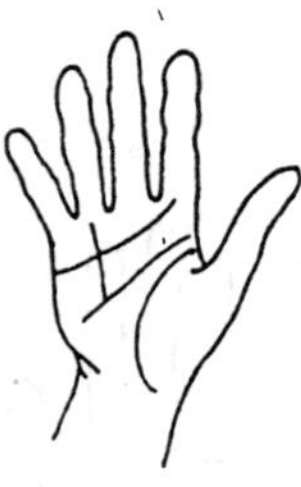

Sun line which starts from the Head Line

The meaning of this line is that this person's success is not dependant on other people or luck, but is achieved as a result of his own talents. Personal ambition and will-power are the basic factor in this person's achievement but success will arrive in mid-life.

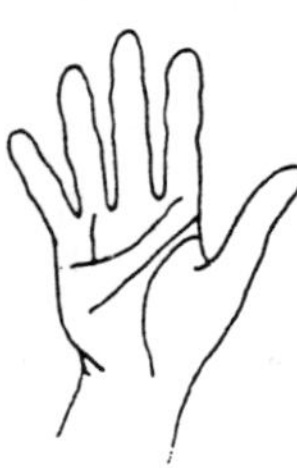

Sun line which starts at the Heart Line

A Sun line which begins at the Heart line is a sign of good taste and a very developed aesthetic sense, as well as of success which would come rather late, at about the age of fifty.

Note: In former times, not much significance was accorded to this line as life-expectancy was much shorter and it was unlikely that the average man would live to this age to enjoy his success. Today many people achieve prosperity and fulfilment at a later age, owing to a much higher life-expectancy.

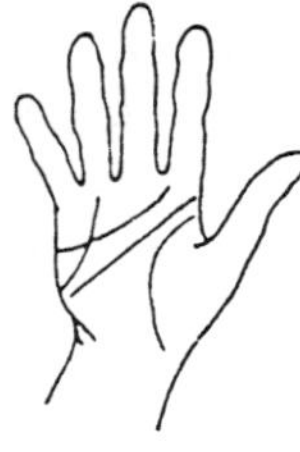

Sun line beginning on the upper Mars Mount

Here there is the possibility of making one's mark in the field of creative writing, the sciences or finance (the specific area can be determined by the other lines of the palm.)

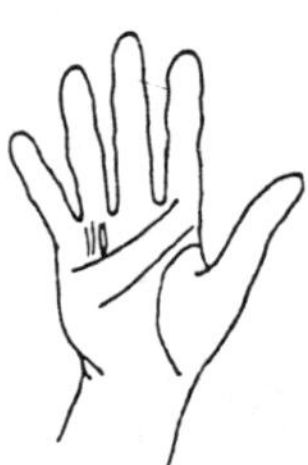

Many Lines on the Sun Mount

Many lines on the mount below the Sun Finger is a sign of an artistic personality and the desire to occupy oneself with various fields simultaneously which may lead to a lack of perseverance. This type of line does warrant fame or repute.

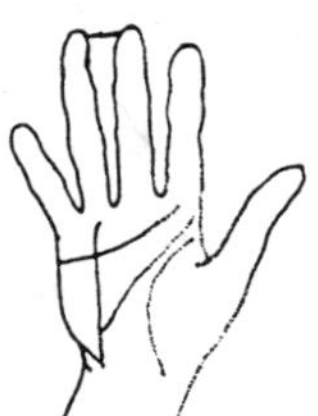

A Saturn Finger and Sun Finger of equal length, with a longer Sun line

This is the hand of the classic gambler in every area of life. When these characteristics are combined with a straight Head line, it indicates the desire to achieve status, power, and money.

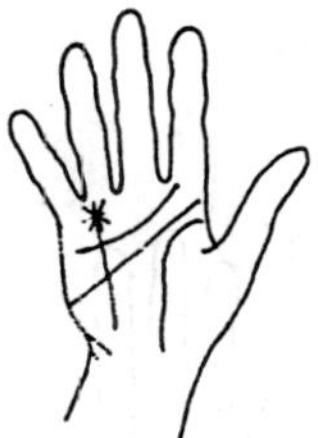

A Star at the end of the Sun line

This is the most wonderful sign one can find on a hand. It is an omen of outstanding success in one's career and an equally good reputation.

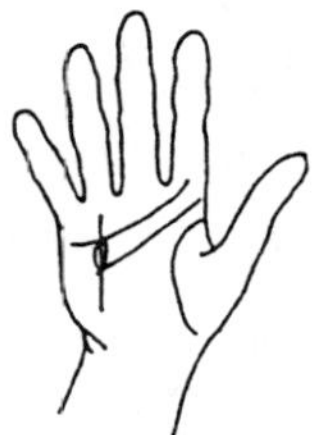

An Island on the Sun line

This indicates a difficult period and a loss of status and reputation, generally as the result of a personal or family scandal. In certain instances, it also denotes financial losses.

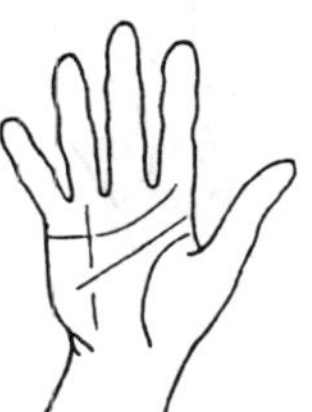

An open break on the Sun Line

This indicates a difficult period generally connected with the loss of money or property.

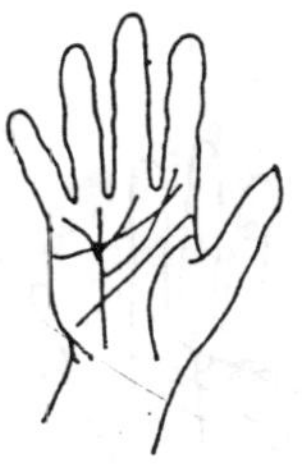

A Sun line emerging in many branches

The significance of every branch emerging from the Sun line is linked to the Mount it reaches.

Note: The age-mark indicated by the Sun line is based on the age appearing on the Fate line.

THE MYSTIC CROSS

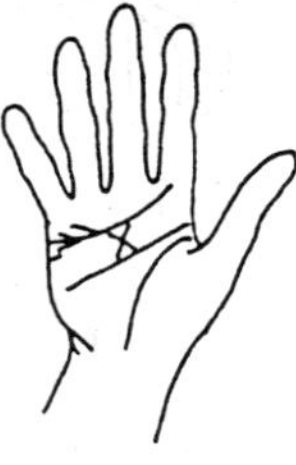

The mystic cross is always situated between the Head line and the Heart line, an area which is called "square". It appears either alone or in a series of crosses, and at times is partly created by the Fate line. People with this cross are blessed with a highly developed intuitive sense and keen sensitivity. They are frequently religiously inclined even if they do not admit it or are not aware of it – they generally prefer to believe in fate or some higher power.

These individuals are psychologically strong personalities. who in a crisis, are not in need of solace from professional care-givers but tend to work out their problems through their own psychological understanding.

When the mystic cross is situated high on the palm, in the direction of the Jupiter finger, the person will believe in mysticism in all matters related to his or her own life: they would want their fortunes told and would be curious to know how or whether their aspirations would be achieved, but they would not show any deeper interest in the subject for its own sake. When the cross is found near the Heart line, it signifies that the persons' intuition will be directed towards emotional matters (lovers, the childrens' problems, feelings towards one's companion). If, on the other hand, the mystic cross is nearer the Head line or forms part of the Fate line, their intuition will be more inclined towards business or a career (such an individual will know when and where to invest his or her money...).

It is known that the Head line has a decisive influence over the mystic cross. If this line is long, it is a proven sign of an interest in mysticism, especially if the cross appears as a sign on its own and not as part of another line. When the Head line is short and makes a sharp turn downward, and carries the mystic cross, this is evidence of belief in superstitions.

When the mystic cross touches the Fate Line or is part of it, this indicates that the feeling for the mystic will actually influence the individual's career in a practical manner.

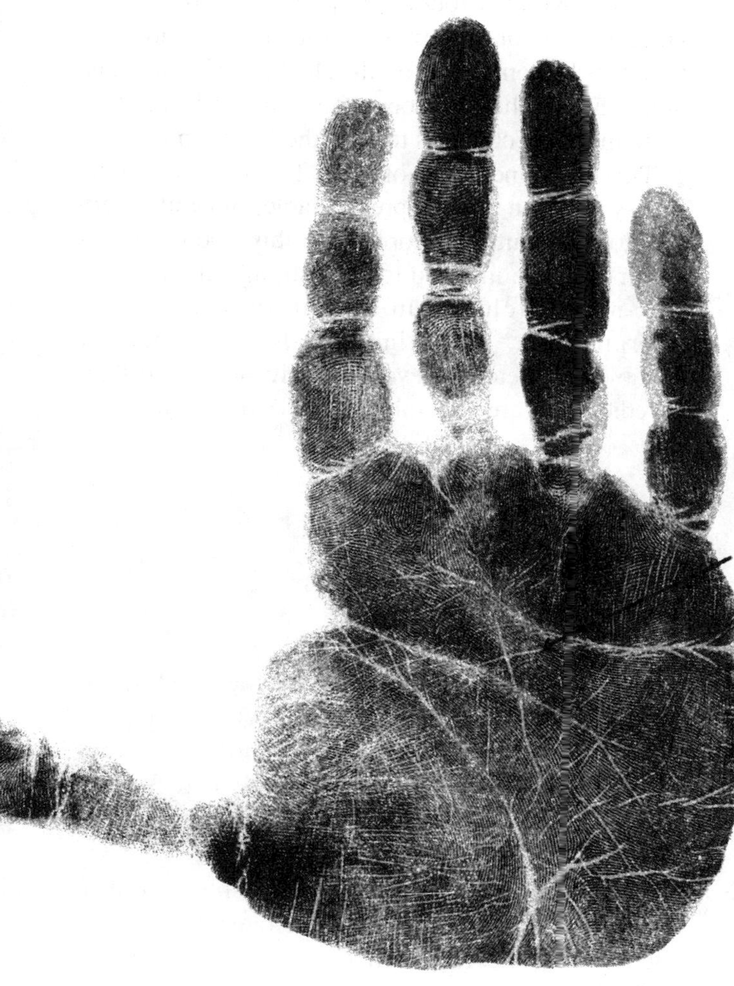

INTUITION LINE

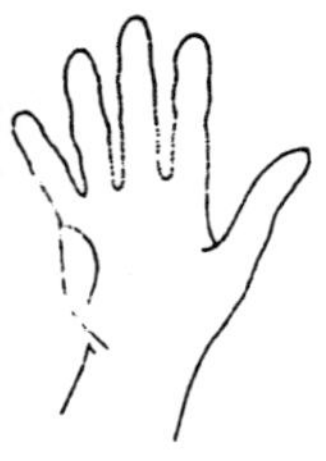

The Intuition Line, also called "Witches' Line", appears at the side of the palm in the form of a crescent, which stretches from the Mercury Mount until the Moon Mount. Frequently it crosses the Health Line or continues alongside it and may therefore be confused with the Health Line (one must note whether the line goes around in the form of an arch, in which case it is termed the Intuition Line.

This line is indicative of a very flexible person who is easy to get on with, impressionable, and with a very developed intuition. People with this line (which is rather rare) are inclined to have strange and colorful dreams which do not lend themselves to interpretation. These individuals are frequently capable of foretelling events in advance – and their "predictions" are generally fulfilled to the letter.

AMBITION LINE

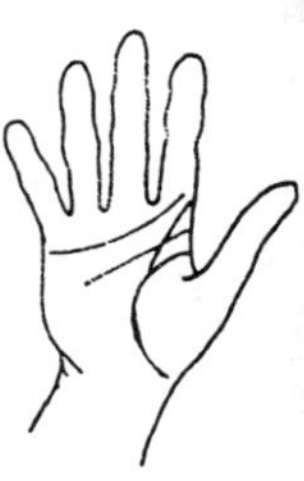

This is the line which emerges from the Life line and ascends towards the Jupiter finger. When it emerges from the Life line before the age of thirty (according to the Life Line's calendar of ages), it is defined as the Ambition Line but when it appears behond this age, it is called the Fate Line.

The Ambition Line points to the aspiration of its owner to reach more significant achievements in his life and is also evidence that from the age it appears on the hand, its owner shows greater drive to improve his intellectual and financial status. In practical terms, this means that he or she may decide to pursue their studies or commercial interests and will also carry out these decisions.

Palm With Intuition Line

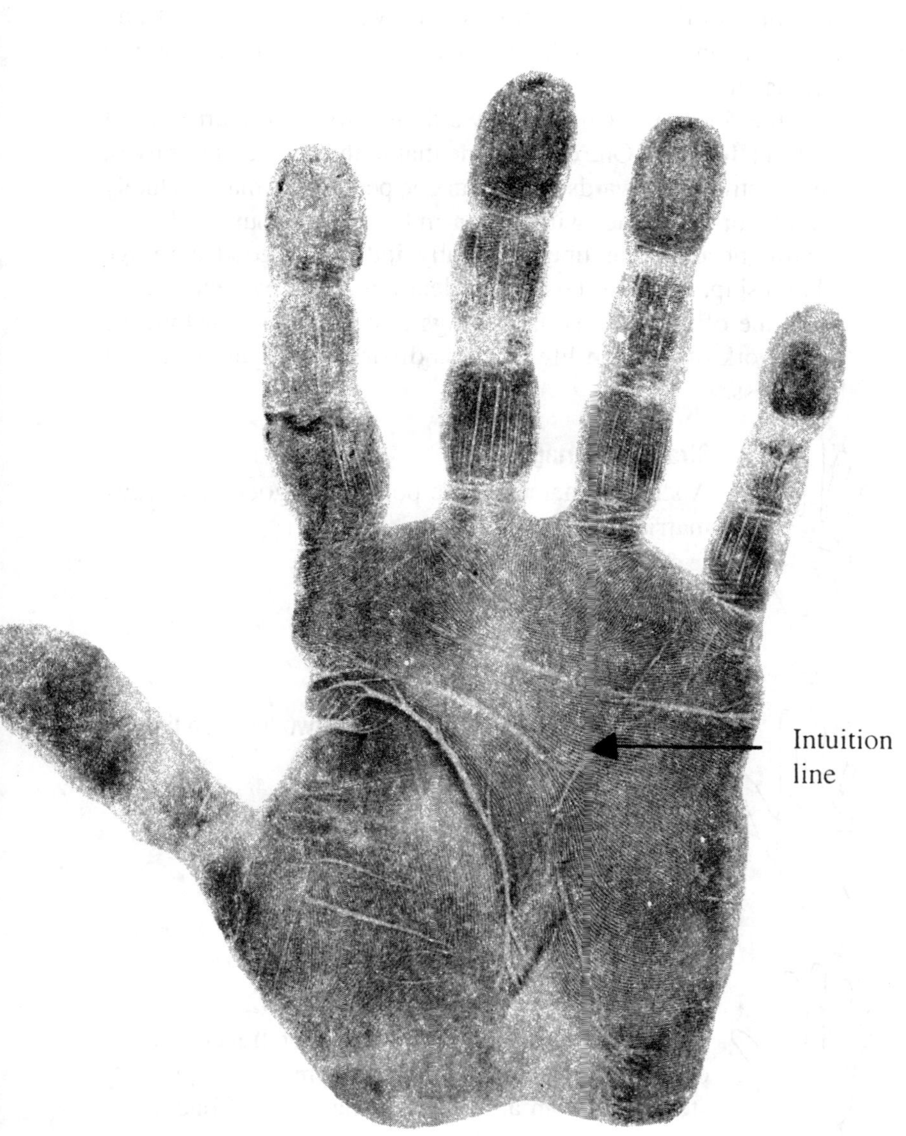

MARRIAGE LINE

The Marriage Lines are little lines which are found on the outward side of the palm, between the end of the Heart line and the beginning of the Sun Finger. It is only when the lines are strong and clear can one claim that the marriage or the relationship is a serious one.

In the science of Chirology, we do not speak of marriage but of strong feelings. One can assume that in the course of our lives, we feel strongly towards more than one person and that it is likely that two or more lines will appear on the palm of our hands.

Straight and clear lines generally indicate a good marriage relationship. It is also possible to learn and find evidence in the Sun Line of the various happenings that may occur within the framework of married life, such as divorce, betrayal or lack of happiness.

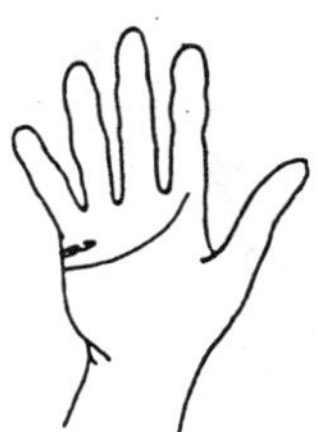

Straight Marriage Line

A straight marriage line points to a good and happy marriage.

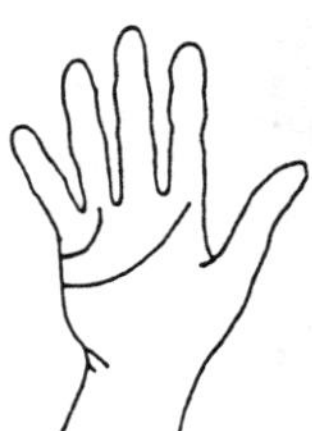

Marriage line which separates into two fork-like lines

Indicates divorce or separation.

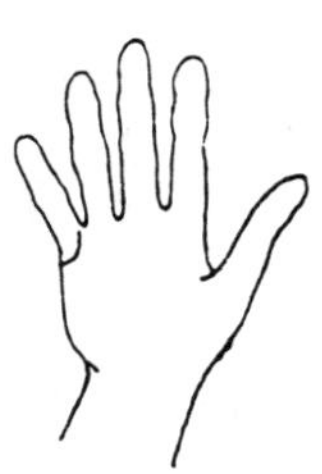

Marriage Line with an island at its center

This indicates a serious problem or tragedy which occurred during the course of the marriage (possibly stemming from an illness or the death of one of the partners), or a possible separation.

Marriage Line bending towards the Heart Line

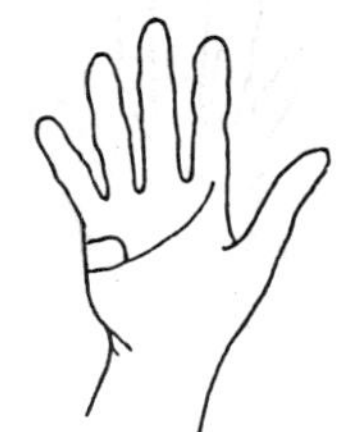

It is to be hoped that the spouse of the individual with this line will depart from this life before he or she does.

Marriage Line which branches off into forked lines at its outset

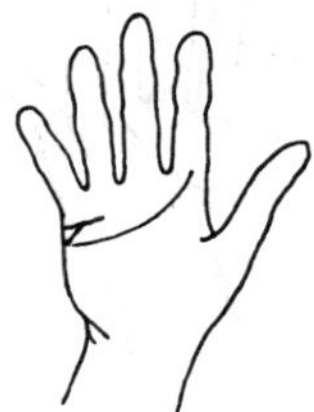

This line indicates problems and delays prior to the marriage ceremony, and at times also a separation before the marriage.

Marriage Line which crosses the Sun Line and descends

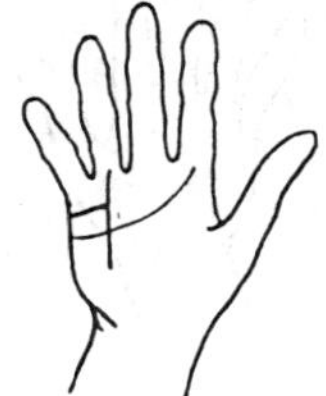

This line warns that the person with this line can expect a decline in his or her social status or property by marrying.

A Line branching off from the Marriage Line and touching the Head Line

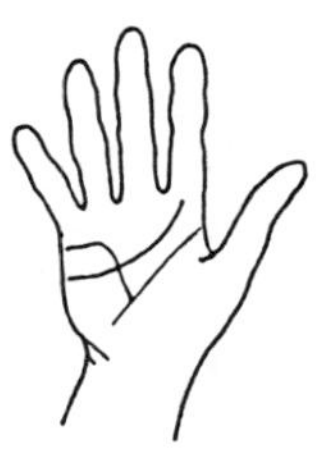

This line is a sign of an unhappy marriage owing to the psychological instability of the spouse or a basic difference of opinions. In every instance, this line is an indication of unhappiness.

A Divided Marriage Line

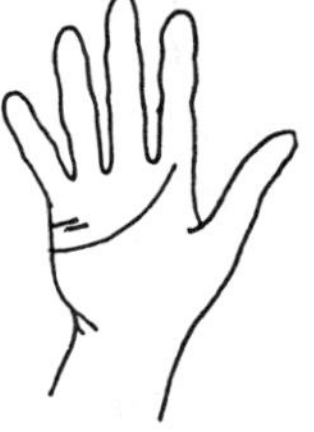

This is a sign of a sudden separation in the course of the marriage.

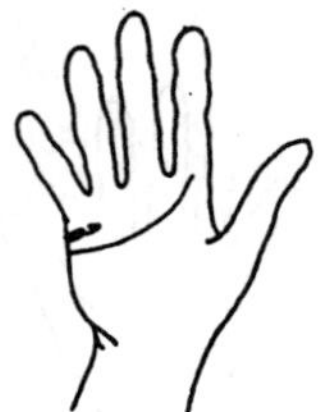

A Marriage Line with many small islands

This is a negative sign, indicating a very unhappy marriage.

A Marriage Line which ascends towards the Sun Finger

This is a very happy indication: the marriage will bring with it wealth and happiness as well as a higher social status.

A small Marriage Line which climbs onto the Mercury Finger

There is the possibility that the owner of this line will not marry at all.

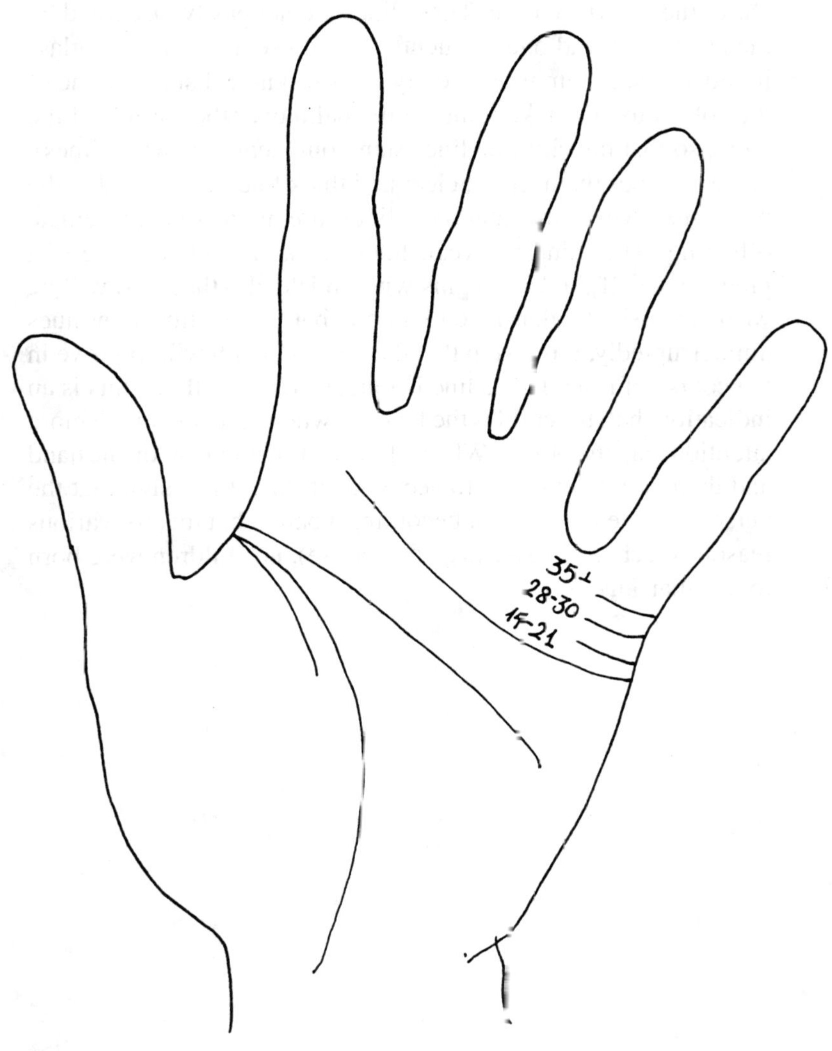

Calendar of Events, which at certain ages left their mark (or will leave their mark) on the ***MARRIAGE LINE***
(See the age along the line)

CHILDREN LINES

The Children Lines are those which are found placed vertically above the Marriage Line. These lines are not easily discerned by the naked eye, and one frequently has to use a magnifying glass in order to see them more clearly. (For instance, I smear some of the color I use to make prints of the palm over the surface of the palm, so that the children lines stand out clearly as white lines). As to the lines themselves: clear and thick lines are related to the male sex, while the diagonal lines are indicative of female offspring. The thin and weak lines are a sign of unsuccessful pregnancies. If the line begins with an island – the child will be weak and sickly during childhood, but if the line continues uninterruptedly, it is a sign that the child's health will improve in the course of time. If one line is longer than the others, this is an indication that this child is the favorite who will enjoy much more attention than the others. When Children Lines appear on the hand and there are no children to account for this, it is a sign that the person had the possibity of becoming a parent but that for various reasons (such as the sterility of a spouse), no children were born to this marriage.

Children Lines

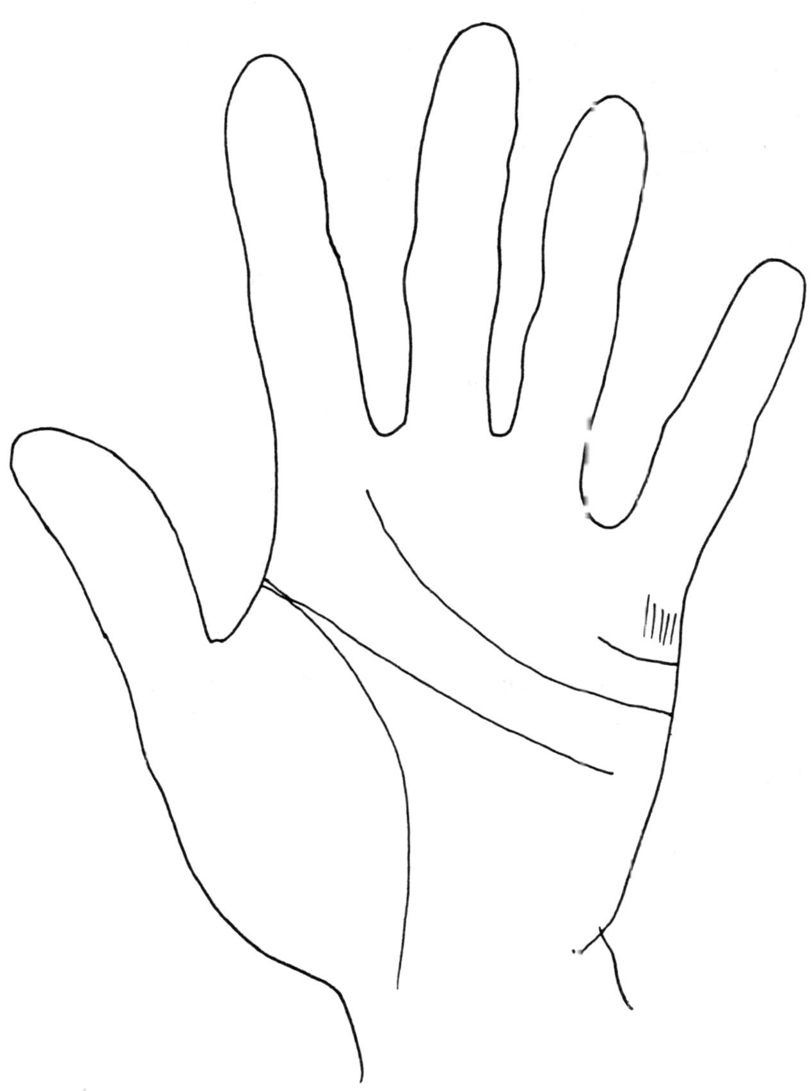

HEALTH LINE

The Health Line is that line which continues diagonally from the Mercury Mount to the Life Line. It must be straight and clear: the straighter it is, the better it is, but it is preferable if the Health line does not appear on the hand at all. If there are two Health lines (or more), one alongside the other, this is a sign of a serious health problem. Faults and islands indicate health problems, but one cannot distinguish what these problems solely from the Health line; the nails, the Heart line and the Life line must also be examined. The mere presence of the Health line in any form is a sign that a health problem exists which must be seen to.

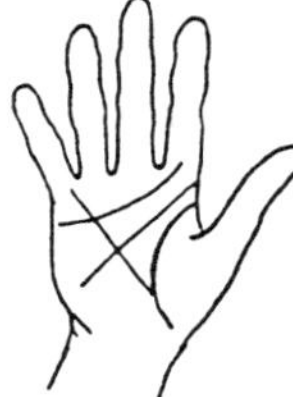

Health Line touching the Life Line

There is a serious health problem at the age indicated by its appearance along the Life line.

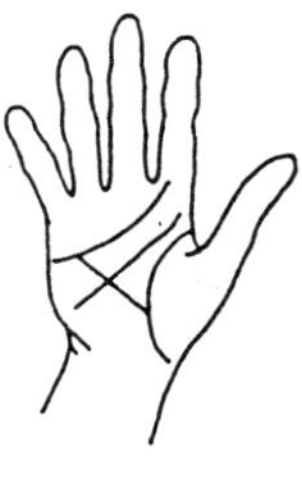

Health Line starting at the Heart Line and reaching the Life Line

This is an indication of heart disease or a defective circulatory system (an island on the Heart line increases the danger of suffering from a heart disease.

Islands on the Health Line

Islands appearing above the Head line point to problems of the upper respiratory system (nose and throat) while islands below the Head Line are signs of problems in the chest and lungs.

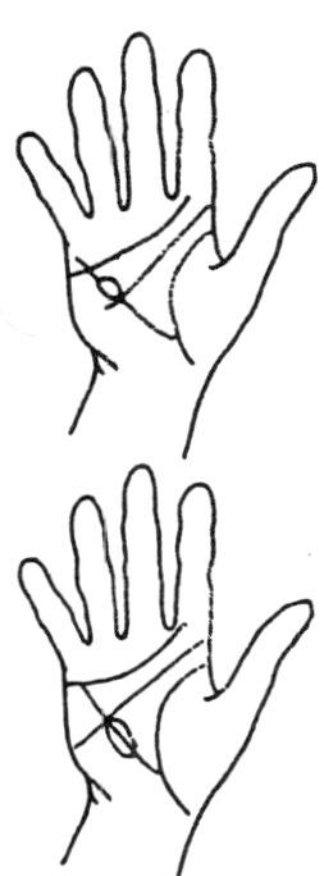

Health Line which crosses the Life Line

The age at which the Health Line crosses the Life line (according to the calendar of the Life line) is a very realistic indication of a fatal danger (which is even more dangerous if there is an open break or overlapping break on the Life line and the Health line crossing it).

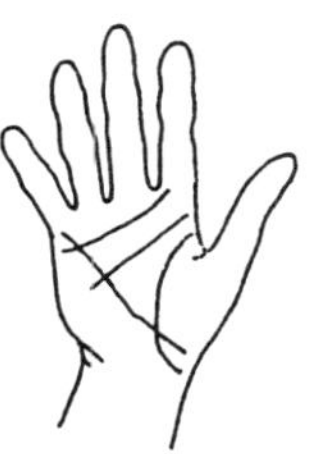

Health Line made up of little sections

Indicates problems and disorders in the digestive system.

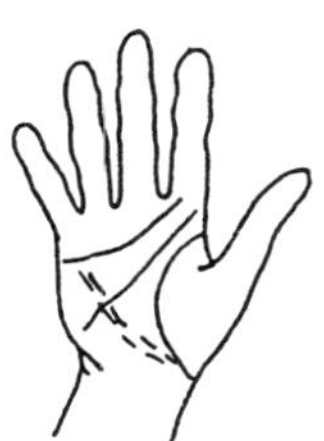

A number of Health Lines bent and irregular line

Indicates weakness in the area of the gall bladder, the liver and the kidneys.

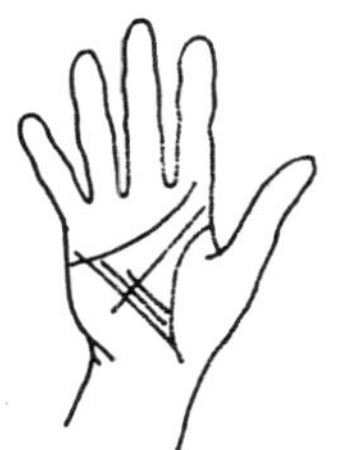

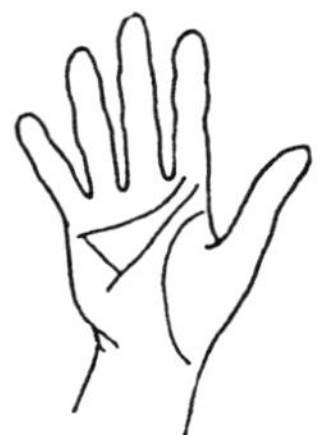

A strong Health Line which only appears between the Heart Line and the Head Line.

There is some possibility here of a mental or psychological disability (when there are many islands on the Health Line, the problem is acute).

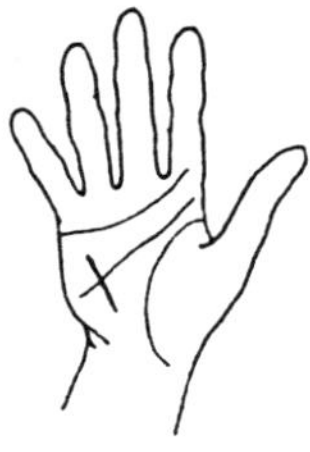

A stressed and thick Health Line at the point at which it crosses the Head Line.

A sign which may point to severe headaches (also when a large island appears on the Head line, it may indicate epilepsy.

A red and deep Health Line

Points to a tendency towards high temperatures and general weakness.

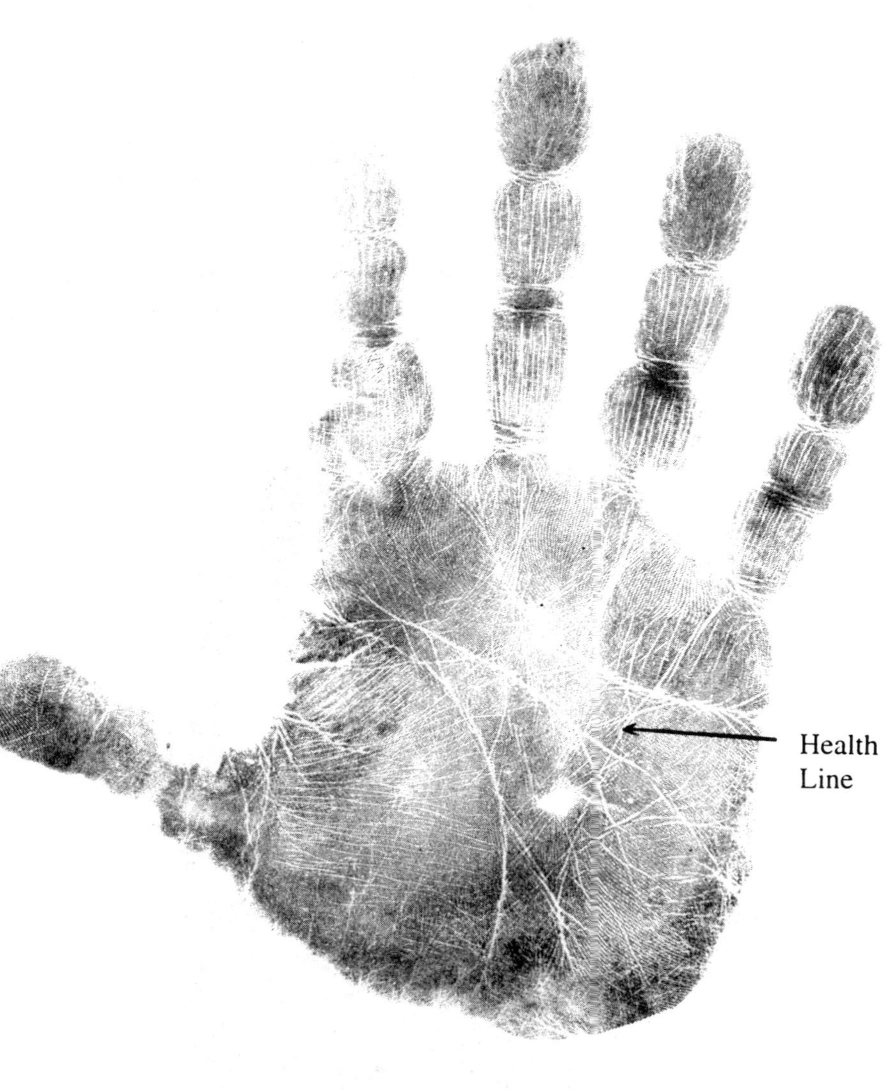
Health
Line

THE THREE BRACELETS

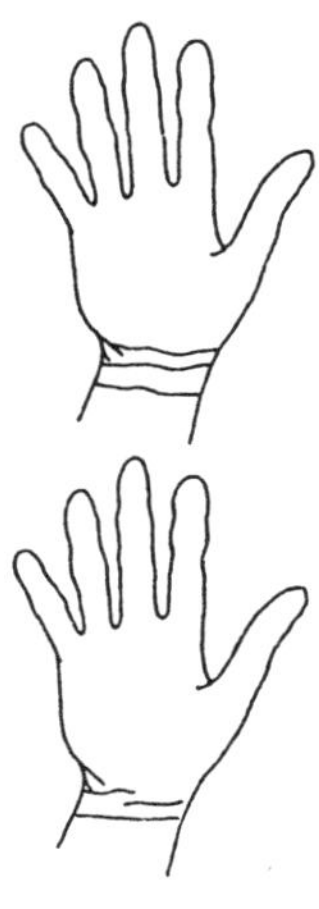

Lines which have not been considered particularly significant in the study of chirology are those of the "bracelets" which appear at the wrist joint. Everyone has either two or three bracelets and according to Cheiro, they indicate the ability to have children. I cannot state unequivecally that this statement is really so but it is credible in connection with women. An interesting detail that I have gathered from my own experience of chirology is that when a break appears on the upper bracelet, it is an indication of gynecologic difficulties which may include sterility.

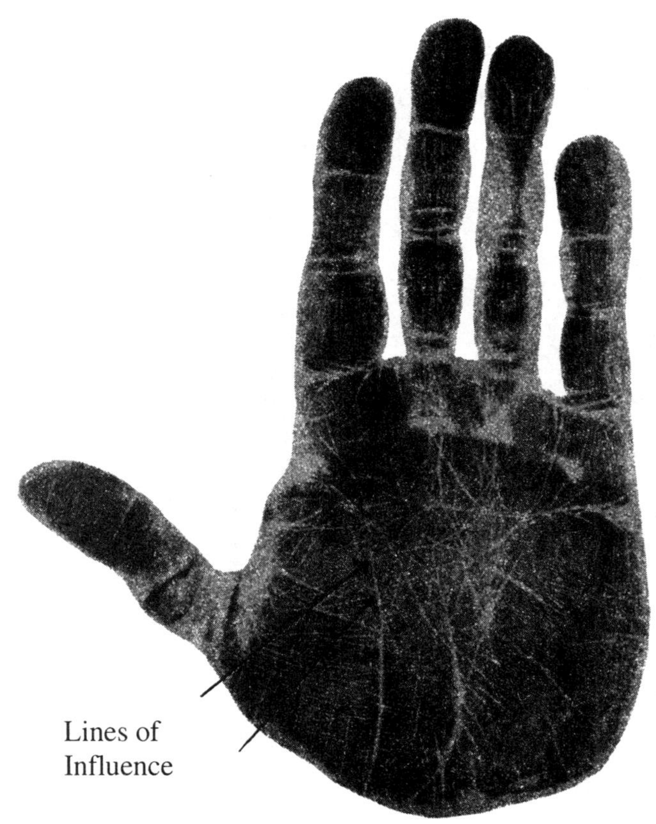

LINES OF INFLUENCE
(or Lines of Interference)

Lines of Influence are those strong and significant lines which cross the Girdle of Venus horizontally.

The line of Influence which crosses the Venus Mount and ends on the Fate line of the Head line indicates that a certain individual had considerable influence on the person's career at the age at which it crosses the Life line. One can determine whether this was a positive or negative influence according to the other lines on the hand.

When the Line of Influence passes the Head line and ends with the Heart line, this is a sign that the influence was very marked and affected by the emotions. The following is an example of this: A young lady worked as a secretary in a certain company for many years. Her boss appreciated her work, helped her to advance within the company and encouraged her to pursue advanced studies. The secretary who was also emotionally involved with him, followed his advice and made great progress. In this instance, it was obvious that the influence was beneficial and one could see this in the quality of the Fate line and Sun Line.

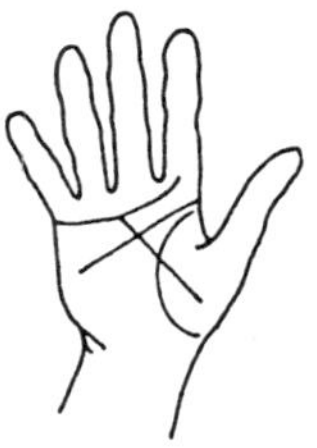

A negative influence is one which objects to a person's life style or decisions on the part of people who can influence the person, and in this case, the line would be termed the Line of Interference. This opposition may not be expressed as interference in practice, but at the same time, it still causes a certain degree of negative stress.

PASSION LINE

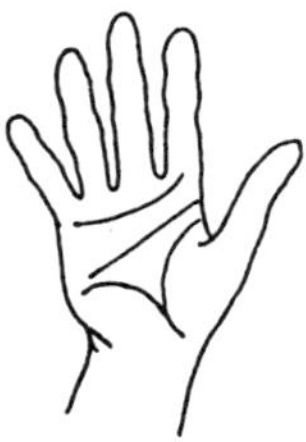

The Passion Line is an arched line which stretches horizontally across the palm, from the Moon Mount in the direction of the Life line. It signifies a strong sexual drive and the need to satisfy these biological urges, at times at any price.

This line generally indicates heightened and uncontrolled sexual yearning but the actual manner in which this is expressed depends on the quality of the hand: when the line appears on a soft hand with pale and unshapely lines, this is an indication of a weak and hedonistic personality which may evince a weakness for drugs and alcohol. If, on the other hand, the hand is hard or elastic (that is, a positive and stronger personality), the sexual urges will play a more balanced role in the person's life.

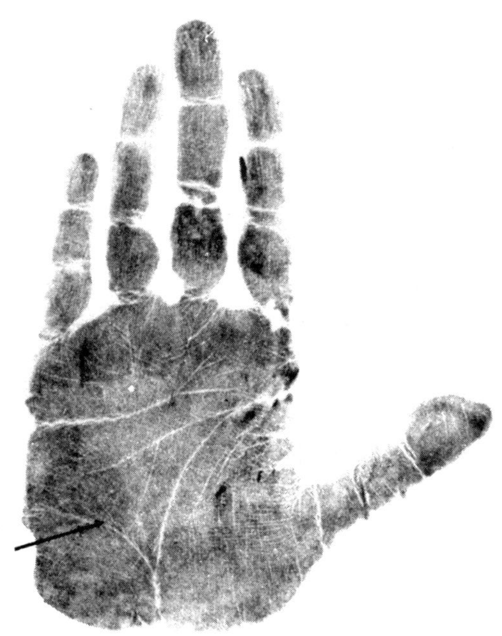

ANXIETY LINES

Anxiety Lines are those thin and delicate lines which are to be found across the Venus Mount and at times cross the Life Line. A person with such lines tends to be fundamentally anxious and suspicious, whose life is filled with apprehension. When one of this person's children is late in returning home, for instance, this parent will become hysterical and will be certain the his or her child has been run-over or at least kidnapped.

When the lower Moon Mount is very active, the situation is even more serious (for then both the imagination and fantasy are hard at work).

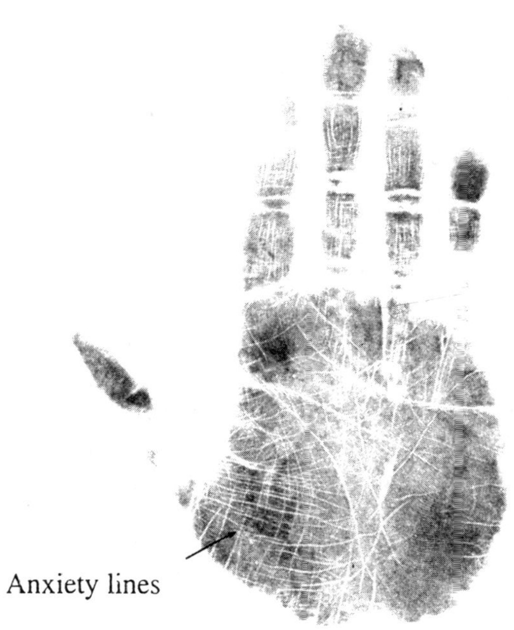

HEALING LINE

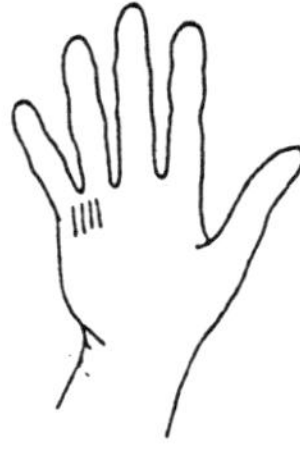

Long lines on the Mercury Mount are called "healing lines".

People with these lines are destined to help others, and they show a strong inclination to support and aid others and work at professions connected with social welfare. These "healing lines" can generally be found on the hands of doctors, teachers, psychologists and various other care-givers

LINES OF RESTLESSNESS (TRAVEL AND JOURNEYS LINES)

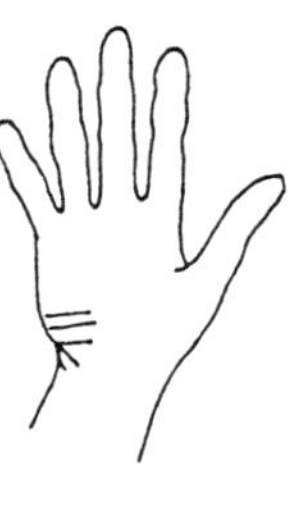

These lines appear at the distended edge of the palm, on the lower Moon Mount. People with these lines are restless, need constantly changing situations and feelings. Boredom and routine are anathema, and they therefore travel extensively and alter the course of their lives in a variety of occupations. The imagination plays an important role in these changes. If the Moon Mount is particularly active, they may sink into their world of day-dreams and permit their fantasies to take over (writers, playwrights, and scriptwriters generally have such lines).

SOLOMON RING

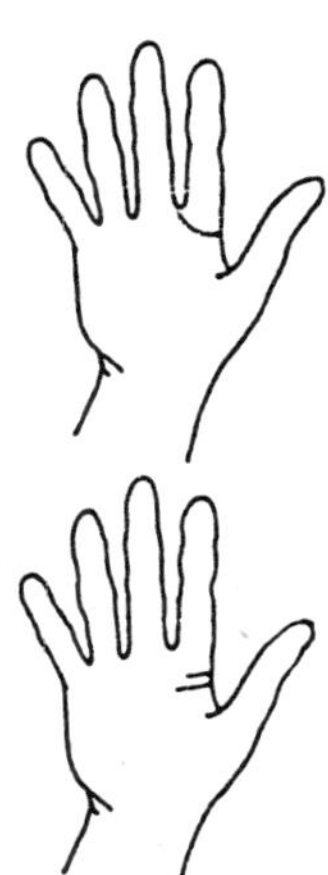

This line appears at the edge of the palm, between the Life line and the base of the Jupiter finger. It may appear as a single line or as two or three lines. This is an indication that the person loves the mysteries of life, studies and researches the subject in the most profound manner, and at times makes use of it in his or her profession. This is also a sign of a highly developed intelligence.

SATURN RING

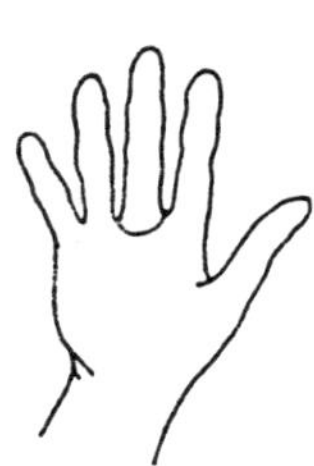

This is a ring line situated on the Saturn Mount, at the base of the Saturn finger, between the first and the second finger. This is quite a rare sign It does not point to success in the life of the person with this line. The lack of success evidently derives from the character of the individual possessing this line: people with Saturn rings are generally full of ideas and wish to reach the peaks, but they lack perseverance and are quick to forsake and abandon an idea even before they attempt to execute it, and therefore they do not generally reach the impressive achievements they had aspired to.

MARGINAL SIGNS

Signs found on the palms

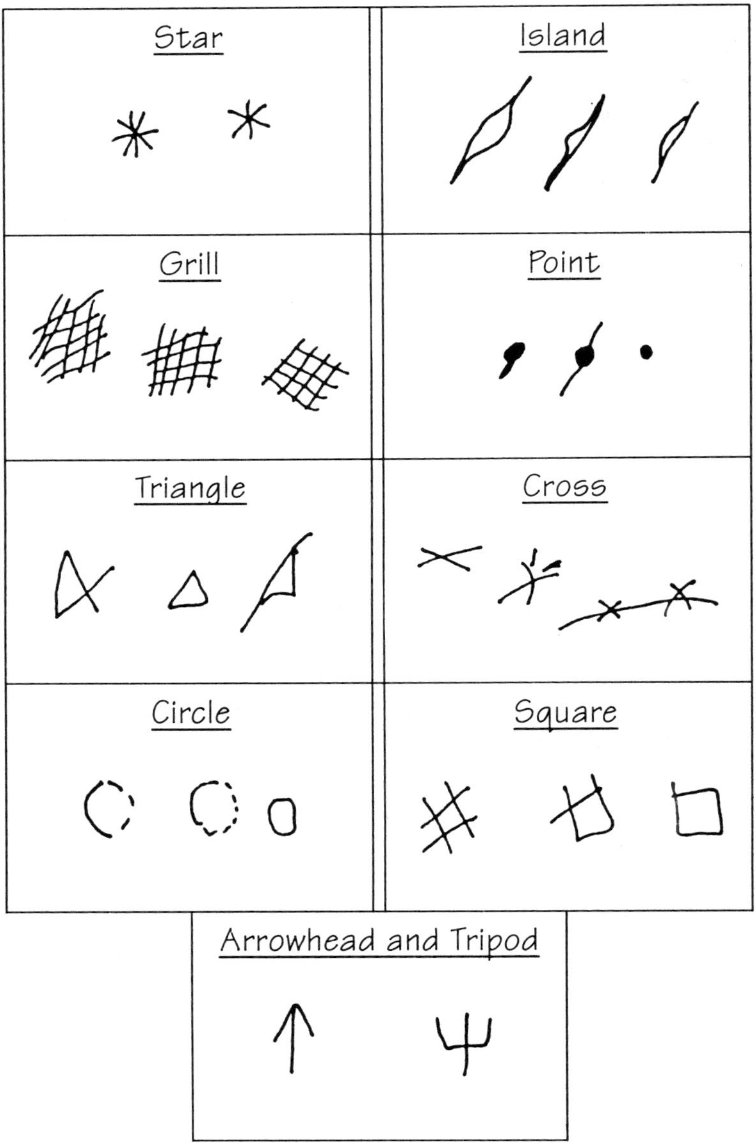

Star	Island
Grill	Point
Triangle	Cross
Circle	Square

Arrowhead and Tripod

THE CROSS

The cross is not a sign which heralds blessings and good fortune – quite the contrary. It signifies dangers, disappointments and troubles and changes resulting from these disappointments. Only is one case does it signify something positive and that is when it appears on the Jupiter Mount.

Note: Various lines which cross one another are not included in this category: the cross must appear as a sign on its own.

A Cross on the Jupiter Mount

Indicates that this person will experience a true and passionate love at least once in his or her life. The position of the cross on the mount indicates the timing of this love relationship: if it is near the Life line, this relationship will take place at an early age; if it is in the center of the mount. the time is in mid-life; and if it is near the Jupiter finger, it occurs much later.

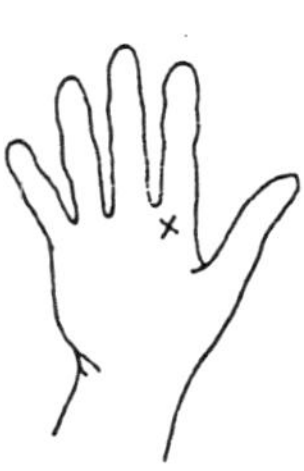

A Cross on the Saturn Mount

When this sign appears as a sign on its own, this is an indication of an increasing possibility of accidents: when it is near the Fate Line – this is a warning of a fatal accident.

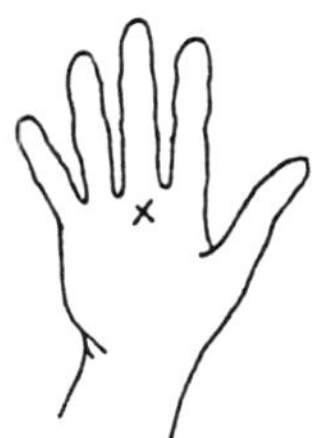

A Cross on the Sun Mount

This points to disappointments in the course of this individual's efforts to gain hoped-for wealth and fame.

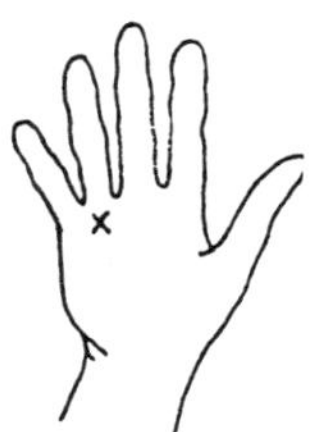

A Cross on Mercury Mount

This is a sign of dishonesty and a two-faced individual.

A Cross on the lower Mars Mount

This sign indicates an aggressive and violent person who tends to lose his or her self-control and is even capable of killing someone during a quarrel.

A Cross on the Moon Mount

In this instance, the imagination overrides this individual's common sense. This type of person tends to boast and praise himself for deeds which he or she have not actually committed or is inclined to diminish the importance of reality (or optimism not based on wisdom).

A Cross on Venus Mount

When the cross is situated near the Life line, it is evidence of quarrels within the family circle. When it is situated at the center of the mount, this is a sign of a serious scandal related to a active love relationship, an affair which may even end up in the law courts.

A Cross on the Mars Plain

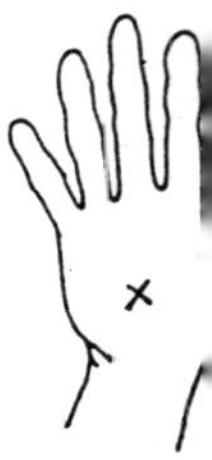

When the cross is alongside the Fate line on the Mars Plain (between the Life line and the Fate line), the individual's immedate surroundings will have a decisive influence on his or her career. When it touches the Fate line near the Moon Mount, it is a sign of disappointments in the course of travelling.

A Cross on the Head Line

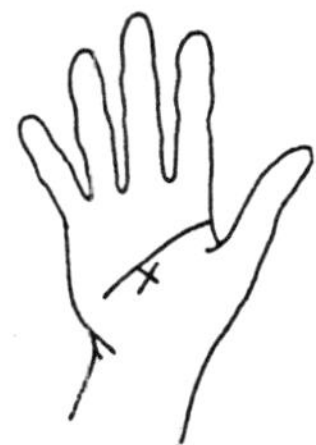

If the cross appears near the Head line, this is a forewarning of a blow to the head. When it appears alongside the Sun Line, this means that the person will not succeed in reaching the goal he or she set for themselves.

A Cross on the Fate Line

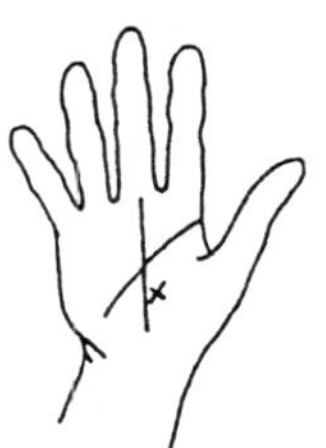

When the cross is clearly on the Fate Line, there will be disappointments and problems connected with money matters.

A Cross above the Heart Line

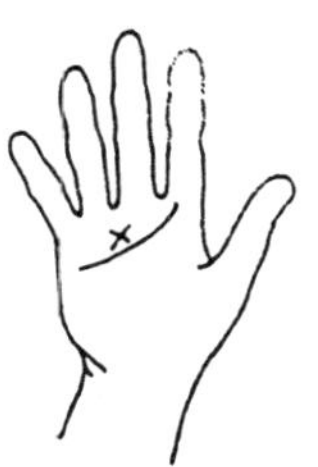

When the cross appears just above the Heart line, this is a sign that the death of a loved one will have a serious influence on this individual's life.

THE TRIANGLE

The triangle is a positive symbol on the hand and is a sign of success: the kind of success would be determined by the mount on which it appears. It is essential that the triangle appears on its own and is not part of a conjunction of lines.

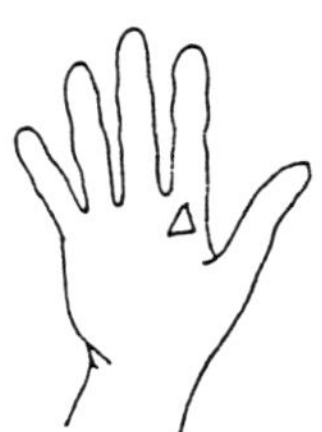

A Triangle on the Jupiter Mount

This is a sign of success in all aspects of administrational and organisational activities – whether in one's career or personal life. People with this sign are capable of successfully managing large and complex projects.

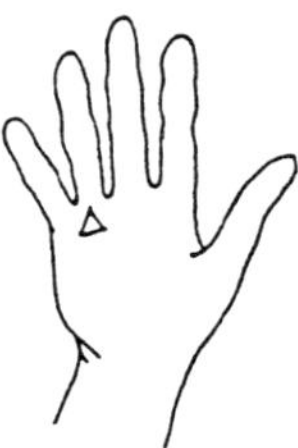

A Triangle on the Sun Mount

Here success will occur in the artistic sphere. This triangle is a sign of an individual who works quietly and confidently, persevering until he or she achieve fame. Even when this person reaches the peak, he or she will remain the same, for success will not spoil his or her character.

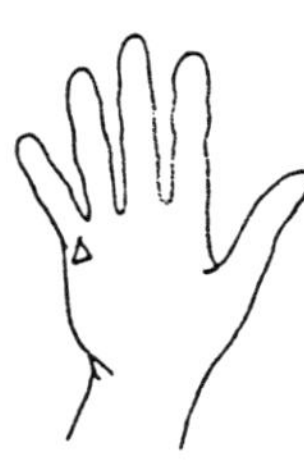

A Triangle on Mercury Mount

Indicates success in all the spheres of mysticism and the occult and a strong tendency to work in these areas.

A Triangle on the Mars Mount.

This is the hand of a person who is blessed with composure and the ability to cope with those stressful situations which turn up during a crisis or danger. This person would be well-suited to a position of command during a war.

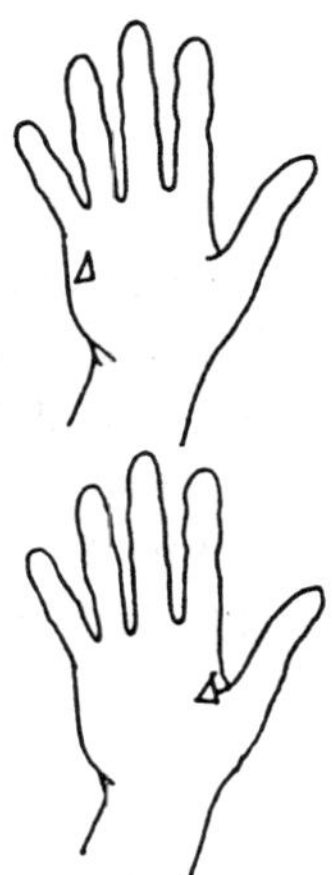

A Triangle on the Moon Mount

Imagination will crown with success every action this person takes.

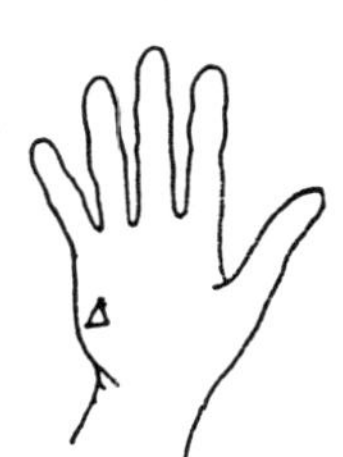

A Triangle on the Venus Mount

Success in love will come to this person as a result of his or her calmness and self control. This is a sign of sound judgment in their search for a suitable mate.

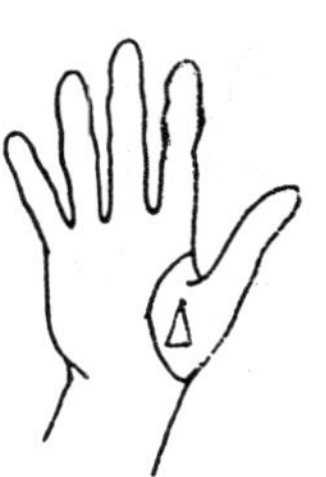

THE STAR

This is one of the most blissful signs to appear on the palm. Wherever it appears, it is an omen of a special kind of luck, dependent on the characteristics of the mount on which it figures.

This is a fairly unusual sign, and when I find it on someone's palm, it has always proven that the qualities ascribed to it are justified (naturally taking into consideration its position).

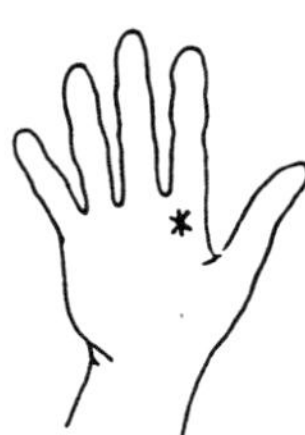

A Star on the Jupiter Mount

This sign indicates success in achieving this person's aspirations. If the star appears in addition to a particularly strong Fate line and Sun line, it is a sign that the person is able to reach an elevated and honorable status while also enjoying the height of success.

As a rule, the star on the Jupiter Mount is indicative of a person with marked ambitions to achieve honor and fame.

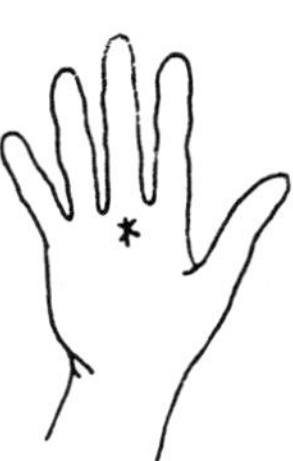

A Star on the Saturn Mount

This is generally accepted as a sign of a terrible catastrophe. A person with a star on the Saturn Mount may, indeed, achieve fame, but this will end in disaster; sometimes this person will achieve fame and recognition only after their death.

Cheiro writes that a person with this sign will have a terribly fatalistic life, full of danger and troubles.

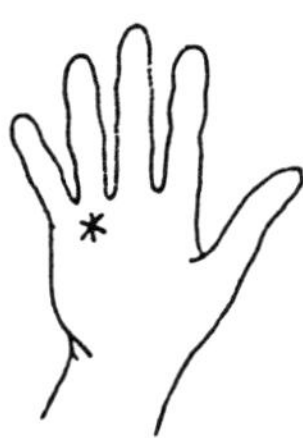

A Star on the Sun Mount

This sign provides this person with wealth and high position, but in most cases, it does not bring with it happiness and peace of mind. If it appears at the end of the Sun Line, this person will reach the peaks in the way of status, reputation and fame in the artistic sphere.

A Star on the upper Mars Mount

A person with this sign will enjoy success and respect owing to his or her personality and a considerable amount of patience.

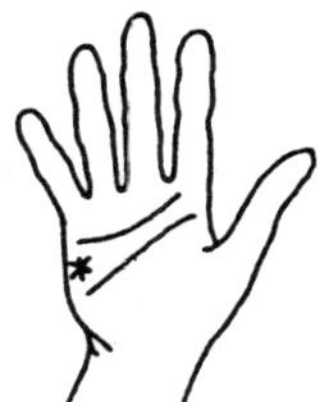

A Star on the lower Mars Mount

This is an indication of fame and honors that will come during and as a result of war, or due to marriage to a person of repute.

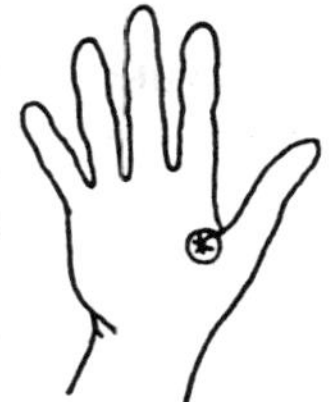

A Star on the Venus Mount

This points to great success in the romantic sphere and in love.

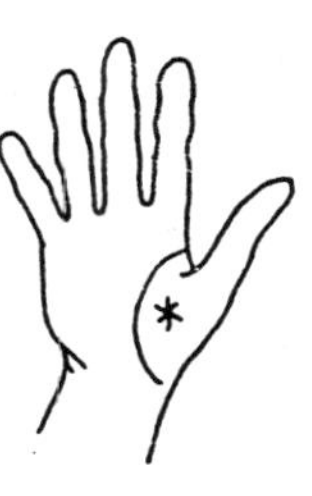

Note: When we are dealing with a star, we have to take into consideration many other factors in order to arrive at a clear and definitive judgment. The quality of the Head line, for instance, is more important when we come to make a decision as to whether the person will indeed reach the heights of fame or not.

THE SQUARE

The square is a defensive line, a sign that the person with this sign is protected from an impending danger. The location of the square indicates what type of potential danger may be involved here.

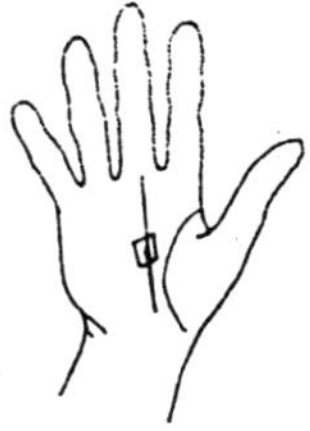

Square on the Fate Line
Indicates the possibility of avoiding financial loss.

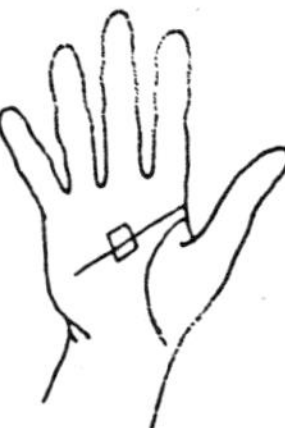

Square on the Head Line
Indicates being saved from an accident or danger connected with a blow to the head.

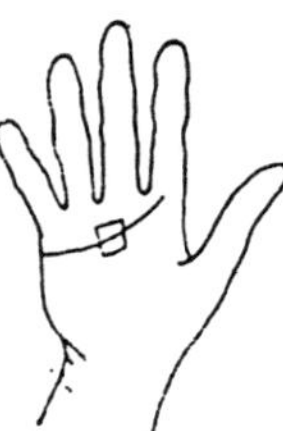

Square on the Heart Line
Protects the individual from a serious problem arising from an emotional relationship.

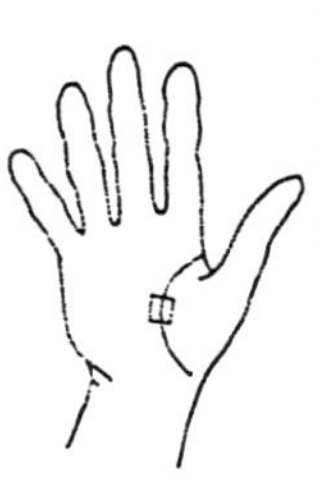

Square on the Life Line
Rescue from death on the date it appears. When the square appears on a certain mount, it protects one from excessive reactions stemming from the character of that mount.

Square on Jupiter Mount

Protection against too much ambition.

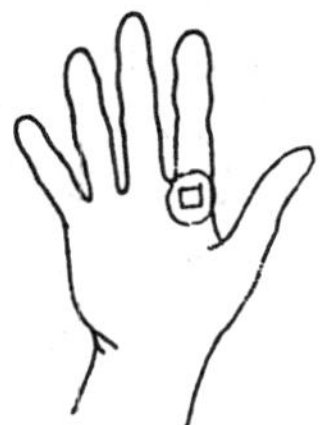

Square on Saturn Mount

Protection against potential accidents.

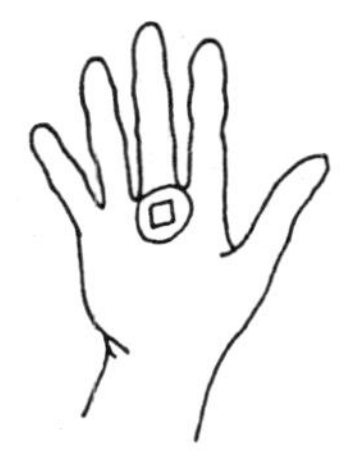

Square on Sun Mount

Protection against too great an effort to achieve fame and repute.

Square on Mercury Mount

Protection against excessive greed as far as money is concerned.

Square on Venus Mount

Protection again the dangers involved in too great a sexual drive.

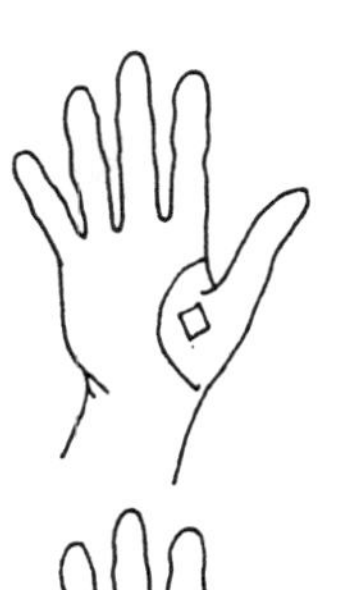

Square on Mars Mount

Protection against possible enemies.

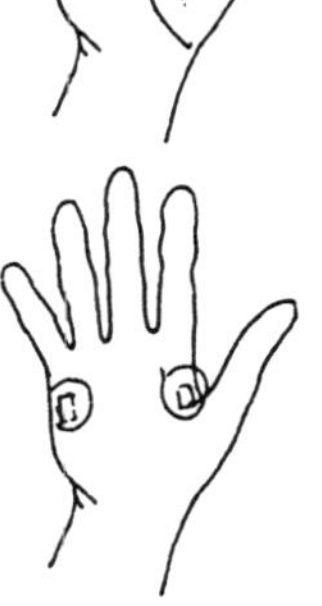

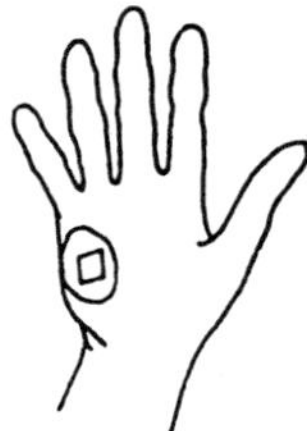

Square on Moon Mount

Protection against an excessive use of the imagination and illusions.

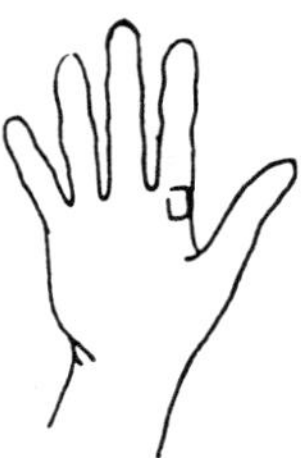

The Teaching Square

The square situated on Jupiter Mount at the edge of the palm is called the "Teaching Square". A person with the square in this location is gifted with the talent for passing on information in a way that is understandable to others. This is definitely the sign of a teacher in the making.

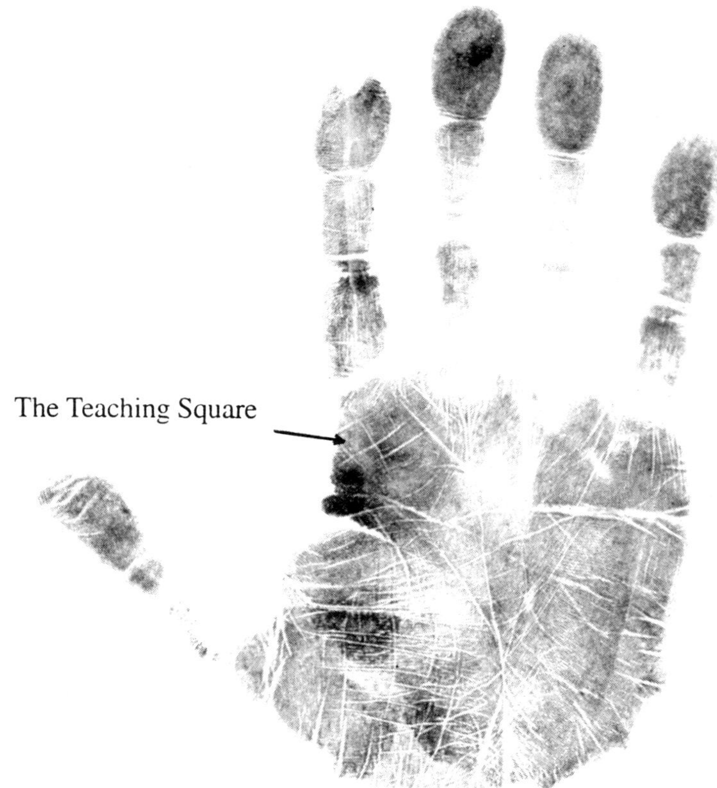

THE GRILL

The Grill is a group of thin lines lacking a specific format but appearing as a horizontal and vertical network. This sign is often seen on the palm, particularly on the various mounts, and indicates the hindrances which may hamper an individual's success. The significance of the problem depends on the quality of the mount on which the Grill appears:

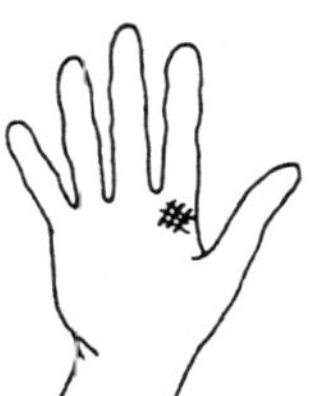

On the Jupiter Mount

Success will be hindered by excessive pride and arrogance.

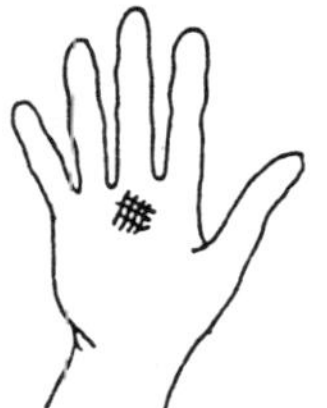

On the Saturn Mount

Success will be delayed as a result of the person's inclination to depression and melancholic moods. This is a sign denoting bad luck.

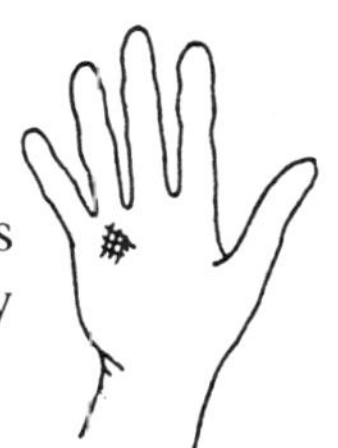

On the Sun Mount

This individual will have difficulty in reaching his aspirations as a result of arrogance and particularly the marked need for publicity and fame.

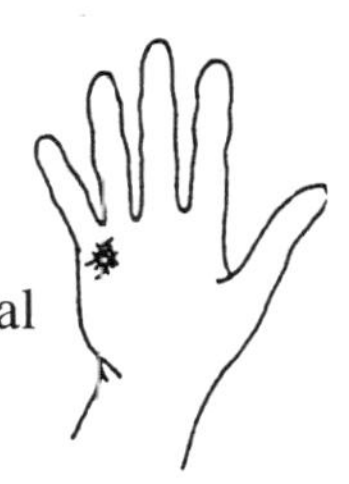

On the Mercury Mount

Success will be delayed by a lack of emotional stability and integrity.

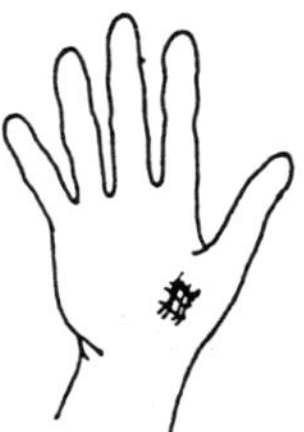

On Venus Mount

Success will be delayed by the person's emotional desires, which distract the individual from rational thought and behavior.

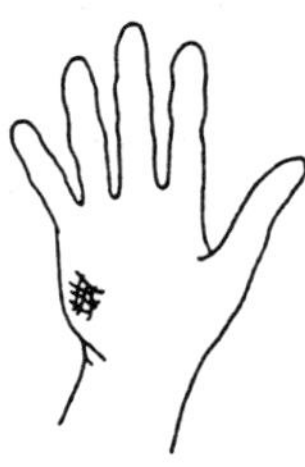

On Moon Mount

Psychological restlessness and confusion owing to an overactive imagination will delay success in this instance

THE SPOT

This is a sign of a temporary health problem.

A Red Spot on the Head Line

Indicates an injury to the head as a result of a fall or a blow. It can also indicate a brain injury resulting from an illness (such as meningitis or a stroke).

A Red Spot on the Health Line

Indicates someone who has had malaria. Frequently this illness leaves certain effects throughout the person's lifetime.

A Black or Blue Spot

Denotes an injury to the nervous system as a result of an illness or severe psychological trauma.

THE TRIPOD or "ARROWHEAD"

This is a very positive sign indicating a successful life.

THE CIRCLE

The circle is an unfortunate sign on any of the palm lines on which it appears. It is an indication of bad luck and a lack of success. It is only when it appears on the Sun Line that it denotes success.

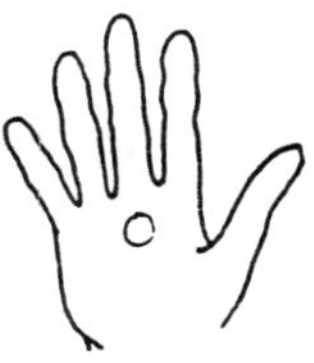

CHARACTERISTIC SIGNS OF PROFESSIONS AND TENDENCIES

Signs Denoting Artists

1) Conical, Philosophic or Emotional Hand.
2) A Huge Venus Mount.
3) A Huge Moon Mount – both upper and lower.
4) A long Sun Finger.
5) A Huge Sun Mount.
6) A Short and Faulty Heart Line – due to emotional inhibitions. (it is easier to express one's emotions through the medium of art)
7) Philosophical fingers.
8) Long Fingers.
9) Shell-shaped fingernails.
10) Narrow and long fingernails.
11) Branches on the Heart Line, up to 5 mm. in length.
12) An arched Head Line reaching the lower Moon Line.
13) Round cushion on the finger-tips.
14) A long and clear Sun Line.

Signs Characteristic of Men or Women in Business

1) A Square hand.
2) A Hard hand.
3) An elastic hand.
4) A short Heart Line.
5) A mathematical Head Line, if it is short (denotes small-business involvement).
6) A long mathematical Head Line, (denotes success in large-scale ventures).
7) A thick and especially long Mercury finger, or one which leans toward the Sun finger (indicating cleverness and shrewdness).
8) A Huge Mercury Mount (a tendency to emphasize the importance of money and property).

9) An active Sun Finger and Sun Mount (indicating a slick talker and an inclination towards gambling).
10) An active lower Mars Mount (denotes the ability to fulfil one's aspirations).
11) A stiff thumb with a good will-joint.
12) A 30-degree thumb.
13) A stiff hand which does not bend backward.
14) Short square fingernails.

SIGNS CHARACTERISTIC OF ARMY OFFICERS

Note: These are also typical of people who hold managing positions in every walk of life.

1) Square or Broad hand.
2) A good Life Line and Head Line without distortions or faults
3) A stiff or elastic hand (which indicates the ability to cope with difficult situations and suffering.
4) An active lower Mars Mount (denoting discretion and courage, traits most characteristic of army personnel).
5) A gap of up to 5 mm. between the Head Line and the Life Line (indicating perseverance and the ability to make decisions).
6) A 45-degree angle of the thumb.
7) A Fate Line which moves past the Jupiter finger (a classic sign).
8) A long Heart Line
9) Small fingernails (denoting quick-wittedness).
10) A long and arched Head Line with a moderate slope.
11) Combination Line
12) A Broad hand plus an active Venus Mount (indicating individualistic motivation).
13) Thumb with a good Reasoning Joint.
14) A long and unbending Thumb.

SIGNS CHARACTERISTIC OF ENGINEERS

1) A Broad hand in all its forms.
2) A Square hand.
3) Developed cushions on the finger-tips (particularly round ones)

4) A Straight Head Line (mathematical) or diagonal.

The following characteristics are especially suited to technical engineers engaged in development and inventions:

5) A Head Line in the form of a restrained arch.
6) Particularly active Moon Mounts – the upper and lower – (denoting a rich and original imagination).

SIGNS CHARACTERISTIC OF TEACHERS

1) Any type of hand.
2) Active Mounts, particularly Mercury (indicating an excellent capacity to espress oneself in writing and orally).
3) A good Head Line – arched: a teacher in humanistic studies. A straight or diagonal Head Line: a teacher of natural sciences.
4) A reasonable gap between the Head Line and the Life Line.
5) An active Sun Finger and Sun Mount (denoting dramatic talent, enabling the person to face an audience and lecture in an interesting manner).
6) An elastic or stiff hand (denoting diligence, self-discipline and the ability to cope).
7) Line on Mercury (denoting sociability).
8) A long Heart Line (humane and child-loving)
9) Square on Jupiter Mount
10) Large fingernails.

SIGNS CHARACTERISTIC OF NURSES

1) Small lines running across the Mercury Mount.
2) A long and strong Heart Line (not faulty), which reaches the base of the Jupiter finger.
3) An arched Head Line, or diagonal and straight.
4) A flexible hand.
5) All the mounts are active.
6) A reasonable gap between the Head Line and the Heart Line.
7) Large fingernails.
8) A waist-like thumb.

SIGNS CHARACTERISTIC OF DOCTORS (Medical Practitioners)

1) A philosophic hand.
2) A long and strong Head Line.
3) A long Heart Line (indicating a very humane approach and the motivation to save lives and help others). Doctors with a short Heart Line are less sensitive, and undoubtedly make good surgeons, particularly when the hand is broad and the fingernails are shell-shaped.
4) A square hand (Doctors with broad hands view their profession scientifically and are more interested in the chemical aspect as well as everything connected with the biology of the body).
5) Tiny lines on the Mercury Mount.
6) A long and developed thumb with an especially long reasoning joint.
7) Large fingernails
8) A reasonable gap between the Head Line and Life Line (a sign denoting good judgment and the ability to make decisions).

SIGNS INDICATING PROBLEMATIC SENSITIVITY*

1) A problematic Life Line in every respect (tiny lines in the form of a network, chains, etc.),
2) A problematic connection between the Head Line and the Life Line.
3) A short Head Line (which can indicate a sense of inferiority).
4) A faulty Head Line.
5) An arched Head Line with a sharp slope (a classic sign).
6) A faulty Heart Line (a classic sign).
7) A stressed or lined Girdle of Venus.
8) A Life Line, Head Line, and Heart Line all linked at their outset.
9) A club thumb
10) A concave hand.
11) An emotional or philosophic hand.

* Sensitivity which may be expressed in the form of psychological problems which call for professional attention.

12) Enormous fingernails.
13) A Saturn finger bent towards the Sun Finger.
14) An enormous lower Moon Mount.
15) A Head Line which emerges from the Life Line.

SIGNS ON THE PALM INDICATING CRIMINAL TENDENDENCIES

Delinquency is here divided into three separate categories:

a) Simple delinquency

This category relates to a person who robs and commits burglary, who became a criminal because he or she did not find another way of getting on, or as a result of anger and the negative residue of childhood experiences which caused him to be an anti-social character. The typical signs of this type of individual are:

1) A very short Head Line
2) A club thumb
3) A short thumb (a primitive element)
4) Short fingernails
5) Elements of the primitive hand
6) Enormous Venus and Moon Mounts (denoting a lack of self-control) when they appear on a primitive hand.
7) A faulty Fate Line (also the absence of a Fate Line may indicate – though not necessarily – frustrations stemming from this fact.
8) A red hand.

B) Delinquency which may derive from the lack of integrity or conscience and avarice.

This is the most dangerous kind of delinquency, for it stems from the motivation to get rich at any cost and in any way, and thus the these offenders do not reject any method in order to achieve their aim, including violent crime which may even lead to murder. They do not respect human life and are generally capable of considerable shrewdness. The typical signs of this type of individual are:

1) A Head Line that emerges from the Heart Line at the very outset, principally when it is the only Head Line on the hand (a classic sign).

2) A straight-mathematical Head Line.
3) A long Sun Finger, almost equal in length to the Saturn finger (denoting an inclination to gamble and play with the lives of others).
4) A Mercury finger bending markedly towards the Sun Finger.
5) A club thumb.
6) A thumb angle of 30 degrees.
7) A red hand.
8) A stiff hand.
9) A primitive hand.
10) Fat and short fingers (denoting the need to satisfy material and bodily desires).
11) A large link between the Head Line and the Life Line.
12) A short Head Line.
13) A particularly short Heart LIne.
14) The gap between the Heart Line and the Head Line is very small- up to 5 mm.
15) Thin and bitten fingernails.

C) White-Collar Delinquency

This category of delinquency refers to people who execute illegal commercial enterprises, or take advantage of loopholes in the law in order to make money or embezzle money. White-collar delinquency is, in the main, connected with a high degree of intelligence. Its characteristics are:

1) A sharp mathematic Head Line, thin and deep, to be found 1 cm. from the end of the Heart Line.
2) A Head Line that rises sharply at its end across the Heart Line (a classic sign).
3) A Sun Finger of equal length to the Mercury finger.
4) A Sun Finger bent in a pronounced manner toward the Mercury Finger.
5) A Mercury Finger bent in a pronounced manner toward the Sun Finger.
6) A very short Heart Line in relationship to the Head Line.
7) Small and narrow fingernails.
8) A stiff hand.
9) A white hand.

SIGNS INDICATING A STRONG PERSONALITY

1) A long and continuous Fate Line (a classic sign)
2) An active lower Mars Mount (indicates the ability to cope successfully)
3) A flexible hand or a stiff hand (denotes the capacity to execute tasks)
4) Fingers which do not bend backward.
5) All the lines on the hand are deep and sharply etched.
6) A long and stiff thumb.

SIGNS INDICATING STRONG SEXUAL DRIVE AND PHYSICAL PLEASURE IN GENERAL

1) A huge Venus Mount.
2) A huge Moon Mount.
3) The presence of a Sensual Line.
4) A short Heart Line.
5) A red Heart Line.
6) A red hand.
7) A short and slack thumb.
8) A Mercury finger which bends easily towards the Sun Finger.
9) Fat fingers.
10) A hand with the elements of a primitive hand.

THE HANDS OF WELL-KNOWN OR INTERESTING PERSONALITIES

THE LATE DR. IRWIN KAPLAN

Plastic Surgeon aged 65

Just writing about Kr. Kaplan excites me. There is no doubt that it was owing to his encouragement, his belief in my gifts and analytic ability, that I wrote this book. He did not let up, urging me on and insisting that I should get my knowledge and experience as a chirologist down on paper. Even when I was having such a difficult time that I was neglecting the considerable amount of work needed to write this book, Dr. Kaplan was a true friend – endlessly advising and offering me guidance.

Naturally, his hand expresses all those wonderful qualities which he displayed and blessed are those who could count themselves among his circle of friends.

Dr. Kaplan was born in Rhodesia (today's Zimbabwe). From childhood onward, he wanted to be a doctor and help other people (see his long and strong Heart Line with the tiny lines on the Mercury Mount), and had already begun his medical studies by the time he reached eighteen. He was an excellent student and displayed impressive achievements in the course of his studies. His first marriage took place when he was twenty-two. He was divorced two years later. During this period of emotional stress, he found it difficult to pursue his academic work as he was unable to concentrate (see an island on the Head Line at this age). Afterward he finished his studies with honors and turned to specializing in the field of plastic surgery (a typical direction for someone with a broad hand, as we have noted, in its wide range of creativity). Until the age of thirty, he worked as a plastic and orthopaedic surgeon and from that age onward, focused on plastic surgery (see the second Fate Line which emerges as this age). When he was 31, he married again, and when he was 34, he returned from England to Rhodesia. From this time onward, there is no good continuity of the Fate lines. Indeed, whenever he managed to establish himself and reach a successful level, he was forced to move to another country and take up residence elsewhere. At the age of 38, he emigrated to Israel and settled in Beersheva in the Negev, where he set up a department of plastic surgery and for a number of years, served as the director of this department. He became quite famous, undoubtedly owing to his

DR. IRWIN KAPLAN

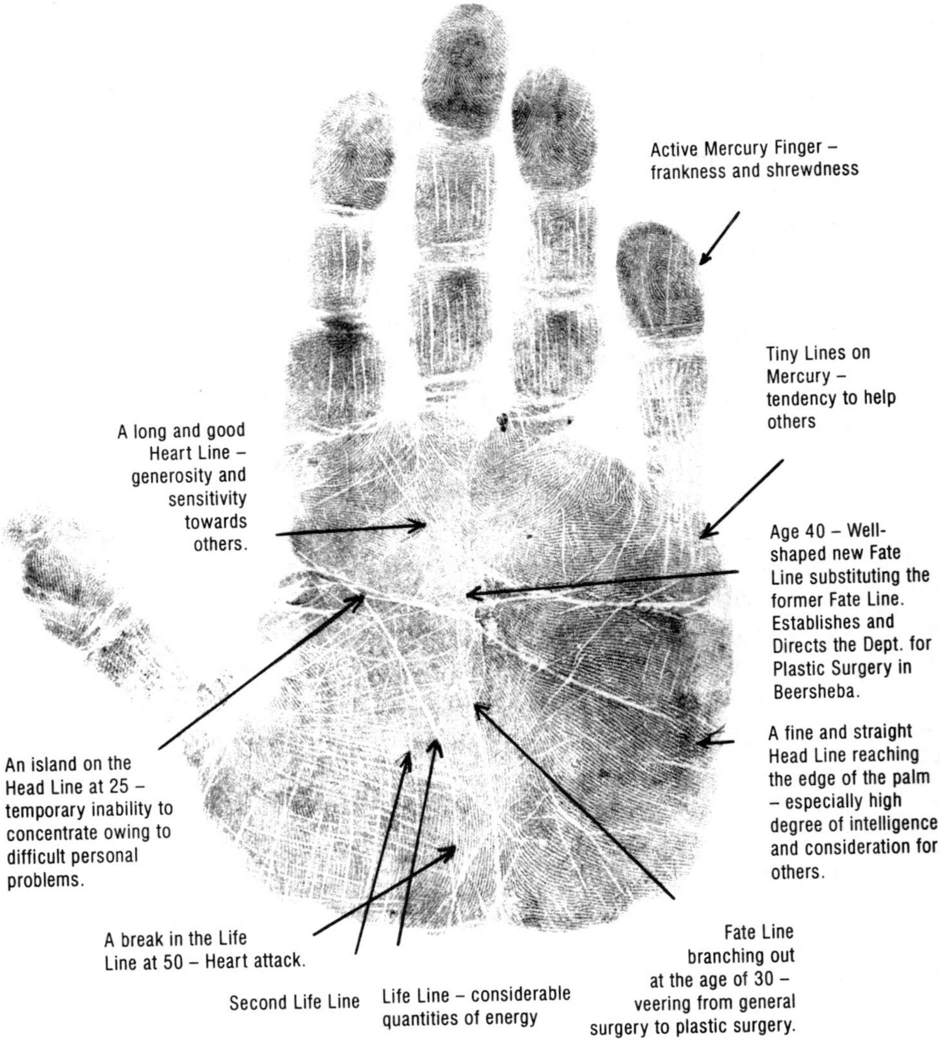

Active Mercury Finger – frankness and shrewdness

Tiny Lines on Mercury – tendency to help others

A long and good Heart Line – generosity and sensitivity towards others.

Age 40 – Well-shaped new Fate Line substituting the former Fate Line. Establishes and Directs the Dept. for Plastic Surgery in Beersheba.

A fine and straight Head Line reaching the edge of the palm – especially high degree of intelligence and consideration for others.

An island on the Head Line at 25 – temporary inability to concentrate owing to difficult personal problems.

A break in the Life Line at 50 – Heart attack.

Fate Line branching out at the age of 30 – veering from general surgery to plastic surgery.

Second Life Line

Life Line – considerable quantities of energy

work during the Six-Day War, when many of the wounded were operated on by him, among them Avigdor Kahalani (see two Fate lines appearing at this age). When he was 43, he returned to England and during his stay there, he specialized in family medicine, returning to Israel at the age of 53. It was this point that he had a heart attack (see the break in his Life line). From that time until his death, he lived in Tiberias.

Dr. Kaplan was every inch a doctor. Today, there are few like him. He was blessed with energy and inexhaustible stamina (see double Life Line). His flexible hand was an indication of his optimism and the ability to cope with both psychological and physical problems at one and the same time. He was an individualist in his approach to life and an original thinker; both a creative person and an idealist (all this information can be derived from the characteristics evident on his broad hand). His major hobby was the building of boats and carpentry in general, while plastic surgergy enabled him to express of his innate creativity. And Israel was his home because his wholly idealistic motives impelled him to do so.

A splendid Head Line stood out on his palm, pointing to a particularly high level of intelligence, while his clearly distinctive Heart line, was evidence of his generosity and his need to make sacrifices for his fellow being. In the light of all this, wouldn't you have wanted him to be your friend?

MENAHEM GOLAN

Script-writer and Director – Aged 60

On contemplating which of those hands of the famous and interesting personalities I wished to include in my book, I looked for significant lines which denoted fame and popularity on a large scale. The long Sun Line... from its beginning until its end is one of these.

Another sign indicating repute is the continuous and splendid Fate Line which moves in the direction of the Sun Mount towards the end. I found such a line in the hand of Menahem Golan, who is a well-known personality in the international world of the cinema. If we carefully examine the print of his hand, we can distinguish the fact that the Fate Line begins on the lower Moon Mount, runs the usual course until the Heart Line and turns in the direction of the Sun Mount. As we have seen, this denotes fame and popularity in both the areas of commerce and entertainment. The second Fate line begins from the Heart line and ascends – together with the Heart line – to the Jupiter finger, which conveys to us that its owner is an ambitious person who is determined to manage and direct enterprises, a very reliable person who loves to do things on a large scale. As is known, Menahem Golan built an international empire of film-making, at first in Israel (Noah Films) and afterwards in Hollywood (Cannon). As to the other aspects of his personality: his palm is that of the broad type, the Life line is diagonal and of a fine quality. The Sun finger and the Sun Mount are very active, and it is these elements which indicate that the man has an adventurous and gambling streak in his personality (particularly in business matters). This sign also points to his creative gift and a very developed dramatic sense.

A huge Moon Mount reveals that Menahem is also engaged in the writing of plays and scenarios for films. We learn from the good quality of the Head line emerging from the Life line, of the sharp-wittedness and wit which characterizes his work; traits which also cause his frequent impatience. His Heart line is also well-formed and ends between the Jupiter and Saturn fingers, which enables us to understand that his emotions are balanced and profoundly felt. It is not surprising, therefore, to find that he is still married to his first love. His Heart Line also indicates generosity and the desire to help others: telling me that on more

MENAHEM GOLAN

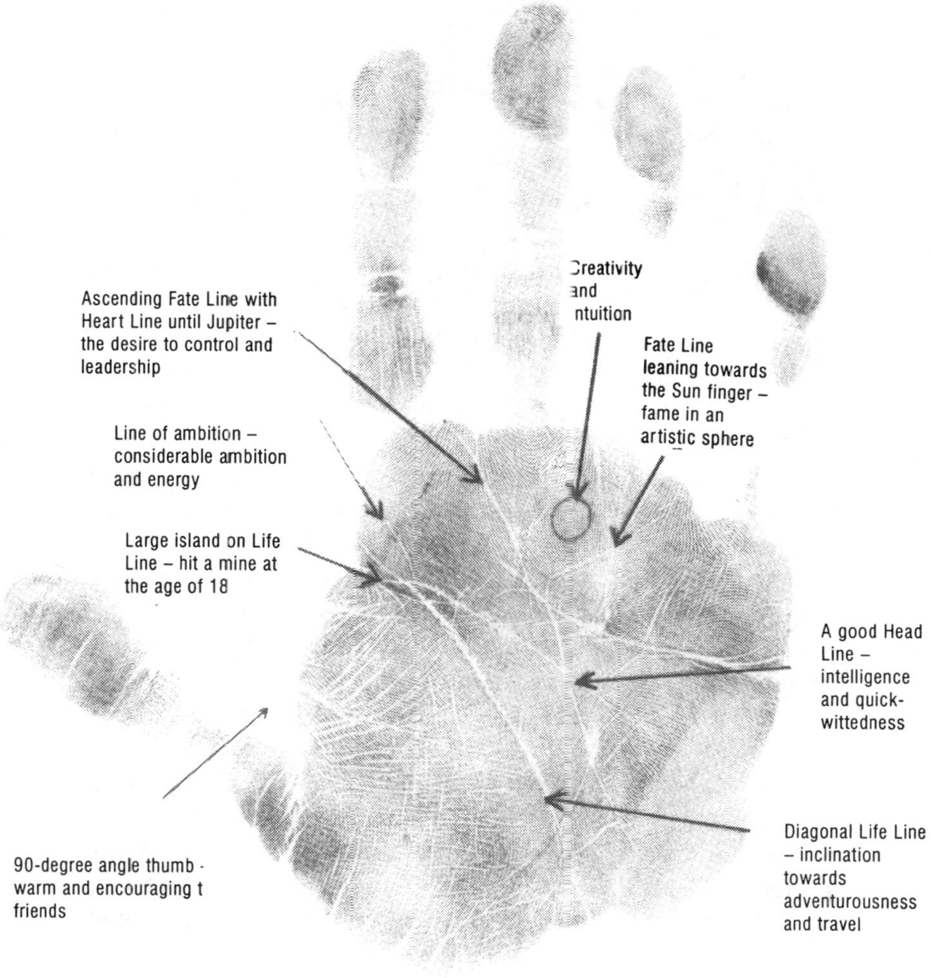

reativity and ntuition

Ascending Fate Line with Heart Line until Jupiter – the desire to control and leadership

Fate Line leaning towards the Sun finger – fame in an artistic sphere

Line of ambition – considerable ambition and energy

Large island on Life Line – hit a mine at the age of 18

A good Head Line – intelligence and quick-wittedness

Diagonal Life Line – inclination towards adventurousness and travel

90-degree angle thumb - warm and encouraging t friends

than one occasion, he landed in a difficult situation because of this trait.

On attempting to summarize his life until now, it is surprising how much the course of his life fits his personality and is easily seen in his hand. During the War of Independence, when he was eighteen years old and serving in the Golani Unit, he was sent on a flying course and fought in the battle over Zemah. Later on, he was Moshe Dayan's personal wireless operator. In the battle to liberate Tiberias in that war, he experienced a nearly fatal experience: his vehicle hit a mine and he was thrown into the air, miraculously staying alive. He played a part in the fierce battles in the Jordan Valley and was frequently in extremely dangerous situations (as we see in the island on the Life line at the age of 18-20).

At the end of the war, he went to London to study stage direction at the famous drama school of the "Old Vic". After returning, he directed many plays at the "Habima", the "Ohel", among them "Eldorado" and "A Streetcar Named Desire". He also directed a number of large-scale musicals and at the age of 25, set up a highly successful children's theater. On reaching the age of 30, he left for the States in order to learn film- making at New York University. Two years later, he returned to Israel to film "Eldorado" – with Haim Topol and Gila Almagor.

Since then, he has directed many films. There were any number of crises, but there were also enormous successes. When he was forty, he went to the United States and established the film-making company "Cannon" together with his cousin, Yoram Globus. Two years ago, he left this partnership and went through a very difficult period, but managed to overcome this and set up a company of his own. At first, he had serious financial problems (as one can see in his left hand – a break in the Sun Line at the age of 58). At the same time, this is a flexible hand which points to the capacity to cope successfully with problems, and there is no doubt that Menahem Golan with be able to contend with this situation satisfactorily.

It should be mentioned that Menahem Golan was quite sceptical about the science of chirology. By the end of our meeting, he was surprised by the accurate analysis of his personality, by the diagnosis of the events which I saw in his hand. He not only showed immense interest in the study but also stated that he intended to study the subject.

IZIK KOL

Executive in Large Company – 57 years old

When I examine the hand of a person sitting opposite me, I attribute almost decisive importance to the shape of the hand, the structure of the fingers and the elasticity of the palm, even before I look into the lines of the hand. The format of the hand provides us with immediate knowledge of the nature of the personality we are dealing with and the person's basic characteristics. It is a serious error to evade these aspects and concentrate merely on the significance of the lines of the palm. We rarely encounter a classical archtype because there are generally elements of different types in the same hand. For instance: a square hand with philosophical fingers, or a rectangular palm with square fingers, and so on.

What caught my attention in the palm of this executive was the fact that this was a classical archetype of the square hand, and everything attributed to this type of hand was indeed characteristic of the person. The square hand, as mentioned above, is indicative of someone who is extremely practical, with logic being the foremost element in the person's make-up. This is indeed this executive's major trait, as is his perfectionism, punctuality, and his determination to achieve the goals he has set out for himself – all of which are characteristics implied by the square hand. His thoughts are constantly occupied with ways to improve or introduce new and constructive ideas into his work, which are immediately translated into practice.

The characteristics to be seen in his hand are indicative of:

All the Mounts in his palm are very developed. The hand is elastic, which provides him with the capacity to cope, the ability to make decisions on the spot and a great deal of energy. The Sun Mount is enormous when compared with the other Mounts, an element which points to a sense of humor and a strong leaning towards the arts in all its various aspects.

The hand itself is small, hence it is clear that he always tries to direct or deal with grand projects. He has little patience for small matters or details (which is typical of the small hand).

He has a double Head line, with the one joining the other, which denotes a complex personality. A many-sided personality can deal

IZIK KOL

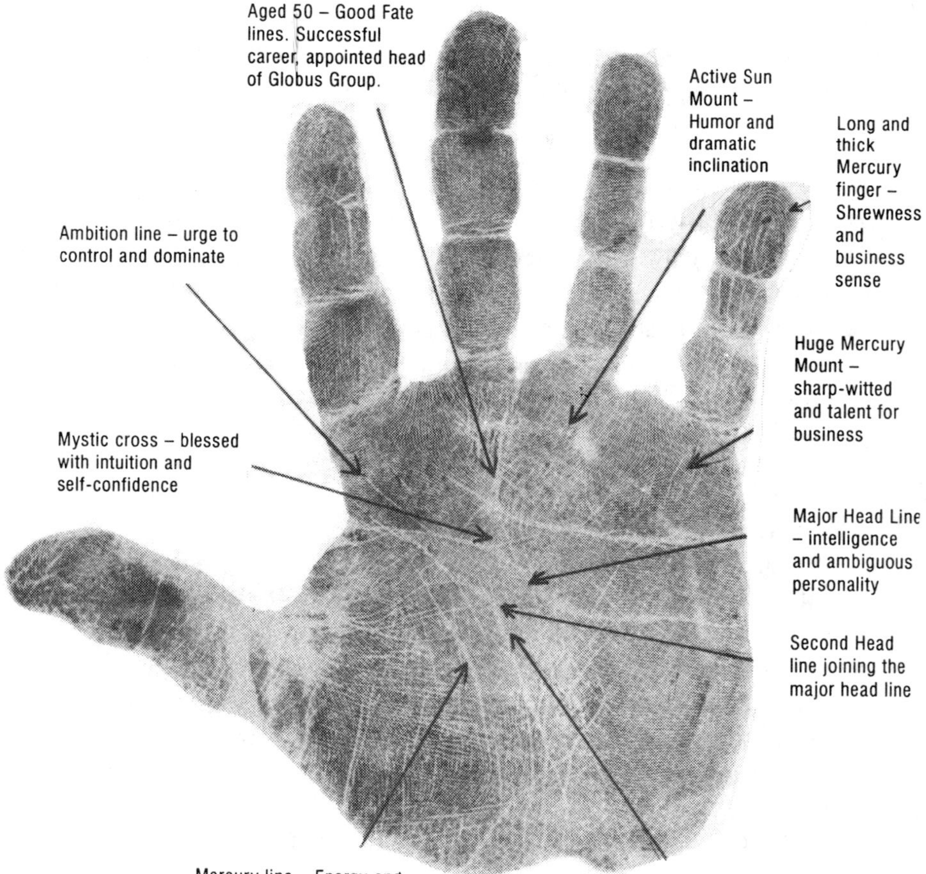

Aged 50 – Good Fate lines. Successful career, appointed head of Globus Group.
Active Sun Mount – Humor and dramatic inclination
Long and thick Mercury finger – Shrewness and business sense
Ambition line – urge to control and dominate
Huge Mercury Mount – sharp-witted and talent for business
Mystic cross – blessed with intuition and self-confidence
Major Head Line – intelligence and ambiguous personality
Second Head line joining the major head line
Mercury line – Energy and charm, persistance and perseverance
At 34 – appointed manager of Herzlia Studios

with different areas simultaneously. A huge Mercury tells me that this is a smart business man, for successful Fate lines indicate success in this area.

About the man:

He was born in Israel. He was a member of a kibbutz until the age of was 27, when he left the kibbutz to become production manager of a film. After this, he served as manager of the Chamber Theater for seven years, and at the age of 34, was appointed general manager of the Herzlia Studios. At 50, he left the United Studios and became overall manager and Cha rman of the Board of Directors of the Globus Group.

DUDU DOTAN

Stand-up Comedian – Aged 42

Within the framework of my research into characteristic signs of the hand, I sought out people who were involved in the world of entertainment. Dudu Dotan's is a typical hand of a member of that group.

In most cases, the Sun Mount is a particularly active feature among people who are involved in acting and entertainment. In Dudu Dotan's case, the Sun Mount is enormous, as is the lower Moon Mount, an aspect which stresses the creative element of his personality. Indeed, Dudu also writes poetry and stories in addition to his professional role of actor and comedian.

In talking to him, I noted that he was logical and weighed his words carefully, despite the fact that the conversation flowed easily. And his hand confirmed this impression:

The Head line is connected to a large extent to the Life line, which denotes a careful person. This sign may also indicate a certain degree of lack of self-confidence, but the quality of this Head line helps him to overcome this trait (Dudu admitted to me that the lack of self-confidence stems from a difficult and emotionally-deprived childhood, and he is therefore always in a tense and anxious state, intent on succeeding). Until the age of 12, his Life line is distorted to a certain extent but it after that it straightens out. This points to a difficult childhood lacking warmth of feeling, and indeed, it evolves that his father spent long periods in prison and the family always suffered from indigence. The most prominent feature of Dudu Dotan's hand are the highly developed Mounts: Sun (humor and acting talent), the lower Moon (imagination and creativity), and Venus (warmth, love, friendship and romantic inclinations). As to the women in his life, he is inclined to adventures and the desire to know women, for whom he has both sympathy and appreciation, but at the same time, he is absolutely faithful to his wife.

The impressive achievements of his career one can ascribe to certain characteristics: this is the hand of a persistent fighter, who does not give up trying and achieves the aims he has set for himself (as we see from the long and flexible thumb). His extremely marked criticism (particularly towards himself) helps him to succeed in his occupations (the square hand plus the defined Head line from the hand's end to end).

DUDU DOTAN

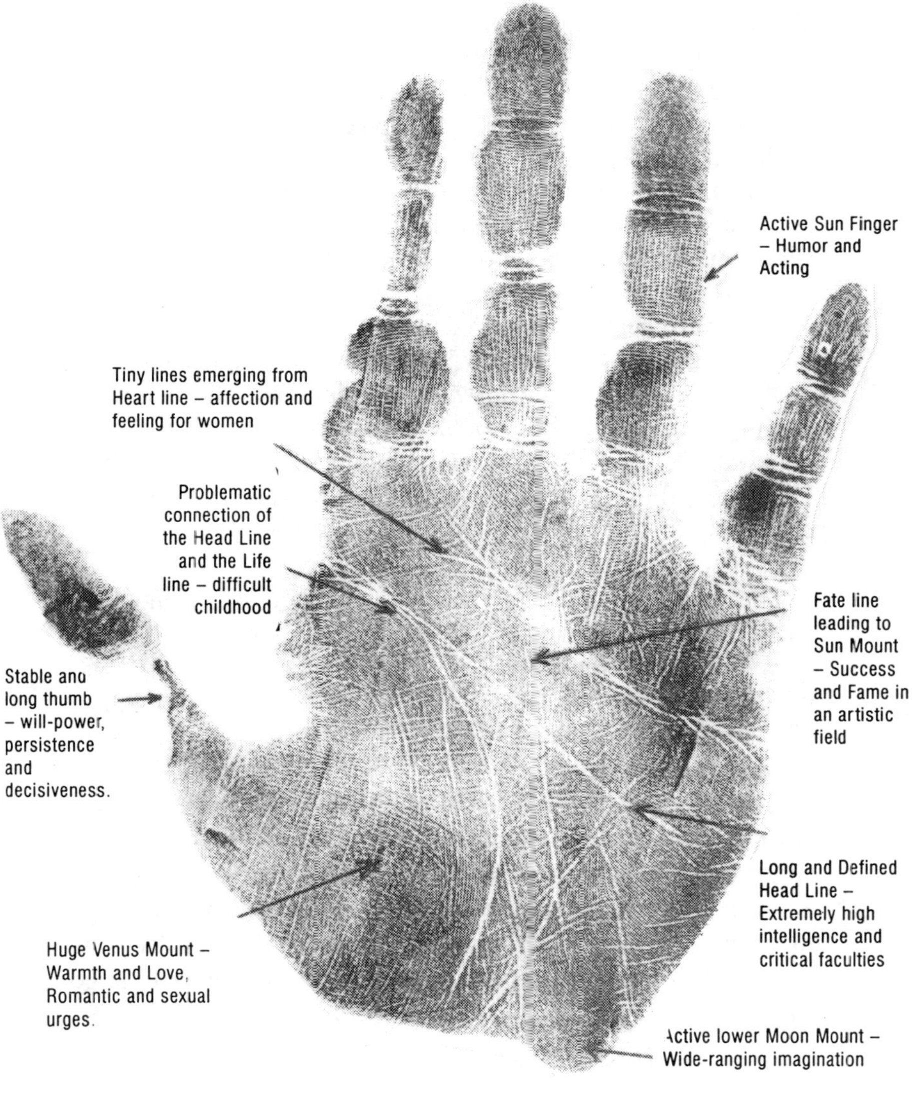

Active Sun Finger – Humor and Acting

Tiny lines emerging from Heart line – affection and feeling for women

Problematic connection of the Head Line and the Life line – difficult childhood

Fate line leading to Sun Mount – Success and Fame in an artistic field

Stable and long thumb – will-power, persistence and decisiveness.

Long and Defined Head Line – Extremely high intelligence and critical faculties

Huge Venus Mount – Warmth and Love, Romantic and sexual urges.

Active lower Moon Mount – Wide-ranging imagination

RAPHAEL EITAN (RAFUL)

Member of the Knesset and former Chief-of-Staff, Aged 62

When I first met 'Raful' I had a preconception of a rigid and stern man who expressed himself in a manner which was "short and to the point", and that he carefully weighed every word he uttered. He scrutinized me unsparingly, with a direct and penetrating look, and trying to understand just what made me tick. When I looked at his hand, I learned that the saying "Don't look at the vessel but at what it contains" indeed fit this occasion.

Inwardly, 'Raful' is a sensitive and generous man who loves to help others. In fact, there is a strong element of making sacrifices for other people in his nature, which on occasion led to his being exploited (the Heart line reaches the Jupiter finger). Such a Heart line, added to a thumb with a "good figure", is evidence of an amiable man who uses tact and sensitivity towards others and is very romantically inclined towards the opposite sex.

The Head Line is quite long, arching slightly and well defined. To a certain extent, it is attached to the Head line and points to an intellectual capacity together with a degree of weighed judgment and caution. This is a man who will think carefully before he commits himself in words or making a decision. The square hand together with the mystic cross, the Intuition Line, the Girdle of Venus, reveals a practical and logical person who can foresee the results of various moves in life and knows how to come to the right conclusions at the right time.

The flexible hand and the excellent Life line denote an energetic individual who is able to bear suffering and is devoted to whatever his goals are. The stiff thumb in a square hand indicates that he is also very stubborn and it is very difficult to dissuade him from the line of thought he has adopted, at times to the point of dogmatism.

All the characteristics mentioned above show that Raful reached the status of Chief-of-Staff – and other positions of command – with the help of these very characteristics. The square above the Jupiter Mount shows the ability to convey a message to others in a very clear and concise manner and indeed, he frequently lectures to various sectors of the public. His large shell-shaped fingernails and the well-formed Sun lines stress his

RAPHAEL EITAN

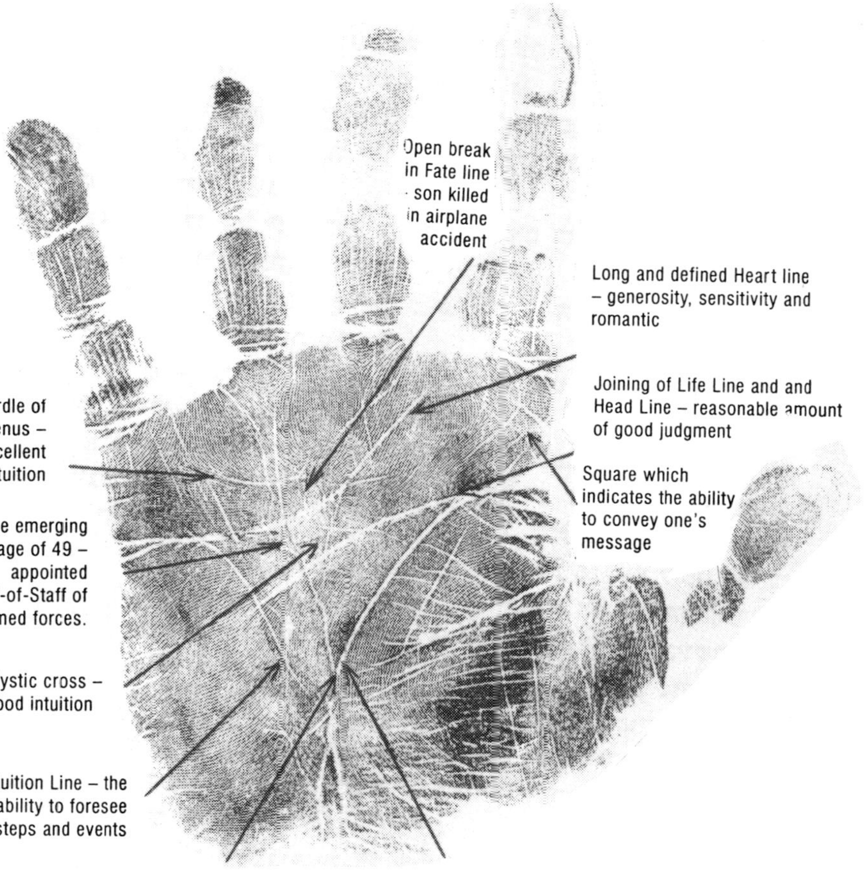

Open break in Fate line - son killed in airplane accident

Long and defined Heart line – generosity, sensitivity and romantic

Joining of Life Line and and Head Line – reasonable amount of good judgment

Girdle of Venus – excellent intuition

Square which indicates the ability to convey one's message

Sun Line emerging at the age of 49 – appointed Chief-of-Staff of the armed forces.

Mystic cross – good intuition

Intuition Line – the ability to foresee steps and events

Appointed head of a battalion in the Paratrooper Force

Deep Life Line – good energies

creativity and leaning toward the arts. And everyone who is familiar with the face knows that his major hobby is wood-carving.

DAN LORENZ

Professor of Physics and Mathematics, Aged 60

In seeking interesting hands to discuss in this book, I tried to locate people who were occupied in a variety of professions and roles, in order to pinpoint the widest range of individual characteristics and special gifts. For instance, the hand of Dan Lorenz, a senior academician, was an excellent opportunity to do just this.

In the chapter dealing with the Fate line, I pointed out that the Fate line which moves in the direction of the Mercury finger indicates great success in the field of commerce or science. How can we determine to which of these fields a person will be inclined? Firstly, we can determine this on the basis of the shape of the hand:

A square hand plus a mathematical Head line (straight) which stretches from edge to edge, plus a short Heart line, points to success in the commercial sphere; A philosophic hand plus a well-defined arched or diagonal Head line indicates success in scientific and theoretical studies. The philosophic hand, as has been mentioned, is not the hand of a business man but of a student, teacher or a researcher.

As to Dan Lorenz' hand, the dominant elements are:

1) First and foremost, a philosophic hand
2) Two parallel Fate Lines, one moving toward the Jupiter Mount and the other towards the Mercury Mount
3) Two excellent Sun Lines, with the foremost arched and the second, mathematival.

A double Fate line and a double Head line indicates that the person is capable of dealing with a number of different areas at the same time, and the quality of the lines reveals that the person will also succeed in all these activities. Dan Lorenz divides his time between various professions: he is primarily occupied with teaching mathematics at the Technion in Haifa, and also serves as the academic director of students'enrolment. At the same time, he also serves as chairman of the inter-university committee for

DAN LORENZ

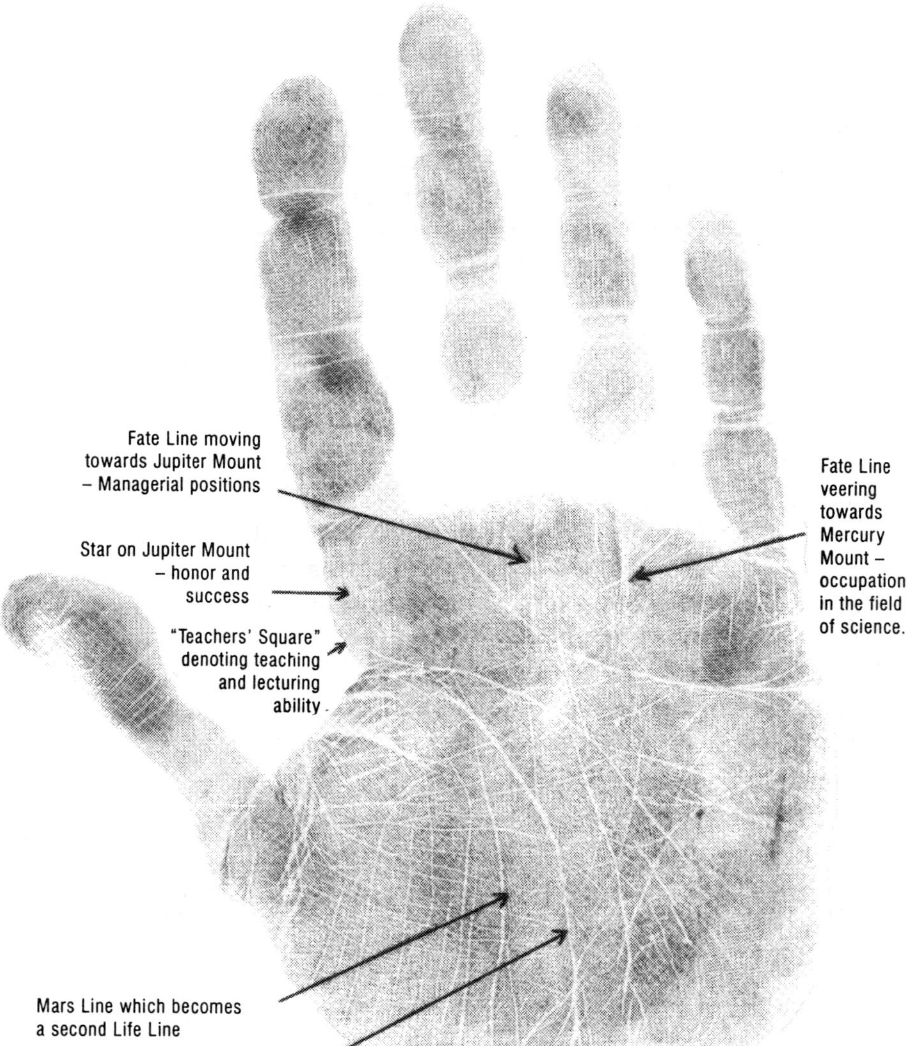

Fate Line moving
towards Jupiter Mount
– Managerial positions

Fate Line
veering
towards
Mercury
Mount –
occupation
in the field
of science.

Star on Jupiter Mount
– honor and
success

"Teachers' Square"
denoting teaching
and lecturing
ability

Mars Line which becomes
a second Life Line

Life Line

establishing a state-wide policy to be applied to the enrolment of students in higher educational institutions.

All these managerial positions are characterized by the Fate line moving toward the end of the Jupiter finger, as well as the "teacher's square" appearing on the Jupiter Mount. Long Mars lines are also prominent in this hand, accompanied by a long and well-defined Life line. Another detail worth noting is the star etched into the Jupiter Mount. This is a very unusual sign indicating that this person has merited, and will merit in the future, a very superior status, honor and success, in everything he does.

ZVI LIDSKY

Lawyer and Writer, aged 57

I first met the lawyer Zvi Lidsky when I was a student at Art School. At that time, I frequently went to swim in the sea and play "beach- tennis", and we met there daily and played ball and swam. Even then it was obvious that Lidsky had excessive energy which expressed itself in the fact that apart from his many interests, he also led an intensive social life. When we met again in order to write this book, twenty-seven years had passed and I was very curious as to whether this tremendous energy was evident in his hand.

If we examine the hand carefully – for the lines in his hand are deeply etched – sharp, smooth and deep, really "like it's written in the books". The Life Line is of a wonderful quality, and in addition, a number of Mars Lines are attached to it, which reveal an enormous amount of surplus energy and an inability to stay in one place for any length of time. Indeed, Lidsky is always on the move, restlessly going from place to place, at a dizzying pace!

His restlessness is also expressed in other traits emphasized in his hand: firstly, a long and fine Head line, denoting a very high degree of intelligence and quick-wittedness. Secondly, the lower Mars Mount is very active, and this element indicates an aggressive and contentious personality. Moreover, according to the format of the palm, it is a classical philosophic hand, and people with such hands are inclined to study human psychology, reading and writing a great deal, while at the same time, pursuing their interest in mysticism. And we find that the lawyer Lidsky has something of a 'mystical' personality, who enjoys all aspects of the mysterious and the occult. He has a fine collection of various and strange amulets, keeps garlic in his car as protection against the evil eye, and will never sit in the 13th row in the cinema. He is very intuitive and clever, with sensitive "antenna" which can sense other people's feelings. The fertile imagination with which he is blessed is very marked in his hand (an enormous Moon Mount). The philosophic hand frequently points to literary talent and indeed, in addition to his legal profession, Zvi Lidsky is a popular writer who has written 15 books to date and has for

ZVI LIDSKY

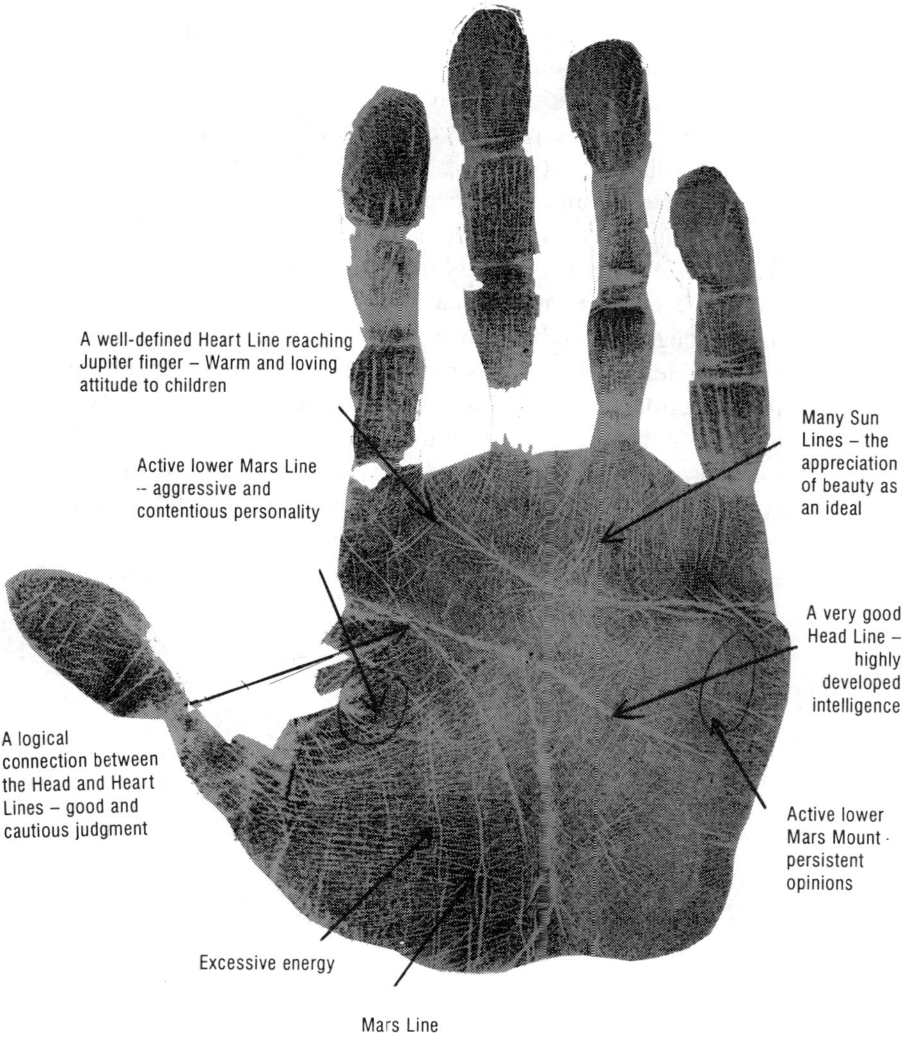

A well-defined Heart Line reaching Jupiter finger – Warm and loving attitude to children

Active lower Mars Line -- aggressive and contentious personality

Many Sun Lines – the appreciation of beauty as an ideal

A very good Head Line – highly developed intelligence

A logical connection between the Head and Heart Lines – good and cautious judgment

Active lower Mars Mount - persistent opinions

Excessive energy

Mars Line

the past 27 years been a contributor to the weekly LA- ISHA, with a weekly column entitled "Stories from Life".

As to his emotional life, if we examine his Heart line, we note that it is well-shaped and that it continues until the base of the Jupiter finger, which stresses his generosity and willingness to help others. Such a Heart line denotes a warm and loving attitude to children and one can assume therefrom that he is also a good father and devoted to his children.

A reasonable link between the Life line and the Head line indicates that Lidsky has an excellent judgment, is not hasty, makes his decisions carefully, and displays an active personality, dedicated to his aims and knowing how to fight couragously for his individual opinions.

He is a very sensitive person with a sharp analytical sense who knows how to gauge people's characters. The same sensitivity is applied to the aesthetic sphere as well: with very strong leanings toward the visual arts and a deep appreciation of beauty as an ideal (many Sun lines). He is constantly surrounded by beautiful women. He is invited to every important and glittering social and cultural event (see the Sun line and the Sun Mount together with the 90-degree thumb). However, a philosophical hand with a straight Head Line denotes an inclination towards isolation and introspection, and he therefore tends to create a barrier between himself and those close to him, and he is capable of spending many hours on his own. Zvi Lidsky is obviously an individualistic type who desires freedom from the restrictions of marriage and is hence unmarried, after two marriages which ended in divorce: at the age of 40, he parted from his wife Nira, who is also a lawyer (see the break in his Sun line at this age.)

HAIM TOPOL

Actor and Director aged 55

Haim Topol is an actor and director of international fame, whose reputation is world-wide.

He was born in Israel in Tel Aviv. His childhood was spent under the shadow of the War of Independence which broke out in 1948. When still a youth, he showed an inclination for the theatre, which was expressed in various ways at school and within the youth movement.

His theatrical career began in an entertainment unit while he was serving in the army, and at a later stage, as artistic director within the army command.

After his release from the army, the theatrical bug had really caught him and from then on until this very day, some 35 years later, he has played in films and plays, many having won international success. Among them one should mention "Salah Shabati", for which he received a nomination for the 'Oscar'.

At the age of 25, he joined the Haifa Theater. He acted in such well- known plays as "The Caucasian Chalk Circle", "The Taming of the Shrew", "Andorra", "The Rhinoceros", and others, and he also directed quite a few plays. However, there is no doubt that his acting in "Fiddler on the Roof" won him a place among the international stars of the theater.

In 1967, when only 32, he was invited to London to perform the same role at Her Majesty's Theatre, a performance which earned endless praise from the critics and the audiences. He was subsequently invited to play in the same capacity in a film of the same story. In 1972, the film was nominated for an Oscar and Topol was also nominated for the Best Film Actor of the year. He did not win the award but succeeded in participating in many films after this, owing to his great performance in "Fiddler on the Roof".

On examining his hand, I naturally looked for certain lines indicating world-wide fame, such as a long and continuous Sun line, from the base of the palm until the beginning of the Sun finger, on which an impressive star would be situated or at least one continuous Fate line veering towards the Sun finger (an element I found in Menahem Golan's hand).

HAIM TOPOL

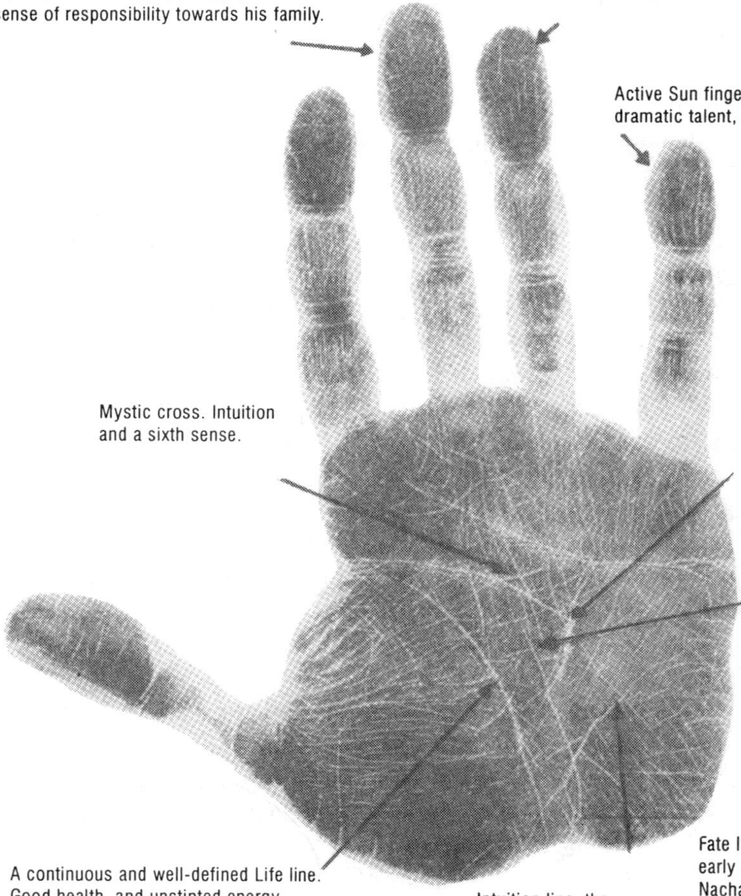

Active Mercury finger. Excellent expressive talent – both orally and in writing

Dominant Saturn. Seriousness and a sense of responsibility towards his family.

Active Sun finger. Humor, dramatic talent, and painting

Forked Head line. Highly developed intelligence and duality of personality.

Mystic cross. Intuition and a sixth sense.

Continuous and well-defined Fate line, starting at the age of 32, breakthrough in his career. Invited to perform the role of Tuvia the Milkman in London production.

Fate line beginning at early age. Success in Nachal Group, 'Green Onions' and others.

A continuous and well-defined Life line. Good health, and unstinted energy.

Intuition line, the presence of a sixth sense.

On the hand's surface, there is no such line, but one can definitely see a number of facets that in summing them up, point to his personality, his occupations and successes. I have already mentioned above that I attribute considerable importance to the shape of the hand, no less than to its lines

I cannot define his hand as an archetypal classic. One can find in it elements of most of the typical hands, and this in itself, indicates a special and many-sided personality who is capable of performing a wide range of activities.

The palm is square – which indicates the capacity to implement roles and projects successfully.

The fingers are long and their shape is conical, with a philosophical element, and they broaden towards the tips, with shell-like fingernails. The philosophical element denotes an analytic mind, keenness, and an interest in everything connected with the human soul, as well as the ability and desire to teach and guide (as we are aware, Topol is also a director). The conical element reveals his interest in various artistic areas and an appreciation of beauty as an ideal.

In addition to his theatrical endeavors, he is also a gifted painter, a talent which he revealed when still a child.

The fingers which broaden towards their tips plus the shell-=like fingernails, are indications of an original personality with vision in both his way of thinking and execution, as well as technical innovation. (He has patented a number of his inventions).

The thumb is well-shaped, with a very dominant will-joint and a 90- degree angle as well as a huge lower Mars Mount.

On the basis of this data, we learn that we are concerned here with a very strong personality, devoted to fulfilling his aims, setting out his goals and realizing them successfully, accompanied in no small measure by his tremendous charm and frank generosity to those who help him (which we learn from the 90-degree thumb, the flexible palm and the long and well- defined Heart line which reaches as far as the Jupiter Mount)

The Fate Line, which actually reflects the course taken by a person's career and the realization of one's personality, is here continuous and already defined from a very young age (19-20), and this is indeed the period in which his career began to take shape (in the Army Entertainment Unit), climbs steadily to the age of 30, at which point we see a number of Fate Lines, indicating a breakthrough through appearances all over the world.

The hand is a network of lines, with a good Life line, which denotes a very energetic personality – both in the physical and the neural sense. According to the number of Fate Lines and Sun Lines, we find this energy well directed along positive lines by the various diverse areas in which he is occupied.

The fork-shaped Head lines emphasize even further the stability of this course (as noted, two Head Lines enable the owner to deal with a number of spheres without one interfering with the other. Thus Topol confirms that he is, at one and the same time, actor, director, script-writer, businessman, painter, etc.)

According to overlapping breaks on a number of Fate lines, we learn that there were also a few failures, which obviously cannot to be avoided in the spheres in which he moves.

What impressed me in particular is his ability to understand people and read their thoughts in a matter of seconds, which may be the crowning peak of all his many achievements. This is indicated by the Intuition Line and the many mystic crosses – a sign which denotes the possession of a sixth sense.

His enormous talent as an actor is expressed by the extremely active Mercury finger, underneath which we find a well-shaped Mercury Mount situated with dignity – a classical sign of the talent to express oneself both orally and in writing. Alongside it, we find a very dominant Sun finger and a huge Mount (a sure sign of dramatic talent). A double Head Line enables him to learn and remember texts by heart and grasp unfamiliar languages with ease (typical of a double Head Line), but at the same time, it also denotes an ambiguous personality and indeed, we often wonder who is the real Haim Topol???.

AVIGDOR KAHALANI

Knesset Member and Deputy Mayor of Tel Aviv, aged 49

In this chapter dealing with the character and abilities of famous people in Israel, it would be impossible to ignore such a dominant and noted personality as former Brig.-General Avigdor Kahalani (Res.) who was closely linked with the state's security forces. On seeking various signs and lines on the hand which are typical of different occupations and professions, such as people in the entertainment world, the theater, medicine, and others, I also looked for signs which indicated that the person could reach a commanding rank in the army.

One of the major characteristics of such a person would have to be a strong love for his country and the desire to contribute to its well-being 24 hours a day. In short, an idealist in every sense of the word.

And I found such a hand in the person of Avigdor Kahalani: Brig.- General in the reserves, Hero of Israel (Gibor Israel) and a member of the Knesset.

A broad hand, a classical sign for politicians and army men (see the chapter dealing with prototypes of the hand, pg.).

A particularly active lower Mars Mount, an element which denotes stubbornness and dedication to a purpose, as well as the ability to keep secrets (a classical sign of people dealing with secret intelligence and similar areas).

A sharp Head line, smooth and deeply etched. Beginning from the Jupiter Mount, touching lightly the Jupiter Mount, and continuing on its course, without faults or disorders, beyond the upper Moon Mount. Jupiter Mount is characterized by an organizational and managerial capacity, and when the Head line emerges from the Jupiter Mount quite naturally, this denotes that the individual with this hand has a talent for organization, good management and wise judgment.

Kahalani indeed has all these qualities. The thumb is firm and rigid, and the will-joint is especially dominant. This is a person who knows how to fight and achieve the aims he has set for himself.

AVIGDOR KAHALANI

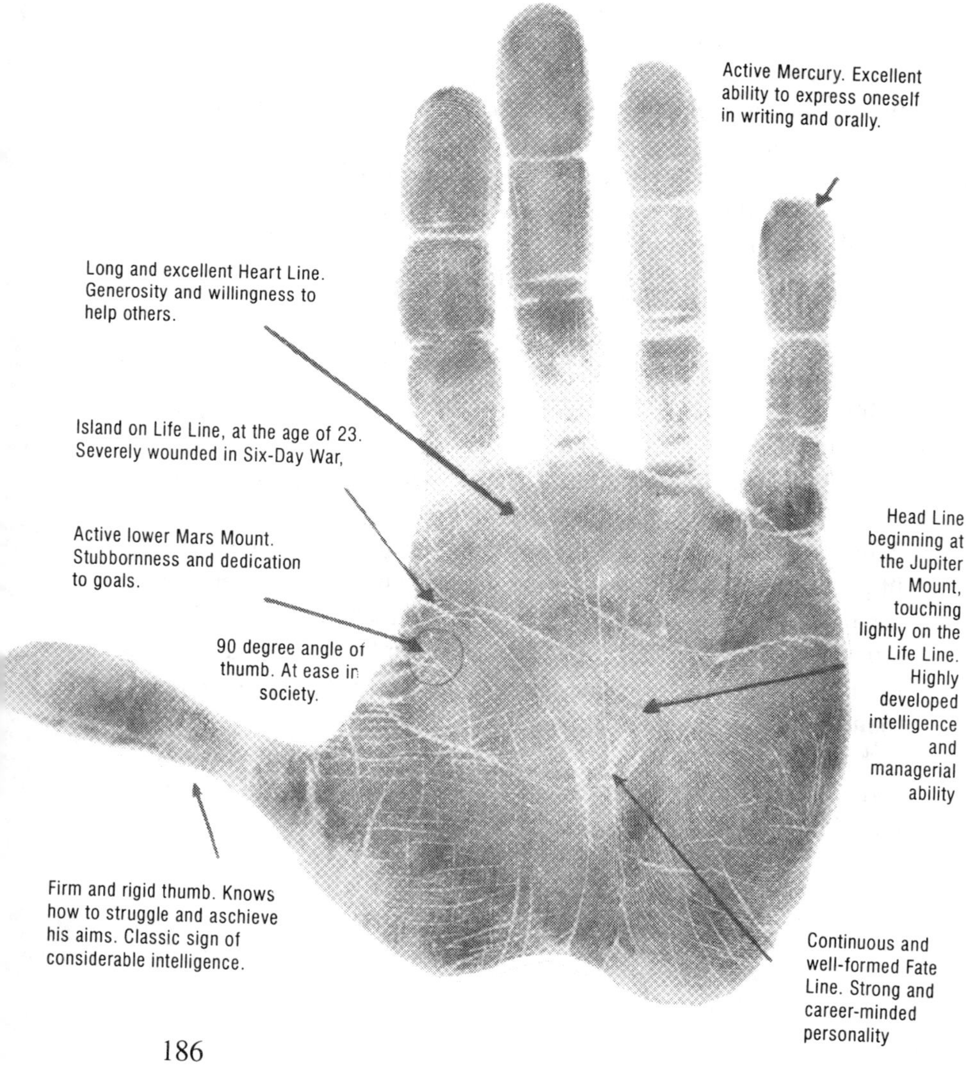

Active Mercury. Excellent ability to express oneself in writing and orally.

Long and excellent Heart Line. Generosity and willingness to help others.

Island on Life Line, at the age of 23. Severely wounded in Six-Day War,

Active lower Mars Mount. Stubbornness and dedication to goals.

90 degree angle of thumb. At ease in society.

Head Line beginning at the Jupiter Mount, touching lightly on the Life Line. Highly developed intelligence and managerial ability

Firm and rigid thumb. Knows how to struggle and aschieve his aims. Classic sign of considerable intelligence.

Continuous and well-formed Fate Line. Strong and career-minded personality

An especially long Heart line, which reaches the base of the Jupiter finger, is a characteristic sign of generosity, sensitivity, as well as a willingness to sacrifice oneself for others. As we are aware, Kahalani was an officer in the armoured corps and commander of a battalion in the various Israeli wars. In the many battles in which he participated, he was always ahead of his men and defended them at great risk to his own life. As a result, he was severely wounded and almost lost his life.

At the beginning of his Life line, one can see a large island (a sign indicating severe body wounds), which appears at approximately the age of 23, when he experienced serious injuries during the Six-Day War as the result of a direct hit on the tank he was commanding. Kahalani suffered 60% burns all over his body and was obliged to undergo innumerable operations until his recovery.

He is one of the few who merited two medals: One award was given him for his stubborn attack during the Six-Day War, and the second, for heroism, for repelling the Syrians in the Valley of Bacha during the Yom Kippur War.

As we can see, the Fate line is continuous and well-formed along the entire hand, a classical indication of a strong and balanced personality, who knows the purpose of life and successfully realizes his potentials in many and varied areas.

The Sun Line begins at about the age of 40 and ascends consistently towards the Sun Mount, a classic sign of success, popularity and fame.

The Mercury finger is very active and the Mercury Mount is huge, while the shell-shaped fingernails indicate a person with a marked ability to express himself in both writing and orally. He chooses his words carefully and can convey whatever his message in a clear and salient manner. It is obvious then that his involvement in politics suits him, particularly when the upper Mars Mount is so active – a typical sign of people who have confidence in themselves and who do not hesitate to say what they think in public. His creative talent is expressed in the writing of books, carpentry and construction in his free time.

In all, we have here a charismatic and energetic personality, who seeks challenges and missions, whose central motive is to better society, and who has proven himself in the present as he has in the past. Avigdor Kahalani is indeed such a man and there is every likelihood that his chances of succeeding in politics and in every other role he takes on are excellent.

DAVID PERI

Lawyer, former Warden of the Central Prison in Ramle, aged 62

The dream of every chirologist is to come across interesting hands with unique and unusual lines which one rarely sees. I always hoped to find a hand with a wonderful Sun line which continues from the base of the hand until the Sun Mount. As I have mentioned above, such a line denotes fame and popularity in whatever occupation this person pursues as well as a large degree of inner happiness. Very rarely, however, does this line appear in its ideal form. I saw such a line in David Peri's hand.

David Peri fulfilled a variety of official executive positions and merited wide-spread public appreciation of the way he carried out these tasks, especially during the time he was head of the prison in Ramle. When I asked him if he was happy, he answered without hesitation, that he would define himself as a happy man, contented with his share of life, especially within the framework of his family and friends.

A Sun line of this kind generally indicates talent in the artistic sphere and creativity in general. Although he is not an artist in the usual sense of the word, David Peri wrote a book about the period during which he served as commander of the Ramle prison, a book which in my opinion is written with considerable skill and is evidence of the element of creativity in his make-up.

In addition to this excellent Sun line, there is also a wonderfully formed Fate Line which veers at its end towards the Jupiter finger. This fact stresses his leadership quality and his ability to fill senior commanding roles, as is reflected in the story of his life. He is a lawyer and criminologist by profession. He served in the area of jurisdiction when he served in the army. As a private citizen, he filled a number of senior functions, among them as aide to the Minister of the Treasury. He represented the government in fiscal trials on behalf of the State Attorney and was also a lecturer on the law and criminology. For many years, he served in the security services. For most of his working years he occupied government functions. At the age of 35, he left an arm of the secret services and moved to the treasury (see an interruption in the Fate Line). At the age of 49, he made a significant change in his life and went to live in a kibbutz (see the break in the Sun Line). At 55, he began

DAVID PERI

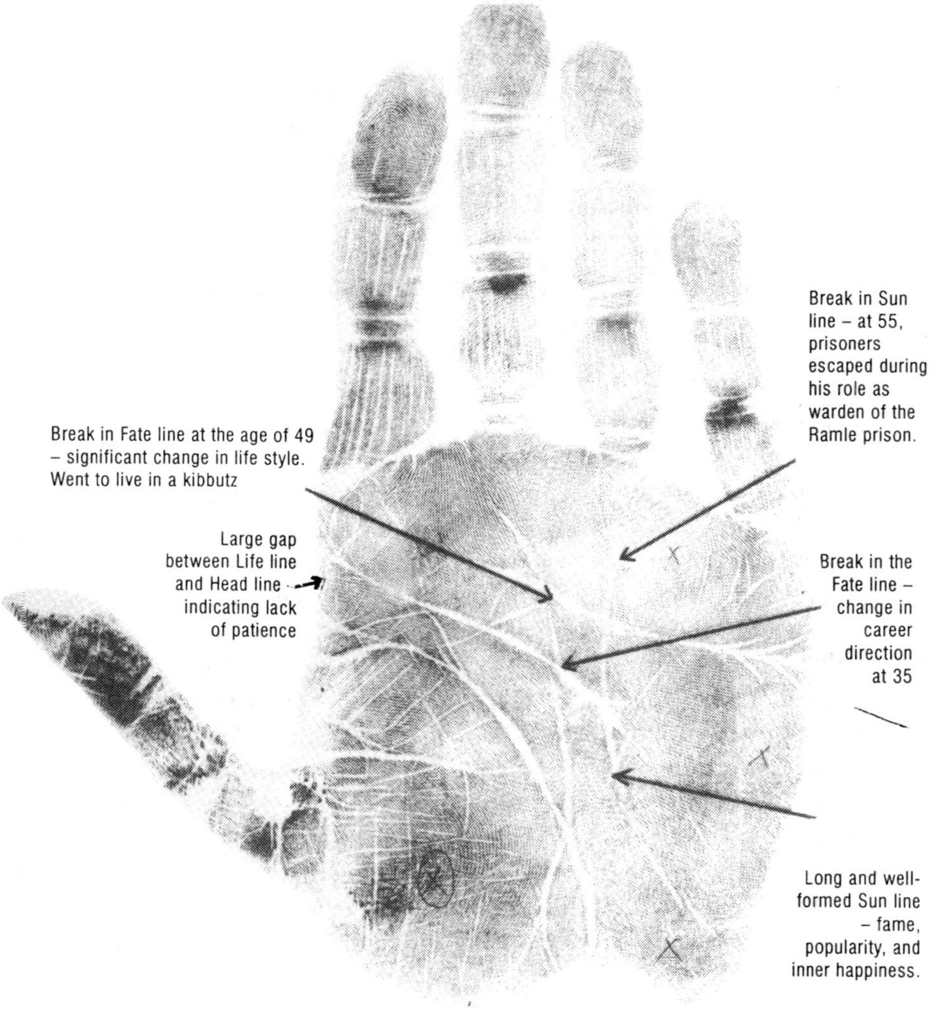

Break in Sun line – at 55, prisoners escaped during his role as warden of the Ramle prison.

Break in Fate line at the age of 49 – significant change in life style. Went to live in a kibbutz

Large gap between Life line and Head line indicating lack of patience

Break in the Fate line – change in career direction at 35

Long and well-formed Sun line – fame, popularity, and inner happiness.

to serve as warden of the prison in Ramle, and when a number of prisoners escaped, (after the event, it turned out that he was not responsible for this occurrence) but after a public scandal revolving around this event (see a break in the Sun Line), he was at first demoted and then upgraded and given additional authority.

Today, David Peri is the director of "Kadourie", an educational institution and village for youth.

JOSEPH R. (Pseudonym)

Joseph D.' hand is a perfect example of the primitive hand. The most striking thing about it are the thick and very short fingers in relation to the size of the hand. The hand itself is short and clumsy: the thumb is small and crude; all the lines are faulty and lacking well- defined forms; and the texture of the skin is coarse.

Joseph suffers from a slight marginal mental retardation. He spends his working day at basic physical and monotonous work in a protected enterprise, and is affected by many physical problems, including a weak heart and defective sight and hearing. A marked tendency to overeat is typical, as is his limited understanding of the world.

All these characteristics are clearly expressed in his hand: the short Head Line indicates his limited mental capacity. However, it also points to the possibility of succeeding at simple and routine tasks. The short and stubby fingers indicate this person's need to satisfy his basic physical requirements, such as excessive eating: the physical defects can be recognized by the disorderly Life line and the Heart line (particularly weakness) and also by the fingernails (small, shell-shaped, pale and blueish and lacking crescents).

THE PALM OF JOSEPH R.
(Pseudonym)

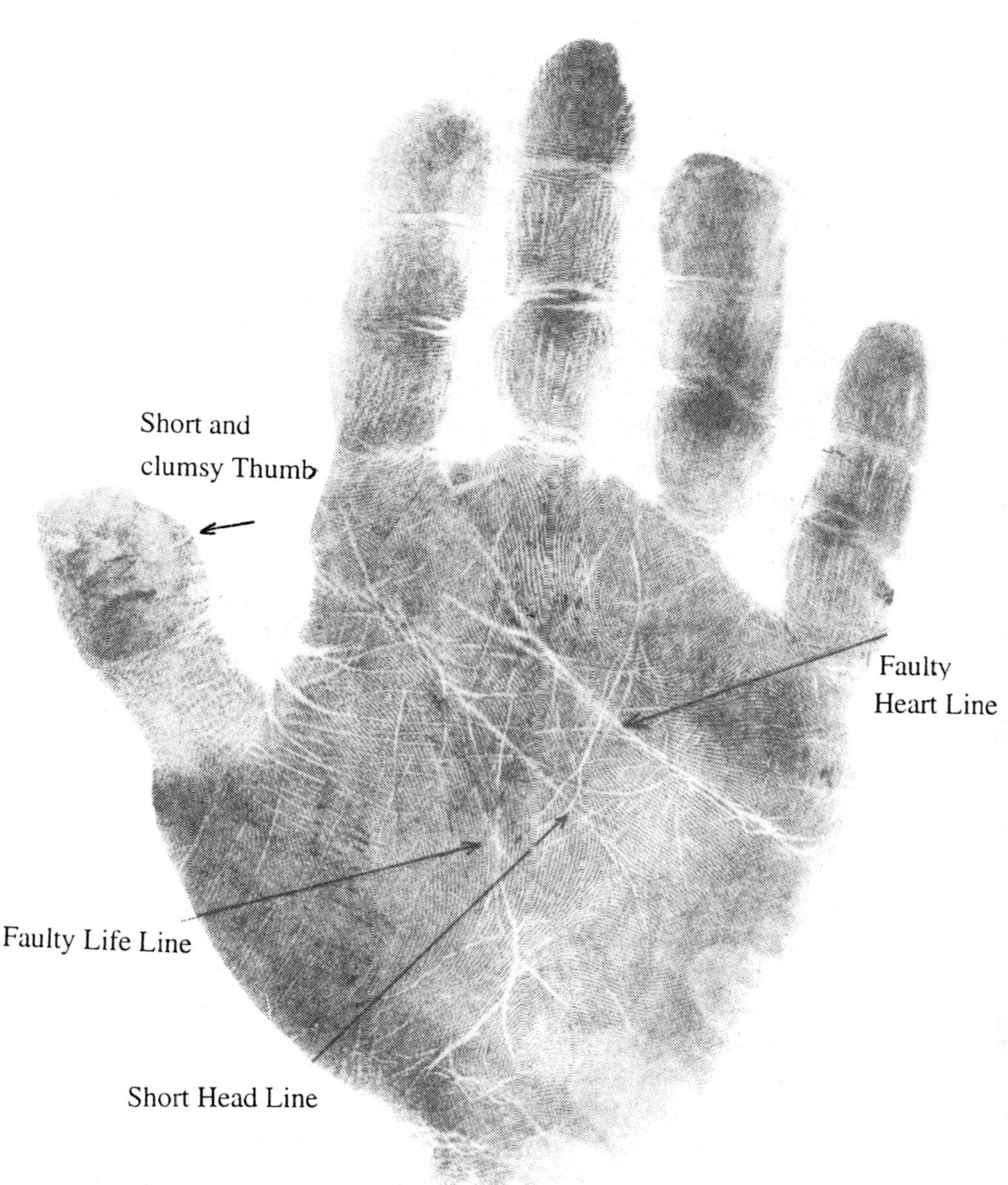

THE HANDS OF ELIAS AND MIRIAM (Pseudonyms)

Some years ago, I decided to renovate and enlarge my house. I contacted a building contractor from among one of the minority groups. As a professional and experienced worker, he carried out a good portion of the renovation himself and worked in my house for days on end and sometimes even late into the night. While at work, he told me about his family and how unhappy he was, placing all the blame for this situation on his wife. I was very curious to see his palm, and I even made a print of it. From the very first glance, it was clear from the connection at the beginning of the three main lines – the Head, the Heart, and the Life Lines – I suspected that much of the responsibility for his failing marriage was really his doing (see the chapter dealing with the Heart Line).

On one of those days on which he stayed rather late, his wife phoned to find out why he hadn't returned home. Jokingly, I said that he probably enjoyed being at my house. It was not long before his wife turned up at my house in a rage. In an outburst of jealousy, she tore up the upholstery in her husband's car, kicked at the machine and inflicted considerable damage in the process. I brought her into the house, tried to soothe her feelings and explained that I had only been joking, while showing her what her husband had been doing and praised his devotion to his work. Taking a glimpse at her hands, I saw that the same problems also existed in her palms (i.e. the connecting three major lines), and it was only then that their marial relationship was revealed to me, a classic situation indicated by the dotted link between the three lines (discussed above in the relevant chapter). The woman mentioned that her husband was very violent and displayed his mistrust and suspicions constantly – accusing her of betrayal, shouting and cursing her in a morbid manner. I had heard from him the same sort of accusations of jealousy on her part and he even told me about a night on which woke up to be faced with her throwing a bottle at him. When I enquired further into their childhood, it seems that they were both the products of broken homes where violence and blows were a permanent factor of their lives.

In the course of my work as a chirologist, whenever I chanced on these three lines connected at their start, it has always indicated the existence of jealousy and violence, together with unhappiness and the inability to function within a family framework.

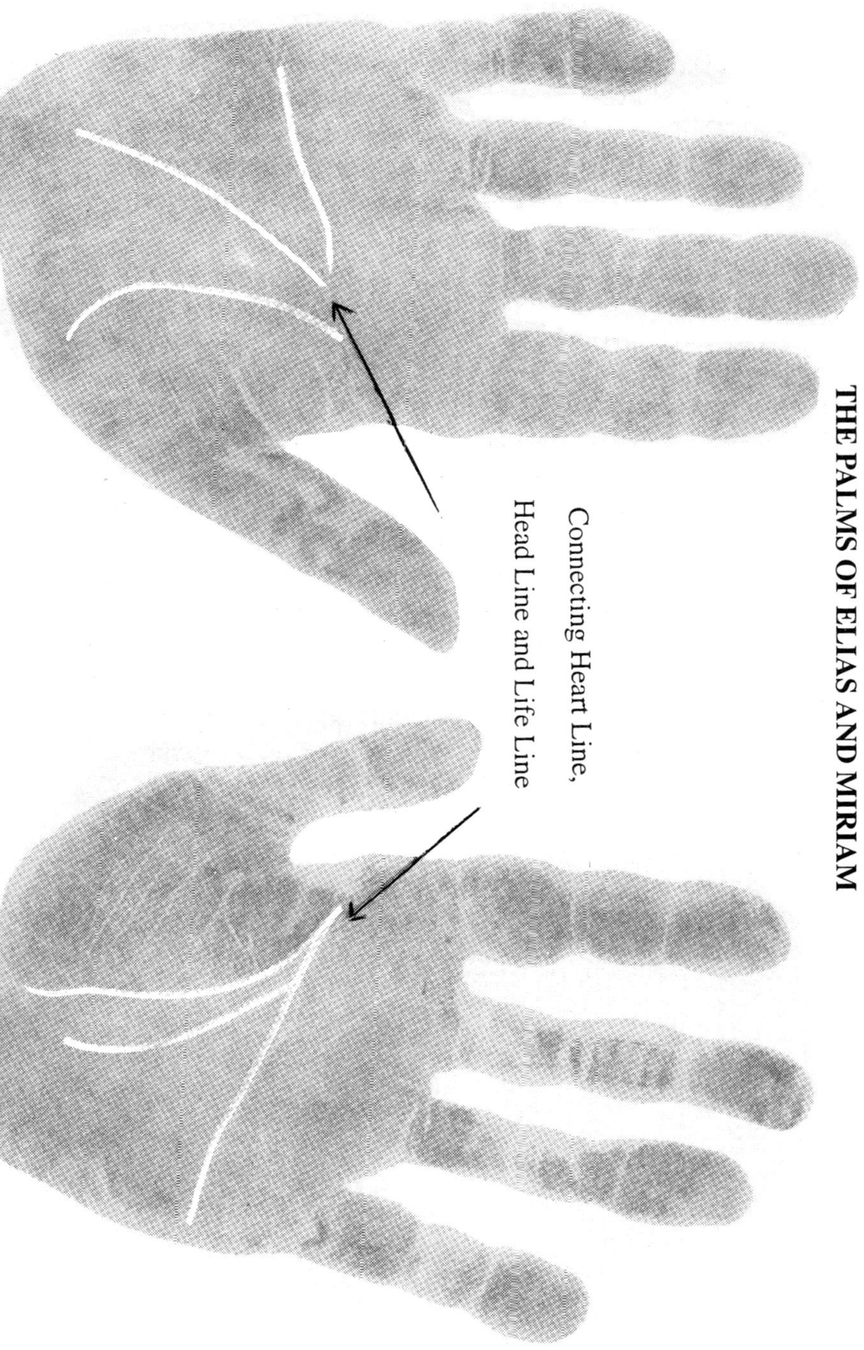

THE PALMS OF ELIAS AND MIRIAM

SHIMON SASSON

Aged 50

The Intuition line is very rare and in all the years of my work as a chirologist, I have as yet met few people who have this line. At any rate, all those whose hands have revealed the presence of the Intuition line have been one of a kind, who could foresee things and events which took place exactly as they had seen them in their minds.

One of these unique individuals was Shimon, one of my former pupils. He was capable – or so it seemed – of simply reading the thoughts of the people he was conversing with, but he could not say just how he was able to do this. Often, he would look into my eyes, then smile and say "You were right", without my having said a word – and it appears that he could really read my thoughts and happened to be quite accurate in his reading. During one lesson, he proved to me and to the rest of the students this impressive attribute, without even intending to.

One of the pupils in that group had had a car accident, and when she arrived at the lesson, I was very excited and upset by the experience which she described in all its details. None of us had had time to hear about the "incident". Shimon was a bit late for the lesson, and when he arrived, he looked into her eyes and began to describe the accident and all its details precisely, to the extent of even describing the kinds of injury other members of the accident had endured. We were all amazed and could not believe our ears. Until today I cannot understand how he could was able to do this. However, I have heard similar stories from all those who have an Intuition line.

PALM OF SHIMON SASSON

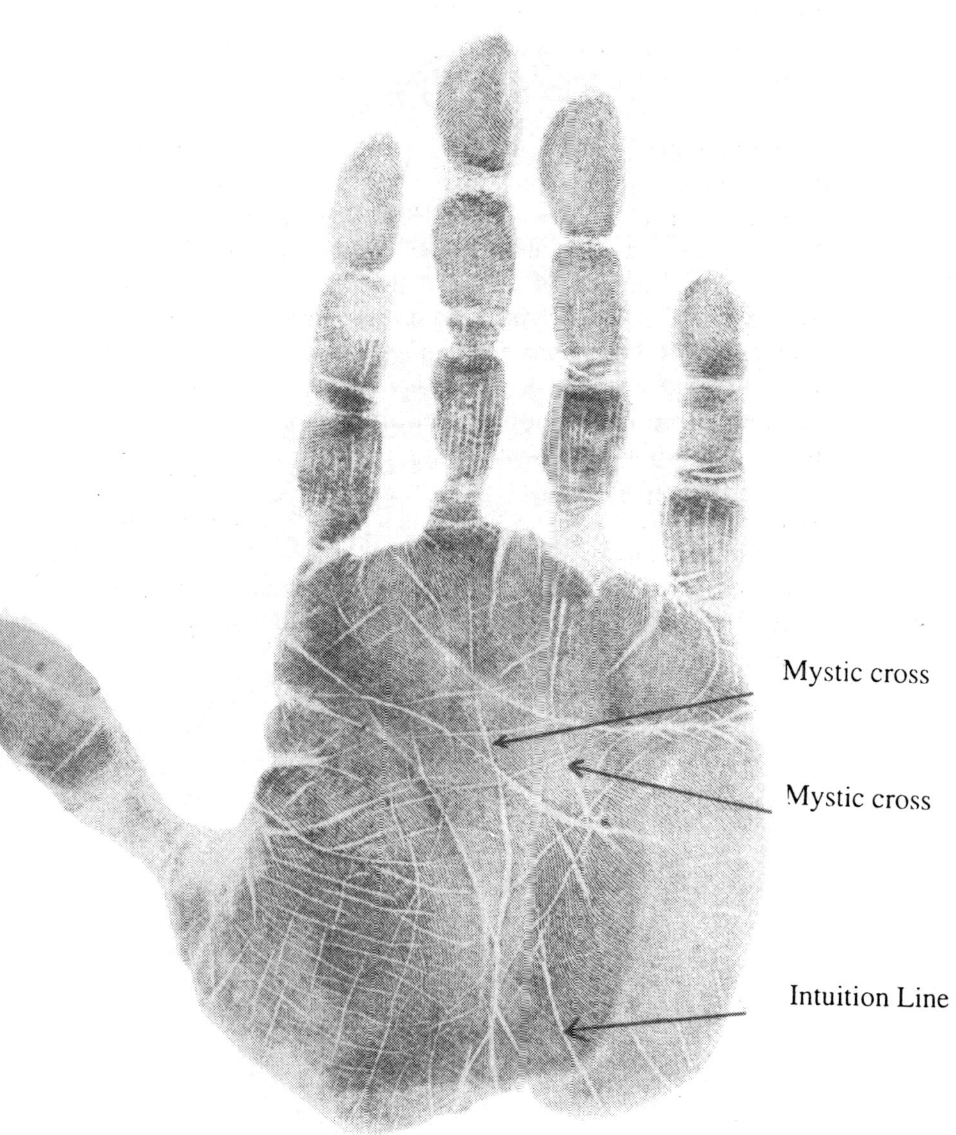

SHAI (Pseudonym)

Aged 28

Not long ago, a young man visited me, and when I looked into his hand, I was astonished by what I saw. There were only two lines in his hand – a Head line and a Heart line. And as one sees in the hand-print, there is no Life line nor is there any other line apart from the two I mentioned. I have never seen such a hand and this is obviously a very rare thing indeed.

I told the man that I could not interpret his palm, but merely that I would try to do so only on the basis of what I saw.

A large island appeared on the Head line, at about the age of 23. From this one could infer that he was injured in the head (see above in the chapter on the Head Line). This was evidently correct. Shai told me that he was hurt in a serious road-accident at this age, lost consciousness, and for half a year, lay prostrate in hospital like a vegetable. When he regained consciousness, it was considered a medical miracle. From this account, we can assume that while he was unconscious, all the lines were erased, and it was as if he had been born anew. When I told this story to some of my colleagues. they though that perhaps he was a creature from another planet.

There is no doubt that this case arouses our amazement as well as questions and thought, for I have no unambiguous answer to these facts.

SHAI'S PALMS (Pseudonym)

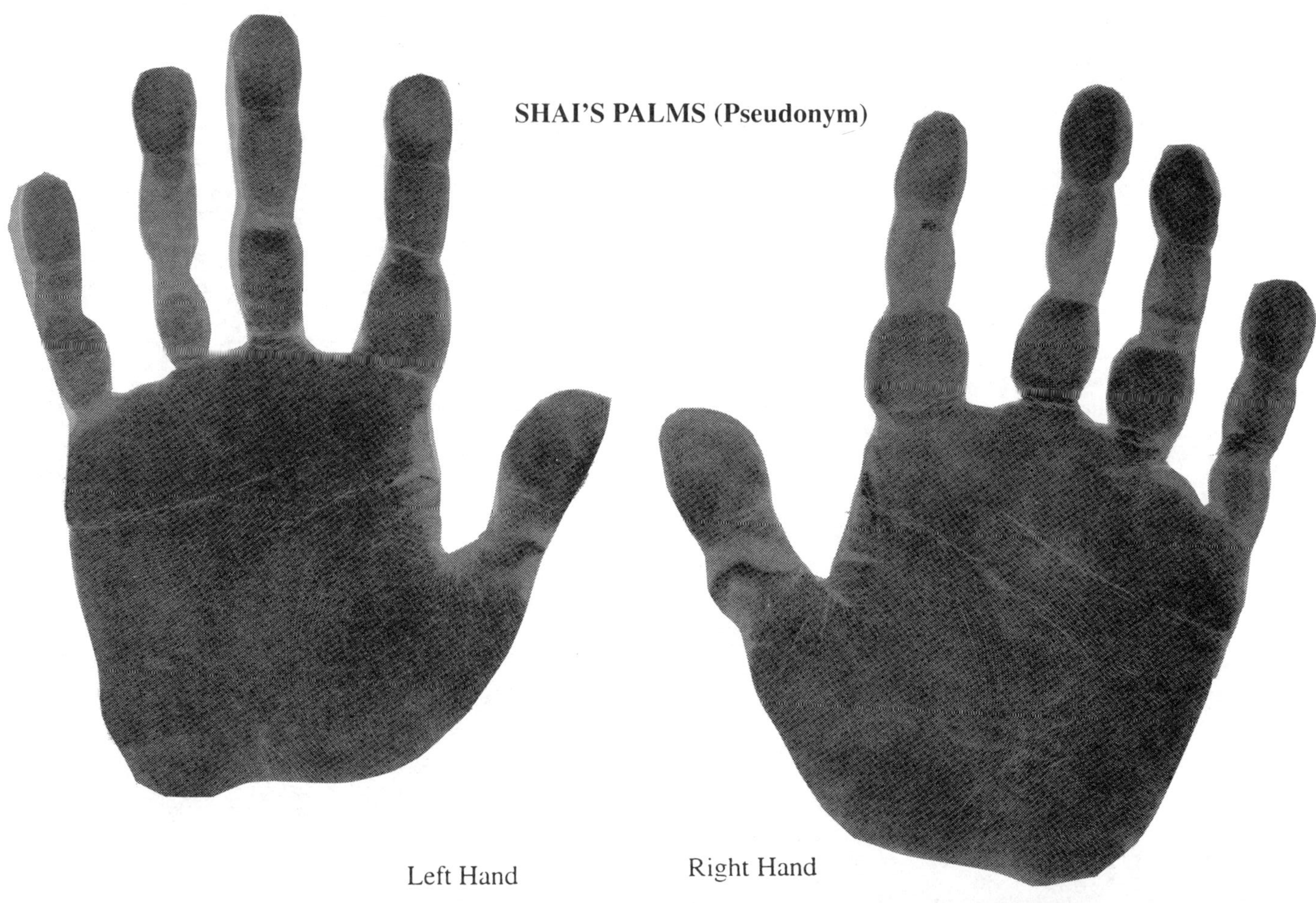

Left Hand   Right Hand

A BUILDING WORKER'S PALM

In the chapter dealing with the lines, I explained that deep and wide lines frequently indicate that this person is engaged in physical labor, or a craft, such as agriculture, a porter or stevedore, carpentry, and the like. This palm is a classic example of the hand of someone employed or occupied in some form of manual labor.

The hand below is that of a building worker and renovator, who does most of the actual work on a renovation site. His Head line is long and curved, which indicates that he devotes a good deal of thought and creativity to his work, and is capable of planning and building houses without the aid of a building engineer.

A BUILDING WORKER'S PALM

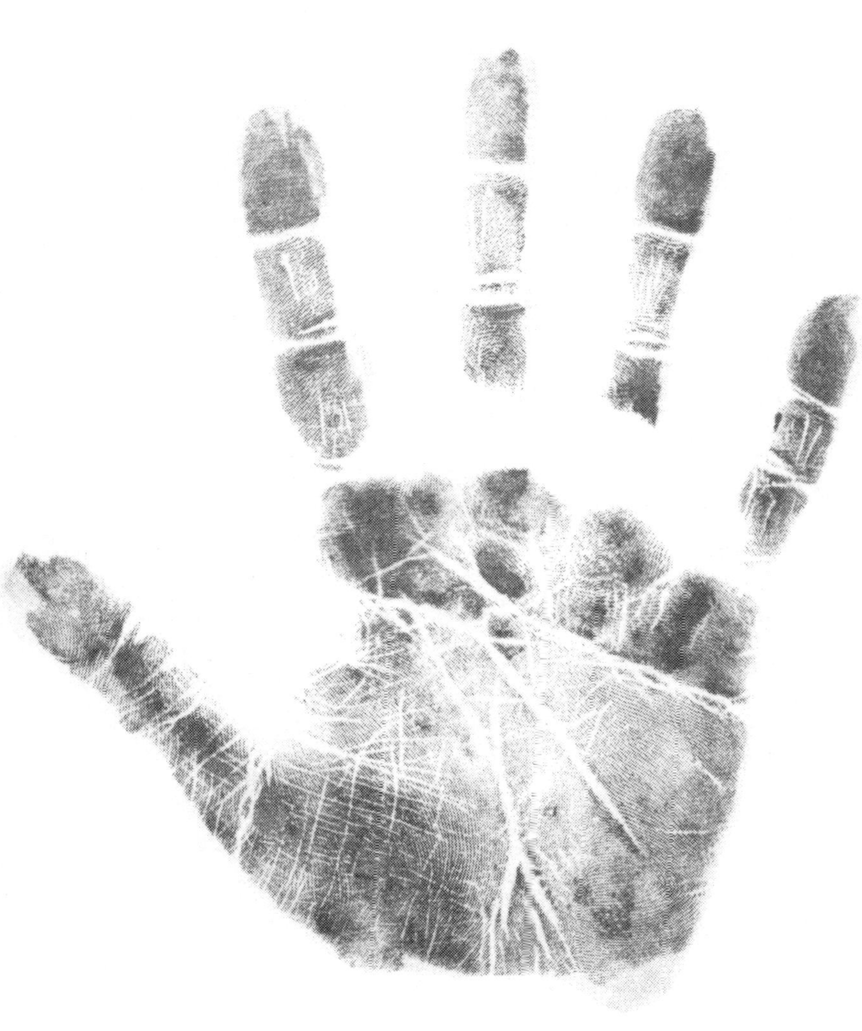

THE PALM OF A MENTALLY RETARDED WOMAN

The print below is that of a woman aged 56 who suffers from severe mental retardation: the level of her mental development is that of a child of 4. As we can see, the lines of her hand are completely disordered: the Head line is defective and interrupted all along it course, and the Heart line is similarly faulty. This woman has spent most of her life in mental institutions, and according to the defects in the Heart line, it is possible to state that throughout her lifetime she has suffered from an absence of warmth and love.

THE PALM OF A MENTALLY RETARDED WOMAN

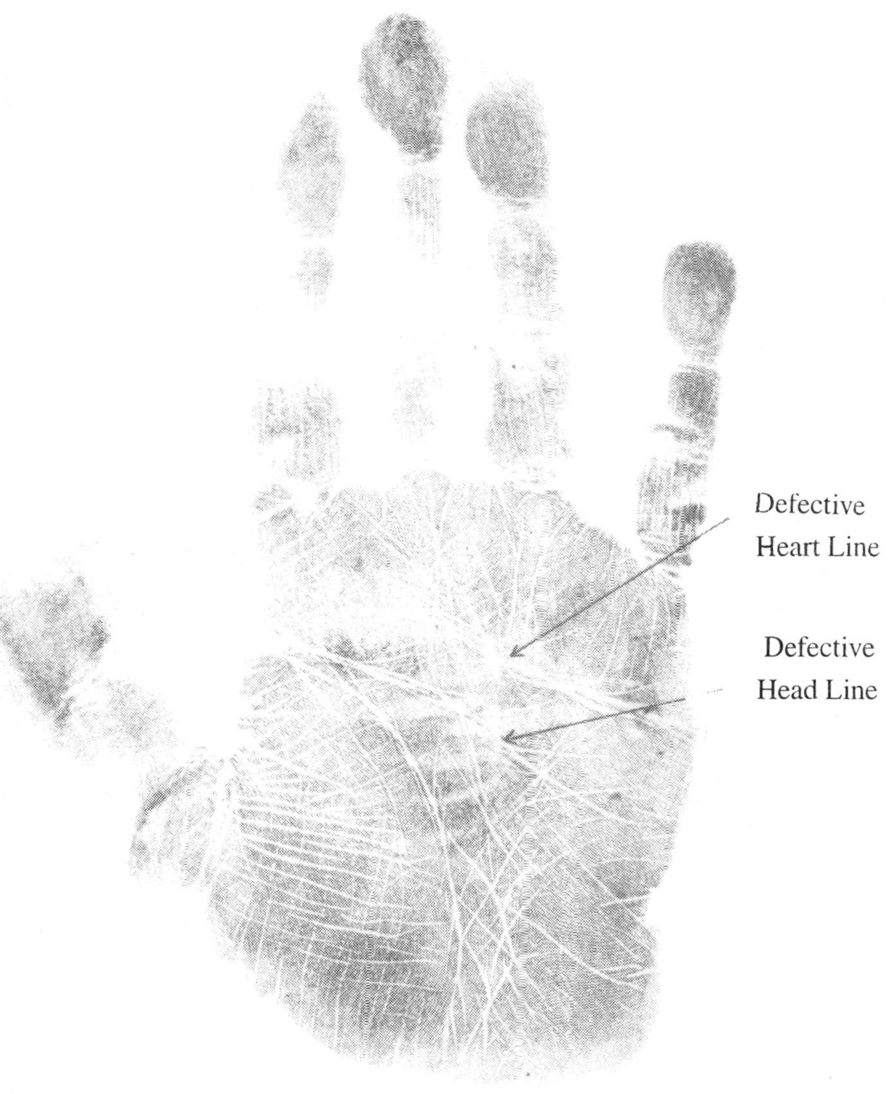

PERSONALITY ANALYSES OF THE PALM IN PRACTICE

When examining someone's palm, the first thing one must do is to find out whether the person sitting opposite you is frightened or calm. Most people are anxious about their state of health and fear death. Hence, do not try to impress him with bombastic truisms, for your first aim should be to quieten the person and see to it that the person is relaxed, and it will then be possible to convey whatever you see in his or her palm and to offer the best possible advice.

Seat the client facing you at the opposite side of the table and tell him to lean his elbow on the table and place his hand so that you can examine the upper surface of the palm. Direct the light of the table lamp so that it focuses on the palm, and proceed as follows:

1) Firstly, determine the type of hand and the prototype to which it belongs.
2) Test the elasticity and color of the hand.
3) Spread black duplicating ink on the palm (with the help of a roller) and make a print of the hand on paper (the print will reveal the little lines and the edges which the naked eye has difficulty discerning).
4) Mark the state of the Mounts on the print – whether they are very active or flat.
5) Note the angle of the thumb in relationship to the fingers.
6) Note the shape of the fingernails, their strength, color and the state of the crescents at their base.

After noting down all this information, weigh them up and consider them for a few minutes, and then tell your client what you see. Firstly, tell your client the good things, that is, the praiseworthy and optimistic things you have seen, and only then – with very careful deliberation over how you choose your words, tell your client the less pleasant facts. Remember – we are all in need of encouragement and support, and the person who comes to you as a client is perhaps more in need of this than anything else. If you admonish him and speak only of his failings, you may arouse his antagonism and from this point onward, your client would no longer take your words seriously even if they are important and may be halpful to him. Also, this client will not come back again and your reputation will be affected as a result.

HOW TO MAKE A PRINT OF THE PALM

The implement generally used to make a print of the palm is the roller used by artists in print-making (and they can be purchased in stationary stores). The ink is that used in duplicating machines. After many years of experimentation, I found this method easy and convenient and the prints made in this way look like clear and good prints that one gets from an x- ray machine.

STAGE ONE:

At first, I put a bit of ink on a sheet of old newspaper, and afterwards spread the color on the newpaper with the help of the roller, passing it back and forth, so that the color is absorbed and covers the paper over the entire surface equally. Now I spread the color over the newspaper with the roller until I achieve the texture I require, that is, neither too thin or too concentrated. Now I move the roller over the surface of the palm, beginning with the fingers and covering the lower parts of the palm until it is completely covered with color, without any excessive streaks of color anywhere.

STAGE TWO:

In advance, I have prepared an round absorbent sponge which fits the hollow of the palm. I place the sponge underneath the sheet of photocopy paper, press the palm of the client on the paper so that the sponge is directly under the hollow of the palm and press the hand down with equal pressure all over and without moving it (in order not to blur the hand print). Then I lift my hand in a single movement – and the print is ready, good and clear.

Do not be disappointed if the print does not turn out well on the first attempt. Try this process a number of times and there is no doubt that you will succeed.

Good luck!

Materials needed for making a print of the palm.

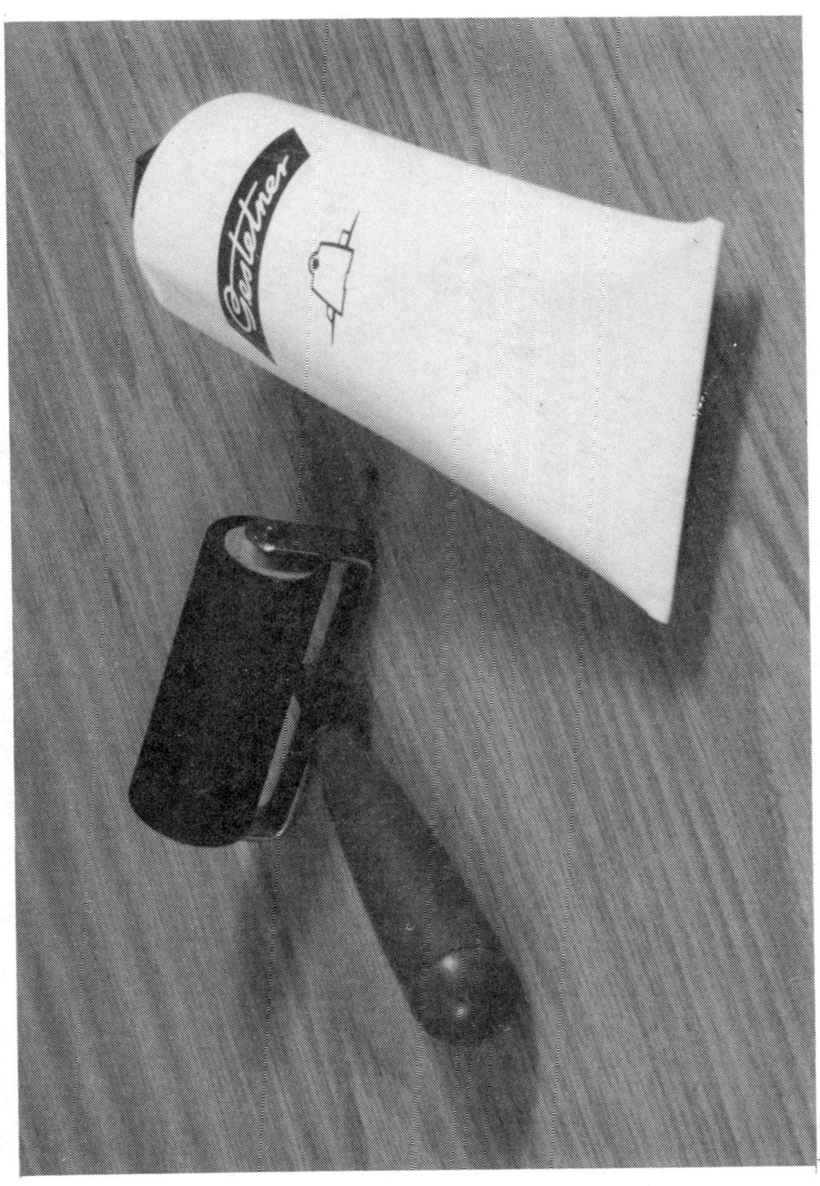

Spread color over the fingers and move downward

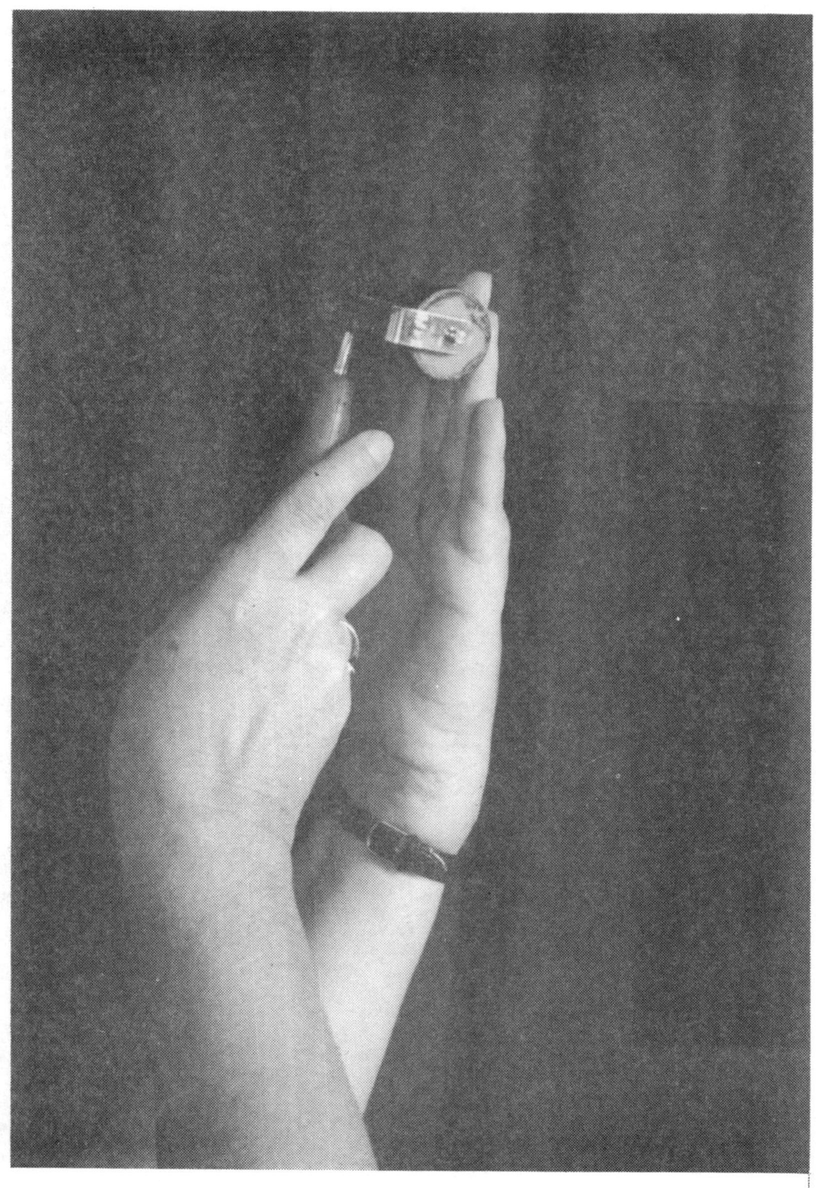

Place the sponge underneath the paper on the table

Place the color-covered hand over where the sponge is situated and press the hand gently and firmly

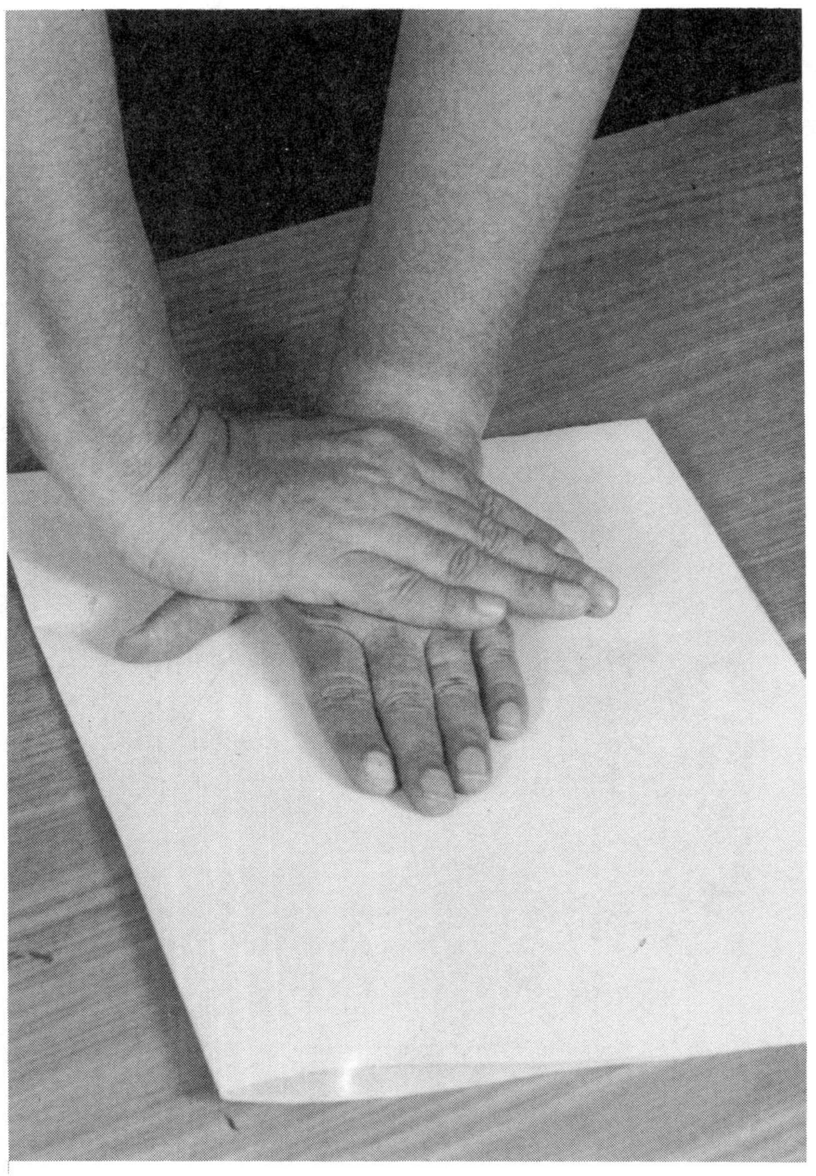

Comparing the print with what you see on the palm.

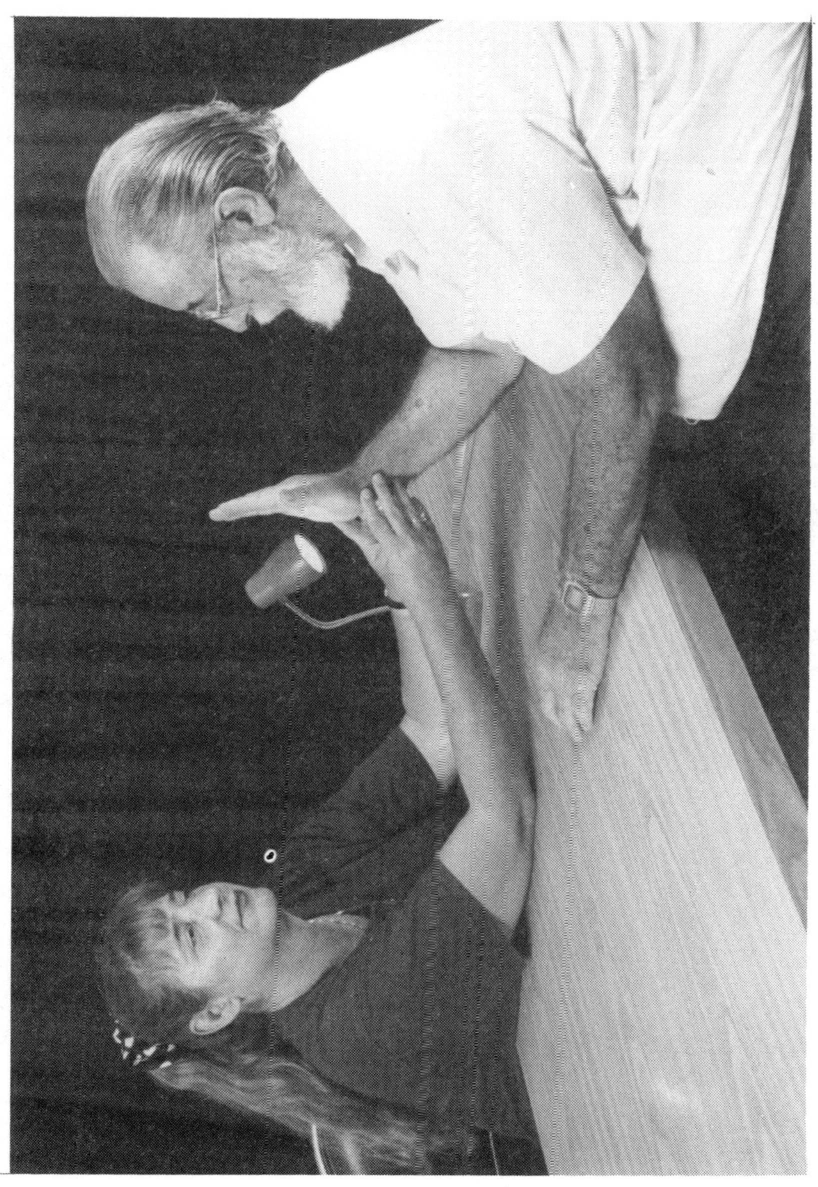